TO PREVAIL

AN AMERICAN STRATEGY FOR THE CAMPAIGN AGAINST TERRORISM

KURT M. CAMPBELL
AND
MICHÈLE A. FLOURNOY

Principal Authors

THE CSIS PRESS

Center for Strategic and International Studies
Washington, D.C.

The publisher gratefully acknowledges permission to reprint excerpts from the September 27, 2001, edition of the *New York Times*.

The publisher gratefully acknowledges permission to reproduce photographs from Hulton I Archive / Getty Images both on the cover and in the interior of this book.

Cover design by Robert L. Wiser, Archetype Press, Washington, D.C.

The CSIS Press, Washington, D.C. 20006
© 2001 by the Center for Strategic and International Studies
All rights reserved.
Printed on recycled paper in the United States of America
05   04   03   02   01   10 9 8 7 6   5   4   3   2   1

ISBN 0-89206-407-2

Library of Congress Cataloging-in-Publication Data
Campbell, Kurt M., 1957–
   To prevail : an American strategy for the campaign against terrorism / principal authors Kurt M. Campbell, Michèle A. Flournoy.
      p. cm.
   Includes bibliographical references.
   ISBN 0-89206-407-2 (alk. paper)
   1. Terrorism—Prevention—Government policy—United States. 2. Terrorism. I. Flournoy, Michèle A. II. Title.
   HV6432 .C36 2001
   363.3'2'0973—dc21
                              2001006787

In memory of
the victims of September 11, 2001, and its aftermath
and
dedicated to our children

May they know peace.

Contents

Preface

To Prevail is the product of an extraordinary collaboration undertaken by the Center for Strategic and International Studies (CSIS) in Washington, D.C., and conceived in the immediate aftermath of the tragedy on September 11, 2001. At the urgings of Sam Nunn and John Hamre, CSIS chairman and president respectively, a Centerwide task force composed of regional scholars, terrorism experts, military representatives, intelligence analysts, former policymakers, and strategic thinkers began meeting intensively to develop a coherent and comprehensive strategy for how to meet the challenge posed by global terrorism.

The task force members participated in a process of rigorous debate and lengthy drafting sessions cochaired by the book's lead editor, Vinca LaFleur, and convened by Stephanie Kaplan, the task force coordinator. Contributions were extensively reviewed and revised, with many assumptions challenged along the way.

The result, we hope, is a synthesized volume that provides powerful insights and recommendations for the way forward. *To Prevail* is meant to be our collective contribution toward sustaining the nation's purpose and resolve throughout this new era for America and, indeed, for the world.

The members of the task force represent the extraordinary talent and expertise at CSIS. Clark Murdock and Walter Slocombe provided essential analysis for chapter 3, "The Imperative to Prevail."

Dan Benjamin authored chapter 4, "The Changing Face of Terrorism," and Robert Orr was the primary drafter of the chapters on coalitions, foreign assistance, and failed states (chapters 5, 12, and 13).

James Lewis authored chapter 8 on law enforcement, with an assist from John Hamre. Dr. Hamre also provided his counsel for chapters 7 and 9 on intelligence and homeland security.

Sidney Weintraub, Murray Weidenbaum, Sherman Katz, Erik Peterson, Robert Ebel, and George Handy all made useful contributions to chapter 10 on economic strategy.

Antony Blinken was the principal author of chapter 11, "Elevating Public Diplomacy," and co-writer with Simon Serfaty of the section on Europe in chapter 14, "Regional Strategies."

Anthony Cordesman drafted chapter 14's sections on the Middle East and Central Asia, with contributions to the latter by Celeste Wallander and Shireen Hunter.

Celeste Wallander's and Sarah Mendelson's keen insights on Russia are evident not only in the chapter's section on Russia, but throughout the book.

The Caucasus section was drafted by Zeyno Baran, Derek Mitchell was the central author for East Asia, and Steve Morrison provided the words and wisdom on Africa.

Teresita Schaffer was the principal author of the South Asia section, and Sidney Weintraub and Chris Sands drafted the section on the Americas.

Jay Farrar, Alex Lennon, Edward Luttwak, Charles Duelfer, and Linnea Raine also served as valuable members of the task force.

Accompanying the text is a collection of archival photographs mostly from the first half of the twentieth century. Together, they convey that Americans have confronted difficult challenges throughout our nation's history and, despite such challenges, have prevailed time and again.

The findings and recommendations are drawn from the text and flow from the insights and analysis of each of the contributors. Still, the principal authors take ultimate responsibility for what is presented

PREFACE   XI

in the conclusion and elsewhere in the text. Any oversight or flaw in the logic is ours, while credit for any presentation of wise counsel belongs to this wonderful collection of contributors.

Kurt M. Campbell
Michèle A. Flournoy
Washington, D.C.

Acknowledgments

This book is the product of many dedicated people affiliated with the Center for Strategic and International Studies whose words, ideas, and inspiration can be found on every page.

Thanks to John Hamre, CSIS president and CEO, and Sam Nunn, chairman of the CSIS Board of Trustees, for their confidence and unyielding efforts to build a strong team at CSIS. Robin Niblett and Erik Peterson provided essential oversight and encouragement.

Special thanks and credit are due to Vinca LaFleur, our brilliant lead editor, who brought out the best of every dimension of this effort. She was the most talented editor for both style and substance any of us have had the good fortune to work with; this book could not have been completed without her devotion to the effort and her commitment to excellence. Stephanie Kaplan served as the task force coordinator and tireless convener. Her masterful management of every detail of the process and her substantive contributions to various chapters were invaluable and took this book from an idea to a reality.

We are indebted to the members of the CSIS task force, who not only contributed their expert analysis, but also endured a series of intense sessions during which we challenged and exchanged ideas.

We are especially grateful to the entire International Security Program at CSIS and to our 2001–2002 Military Fellows—Robert Bateman, Mark Brilakis, Patrick Kelly, Kevin McLaughlin, and Renwick Payne. Members of the ISP helped to articulate ideas, conduct research, and photocopy proliferating chapters at a moment's notice. Many thanks are owed to Rob Gile, David Fuhr, Andrew Peterson, Pete Schroeder, and Michael Stanisic. We especially thank Jessica Cox and Elizabeth Latham for their unwavering support and for serving as purveyors of sanity during the course of this intensive project.

We thank Alex Lennon, of CSIS's *Washington Quarterly,* who served as a sounding board for many of the book's arguments, especially for the concluding chapter.

We extend our deepest appreciation to the CSIS Press, directed by Jim Dunton, a master at his craft. Under his direction, Roberta Howard, Donna Spitler, Divina Jocson, Maria Farkas, Heidi Shinn, and Mary Marik were absolutely essential to the high-quality production and timely delivery of this book. In addition, we thank the entire CSIS External Relations Department, especially Jay Farrar, Moira Whelan, and Mark Schoeff, who supported every aspect of this task force both logistically and intellectually.

Many other friends of CSIS played a useful role in developing this book's message and recommendations, in particular the Center's Congressional Fellows and the members of the Ambassadors Roundtable.

Thanks lastly and most of all to our families, who put up with long days and late nights of work. We hope they will be proud of what we have produced.

Taking the Pledge, circa 1965. Elementary school students stand to recite the Pledge of Allegiance.
Photograph: Hulton | Archive/Getty Images.

Chapter 1

Introduction

"This is our calling. This is the calling of the United States of America, the most free nation in the world. A nation built on fundamental values that rejects hate, rejects violence, rejects murderers, rejects evil. And we will not tire. We will not relent. It is not only important for the homeland security of America that we succeed, it is equally as important for generations of Americans who have yet to be born."

— President George W. Bush
FBI Headquarters, Washington, D.C.
October 10, 2001

On September 11, 2001, the post–Cold War sanctity of American life was shattered. Nineteen men, armed with box cutters, knives, and the skills to fly jet planes, hijacked four U.S. airliners bound from Boston and Washington to California. At 8:45 A.M., American Airlines flight 11 slammed into the north tower of New York City's World Trade Center, igniting a massive explosion. As horrified New Yorkers and Americans across the country watched the blaze in person or on TV, United Airlines flight 175 struck the south tower some 17 minutes later.

At 9:40 A.M., the Federal Aviation Administration halted all flight operations at U.S. airports for the first time in American history. But it was too late. At 9:43 A.M., American Airlines flight 77 plowed into the Pentagon outside Washington, D.C., slashing a hole in the building's side and forcing its evacuation.

Inside the Twin Towers, the jet fuel inferno reached temperatures above 1000 degrees—powerful enough to melt the steel supports that girded the buildings. At 10:05 A.M., the south tower collapsed—crashing down upon hundreds of rescue workers and others trapped inside. A storm cloud of dust, debris, and acrid smoke engulfed the downtown area. At 10:28 A.M., the north tower crumbled—its trademark antenna riding the terrible wave of death to the ground.

All that stood between another Washington landmark struck and more innocent lives stolen was a group of passengers on United Airlines flight 93 who were not prepared to die sitting down. After using their cell phones to call loved ones on the ground, a number of passengers learned of the terrifying events that already had transpired. Empowered by knowledge, a group voted to attack their hijackers. Their plane crashed in rural Pennsylvania. No one on board survived.

In the space of two hours, one sunny fall morning, 19 terrorists murdered almost 4,700 people on American soil.

September 11 is already seen as a turning point in history, a gash in America's national psyche. Historian Leo Ribuffo observed, "Before September 11, we all thought we were going to get richer and richer and we would live forever." Now, suddenly, the United States must again engage in a long twilight struggle—this time against shadowy adversaries based in countries across the globe, even our own. The need to meet this challenge with both urgency and patience promises to test the very essence of our national character.

In the fall of 2001, military forces including aircraft, special operations forces, and naval assets from the United States and other nations began a protracted fight against a desperate but tenacious enemy in Afghanistan. Yet, in a fundamental sense, the United States is at war on the home front as well. Since September 11, anxieties have been compounded by a series of lethal anthrax attacks delivered through the U.S. mail. Many of our national buildings and institutions have been evacuated, as emergency workers in full-body "haz-mat" suits test for traces of the dangerous spores. Postal workers have been involuntarily conscripted to the front lines of the campaign: Inhaling a dose of anthrax smaller than the period at the end of this sentence is enough to cause infection and death.

With so much misery and anxiety, it is natural for Americans to turn to history for perspective, comfort, and courage. We have deployed analogies to help make sense of our altered global and domestic realities—from the American Civil War to Pearl Harbor; the Cuban Missile Crisis to the war on drugs. Yet the best analogies from America's past can only provide imperfect insight and inspiration for what lies ahead. In the fight against global terror, we face unprecedented challenges in uncharted political waters.

More Americans died on September 11, 2001, than on any single day on the bloody battlefield of Antietam. The strategic surprise of the twin assaults on the World Trade Center and the Pentagon was greater than the Japanese attack on Pearl Harbor. While tensions ran high during the Cuban Missile Crisis, a resolution emerged after only 13 days; there will be no comparable short-term respite in the campaign against global terrorism. And while drug traffickers respond to the logic of supply and demand for illicit products, the September 11 terrorists were driven by religious fanaticism and hatred that does not conform to the profit motive.

President George W. Bush, his administration, and Congress, temporarily absent bitter partisan divides, have called for a lengthy, multifaceted campaign aimed at wiping the scourge of terrorism from the earth—"to draw the line in the sand against the evil ones."

This bold challenge raises the prospect of a unifying and overriding national mission pursued with unyielding intensity. Yet there are vital questions associated with virtually every facet of this new national agenda, from the role of presidential rhetoric to the nature and durability of an international coalition, the steps necessary for preserving economic vitality both at home and abroad, new intelligence requirements, challenging institutional innovations, and the need to protect civil liberties in an environment of heightened internal security.

While Presidents Jackson, Lincoln, Roosevelt, and Kennedy all faced extraordinary challenges in a time of war or crisis, each was able to conceptualize early on a vision for ultimate victory. Will President Bush be able to articulate a clear vision of victory in our current struggle and, furthermore, how to get there from here? Will our national leadership—conceivably stretching across several administrations—be able to rally the collective American will to sustain a new national calling involving both vigilance and sacrifice? Americans have a newfound confidence in their government leaders and institutions for the first time since Watergate, but can this confidence be sustained in the face of the inevitable setbacks ahead?

During the Cold War, political differences were meant to disappear at the water's edge. The September 11 and subsequent attacks will now require that political opponents muster greater cooperation inside the water's edge as well. Will the United States be able to settle on the right blend of political cooperation combined with the necessary checks and balances to achieve a successful national consensus? Perhaps more profoundly, will September 11 lead to political realignment inside and between political parties and ideologies?

Related to the challenge of sustaining a new national mission is how to make the new priorities mesh with those that already existed, such as managing the rise of China, the search for a stable peace in the Middle East, confronting the spread of infectious diseases like HIV/AIDS, dealing with the deteriorating situation in Colombia, and efforts to develop a viable national missile defense. All of these challenges will reassert themselves, though perhaps in a different light or form, after the nearly exclusive focus on international terrorism subsides. How will these relative and shifting priorities be influenced by a wholly new domestic and international agenda?

The creation of an international coalition against terrorism—or, more accurately, a coalition of coalitions—is an essential component of the American strategy. It will be more difficult than assembling the Gulf War coalition, but far less formal and more ad hoc than erecting the original NATO alliance, although members of both will contribute in varying degrees. Coalition membership will be based on relations with the United States, regional realities, and a careful weighing of perceived threats and opportunities. Can the United States maintain a broad coalition against terrorism without diluting the will to take decisive action in the international arena?

Further, arriving at an international consensus on the definition of terrorism will prove vexing. By framing our new battle as a "war on terrorism," we risk setting out to do battle with a tool and not the people, ideologies, and movements that subscribe to terrorism as a means of propaganda or political change. Will the United States be able to promote a consensus on definitions of "terrorism" and "terrorism of global reach" as it seeks to assemble the broadest possible coalition to wage this campaign?

Before September 11, a debate was under way about the threats the U.S. military would be called to meet in the coming years. The prevailing wisdom was that rising powers, like China, presented the greatest challenges to U.S. security—and that the greatest danger to the U.S. homeland was the risk of long-range missile attack. Now it seems clear that the United States is endangered as much by other states' weakness as by their strength—and that the likeliest attacks on American soil will be launched right here at home. What does this mean for the military's future purpose, posture, and organization? Does the military have the capabilities it needs to tackle a dispersed and shadowy foe? And, crucially, after virtually bloodless campaigns in the Gulf War, Kosovo, and Bosnia (bloodless for U.S. military forces and personnel, but not for their adversaries, of course), will the public be prepared to sacrifice American troops and treasure toward the elusive and somewhat undefined goal of eliminating global terrorism?

Similarly, it is clear that both the intelligence and law enforcement communities will need to modify their practices and enhance their capabilities to prevent another catastrophic terrorist strike. Yet, in the quest to ensure the public's safety, we also need to preserve the individual protections that distinguish the United States from those we are fighting. How can U.S. leaders develop effective capabilities to defeat terrorist outposts on American soil without sacrificing individual freedoms and other liberties we hold dear?

September 11 and subsequent terrorist assaults have obliterated the American public's sense of invulnerability. The six-story rubble of the World Trade Center, the charred Pentagon, and the hand-addressed envelopes carrying anthrax spores are irrefutable proof that America's original buffers—vast seas and friendly neighbors—provide little protection in an interconnected world, where new technologies enhance the efficiency of evil forces no less than of good. It is clear we need a more integrated and effective system for homeland security, requiring much greater cooperation of agencies with both international and domestic mandates. Will the United States be able to create the appropriate institutions, and the bureaucratic fusion within and between public agencies and private companies, that are needed to mount an effective homeland defense against future terrorist attacks?

September 11 has also created opportunities for a fundamental realignment of relations in the international arena, in ways both good and bad. There are new possibilities for U.S. dialogue and partnership with myriad states, including Russia and China, and the potential for renewed tensions between India and Pakistan over the thorny issue of Kashmir. Will these new avenues for diplomatic cooperation—and increased possibilities for conflict—be fleeting or fundamental as the campaign against terrorism drags on?

President Bush told Americans in the immediate aftermath of September 11 that the country was facing "the first war of the twenty-first century." Vice President Dick Cheney predicted that the coming conflict would be "global in scope." What is also true but less understood is that this will be the first major conflict to occur in the age of globalization.

Much has been written about how globalization—the relentless expansion of market forces and the constant search for realizing greater economic efficiencies—influences everything from indigenous cultures to patterns of productivity. We have come to understand globalization as representing an inexorable economic force that alters everything in its path. If that is true, what will happen when the patterns of globalization collide with the passions of global conflict? How will economic tools and factors, both at home and abroad, be utilized in and influenced by the campaign against international terrorism?

In addressing these and other questions, *To Prevail* aims to provide an integrated vision for the formulation and execution of a sustained campaign against global terrorism. We recognize the difficulty of trying to set out a durable framework for U.S. policy even as the forces of history are swirling all around us. But we also believe that, in this time of national challenge, scholars, commentators, and practitioners alike have an obligation to help sort out the new global realities America confronts—and to help the public gain a complex understanding of the hard choices, tough battles, and inevitable setbacks ahead as we work to defeat terrorism and defend our homeland from an insidious and deadly threat. Not since the early days of the Cold War have Americans been so open to considering our place in the world and the implications of a greater American interconnectedness in international affairs.

Americans have not waited, however, for the judgment of experts and theorists to decide for themselves whether these dangerous last few months will become an era. There has been a broad rediscovery of world affairs, with many in our country paying close attention to international developments for the first time since the Gulf War. But in contrast to that conflict, which now looks more like a blip in the rear-view mirror of history, there are indications that the public views the campaign against terrorism as an open-ended struggle that will change or taint much of what is cherished about American life.

To Prevail offers an overview of the numerous domestic and foreign policy arenas that will be affected, while also demonstrating the degree to which the borders between those distinctions have blurred. Throughout its examination, the book seeks to take readers over the horizon, and to help them understand the long-term goals that any short-term decisions in the campaign against terrorism will need to take into account. We see *To Prevail* as trying to lead public understanding and frame the national debate. Our goal is to have one of the first words. We know we will not have the last.

Chapter 2, September 10, 2001: The Way We Were, is both a nostalgic exploration of a simpler American way of life and a review of the conditions that permitted the September 11 strikes to occur and succeed.

In the third chapter, The Imperative to Prevail and the Nature of the Campaign, we underscore the urgency of the terrorist threat and the commitment required to defeat it. We attempt to define the meaning of victory in this unconventional campaign and describe the tools necessary in order to wage it. This chapter also delves into the long-term impact of the terrorist threat on people's daily lives—the accommodations and sacrifices people will be asked to make, the requirement for strong national leadership, and the challenges for U.S. authorities in sustaining official and public resolve as time goes on.

The Changing Face of Terrorism, chapter 4, describes for readers what sets the new terrorists apart: the explicitly religious terms in which their grievances and goals are expressed and the effort to create massive bloodshed. It also reviews their organizational structure, goals, capabilities, and modes of operation—and, in so doing, helps to clarify why the new terrorists are so difficult to deter.

The bulk of the book describes the elements of an integrated, long-term strategy to combat global terrorism. Many chapters look at functional areas, like improving military capabilities, strengthening intelligence and law enforcement, building and sustaining international coalitions, and enhancing homeland security. These chapters examine the ways in which the events of September 11 and subsequent attacks have shaken priorities, revealed organizational and operational shortcomings, and made plain the need for change—while also considering the long-term implications of redirecting our focus and resources to the fight against global terrorism. The book also explores how neglected aspects of U.S. foreign policy—from public diplomacy to capabilities for rebuilding failed states—must be strengthened for the challenges ahead.

Other chapters examine policy choices tailored to specific regions around the world. We structure our observations around four basic questions: What is the regional context in which the September 11 attacks occurred? What is the threat of terrorism in that region? What is the United States likely to ask from the leading states in that region over the long term? And, how is the region likely to respond? We seek to point out new opportunities for strategic cooperation, while raising red flags over the difficult compromises that might be required to sustain that cooperation—and the unintended consequences the United States may be forced to deal with down the line.

A chapter called Implications for Globalization explores whether the process of globalization—so dependent on openness, efficiency, and speed—can coexist with a war on terror that demands tighter borders, tougher security, heightened inspection, and fewer choices for producers and consumers alike.

In the concluding section, we present key findings drawn from the preceding chapters, as well as specific recommendations for policymakers and practitioners on subjects ranging from organizational innovations to a new U.S. strategy for the Middle East.

The appendixes—a collection of some of the key speeches by American and international leaders in the wake of September 11 and an overview of major terrorist groups and the acts they have perpetrated—will make this volume a useful teaching and reference tool. The rhetoric of resolve coming from leaders as diverse as President George W. Bush, Prime Minister Tony Blair, and Mayor Rudolph Giuliani powerfully illustrates the importance of inspiration during times of national crisis.

At the start of a new century, as the United States contemplates an open-ended, multifaceted campaign, *To Prevail* strives to inform understanding of the complex global realities our nation confronts. Through this effort, we seek to join and hopefully shape the national dialogue on how best to defeat the purveyors of international terrorism, preserve American liberties, and defend this nation and its citizens from a threat to our very way of life.

Dizzy Buildings, 1971. A worm's eye view of the World Trade Center, New York, under construction.
Photograph: Hulton I Archive/Getty Images.

Chapter 2

September 10, 2001:
The Way We Were

For most Americans, September 10, 2001, came and went without fan-
fare. A day calendar found by firefighters in the six-story rubble of
what were once New York City's twin towers bears poignant testa-
ment to the passing of an age. The calendar's paper edges were burnt
and crumbled, covered in pulverized cement powder. Written in the
margins were a few social appointments and a smiley face from the
September 10 of someone's life, followed by a vacant box on the next
day, September the eleventh.

Indeed, for a moment that would be seen in hindsight as the end of
an era in American life, there was nothing particularly significant about
the day's headlines or national agenda. The day before catastrophic
terrorism came home to America was in most ways a day like any
other.

New York's newspapers carried below-the-fold coverage of the may-
oral primaries scheduled for the following day, amid universal sentiment that Mayor Rudolph Giuliani's last months in office had not
lived up to expectations. The *Washington Post* covered Michael Jordan's
impending announcement of his return to professional basketball and
what it would mean for the capital city's battered sports psyche. The
Los Angeles Times published a story on immigration, citing business
leaders from the San Fernando Valley who wanted to remove hurdles
in the immigration process to deal with anticipated shortfalls in
California's labor pool. The *Financial Times* ran a front-page story
indicating that Treasury Secretary Paul O'Neill believed the U.S.

economy was in a shallow cyclical downturn and would bounce back by the end of the year.

In international coverage, the *Boston Globe* chose the banner headline, "In Surge of Violence, Mideast Blast Kills 8," for a story detailing the escalating pattern of armed attacks and reprisals between Israelis and Palestinians. In an interview with an Indiana paper, former senator John Danforth, the newly appointed presidential emissary to Sudan, expressed his hopes for bringing a measure of peace to that troubled African country. A Newport News navy newspaper featured a color picture and a proud piece on the USS *Cole*, badly damaged in a terrorist attack in Yemen in December 2000 but now repaired, replenished, and ready for sea duty.

A few newspapers carried brief stories cobbled together from wire dispatches about the reported murder of Ahmed Shah Massoud, the charismatic leader of the Northern Alliance, in the mountains of Afghanistan. While details were unclear, it appeared Massoud had been attacked by suicide bombers posing as a television crew.

Washington was in the midst of some of the fiercest partisan political struggles in years, as Republicans and Democrats in an evenly divided Senate and House fought it out on issues ranging from health care benefits to tax cuts. President Bush had recently returned to the White House after a lengthy "working vacation" at his Texas ranch, and he and his staff were busy planning their agenda for the fall political season. There were mounting concerns abroad over President Bush's "unilateralist" foreign policy on issues such as global warming and ballistic missile defense, and even close allies like Britain and Japan were expressing private concerns. U.S. relations with Russia and China were uneven at best. The conventional wisdom in Washington was that the American military had to gear up for potential high-tech challenges that would confront the nation toward the end of the next decade.

One of the autumn highlights on the East Coast was visiting the nation's capital by air. Experienced travelers flying one of the many airline shuttles from New York's La Guardia to Washington's Reagan National Airport could arrive at the airport 10 minutes before their flight's departure, breeze through security, and still have time to grab a coffee and bagel before boarding with e-ticket in hand. No one worried that powdered sweetener or coffee creamer might be anthrax. Minimum-wage airport security personnel haphazardly scanned personal possessions. Passengers could even board their aircraft legally with a four-inch bladed knife in their carry-on bags.

The weather was especially clear on September 10, allowing airborne travelers leaving New York a magnificent view of the World Trade Center, gleaming in the crisp autumn skies.

An airliner's descent into Washington from the west along the Potomac River was a combination sightseeing tour and roller coaster ride. Planes flew a few hundred feet over the headquarters of the Central Intelligence Agency, banking to the south while providing a panoramic view of the Capitol dome, the National Mall, and federal buildings. Final descent brought planes breathtakingly close to the Pentagon before touchdown at Reagan National Airport.

The civilian air traffic control system manages thousands of civilian flights up and down the eastern seaboard, but on September 10, there had never been any cause to contemplate how armed fighter aircraft might need to intercept civilian aircraft commandeered by terrorists and turned into hurtling suicide bombs. In the event of a hijacking, pilots and flight crews were advised to cooperate with their assailants. Experience taught that such episodes generally ended on the tarmac with the hijackers dead or in custody and the majority of passengers unharmed.

Precautions against terrorist attacks of a conventional nature—a car bomb or a case of smuggled explosives—had been taken by both the Pentagon and World Trade Center occupants in recent years.

The Pentagon was in the midst of a major renovation, scheduled to last several years at a cost of more than a billion dollars. The five wedges of the Pentagon were being renovated in turn, and the army and navy staffs had just resumed occupancy of their newly finished digs along the outside corridors of the building facing the south. The new offices boasted specially reinforced glass designed to withstand explosions and gunfire.

A huge new facility adjacent to the building had just been completed to screen all incoming packages for signs of explosive devices or chemical agents. And Pentagon authorities had spent the past few years trying to perfect a hydraulic barrier to deny access to building entrances by speeding vehicles potentially rigged as suicide bombs. While there had been no attempts to drive a bomb to the Pentagon's doorstep, several distinguished visitors to the building, including the defense ministers of Japan and Germany, had been injured when the barrier suddenly opened, smashing their speeding limousines. After one such accident just yards from the Pentagon entrance, one defense minister and several of his officers had waited for more than an hour for an ambulance to take them to a nearby hospital.

Several of the businesses occupying space in the World Trade Center complex had provided their employees with survival kits in the wake of the terrorist bombing of Tower One in February 1993. One company issued red nylon emergency pouches filled with flashlights, water, whistles, a phosphorescent stick that glowed in the dark, and breathing masks. Companies occasionally practiced emergency evacuation procedures, but employees focused on work demands found these civil defense exercises bothersome, and the exercises declined in urgency as the 1993 bombing receded farther into memory.

Fears about the potential for domestic terrorism had ebbed and waned in the years before September 10, 2001. Most Americans believed that the primary threats to the United States were overseas, and targeted at symbols of the U.S. government, from our East African embassies to the USS *Cole.* In the immediate aftermath of the bombing of the Murrah Federal Building in Oklahoma City in 1995, there had been unsubstantiated speculation that Middle Eastern groups were involved, followed by a sense both of shock and relief when a former U.S. soldier named Timothy McVeigh was apprehended while fleeing from the scene. This tragic case of homegrown terrorism proved to be an isolated attack by an unsophisticated protagonist. The FBI worked aggressively in the wake of Oklahoma City to infiltrate and dismantle right-wing hate groups made up largely of white extremists.

A number of blue-ribbon panels and presidential commissions had been established to explore new security challenges from biological weapons to cyber attacks—especially after a bizarre cult named Aum Shinrikyo unleashed sarin gas in a Tokyo subway in 1995. These efforts—including the Bremer National Commission on Terrorism, the Hart-Rudman Commission on National Security/21st Century, and the Harvard working group on responses to catastrophic terrorism—all issued handsome and well-received reports. Little, however, fundamentally changed in the way of bolstering homeland defense or preparing for a national disaster brought on by a catastrophic terrorist strike.

On September 10, 2001, there were large and growing Islamic communities scattered across the United States, composed primarily of patriotic citizens living normal lives. There was evidence, however, of a growing group of Islamic fundamentalists inside U.S. borders who were intent on striking a blow against America. The FBI had known for years, even before the first World Trade Center bombing in 1993, that cells from Osama bin Laden's Al Qaeda organization were operating freely inside the United States, using false identities, encrypted e-mail, and secretive bank accounts. Despite the fact that the FBI in the past decade had tripled its spending on terrorism prevention, quintupled the number of intelligence operatives it employs, and worked to revamp its stove-piped and technologically challenged bureaucracy, the bureau still demonstrated serious deficiencies in the fight against terrorism. There were significant shortages of agents and interpreters fluent in Arabic, Farsi, and Pashto.

The CIA, with its exclusive international charter, tracked the same suspicious individuals as they entered and reentered the United States, in some cases over the course of several years. Yet the handoff to domestic law enforcement agencies once these suspicious aliens entered the United States was often messy, reflecting a history of entrenched bureaucratic resentment and distrust between the CIA and the FBI.

The ultrasecret National Security Agency collected reams of data from overseas communications of every kind but, with a communications haystack that had grown exponentially while the size of the needle stayed the same, worthless gibberish tended to crowd out intelligence gems. Literal stacks of potentially important intercepts and communications accumulated without the necessary translation or interpretation. In any event, on September 10, tracking Al Qaeda operatives was just one of many demands on law enforcement and intelligence agencies. Bin Laden's disciples were able to scheme and prepare with little fear of detection or capture.

For years, the war against terrorism had been waged in secret by intelligence operatives and U.S. special operations forces in every corner of the globe, yet the only evidence of this campaign was a few nondescriptive line items in the federal budget. Though Clinton administration officials had tried to disrupt Osama bin Laden's financial activities and either kill or capture him after the first attack on the World Trade Center, they had little to show for it publicly. A cruise missile strike on a training camp in Afghanistan and an assault on a drug manufacturing factory in Sudan—purportedly involved in the development of chemical agents and linked to a bin Laden associate—were both high-profile gambles that did not have the desired effect once the rubble was cleared. Some reporters even speculated that the former president had launched the raid against Afghanistan to distract American attention away from a particularly difficult chapter in the Monica Lewinsky scandal.

Those missile strikes plus a host of other grievances held by some in the Middle East helped Islamic militants stoke rage and resentment against America throughout the region. The presence of U.S. military personnel in Saudi Arabia, the protector of Islam's most holy sites, had been a source of enduring tension since the end of the Gulf War. Many Arab citizens blamed U.S.-led sanctions for the starvation of Iraqi children. America's perceived bias toward Israel in its struggle with the Palestinians caused popular outrage in the Arab street. In some Arab states, America's "soft power"—its music, information, and values—was seen as leading to the erosion of traditional structures and cultures. Indeed, Arab intellectuals and wealthy Saudi families would openly vent their anger and suspicions about the role of the United States in the Middle East. Arab newspapers were generally overwhelmingly critical of America's regional focus and priorities.

Among the hundreds of thousands of Afghan refugees who grew up in the camps along the Pakistan border, these grievances had led scores to make the journey to training camps inside Afghanistan to commit their lives to the destruction of every aspect of American life. Joined by the disaffected and fanatic from Egypt, Algeria, Saudi Arabia, Yemen, and Sudan, these men were given terrorist tools and training to carry out that mission.

Increasingly, Osama bin Laden was viewed by radicalized Islamic militants and counterterrorist operatives alike as the personification of the jihad against the United States. Bin Laden had made Afghanistan his base of operations since the mid-1990s, and the Taliban treated him and his commanders as their "honored guests." All Middle East states, even Pakistan, feared the brutal Taliban regime, even though the Taliban maintained only a perilous hold on one of the poorest and most war-torn states in the world. The Taliban's style of rule ranged from the barbaric to the bizarre: Women could be publicly stoned and lashed for letting their faces or ankles show; singing a song or flying a kite was a punishable offense. Yet, much to the chagrin of many Arab rulers, the Taliban's brand of Islamic fundamentalism had drawn converts and admirers throughout the Muslim world.

Bin Laden had kept a low profile in the weeks preceding the terrorist attacks against the United States. On September 10, some observers even argued that bin Laden's charismatic hold on his "Arab Afghan" followers was loosening. In any event, virtually no one in America expected bin Laden would be able to launch such an audacious strike from his medieval mountain camp—wreaking destruction on the twin symbols of American capitalism and national defense.

The next day, however, by 9:03 A.M. eastern standard time, as the second jet slammed into the World Trade Center and obliterated our desperate hope that the first had been a freak accident, America's national consciousness was raised—both to our domestic vulnerability and to our place in a dangerous world.

Osama bin Laden and his fanatic faction had succeeded in carrying out the most devastating attack against the United States in its history. Thousands of lives were lost—and so too was an era in American life. A new era, whose contours were still uncertain, had suddenly, dramatically begun.

War Birds, circa 1935. War birds (army planes) fly over the Statue of Liberty, New York. Photograph: Hulton I Archive/Getty Images.

Chapter 3

The Imperative to Prevail and the Nature of the Campaign

"[O]ur war on terror will be much broader than the battlefields and beachheads of the past. This war will be fought wherever terrorists hide, or run, or plan. Some victories will be won outside of public view, in tragedies avoided and threats eliminated. Other victories will be clear to all. Our weapons are military and diplomatic, financial and legal. And in this struggle, our greatest advantages are the patience and resolve of the American people. We did not seek this conflict, but we will win it."

— President George W. Bush
Radio Address to the Nation
September 29, 2001

The United States must prevail in the campaign against global terrorism. As President George W. Bush said of Osama bin Laden, Al Qaeda, and their ilk, "These terrorists kill not merely to end lives, but to disrupt and end a way of life." In the words of British prime minister Tony Blair, "There is no compromise possible with such people, no meeting of the minds, no point of understanding with such terror. Just a choice: Defeat it or be defeated by it. And defeat it we must."

This is a struggle we must win—yet the contours of victory are still imprecise. For the American people, victory must come to be seen as a process rather than a defined endpoint. It will require citizens to focus their attention on the conduct of the campaign and the essence of national solidarity, rather than trying to conceptualize the conclusion of a conflict that is likely—to paraphrase Hobbes—to be nasty, brutish, and *long*. Thus, pursuit of victory must involve steps to sustain American purpose and resolve in the face of repeated unthinkable attacks, or in their absence, possibly for years to come.

The most important task for national leadership at the outset of the campaign against terrorism is to try to conceptualize what is desirable and achievable in this effort. The overarching goals of the United States in the campaign should be to reduce the threat of global terrorism, to enhance the security of Americans at home and abroad, and to sustain the resoluteness of U.S. and international purpose. The specific objectives of the campaign are clear: To attack and destroy global terrorist networks; to punish states sponsoring terrorism until they stop; to build stronger capabilities to combat terrorism and secure the U.S. homeland; to strengthen international norms and actions against terrorism; and, over time, to ameliorate the conditions that provide fertile ground for terrorists.

Much has been said and written about the various tools to be employed against terrorism, but the measurements of success are likely to evolve for the simple reason that no one yet knows what is possible in this unconventional conflict. Victory cannot be realistically interpreted as stamping out every terrorist. In the simplest terms, it will mean reducing terrorism to the point where it is no longer a daily preoccupation and the nation can once again return to a more normal state of affairs.

Secretary of Defense Rumsfeld has been among the most rigorous in his thinking about the meaning of national victory in this campaign. "I think the idea of eliminating it [terrorism] from the face of the Earth is setting a threshold that's too high," Rumsfeld said during a Pentagon briefing. "What we are attempting to do is to assure that we can prevent people from adversely affecting our way of life." He further refined his thinking in writing: "Victory means crippling the ability of terrorist organizations to coerce and terrorize and otherwise disrupt the way of life of the men and women in the United States and our friends and allies around the world."

Indeed, one of the most pernicious aspects of the terrorists' threat is that not only have they breached our borders, but that they have infiltrated our minds. The attackers have pierced America's sense of invulnerability, and this sudden awareness of being at risk is a now a hallmark of everyday life, felt at a very personal level. One measure of victory in the campaign against terrorism will be our ability to hold on to what distinguishes us as a nation—the openness and tolerance of our society, the optimism of our national character, the fundamental freedoms we experience in our everyday lives—even as we come to terms with new dangers, and establish new defenses. Sustaining the American spirit, and the spirit of individual Americans, will be an enduring challenge for our national leaders, spiritual counselors and clergy, teachers, parents and role models everywhere.

As terrible as the suicide airplane bombs and anthrax attacks have been, it is not hard to imagine even more terrible attacks that could place huge burdens on American tolerance and forbearance, deeply straining our national institutions and ideals. Preserving our cherished institutions and liberties may turn out to be one of the most challenging aspects of the campaign. The extraordinary task for American political leaders will be to motivate Americans to be at their best while preparing for highly stressful and unpredictable conditions that may find us at our worst.

Prevailing in the war on terrorism must be our primary, immediate priority. It must be "our calling," as President Bush has said—not in a religious sense, but in the sense of meeting a challenge that will define this moment in the history of our nation and of Western civilization. Nevertheless, even in the face of a continuing threat, the campaign against terrorism should not be made the sole organizing concept for the totality of U.S. foreign and domestic policy. It should not trump indefinitely or negate the rest of our national agenda.

Indeed, it must be weighed and balanced against the other priorities that will continue to affect the vital interests and character of the nation. For example, problems that existed on September 10 still existed on September 12—from nuclear proliferation to the global economic downturn to the spread of HIV/AIDS. And important opportunities, from reducing barriers to free trade around the world to laying the foundations for a durable peace in places like the Balkans, Northern Ireland, and the Korean peninsula will be lost without sustained U.S. engagement. Similarly, domestically, improving homeland security will not fix the U.S. health care crisis, improve education, or alter the fact that one in six American children lives in poverty; however, it could, if pursued without adequate reflection and debate, erode key civil liberties.

The strategic mantra during the Cold War was the maintenance of the balance of power. In this new campaign against international terrorism, a better mantra may well turn out to be the power of balance, where the ultimate effectiveness of our national effort will require balancing many competing demands and priorities.

Achieving this balance will be very difficult if the nation continues to feel under attack. But as we conduct the long campaign against global terrorism, there is good reason to resist the sort of all-consuming national passion that characterized the early Cold War era. McCarthyism and covertly staging coups in the name of anti-Communism were not high points in recent American history. In the final analysis, it is hard to imagine much domestic tranquility or the pursuit of other worthy foreign policy or domestic priorities without advances in the war against terrorism. But in making the campaign our top national priority, we must take care not to neglect or abandon all other foreign and domestic policy objectives.

The Nature of the Campaign

The campaign against terrorism was actually being waged behind the scenes for years before September 11, 2001—at least since the first attack on the World Trade Center in 1993. The battle against bin Laden and his creed was directed by a small band of U.S. and allied intelligence operatives and national security officials, and played out largely through clandestine efforts and intelligence operations. After September 11, this hidden struggle became a national campaign.

Almost immediately, the public and official reaction to the spectacular assaults and their terrible human cost was to label them "acts of war" and declare that the United States was "at war" with terrorism. But what does it mean to be "at war" against this enemy? How we will conduct the war, ensure we stay the course, and win?

Perhaps the most important difference between this campaign and more conventional wars in our history is that the traditional means by which the United States has won its "good" wars—massive production sustaining mobilization of large, magnificently equipped military services, supported by an essentially unscathed and invulnerable home front—are either not decisive or not available here. And the traditional objectives of wars, total or limited—either complete surrender by the enemy or a negotiated compromise—are not applicable in this case. However else this war ends (if it ends), it will not be a ceremony on a battleship or in a school or railway carriage; still less will it be a formal agreement leaving the terrorists in place in exchange for commitments to change their ways.

This war carries with it an added imperative about the way we wage the campaign on the home front. We must find a way to strike a balance between more stringent security measures and the need to preserve civil liberties. History reveals that virtually every wartime U.S. president chose to curtail civil liberties when confronted by perceived internal threats. John Adams signed into law the Alien and Sedition Act during a period of intense anti-French sentiment, Lincoln suspended habeas corpus and subjected anti-war organizers to a form of martial law, and Franklin Roosevelt signed the executive order that sent Japanese Americans into internment camps during World War II. After each crisis ended, civil liberties were restored and in most cases came back stronger than before; yet still, Adams, Lincoln and Roosevelt, patriots all, took egregious steps to silence perceived domestic critics or arrest fellow travelers—even when there was little evidence to support such draconian measures. This time, ironically, there is a clear and present danger on the home front, which makes President Bush's restraint on these matters all the more impressive.

The question is whether this restraint can persevere in the face of new and deadly attacks. Leaders and lawmakers alike have been judicious so far about offering up initiatives that would unduly interfere with fundamental personal freedoms. Yet, further attacks at home could lead to calls for more intrusive law enforcement surveillance, racial profiling, and temporary suspension of travel rights. Reports indicate some one thousand suspects have been swept up in the post–September 11 dragnet. Another catastrophic act of terrorism could see that number soar higher, and even lead to the imposition of martial law. As we get thicker into this grim campaign, it is likely that the nation will confront some of its most difficult challenges since the founding of the Republic.

In many respects, the war on terrorism more resembles the wars on drugs and organized crime than it does the war against the Axis, the war to the save the Union, or even the wars against Saddam Hussein and Slobodan Milosevic. Obviously, there is no distinct state entity as the enemy; moreover, not only individual terrorists and cells, but the very concept of "terrorism" can be difficult to pin down. Of course, the enemy includes nation states that harbor and support—and even those that tolerate—terrorists, and they may well find that their choices have made them the target of U.S. actions, and even of U.S. military force. But the real enemy is the terrorists themselves, and even Al Qaeda is a loose network of many cells, while Osama bin Laden and his henchmen are by no means the only terrorist grouping that could conceivably threaten us. Indeed, September 11 may come to serve as a model and inspiration for other terrorist groups opposed to the United States.

Furthermore, the war metaphor does not accurately capture the element of reconstruction and renewal that will be an essential component of the overall campaign. Given that failed states in the Middle East and Africa have been a central breeding area and recruiting zone for Islamic terrorism, the United States, with the full support and resources of the international community, must develop long-term strategies to help failed states recover and to assist in post-conflict reconstruction. This is more akin to waging peace than fighting a war.

The most difficult element in this strategy is its starting point, Afghanistan, where the United States must work relentlessly to convey an essential truth: America is neither imperialist Great Britain playing the Great Game in South Asia nor the expansionist Soviet Union seeking to install a puppet regime in Kabul. The United States wants simply for Afghanistan to be governed by people who will direct their energies toward lifting the lives and enhancing the opportunities of Afghanistan's citizens—not using their country as a base for terror against the civilized world. In this fundamental battle for hearts and minds, we must pursue a course that highlights that our interests are practical and humanitarian, not materialistic or imperialist.

Nonetheless, in many respects, the war model is appropriate, and in ways that go beyond symbolizing national commitment, unity, and extraordinary effort in the face of mortal danger. Indeed, the most useful part of the war analogy may be the degree to which it helps us understand the hardships and challenges ahead: patient acceptance of setbacks and losses, petty inconvenience for all and unevenly distributed sacrifice for a few, continual unpredictable risk, defeats as well as success, profiteers as well as heroes, selfishness and opportunism as well as unity, folly as well as courage. If we are to be successful in sustaining the war that has been thrust upon us, we need to be honest about the real costs, and what it will take to win.

"War" implies the use—even the unlimited use—of military force, and military force is a field in which the United States has a huge comparative advantage. This time, however, as the Bush administration has rightly and even courageously stressed, military operations—and particularly those that are visible and clear cut—have only a limited, though vital, potential to contribute to success.

A new willingness to use—and public and international acceptance of—extreme measures, martial and otherwise, will be needed. But, paradoxically, rhetorical dropping of constraints may itself contribute to impatience, because the public and the world may be led to expect fast results. There are no high-confidence military (or indeed other) instruments waiting to be employed to assure quick eradication of terrorists. While the continued success of terrorists demonstrates that not enough has been done in the past, it is naïve to think that inadequacies have been the result of a lack of toughness about whom we hire as spies, whether military force should be used against identified and located terrorists, or insistence that our intelligence match a juridical standard of evidence.

Intelligence is crucial in any war, but it comes close to the defining factor in this campaign. The intelligence problems of identifying and locating terrorists, and understanding their support networks, are formidable, even with a very relaxed standard of what is a legitimate target. The difficulty of finding a man or members of a shadowy organization that can select its targets at will and otherwise works chiefly to hide in countries with dysfunctional governments and sympathetic elements of the population cannot be overstated. The whole world is a haystack. And intelligence is perhaps the hardest instrument of national power to mobilize and deploy quickly. Insofar as success depends on building both technical and other collection capabilities, effective webs of agents and cooperators, and analytic prowess, time and patience will be needed.

In addition, our inability to function as an integrated network or "system of systems" contributed directly to the failures that led to September 11. Communication between our law enforcement, intelligence, and military "stovepipes"—or nodes, to use a less pejorative term—is better than it has been, but is far from seamless. Our military is organized to fight regional aggressors, not global, elusive, transnational entities. Bin Laden and his Al Qaeda network are already practiced in the art of net-war. They operate globally in small, dispersed, Internet-enabled units that, on September 11, "swarmed" and struck a catastrophic blow against an unprepared America. To degrade, defeat and destroy twenty-first-century terrorist networks, we must learn to fight as a network ourselves, one with global reach and an ability to bring to bear at the right time the right tool for maximum effectiveness. Hierarchy is necessary at the "system of systems" level to ensure strategic direction and unity of purpose, but we must break down our "stovepipes," each with their own hierarchies, to operate as an integrated network.

Finally, most of the important and enduring elements in the campaign against terrorism will involve the United States acting with other states, rather than acting alone. So far, the Bush administration has preferred to act internationally through the creation of a number of loose and informal coalitions involving a range of states. These coalitions offer the greatest flexibility, less formal than security organizations like NATO, and providing more room for maneuver than would be possible inside a broad-based multilateral political institution like the United Nations.

While there will inevitably be circumstances ahead when the United States must consider acting alone, the Bush administration has rightly placed a high priority on assembling the international coalition necessary to fight global terrorism in all its manifestations. Effective measures from law enforcement and intelligence collection to the prosecution of the military campaign all require international cooperation; indeed, without it, U.S. efforts will fail. When contemplating unilateral action, we must balance the potential gains against potential losses in the form of resulting defections from our antiterror coalitions.

A New Meaning to National Mobilization

The United States is entering its first true national-level campaign since 1941, but this time the signs of national mobilization will be strikingly different from those of more traditional conflicts. In this campaign there have been and will be significant civilian casualties on the home front—almost certainly more than the fatalities of all soldiers, clandestine operatives, and diplomatic representatives operating overseas combined. This blurring of soldier and civilian will have many implications for American life, not least of which will be the redefinition of "duty stations" beyond its narrow military application. Our new national battle stations include post offices, businesses, metros, malls, and schools; in short, everywhere that you are liable to encounter Americans going about their daily responsibilities.

The national mobilization will not involve a harnessing of vast economic resources for exclusively military ends. Indeed, the new military requirements associated with fighting terrorism are likely to be incremental innovations in existing capabilities, such as placing precision-guided munitions on unmanned aerial drones. Instead, the fundamental areas of new mobilization are likely to involve efforts at homeland defense, from greater vigilance in neighborhoods to better technologies for detecting dangerous microbes in the air or water. There will be much more effort focused on all aspects of domestic security from prevention to detection and to emergency response, and these steps will go beyond simply a small cadre of technical specialists. There is a role for every American in maintaining a higher degree of national vigilance and preparedness. Everyone will have an answer to the perennial question: What did you do during the war?

We are up against a set of enemies whose optimal strategy would be to outlast us—and the best way to outlast us would be to create a pervasive insecurity inside our national borders in the hope that our tolerance for fear and random suffering is lower than theirs. Indeed, it is reasonable to argue that no nation has ever fought the United States except in the hope of wearing down public support by increasing the cost, not defeating us directly. That was Japan's plan, and North Vietnam's. It will be the terrorists' too.

Thus, our response must recognize that the goal of terrorists is not simply killing or destruction as such, but terror—that is, destroying the will of the opponent by sowing fear and division. Here, the terrorists have almost certainly miscalculated. All the signs in the wake of September 11 point to greater resolve and national unity. The real concern is that future strikes against the American homeland will lead to greater pressures for the United States to retaliate abroad.

Continued insecurity at home may provoke more urgent calls for stepped up military attacks, which could force our military campaign out in front of the political and diplomatic dimensions—causing ruptures in the international coalitions on which success depends. Paradoxically, "stronger" U.S. retaliation could actually weaken our chances for a long-term, comprehensive victory against terrorists. Devastating U.S. military attacks abroad with the real potential for the collateral deaths of innocents could inadvertently spur further anti-American resentment and assist bin Laden (or his successors) with recruitment.

The nature of the casualties in this campaign—coming both at home and abroad—may also lead to wholesale reconsideration of the nature of public tolerance for sustaining battlefield losses. The Vietnam syndrome rests on the assumption that the American public will be profoundly anxious about extensive casualties coming in an ambiguous fight, while the so-called Kosovo syndrome suggests the American public has come to expect that maximal foreign policy objectives can be achieved with minimal U.S. casualties. The campaign against terror is likely to write a new chapter in U.S. attitudes about "acceptable" wartime losses for the simple fact that citizens are now conscripts and we have already suffered significant casualties on the home front. We can limit the potential for the kinds and numbers of casualties in conventional military operations abroad, but the number of American fatalities at home is in large part determined by the tactics of a merciless enemy.

The campaign on the home front will have powerful ramifications for many domestic pursuits that are even now hard to fully appreciate. For instance, architectural and construction codes for projects as diverse as skyscrapers, nuclear reactors, and water purification plants, will all need to be reconsidered after a careful review of the lessons learned from September 11.

The challenge in this—as in other, simpler, wars—will be sustaining the effort in the face of delay, inevitable setbacks and losses, frustration, and yes, compromise—all along with the prospect of continued terrorist successes against the United States. Estimates that the effort will take only "a year or two" are almost certainly too optimistic. Yet patience is not the most obvious characteristic of American public opinion—and understanding of delays, mistakes, compromises and problems not the most notable characteristic of the American media or American politicians.

The role of presidential communication—visible, stirring, straightforward and sustained—to explain U.S. goals and rally national morale cannot be underestimated. In the face of the horror of September

11, many Americans were left speechless. Yet, words have not failed us—to the contrary, words will help get us through this crisis. Just as Churchill and Kennedy moved nations in earlier eras of conflict, our leaders must speak clearly to the American people about not only the righteousness but also the difficulty of the path ahead, urging vigilance, counseling patience, lifting and soothing spirits.

So far, the public statements of President Bush, Prime Minister Blair, and New York mayor Rudolph Giuliani have been among the most impressive in modern memory. But as the campaign enters a more intense stage when Americans will seek more information as well as comfort, our national leaders may be called upon to clarify the exact nature of war aims, or the precise characteristics of this or that disease's transmission. Given the unconventional and in some cases unprecedented new circumstances we face, explaining clearly what is happening, what we know and what we don't, along with providing necessary technical information, will be among the more challenging missions of the campaign to keep the public trust. As the struggle grinds on, true leadership will help inspire a combination of patriotism and introspection, as well as provide the essential information for citizens to make choices in their everyday lives.

The New Politics

President Bush came to office pledging to change the tone of political discourse in Washington. In the space of a day, the events of and national response to September 11 achieved that goal. The lawmakers who gathered on the steps of the Capitol to pledge their unity and sing "God Bless America" became one of the earliest symbols of a new national solidarity and resolve. A bipartisan spirit has largely prevailed since then, with political disagreements mostly civil and within the confines of seeking to do what is best for the country.

Nevertheless, we should be wary of this new sense of unity becoming an imperative that stifles debate. Nor should it be allowed to cast doubt on the patriotism of those who would question the administration's priorities, plans, or proposals for the campaign against terrorism. The goal here should not be unanimity at any cost, but rather unity of purpose reached through the discussion, debate, compromise and consensus building that has served our nation so well since the founders first conceived of checks and balances. The real standard of the new bipartisanship should be vigorous debate of the merits of the antiterror measures proposed. At the end of the day, hard-won unity will serve the country infinitely better than forced unanimity.

Both parties have already learned important lessons from the September 11 tragedy and its aftermath, sometimes coming at the expense of party orthodoxy. For Democrats, the priority of defense, intelligence, and other security issues has been reinforced. For Republicans, the government's role and relevance in the daily lives of American citizens has been elevated. These new alignments have already resulted in some surprising common ground; for example, members from both the right and the left have raised profound concerns about the potential long-term implication for civil rights of various proposals designed to combat terrorism at home. The tragedy also appears to have energized the vital center in American politics, at least in the Senate, with key leaders like Senator John McCain and Senator Joseph Lieberman transcending party labels to work together to get things done.

There is broad support in both parties for extensive fiscal stimulus, even if it means substantial increases in government expenditures in the short run. To some degree, we are all Keynesians now in our support for federal stimulus and spending. We are also likely to see virtually every major initiative in Congress—from enhanced trade authorities to new minimum wage laws—described by its proponents as an essential tool in the fight against terrorism. This propensity to get on board the antiterrorism spending wagon is not a new phenomenon. After all, one of the primary rationales for the National Highway Act in the 1950s was that better roads were said to be essential in the event of a major conflict with the Soviet Union. Increased continental travel, transport, business, and tourism were cited only as incidental benefits in congressional debates.

On some issues, however, partisanship has survived the September 11 attacks. For instance, the question of "federalizing" the airport security function caused concern in Republican ranks about the potential for a large new organization with ties to organized labor, and Democrats railed against Republican plans in the House to give the majority of post-September 11 financial relief to corporations rather than individuals. Inevitably, there will be a return to more partisan politics in time, but the hope is that future dialogue and debate will be characterized by civility, rather than the rancorous point-scoring that set the tone in the 1990s. The real enemy does not sit across the aisle, but is making preparation to attack America again.

Americans Are Now More Focused on the World

A striking and important aspect of the campaign against international terrorism is the renewed involvement of the American public in foreign policy. Over the last decade, national leaders have largely conducted foreign policy in a vacuum, virtually disconnected from broad public interest or support. The common denominator associated with the Bosnia and Kosovo campaigns, the NATO expansion debate, and the push for the North American Free Trade Agreement was a disinterested American public. Leaders in the executive branch and some members of Congress have devoted inordinate amounts of time and energy—largely in vain—to reengage the U.S. public in a national dialogue about American purpose abroad. The reality, however, is that just as there have been significant and apparent downsides associated with public indifference to foreign policy, there were also some unspoken benefits, such as the ability to escape serious public scrutiny.

Now, suddenly, Americans are paying close attention to events transpiring overseas and how they affect us. And while greater public interest in and focus on foreign affairs may be one of the unanticipated pluses to emerge from the ongoing crisis, the Bush administration will have to cope with a better-informed U.S. citizenry that suddenly has more questions and concerns.

Hopefully, this renewed interest in world affairs will lead to greater interest in language training and international travel for American citizens both in schools and later in life. Reportedly, enrollment in Arabic language courses already has risen sharply on campuses from Princeton to the University of Chicago. Ultimately, a more cosmopolitan citizenry well informed about regional politics and dynamics, and perhaps even more familiar with how America and Americans are seen overseas, may turn out to be a central element in a sustained strategy against international terrorism.

Yet, it is not a given that the public's reengagement with foreign affairs will translate into durable support for America's engagement beyond our borders. In the wake of September 11, the Bush administration

has reached out to other states worldwide for support and cooperation, and so far, Americans have solidly backed this outward-looking
approach. Indeed, public opinion polls have shown strong levels of
American support for U.S. engagement in the world. Yet, as the campaign against terrorism progresses, public support for engagement may
wane—particularly if we suffer setbacks overseas, or the United States
encounters mounting criticism from abroad. U.S. leaders must be alert
for—and must seek to reverse—signs of public disenchantment with
America's international engagement.

It would be a tragedy for our nation and the world—and a victory
for the terrorists—if American leadership and engagement in the world
became a casualty of September 11. Indeed, if September 11 has taught
us anything, it is that our security and prosperity at home are directly
affected by forces far beyond our borders. The United States cannot
escape the world. But we can, and must, work to shape it.

Employing Leverage

Our greatest leverage—military and otherwise—is probably not on the
terrorists themselves, but on those people, organizations, and individuals who support, assist, tolerate and apologize for them. We can reasonably expect to gradually grind down this infrastructure of sympathizers and supporters, but success will be neither simple nor swift.

The countries that offer outside support may be more open to pressure. Their support may reflect actual sympathy with the terrorists' goals,
or a judgment that the costs of cooperating with the terrorists are lower
than the costs of not. Now is the time for the civilized world to raise
those costs dramatically. For the Taliban as the most direct and open
state supporter of bin Laden, a combination of military action, backing
armed opposition, and less visible pressures, all calculated as much to
exploit fissures in Afghan politics as to win a military victory directly,
will likely eventually produce a change in the power structure.

However much we rightly insist on the principle that we will do
what we must to protect the United States, what we are able to do will,
in most cases, be conditioned by the degree to which we can sustain
the support of other nations. Reliance on coalitions is less a choice
than a necessity, as illustrated by considering the near-impossibility
of a serious military (or intelligence) campaign against the Taliban if
we did not have the direct support of neighboring states like Pakistan

and Uzbekistan, and the acquiescence of Saudi Arabia, Russia and the Europeans. We do not need everyone's support every time, and no single nation's help is indispensable, but without some foreign support, we are likely to be frustrated in our efforts.

Yet, we cannot realistically expect others to join in the struggle simply because of the justice of the fight or its importance to the United States. Other nations will have their own interests that they will want us to advance if they help us—some even related to U.S. support against those they consider terrorists. Nor will other foreign policy problems and conflicts evaporate just because the United States wants the world to focus on the fight against terrorism. But the compromises and compensations involved in getting essential outside support can create problems in maintaining support at home. Some of our "new friends" will inevitably disappoint American official, public, media and congressional expectations. Continued realism from the administration about the need for foreign support—and the limits on what we can expect—will be required.

Compared to the international effort, military and otherwise, the problem of enhancing homeland security is even more important and challenging, not only in itself, but in terms of its impact on public morale. The country is likely to be far more tolerant of delays and uncertainties, even of blunders, in overseas operations than of repeated terrorist incidents at home. Yet, with clever, well-financed people prepared to die and indifferent to the consequences of mass bloodshed to their own cause, complete defense is all but impossible.

In the short run at least, prevention, better intelligence, security measures and defenses will be the main means to homeland security. We can make attacks harder, and frustrating a substantial fraction of attempts will inhibit bin Laden and other terrorists' ability to recruit volunteers with the promise of success and an image of power. But measures to prevent terrorism, whether security checks at public arenas or national identity cards, tend not to produce direct results, because their purpose is largely deterrent—yet they almost inevitably result in costs, from mere waste of time to serious compromises of traditional liberties. Many successful operations against attempted attacks will remain unheralded (not so much because of secrecy as the uncertainty of "proving" that an attack was really being planned); and most problematic, even a very high rate of success in preventing or stopping attacks will see a few strikes still evading our protective measures.

We will need, in homeland security, to guard against the tendency to prevent the last attack and not the next one. Besides doing a lot more to stop airplane seizures, we need to worry both about more traditional hostage and blackmail situations, small-scale bombings, attacks on airliners landing or taking off—and about other unconventional modes of attack, such as chemical, biological or cyber attacks. While Al Qaeda seems to prefer well-orchestrated, spectacular assaults, low-level attacks, more frequent and widely distributed—letters filled with anthrax, for example—could prove to be more effective in dividing and demoralizing the nation.

Rationally, it is still true after September 11 that an American is far more likely to be killed on the highway—or by a fellow-citizen's handgun—than by a terrorist. People are not nearly so worried about the statistically greater risks from familiar sources, partly because they have a better sense of their actual scale, but partly because they feel, rightly or wrongly, that they can have some control over them, whereas terrorism presents the specter of random, uncontrollable violence.

It follows that measures that would give ordinary citizens a greater sense of being able to contribute to their own protection would pay double dividends: Wisely chosen, they would in fact greatly reduce the risks, but they would also give a sense of confidence and security. In this connection, such public health measures as a commitment to have the proven vaccines against smallpox and anthrax available for anyone who wanted to be inoculated would be helpful. Well-planned measures of what used to be called "civil defense"—evacuation plans, preparation to remain sheltered in residences for an extended period, basic training of a very broad-based, voluntary national service "reserve" in useful skills ranging from first aid to traffic control—would not only help in the event of a terrorist attack (and in other likely cases of disaster, natural and man-made), but would foster a sense of participation and contribution that would help sustain the national mood of collective purpose and unity.

Going Forward

September 11 has already altered many national trends in its wake. Church attendance is up; most manifestations of crime are down. Gun sales have risen; travel and tourism have slumped. Marriage proposals apparently rose in the aftermath of the tragedy as stories of loss and last phone calls to loved ones inspired people to want to join their lives together. Public trust and confidence in our leaders and vital public services is up considerably. Volunteerism is up; classes in international relations are oversubscribed on university campuses; and larger phone bills and Internet usage suggests a national dialogue of sorts under way. Newspaper sales have increased, as has coverage of international politics—particularly related to September 11 and its aftermath, of course.

Consumer purchases point to a mini-boom in home improvement supplies even in the overall context of negative economic trends, suggesting that Americans are hunkering down at home with their families. And a recent poll of Hollywood producers reveals a great interest in developing film stories that look with nostalgia at the easy life of the 1990s, a time that can now be thought of as an interwar period.

Some of these trends will endure while others will subside, but it is clear that September 11 has altered the fabric of American life.

One can hope that, despite our grief, anger, and uncertainty, some lasting good may emerge from the tragedy we have suffered. Inwardly, we may be more united, and more conscious of our responsibilities to one another and to our homeland. Outwardly, we may be less self-absorbed; more interested in events beyond our borders and the way our policies are perceived by others. Domestically, our political actors may focus more on the common good than on narrow partisan gain. Internationally, we may prove more willing to collaborate with other nations on issues of concern to them—just as we depend on their support in the campaign against global terrorism.

The United States did not choose this conflict, but we cannot choose not to fight. The costs of a failure of persistence and resolve are too great to contemplate, however hard and long the campaign. There is an imperative to prevail and, in the words of President Bush, to "lift a dark threat of violence from our people and our future." We cannot go back to September 10—innocence lost can never be regained. But we can set our sights on a future in which the sense of optimism, hope, and boundless possibility that defines us as a nation is restored.

Gas Mask Passengers, December 19, 1938. Railwaymen in a specially adapted coach attending a training lecture and demonstration. Photograph: Hulton | Archive/Getty Images.

Chapter 4

The Changing Face of Terrorism

"The men on the wall here have put themselves on the list because of great acts of evil. They plan, promote, and commit murder. They fill the minds of others with hate and lies. And by their cruelty and violence, they betray whatever faith they espouse."

— President George W. Bush
Unveiling the FBI's Most Wanted List of Terrorists
October 10, 2001

The catastrophic events of September 11, 2001, demonstrate beyond any doubt that terrorism has changed dramatically from the phenomenon with which Americans had become familiar in the postwar period. By many multiples, September 11 was the most devastating terrorist attack in history—more lethal than all attacks against Americans in a half century combined. The discontinuity between this and what was commonly known as terrorism before is so radical as to almost stretch the term beyond recognition. The new terrorism, as it has come to be known, aims to achieve change on a scale that was unimaginable to earlier terrorists. It seeks nothing less than a vast redistribution of global power and a geopolitical revolution that would end the hegemony of the United States and its Western allies.

The contrast between the two principal forms of terrorism of the postwar period—national liberation and state-sponsored—could hardly be starker. Those types of terror sought incremental change in a manner that avoided massive bloodletting. Thus, for example, violence caused by Palestinian groups from the late 1960s onward or by the Irish Republican Army and its splinter groups in roughly the same period aimed at gaining potential sympathizers and winning for those groups a place at the bargaining table, where the status quo could be revised. An essential part of that strategy was the calibration of violence to prevent the groups from being deemed too barbaric for inclusion in any political process. Double-digit casualties were the hallmark of a major attack, and groups sought through their violence to create a psychological and theatrical dimension that magnified its impact. Thus, no matter how horrifying the Munich Olympics massacre or the *Achille Lauro* hostage taking, Americans could take some consolation in the certitude that terrorist groups did not want to be labeled monsters and hunted to extinction. Instead, the terrorists sought a blaze of publicity and a place at the negotiating table.

State sponsors of terrorism also carefully calibrated their violence. Their goal was to affect U.S. policymakers' thinking and influence public opinion but to avoid eliciting a major retaliation or starting a war. So, for example, the 1996 Khobar Towers bombing in Saudi Arabia appears to have been organized by hard-line leaders in Iran in an effort to undermine support for the American presence in the Persian Gulf. By ensuring that casualties would be relatively limited—and by making the connection to Tehran difficult to quickly ascertain—the Khobar Towers attack succeeded in making a strong counterstrike unlikely.

By contrast, practitioners of the new terror have deliberately worked to maximize the carnage. This can be said because September 11, for all its uniqueness, did not come without precedent or warning—indeed, a number of conspiracies in the past eight years could well have resulted in comparable bloodshed. The first true landmark of the new terrorism occurred in 1993 with the first bombing of the World Trade Center. In the aftermath, it was largely forgotten that an incremental increase in the amount of explosive or better placement of the vehicle carrying the bomb could well have caused the cataclysm that the terrorists had sought: toppling one tower into the other, killing thousands. Two years later, the mastermind of the World Trade Center attack, Ramzi Yousef, attempted to blow up 12 U.S. 747 airliners in flight over the Pacific Ocean—a plot that was foiled.

Shortly before the millennium celebrations, Jordanian intelligence uncovered a conspiracy by terrorists affiliated with Osama bin Laden's Afghanistan-based network that aimed to level Amman's Radisson Hotel, then filled with American tourists, and kill hundreds of Americans visiting religious sites at Mt. Nebo and the Jordan River. On the Canadian-U.S. border, an Algerian with links to the Afghanistan network and the Armed Islamic Group (GIA), Algeria's most extreme Islamist group, was apprehended with a car full of bomb-making matériel and a plan to attack Los Angeles International Airport and perhaps other targets. These plots sought a level of carnage considerably greater than anything known in decades—including the bombing of Pan Am 103 or the U.S. Marine barracks in Beirut.

The determining difference between the older forms of terrorism and the new terrorism lies in the realm of motivation. Specifically, the key characteristics of the new terrorism derive from the explicitly religious terms in which grievances and goals are expressed. Thus, bin Laden's message comes first and foremost in the form of his *fatwas,* or religious rulings, and he casts his positions in clear religious terms. An example is the famous 1998 *fatwa* demanding that "all those who believe in Allah and his prophet Muhammad must kill Americans wherever they find them." The need to expel the United States from the Arabian peninsula is stated as removing a blasphemy, a violation of religious law.

Bin Laden and his associates draw on specific Koranic verses and religious authorities to justify killing. Many analysts argue that the goals in all terrorism are ultimately political, but it is important to note that a core belief of most extreme Islamists is that the categorical division between politics and religion is a false one. The West must take them at their word and recognize that, at least on the side of our opponents, religious beliefs are central.

The belief that violent struggle is divinely mandated underlies the defining characteristic of the new terror: the effort to create massive, history-changing bloodshed. The terrorists' conviction that they are involved in a metaphysical struggle changes the entire calculus about violence. Instead of using it sparingly, like traditional political terrorists, the need to fulfill divine commands leads to a sense that the greater and more spectacular the violence, the more pleasing it is to the deity. The usual reluctance to use brutality indiscriminately disappears. The

East Africa bombings, for example, resulted in a large number of Muslim victims. Traditional terrorist groups avoided such killing because it would alienate potential sympathizers.

This high priority on carnage as a goal in its own right conditions other characteristics that distinguish the new terrorism from the old:

- **A deemphasis on terrorism as a tool first and foremost of psychology.** Virtually every modern definition of terrorism revolves in some way around the concept of influence. The United States Code Section 2656f(d) calls terrorism "premeditated, politically motivated violence perpetrated against noncombatant targets by subnational groups or clandestine agents, usually intended to influence an audience." Clearly, in an event such as September 11, the intended psychological effect remains important, but it is nonetheless derivative of the violence itself. To put it another way, it resembles the use of massive violence in war as psychological tool—as in, say, the firebombing of cities in World War II.

- **A general independence of state support.** It is too early to rule out definitively some connection with a hostile state in the September 11 bombing. But as a rule, state sponsors of terror have not been linked to the new terrorists, whose agenda and independent resources make them uncontrollable, excessively violent, and therefore dangerous to the interests of state sponsors. The sanctuary given to bin Laden's network in Afghanistan is more symptomatic of the terrorists' reliance on failed states as places in which they can operate than a case of symbiosis between a state and a terrorist group.

Who Are the New Terrorists?

If religious motivation and a desire to cause bloodshed on a grand scale are the key determinants of the new terrorists, who rightly belongs in this category? Several non-Islamic terrorists or groups demonstrate those characteristics. Timothy McVeigh, for example, wanted to cause maximum carnage and had been influenced by the Christian Identity movement. Aum Shinrikyo had an apocalyptic, quasi-religious ideology that also demanded enormous violence.

At this time, however, the only group that deserves the designation is the jihadist network affiliated with Osama bin Laden. It is the only group with the "global reach" President Bush noted, which represents a strategic threat to the United States. Nonetheless, the appearance of violent groups in so many religious traditions and among recently created cults suggests that Al Qaeda may not be the last new terrorist group with worldwide capabilities.

At least two other major terrorist groups merit further consideration. Hamas and Hizballah both seem to fall in a nether zone between old-style political terrorism and religiously motivated terror. Both groups have conducted relentless campaigns of violence against Israel. But neither has thus far managed attacks that left anything like the toll of September 11. Neither, for that manner, do these two groups have a demonstrated ability to conduct large-scale operations outside of the Middle East. As a matter of political consistency, the persistent, high-profile threat these groups represent must be countered in the course of any "war on terrorism." In addition to the crimes these groups have already perpetrated, a question for the future will be whether the "success" of bin Laden's organization will lead these and others to attempt more violent attacks as a way of showing their capability and determination to both their operatives and supporters.

Nature and Attributes

The advent of the new terror has been possible because of the creation of an elaborate international network. The network has a hub-and-spokes configuration, with the leadership hub based in Afghanistan since 1996. (Earlier, it was based in Sudan, until the United States successfully pressured the National Islamic Front regime in Khartoum to evict bin Laden and his associates.) The spokes are cells, affiliated organizations, and perhaps also individual operatives.

With this organization, the network has managed to maintain operations in upwards of 60 countries. Among the constituent groups in the network are bin Laden's own Al Qaeda; the Egyptian Islamic Jihad (EIJ), which enjoys a privileged position; and a range of others including, for example, the GIA in Algeria, the Harakat al Mujahedin that is based in Pakistan and operates principally in Kashmir, the Islamic Movement of Uzbekistan, and Abu Sayyaf in the Philippines. Al

Qaeda, EIJ, and GIA cells have been found in numerous countries in Europe, Africa, and the Islamic world.

Bin Laden's achievement in forging this network is often attributed to the personal fortune that he invested in the effort, and his own contributions have probably long since been supplanted by other sources. Yet, money is only a part of the explanation. In large measure, bin Laden's achievement is also due to his ability to create an overarching religious ideology that has subsumed the particular agendas of the many groups. By redirecting much of the energies of these groups from unsuccessful efforts to cause upheaval in their home countries into a broader assault on the West, bin Laden has created a genuine strategic threat. This ideological bridge maintains emphasis on, for example, liberating Kashmir from Indian control and Chechnya from Russian domination. But by operating transnationally, the groups have found a way to get out of the box of facing off solely against national police in isolated theaters—conflicts they usually lose. Instead, operational cells are small and typically attack third-nation targets.

The combination of network structure and ideological cohesiveness suggests that the organization will have staying power, even as it is targeted for destruction in the wake of September 11. Effective decapitation of the network—the removal of the top layer or two of leaders—would undoubtedly disrupt operations for some period of time. But because so much of the network in the form of cells outside of Afghanistan might survive, Al Qaeda or a successor group could be in operation again in a matter of months. It seems likely that the complex system for funding the group could be largely maintained. The unknown variable is whether a charismatic leader would be necessary and is waiting in the wings.

Another key to the organizational success of the jihadist network is the ability to exploit the sanctuary offered by failed states. These states have no real functioning government that can be called a part of the international community. As a result, it is difficult or impossible to exert pressure to expel the terrorists. In the case of Afghanistan, the Taliban has never gained international recognition and there is little outside of food assistance that can be interdicted to achieve leverage. Moreover, the Taliban's inability to conquer territory controlled by the Northern Alliance has made bin Laden's power base—the heavily armed, battle-seasoned "Afghan Arabs"—an invaluable asset for the Kandahar-based regime. Bin Laden has not only endeared himself to the Taliban's leader, Mullah Muhammad Omar, because of their similar religious outlook, he has also made himself valuable to Taliban field commanders by detailing fighting units to them and giving them financial and weapons support.

Should bin Laden flee Afghanistan—and should he survive transit to another country—he is most likely to seek a haven in another failed state: Somalia or Yemen, where substantial regions are virtually independent of central control, or the war-torn Caucasus.

Goals

Another telling indicator of the distinctiveness of the new terrorists is the scale of their goals. Traditional terrorist groups sought change that, while significant, was nonetheless incremental in nature. Palestinian efforts over several decades combined political efforts to build support with violent attacks to call attention to their cause. For most activists, however, the ultimate goal was to begin a political process of revision of the status quo and the establishment of a Palestinian entity in Gaza and the West Bank. The Palestinian cause has been undermined by its leaders' inability to control those activists who seek a far greater revision—to destroy Israel and create a Palestinian state in its place. Nonetheless, the dominant desire to create a Palestinian state alongside Israel represents change of an incremental nature.

In comparison, bin Laden's aims are enormous. His primary objectives are to

- expel the United States from the Arabian peninsula, essentially ending its presence in the Persian Gulf;
- drive the West out of the traditional lands of Islam, which stretch at a minimum from Spain to Afghanistan, and reestablish a caliphate—the Muslim empire of the seventh and eighth centuries;
- end the repression of suffering Muslims everywhere, a phrase that suggests a defense of Muslims in every country where they may live; and

- end the rule of virtually all the regimes in the Islamic world and usher in an era in which shari'a is the universal law governing Muslims.

Increasingly—and especially since September 11— bin Laden has elaborated on these goals, mentioning the imperative of rescuing the Palestinian people from Israeli oppression and ultimately destroying the state of Israel. He also has spoken more directly about the suffering of Iraqi children due to UN sanctions. His espousal of these causes can be explained as an effort to widen his base and cast himself as the champion of the causes of greatest concern in the Islamic world. In donning the mantle of Palestinian nationalism, he has been especially shrewd, making it harder for Muslim leaders to attack him and eliciting new demands for Israeli concessions from European and other countries that see the Palestinian issue as a root cause of the new terror.

Capabilities

The jihadist network has shown itself extraordinarily innovative in designing acts of terror. Virtually no two attacks have been alike. In East Africa, the mode of attack was traditional—truck bombings—but the coordination of two attacks hundreds of miles apart was unprecedented. The bombing of the USS *Cole* was similarly unprecedented in that it was the first major terrorist attack on a warship by another vessel, and the "shaped charge" that was used represented a leap forward in the use of explosives. Finally, September 11 demonstrated an ingenious ability to turn American infrastructure against America—the use of passenger airliners as cruise missiles to destroy major buildings.

In preparing these and other attacks, the bin Laden network has proved itself highly adept at a number of the skills necessary for terrorist operations:

- **Sophisticated use of computer and telecommunications links.** The terrorists have used a variety of e-mail, cellular, radio, and other communication, including, reportedly, encrypted messaging. By varying the means of communication and using the lowest-tech means—couriers and face-to-face conversation—they have leaped ahead of U.S. intelligence capabilities.

■ **Surveillance techniques.** Surveillance was clearly employed at American airports in 2001 and around the East African embassies in 1998. Information technology has also been used to store and transfer targeting information.

■ **Document forgery and theft.** Through high-quality printing and forgery techniques, the terrorists have managed to gain access to country after country. In preparing for the September 11 attacks, they evidently also stole the identities of others.

■ **Sleeper operatives and cells.** Post–September 11 reporting has emphasized the recent arrival in the United States of the 19 hijackers. It is inconceivable, however, that these attacks could have been pulled off without a long-term presence in America. Otherwise, it would have been impossible to defeat airport security measures or to know airline operations so that timing and execution of the hijackings could be carried out. In East Africa, cells were in place for five years before the actual attacks were carried out.

■ **Finances.** The network also possesses a highly elaborate system of finances, which has allowed it to field hundreds of operatives and a large support structure. Elements of this system include

> **Legitimate businesses.** Legitimate businesses function as a cover for terrorist operations and provide necessary income. In Sudan, for example, bin Laden operated numerous companies that engaged in everything from construction to agriculture, from a bank to an import–export firm.

> **Use of nongovernmental organizations.** A network of financial pipelines through Islamic nongovernmental organizations allow funds to be shuttled to various operatives and donors to contribute to the jihadist cause. These contributors include wealthy, radical sheikhs and businessmen in the gulf region and the *zakat,* or mosque collection plate, from poor believers in countries around the world.

Criminal operations. Some cells, like the Algerian one based in Canada, have managed to live off the land through petty crime, credit card fraud, and the like.

Narcotics. Evidence is sketchy, but just as the Taliban has been deeply involved in the heroin trade, there is reason to believe that bin Laden's network has been as well—possibly as a middleman, or by taxing producers, or through providing protection.

- **Public relations.** Al Qaeda also possesses a well-tuned public relations operation—indeed, there is a committee just below the top level of leadership devoted to the issue. The group's media dealings with the West have successfully driven home the grievances that motivate the terrorists and created in the image of bin Laden a figure of mythical dimensions. No other new-terrorist organization has mounted anything of comparable sophistication.

More so than with any other major terrorist group, Al Qaeda's public relations are directed toward potential sympathizers—not the enemy. In the Arab-language press—especially offshore publications like the London-based newspaper *Al Hayat,* or Al-Jazeera broadcasting, Al Qaeda has conducted a major campaign to establish bin Laden as the true leader of Islam, the champion of a long-repressed Muslim *umma.* Al Qaeda has telegraphed attacks well ahead of time to notify Muslim spectators that something is coming, and while avoiding direct claims of responsibility that would contradict the position of its Taliban hosts, it has then applauded the attacks and described them as part of the world jihad. All of this is carefully crafted to increase bin Laden's appeal and to establish him—in contrast to the supposedly corrupt leaders of Muslim nations—as the true leader of Islam.

Modus Operandi

Based on the record of the past eight years, some generalizations can be made about how the new terrorists design and carry out attacks.

Probably the most comprehensive statement about their tactics is that no mode of violence will be ruled out in pursuit of their goals. Large-scale attacks are clearly preferred but, in the multiple constituent plots that made up the millennium conspiracy, plans included spraying gunfire at visitors to the John the Baptist pilgrimage site on the Jordan River, Mt. Nebo, and at a crossing between Israel and Jordan. These attacks, if carried out, would probably have resembled the massacre of European tourists carried out at Luxor, Egypt, in 1997 by members of the Al-Gama'a al Islamiyya, an Egyptian jihadist group that has had on-and-off relations with Al Qaeda. Indeed, Egyptian government officials have recently contended that bin Laden had a role in that attack.

More frequently, however, the attacks are aimed at achieving spectacular impact—a characteristic that is meant to be a corollary of the world-historic goals of the group. Although Al Qaeda's precise role in the September 11 attack has still not been determined, achieving impact was already evident in the first attack on the World Trade Center, the Manila Air conspiracy, and the plan to destroy New York tunnels and landmarks.

Another typical characteristic of an Al Qaeda attack is multiplicity. A series of massive blows are struck in a short time—as on September 11, the embassy bombings, and many of the failed conspiracies. Indeed, as senior officials remarked after the embassy bombings, other plots were then in train. Although it has been noted that for these terrorists, the psychological dimension of terror is of secondary concern after causing mass casualties, these highly coordinated attacks do have a profound psychological impact. They create an impression of unprecedented proficiency. And they appear not as set pieces with a distinctive beginning, middle, and end but rather emphasize that the violence is without end. In a phenomenon reminiscent of the Tet offensive during the Vietnam War, the spectator is left unsettled and fearful by the lack of certainty about whether the violence is over or has just paused.

The symbolism of the attacks is also noteworthy. Speculation had been that as targets such as overseas embassies became "harder," the terrorists would shift to "softer" ones such as cultural centers or schools. Instead, the terrorists have maintained a focus on icons of American power. The successful attacks of the past three years have in fact shown a kind of escalation: first embassies, then a U.S. warship, and finally the World Trade Center, symbol of American economic might, and the Pentagon, irreducible symbol of American military might.

Other notes have also been struck along the way: The millennium conspiracy telegraphed the religious dimension of Al Qaeda's struggle against "Crusaders and Jews." A large percentage of the inhabitants of the Amman Radisson at the time the plot was set to go forward were Christian pilgrims, mostly American, visiting sites of religious significance such as the site associated with John the Baptist on the Jordan river. Mt. Nebo's fame owes to its designation as the summit from which Moses, before dying, gazed up at the promised land of Israel.

A final operational aspect to note is the use of suicide operatives, who have been a standard feature of Al Qaeda operations. Although the employment of one or two suicide bombers has been routine for groups such as Hizballah, Hamas, and even the Sri Lankan Tamil Tigers, Al Qaeda has used larger numbers of such operatives per conspiracy than other groups. In the embassy bombings, at least four terrorists were to die in the bombings, although during the event one ran away and was later captured. The bombing of the USS *Cole* used two. And, of course, the use of 19 suicide operatives on September 11 was another aspect of the attacks that transcended anything in the past by a large factor. That these operatives were mostly educated, capable individuals in their late 20s and 30s and not the usual brainwashed teenagers also conveyed a sense of Al Qaeda's unique determination.

Weapons of Mass Destruction

The consensus in the scholarly community has long been that terrorists are, in the main, unlikely to use chemical, biological, or nuclear weapons and are more inclined to seek to acquire them for the purpose of blackmail. Aum Shinrikyo's use of sarin in the Tokyo subway is depicted as a fluke owing to the bizarre theology of the group, and the difficulty this group had mounting this attack after numerous failures is a discouragement to others. Some experts have maintained this position even in the aftermath of September 11.

To believe this, however, is to miss Al Qaeda's drive to make the scale of its violence match the scale of its goals. Attacks that have not merely terrestrial but also metaphysical aims require the greatest available weapons. The CIA has on numerous occasions going back at least as far as the embassy bombings stated that Al Qaeda seeks to acquire chemical and nuclear weapons. Court testimony supports these assertions, and it is believed that the group has at a minimum a "crude" chemical weapons capability—probably the ability to use poisons in small-scale attacks. More recently, the intelligence community has also reported that the jihadists seek biological weapons as well. Although the evidence provided by training manuals needs to be considered carefully, these texts do discuss chemical and biological devices. And, given the weak security on former Soviet bioweapons installations or the possibility that agents could be obtained from a state sponsor, these warnings are highly credible.

As of this writing, a rash of anthrax attacks in Florida, New York, and Washington, D.C., has not been scientifically linked to Al Qaeda. While the limited nature of the attacks is atypical of jihadist violence, the willingness to try virtually any approach to violence means that an Al Qaeda link needs to be considered a genuine possibility. Indeed, in the wake of September 11, it is both analytically necessary and, as a matter of policy, prudent to believe that Al Qaeda terrorists will use weapons of mass destruction if they have them and are confident that they can be employed successfully to cause mass casualties. Bin Laden himself has said in interviews that Muslims would be justified in using such weapons, and the grim record suggests that he should be taken at his word.

General Assembly of the United Nations, September 22, 1960. Photograph: Hulton I Archive/Getty Images.

Chapter 5

Building and Sustaining a Coalition of Coalitions

"The message to every country is, there will be a campaign against terrorist activity, a worldwide campaign . . . . Now, this is a campaign in which nations will contribute in a variety of ways. Some nations will be willing to join in a very overt way. Other nations will be willing to join by sharing information—and information in a campaign such as this is going to be incredibly important . . . . [T]here needs to be a financial component of the campaign, where we need to cooperate to make sure we cut off funds, find these organizations that serve as front groups for funding these terrorist cells. And so my message to all nations is we look forward to full cooperation."

— President George W. Bush
September 19, 2001

The September 11 hijackers carried passports from Saudi Arabia, the United Arab Emirates, and Lebanon. Their apparent ringleader, Muhammad Atta, was Egyptian. In the months and years before they launched their attack, some of them had lived or traveled in Germany, Spain, the Czech Republic, Malaysia, and Canada, among other nations—as well as U.S. states from California to Virginia, Florida to Maine. Their suicidal strike on the World Trade Center and the Pentagon claimed victims from more than 60 countries. The September 11 attack may have been directed at Americans, but it was international in both its inception and implications.

Global Threats Demand Global Responses

Such a global threat demands a global response, and the long-term, multifaceted campaign against terrorism will require constant international coalition building and maintenance. Yet there is no single, monolithic coalition that can fulfill all U.S. objectives. Rather, the United States will have to build and sustain a series of interconnected coalitions around each key aspect of the campaign. Each coalition will be composed of distinct actors, though their membership may overlap. As with a suit of armor, the ultimate ability of these various coalitions to help protect the United States will depend not only on each individual coalition, but also how they are fused together and the seams are reinforced. The coalitions will need to be engaged at varying levels of intensity over different time periods—with activities sequenced carefully—and they all will need to evolve as circumstances change.

The United States will need to balance carefully the various coalitions throughout this process. While some coalitions will be mutually reinforcing, especially if their actions are sequenced properly, action by some of the coalitions on certain issues will inevitably increase tensions in others and restrict options in one or more spheres. This will be most true of military action, especially if undertaken unilaterally.

The United States has a right and a duty to protect its citizens, including through unilateral action when necessary. Indeed, effective military action that achieves broadly accepted objectives, and that limits collateral damage, has the potential to enhance U.S. credibility and leadership in other areas as well. That said, military action, especially when undertaken unilaterally, might severely restrict the U.S. ability to mobilize key countries to support other priority fronts in the fight against terrorism.

The campaign against terrorism will call for more multilayered, multilateral cooperation than the United States has ever engaged in to date—and at a time when the reputation of the U.S. administration abroad has been one of high-handed unilateralism. In the initial period following the September 11 attacks, the Bush administration has done a good job of coalition building and using multilateral forums including the United Nations, NATO, and more than 40 other international organizations to create a sense of common purpose. The real challenge, however, will come as the searing memory of September 11 recedes and the fight against terrorism expands to directly affect more countries.

To maintain broad-based international support over time, the U.S. government will need to prove consistently its collaborative, multilateral bona fides. The campaign against terrorism will suffer if it is the only foreign policy priority the United States handles in this fashion. The more the United States can participate in collaborative efforts on issues of concern to other countries, such as missile defense, the International Criminal Court, and even climate change, the more partners the United States will have in its struggle against global terror.

Maintaining the various coalitions outlined below will require monumental effort. The United States cannot and should not aspire to lead them all. While U.S. participation is necessary across the board, the Bush administration should actively recruit countries and international organizations to take the lead on some of the coalitions at the earliest possible stages of the campaigns. In fact, the success of some of the coalitions outlined below might depend on a low U.S. profile.

It should be noted that while the United States will need to call on its allies, as it has already done with NATO, the coalition-building effort must involve much more than simply mobilizing existing regional alliances. Overdependence on preexisting alliance machinery could inhibit more creative and appropriate arrangements from developing.

A Coalition of Coalitions

To prevail in the long-term struggle against terrorism, the United States will need to maintain a coalition composed of at least seven distinct political coalitions.

9-11 Coalition

The first coalition must work proactively to identify, isolate, and destroy Al Qaeda and any other networks directly linked to the September 11 attacks. This effort will itself require a series of overlapping alliances and agreements among a broad array of states and their intelligence, financial, diplomatic, law enforcement, and military assets. This multifront effort will also need to focus on preventing key states, including in the first instance the current Taliban regime in Afghanistan, from being able to continue sponsoring terrorism.

The first piece of this coalition will be the frontline states—Pakistan, Tajikistan, Uzbekistan, Turkmenistan, China, and to an extent Iran—as well as Russia. These countries will be essential for providing intelligence, cutting off military supplies, enforcing sanctions, providing military access, ensuring humanitarian access, and, potentially, helping in the rebuilding of Afghanistan once political conditions in the country permit. For obvious political reasons, as well as important intelligence reasons, key Arab states—from Saudi Arabia and the Gulf States, to Egypt, Jordan, and Morocco—must also form a key part of this coalition. NATO countries will provide some level of support for military action; European countries will also be crucial on the financial, intelligence, and law enforcement tasks. Finally, a wide range of countries from Africa, Asia, Europe, and North America—especially those that may be host to Al Qaeda operatives or whose financial centers have been used to help fund the network—should be involved as the need arises.

Norms and Legal Foundations

A second coalition, one that can and should be pursued simultaneously with the first, should focus on further broadening and deepening a clear set of norms and international legal instruments to combat terrorism. These norms and laws would both solidify the legal basis for going after Al Qaeda and other networks, and create a stronger deterrent to groups that might have otherwise considered terrorism a viable alternative.

Between 1963 and 1999, 12 UN-sponsored antiterrorism conventions were passed on issues from hostage taking to plastic explosives to the safety of civil aviation. Now the U.S. Senate should work expeditiously to ratify the last two of these—the 1997 Convention for the Suppression of Terrorist Bombing and the 1999 Convention for the Suppression of the Financing of Terrorism. The Bush administration should also work with friends around the world to quickly secure the final 18 country ratifications necessary to bring the Convention for the Suppression of the Financing of Terrorism into force as soon as possible. While this is an important and not particularly controversial convention, getting it into force quickly with as many signatories as possible will help in the crucial efforts against the monetary lifeline for terrorists.

In addition, the United States should strongly support, though not visibly lead, the effort to negotiate a thirteenth UN convention that would fill in the gaps and strengthen mechanisms for implementing the previous twelve. Although strong UN General Assembly and Security Council resolutions were passed in the days and weeks following the September 11 attacks, a binding international convention that obligates action on a broader range of issues and that overcomes long-standing disputes on defining terrorism would provide the best possible umbrella of legitimacy for a broad, sustained antiterrorism effort.

This international legal framework would facilitate participation of states with domestic political constraints, especially in the Islamic and the broader developing world. It would also bring into the process countries that may be called upon to participate in antiterror efforts in coming years, but that do not currently seem to merit priority attention.

Finally, it should be emphasized that further elaborating international antiterror norms will not require the United States to seek UN "approval" for all its actions against terrorism. Indeed, the United States already has authority under Article 51 of the UN charter to exercise the "right of self defense." But while the United States is free to combat directly those who have attacked our nation, Security Council resolutions specifically identifying parties who have violated the abovementioned norms will assist the United States in securing the broadest possible support for its campaign.

Other Networks

A third, action-oriented coalition would seek to dismantle operative terrorist networks, whether or not they have any link to the attacks of September 11, 2001. In fact, this would need to be a series of coalitions, each one focused on a specific network. Like the battle against the perpetrators of the September 11 attacks, this broader series of battles would need to encompass political, financial, intelligence, and law enforcement dimensions, among others.

This series of coalitions targeted at other terrorist networks poses some significant dilemmas.

First, expanding the battle opens numerous opportunities for potential partners to demand cooperation on their own top-priority terrorists, even as the United States focuses on the perpetrators of September 11.

Second, calling on partners to pursue other networks is certain to affect cohesion of the 9-11 alliance—for example, a number of European allies would not support immediate action against networks supported by Iraq, Iran, or Syria. This is not to say that these battles should be avoided, only that they must be sequenced carefully and underpinned by convincing public "proof" of the culpability of the networks and states in question. Significant progress on the 9-11 and Norms and Legal Foundations coalitions outlined above may facilitate progress in pursuing other networks later.

At very least, the U.S. government must be careful about opening too many "fronts" in this war simultaneously. There is no clearer recipe for dissipating the cohesion so crucial to securing our objectives.

Global Growth and Development

The United States cannot let the long-term struggle against terrorism consume other fundamental goals. It must continue to work actively to advance other global economic and political priorities such as promoting global prosperity, alleviating poverty, and combating HIV/AIDS and environmental threats to self-sustaining, inclusive social and economic development. The G-8 countries will be central in advancing an agenda to bolster global economic health, including progress on trade (through accelerated progress on a new round of the World

Trade Organization) and sharing the benefits of globalization with the have-nots around the globe.

This latter goal will require renewed efforts to reduce the crushing debt burden on developing countries through the highly indebted poor countries initiative and other efforts; overcome the increasing digital divide; ensure full capitalization of the World Bank and regional development banks; and implement a wide range of development priorities identified for the UN-hosted International Conference on Financing for Development that will take place in the spring of 2002. The success of all of these efforts will depend on engaging key developing countries from the Middle East, Africa, Latin America, South Asia, and Southeast Asia.

Not only is advancing the global economic agenda intrinsically valuable and necessary, it will provide incentives for countries around the world to eschew support for terrorists in exchange for a chance to participate in the international system. And the more hope people have for their future, the less susceptible they will be to violent extremists. By helping to give people something to live for, we may rob terrorists of suicide recruits.

Humanitarian Relief

A fifth coalition should focus on meeting massive humanitarian needs—not only in the short term but for an extended period.

Even before September 11, Afghanistan had earned the sorry distinction of being the world's largest source of refugees, with approximately 4 million Afghans seeking refuge in neighboring countries—and nearly 1 million more Afghan people displaced within their own homeland. In the weeks since September 11, a new wave of refugees has begun to reach the borders; many more are likely to follow as the campaign against terror progresses.

Behind these sterile statistics are real-life stories of immense human misery. And if not addressed in exemplary fashion by the international community, these refugees pose a very real threat to the stability of neighboring countries—especially Pakistan—and could end up providing new recruits to radical causes, including Al Qaeda. Addressing the refugee crisis will require not only major financial support from donors, but also complete access and political support from all the receiving front-line states. Should military action be taken in countries beyond Afghanistan, the focus of this coalition may need to broaden.

A problem even larger and more challenging than refugee flows is the intense humanitarian crisis within Afghanistan. According to the United Nations, in Afghanistan already approximately 7.5 million people—a number equivalent to the entire population of Virginia and Washington, D.C., combined—are defined as "highly vulnerable." Even before September 11, more than 3.8 million Afghan people depended on UN food aid for survival. While the numbers of hungry and homeless increase, the UN's ability to reach them has dwindled, given the rising risk to foreigners in Afghanistan and the evacuation of relief personnel.

In 2000, the UN's $220 million humanitarian appeal for Afghanistan generated only 48 percent of that amount. The humanitarian coalition will have to be more resolute about addressing the sweeping needs in Afghanistan. The United States, long the largest donor to humanitarian work in Afghanistan, has led the way with pledge of an additional $320 million for food, medicine, and other critical needs. Europe, Japan, and other donor states must join this effort at comparable levels. Indeed, given the scope of the needed efforts and the sensitivities aroused by military action, the U.S. government should ask the EU, Japan, the World Food Program, and the UN High Commissioner for Refugees to head this humanitarian coalition.

The humanitarian problem goes far beyond financing. The international community must begin to address the very real legal, political, and bureaucratic impediments to meeting the needs of internally displaced persons who have all the needs of refugees, without any of the protections of the international system. The UN should authorize and establish camps and food distribution centers within Afghanistan wherever security conditions permit. Only in this way will the massive needs be met and a humanitarian catastrophe avoided. In addition to helping the people who most need it, such an effort would also decrease the flow of refugees to neighboring countries where they pose a threat to stability, and it would help retain the internal economic and governance structures that will be needed to rebuild the country. If there was ever a time to set a new precedent for protecting the lives of the internally displaced, this is it.

Repairing Failed States

A sixth coalition that will be required in the long term must "drain the swamps" that have bred and sustained terrorist networks in recent years. This will involve concerted efforts to rebuild failed states whose collapse has left vacuums in the international system that have been exploited by terrorist networks.[1]

In the first instance, a serious effort to rebuild a viable state in Afghanistan would need to be undertaken once the Taliban government is replaced, or at least the elements that have supported Al Qaeda are removed. If terrorism is to be denied the ideal safe haven over time, the international community will need to remain engaged in Afghanistan as it failed to do following the Soviet pullout in 1989. The scope of such an effort would potentially dwarf recent efforts at postconflict reconstruction in Somalia, the Balkans, Haiti, and East Timor. Because of the scope of the challenge and the regional sensitivities, this rebuilding effort would have to look very different from those previous efforts as well.

The key to any rebuilding effort will be the creation of a legitimate, inclusive government that will work to expel Al Qaeda and all terrorists from Afghanistan's territory. The United States should strongly support a UN political lead in this area. One useful mechanism would be to broaden and deepen the 6+2 diplomatic formula used previously (the six frontline states plus the United States and Russia) and establish a powerful group of friends of Afghanistan. To avoid some of the problems encountered by the 6+2, no state can be given veto power over what happens in Afghanistan. Only by ensuring tight collaboration among all parties with a major interest in Afghanistan's future will sufficient stability be returned to the country.

This friends mechanism, which should also include an EU representative, could work with the UN and the development banks to provide the operational capacity necessary to reconstruct the country. This would be the only acceptable alternative, because UN administration of Afghanistan is not an option either politically or operationally. This effort would need to include programs to address four major pillars of reconstruction: security, justice and reconciliation, economic and social well-being, and governance and participation.

To meet the immense needs in each of these areas, the United States would need to help mobilize a broad coalition of donor states and multilateral development banks in addition to the United Nations. While U.S. support to this coalition would be needed throughout, the United States should not attempt to lead it overtly or even take an inordinate role behind the scenes.

Finally, note that Afghanistan is not the only failed state that has provided fertile breeding ground for terrorist networks. This issue will have to be addressed more broadly, from places like Somalia and Yemen to the Caucasus, Northern Nigeria, and parts of the Philippine and Indonesian archipelagos.

Supporting Islam

The long-term struggle against terrorism will not succeed if Muslims around the world perceive it as being anti-Islamic in any way. While clear, repeated pronouncements from world leaders that the struggle is not against Islam will help, rhetoric alone will not be enough. There must be corresponding action. A seventh coalition would work to buttress viable moderate, democratic, Islamic alternatives in key states around the globe—from Jordan and Indonesia to Turkey and Nigeria. Other difficult but crucial cases like that of Egypt should be addressed as well.

This coalition would involve serious economic and political efforts to ensure the viability of these states in the face of radical alternatives. It could proceed much as the Alliance for Progress was envisioned for Latin America in the 1960s—a broad economic, social, and political project that would not only strengthen relations with the United States but, even more important, give national leaders the support to reform their societies and defeat radical alternatives within. Also, like the Alliance for Progress, the beneficiary states would serve as key protagonists in mutually supportive political efforts.

Success would require large amounts of political and financial assistance from the United States and other G-8 countries, although overt leadership would most usefully come from countries other than the United States. This coalition would be helpful not only in terms of the importance of stabilizing and strengthening these crucial states, but also in proving to the world that any ongoing military action against terrorists is against terrorism, not against Islam. So as not to compromise the efforts, however, the rubric under which these efforts might be pursued could vary on a case-by-case basis—from supporting key regional states to furthering democratization and good governance.

Three Areas for Action

Building and maintaining these, and perhaps other, coalitions will be difficult but essential. To promote success, the United States should take three key steps immediately.

First, the administration and Congress must fundamentally rethink, renegotiate, and reinvigorate the patchwork compact on foreign assistance that has evolved over the past four decades. Coalitions must be created on the basis of mutual interest, and the United States cannot and should not expect to be able to "buy" partners. At the same time, an outdated and underfunded U.S. foreign assistance program has dramatically limited U.S. abilities to help solve problems of interest to potential partners around the globe.

It has been more than 30 years since the UN endorsed the target of 0.7 percent of GNP for official development assistance from donor countries. The United States never reached that target and, over the past 40 years, development assistance has dropped virtually in half in constant dollars—declining from almost 0.6 percent of GNP to 0.1 percent of GNP. This leaves the United States with a very limited supply of "carrots" to offer governments and a much-reduced presence in places where a positive American role could help counter other influences.

The problem is not just diminished money and presence, however; it is also the limited flexibility and effectiveness of the assistance programs themselves. Development assistance is currently subject to more than 120 distinct congressional earmarks. This has led to fragmented programs and a dangerously uneven allocation of resources. It is time to address the problem comprehensively and strategically. Congress should maintain an active role in the development of assistance priorities and program oversight but must also recognize that these programs cannot succeed if they continue to be fragmented and micromanaged.

Combating terrorism will not only require significantly more money and a more rational mechanism for dispersing it. It will also finally require a greater appreciation for the value of foreign assistance. Programs that promote democracy and alleviate poverty are fighting terrorism by other means. Only by reengaging on a broad range of development issues will the United States be able to win the hearts and minds of some of the most vulnerable populations and countries around the globe.

Second, the United States must lead in promoting a thirteenth overarching UN convention on terrorism, which would tie together previous conventions, create enforcement mechanisms, fill gaps in the patchwork of previous agreements, resolve some key long-standing differences, and provide a definitive legal basis for international efforts against terrorism.

The extent to which many countries will be able and willing to participate in antiterrorism coalitions will depend on the level of international sanction such efforts have. While UN General Assembly and Security Council resolutions have strengthened the international legitimacy of the struggle against terrorism, the binding nature of a convention and the inclusive process of negotiation could broaden and bolster support. This process could also help force the hand of governments that have wavered in the fight against terrorism and, if successful, could deter other groups from choosing terrorism as a means of pursuing their aims.

Third, the Bush administration must drive a stake through the heart of the widespread perception of U.S. unilateralism. While the United States can, should, and will maintain the right to act unilaterally, the coalitions outlined here will require the ongoing good will of many states. The more that the United States acts under multilateral auspices, the more cooperation it will get. In addition, opportunities should be sought to demonstrate that the United States is a committed, col-

laborating partner on a wide range of issues of interest to coalition partners. The campaign against terrorism will be difficult and long. We cannot expect others to be there for us if we are not there for them.

Note

[1] The subject of failed states will be treated in greater depth in chapter 13, "Rebuilding Failed States: Test Case Afghanistan."

Parachuting Marines, January 1, 1940. U.S. Navy Marines parachute down to an airport during a training exercise. Photograph: Hulton | Archive/Getty Images.

Chapter 6

Improving Military Capabilities

"This war will not necessarily be one in which we pore over military targets and mass forces to seize those targets. Instead, military force will likely be one of many tools we use to stop individuals, groups, and countries that engage in terrorism. Our response may include firing cruise missiles into military targets somewhere in the world; we are just as likely to engage in electronic combat to track and stop investments moving through offshore banking centers . . . . While we may engage militarily against foreign governments that sponsor terrorism, we may also seek to make allies of the people those governments suppress. Even the vocabulary of this war will be different. When we 'invade the enemy's territory,' we may well be invading his cyberspace. There may not be as many beachheads stormed as opportunities denied. Forget about 'exit strategies'; we're looking at a sustained engagement that carries no deadlines."

— *Secretary of Defense Donald H. Rumsfeld*
New York Times
September 27, 2001
(reprinted with permission)

The terrorist attacks of September 11, 2001, forced a paradigm shift in our thinking about U.S. national security. Before September 11, we tended to conceive of ourselves as a nation with global interests that could be protected via active engagement abroad, but whose homeland was relatively insulated from chaos and conflict overseas. After September 11, we know we are not invulnerable. Wars will be brought home to us in unexpected and horrific ways.

We now understand, all too painfully, the lesson that many of our adversaries, and would-be adversaries, took home from the 1991 Gulf War: If you are going to challenge the United States, don't take on the conventional might of the U.S. military; rather, use asymmetric means like terrorism, cyberwar, or weapons of mass destruction to exploit America's vulnerabilities and avoid its strengths. Indeed, the fact that asymmetric threats were on the rise had become a common refrain among U.S. national security experts over the past decade,[1] but it did not sink into our collective consciousness or fundamentally change our national security priorities—until now.

The U.S. military remains, by any standard, the most powerful in history. Yet, the events of September 11 raise some crucial questions. Does that catastrophic terrorist attack fundamentally change the purpose and orientation of the U.S. military? Should it change the posture of our forces around the world? What is the appropriate role of the U.S. military in the war against terrorism? Does the military have the capabilities it needs to play this role? And, does the Department of Defense need to be reorganized for this mission?

Purpose of the U.S. Military

The U.S. military's purpose has often been described as "fighting and winning the nation's wars." In truth, the purpose of our armed forces is both broader and more basic: The U.S. military is an instrument of national power that should be used to protect and advance a broad range of U.S. national interests. A succession of presidents have recognized this fact—emphasizing not only the importance of being able to decisively defeat aggression when it occurs, but also to defend the American homeland, reassure allies and partners, deter and dissuade potential adversaries, and conduct other missions like smaller-scale contingency operations when they support American interests.

This basic purpose has not changed in the wake of the attacks on the World Trade Center and the Pentagon. What has changed is our understanding of what is needed to fulfill this purpose in the post–September 11 world. As a result, military missions like combating terrorism and defending the U.S. homeland, which in the past were seen as either specialized or secondary missions involving only small portions of the force, will and should be given greater priority.

This is not to argue that the entire U.S. military should be focused on these missions alone. Terrorist attacks on the United States are not the only threat against which we must defend; other forms of aggression against U.S. interests abroad persist and are ignored at our peril. Rather, it is to say that these missions should now move from the periphery to the mainstream of U.S. defense planning, programming, and budgeting.

U.S. Military Posture Overseas

In the wake of September 11, as in the aftermath of the terrorist attacks on Khobar Towers in Saudi Arabia in 1996 and the USS *Cole* in Yemen in 2000, some questioned the appropriateness and desirability of deploying thousands of U.S. military personnel in key regions of the world, particularly the Persian Gulf. Such a large U.S. military presence in the gulf, it was argued, feeds anti-American sentiment in the region, makes the Arab regimes that host U.S. forces even less popular with their own populations, and gives terrorists highly lucrative targets at which to strike.

However, this argument overlooks the fact that U.S. military presence in the region serves as a deterrent to would-be aggressors, such as Saddam Hussein; that it underwrites the regional stability that allows for the unimpeded flow of petroleum products to the rest of the world; and that it reassures Arab allies that do, in fact, want U.S. forces to stay. Furthermore, a wholesale U.S. withdrawal from the region in the wake of September 11 would hand the terrorists a strategic victory while it would send an open invitation to other potential adversaries: If you want to force the United States to abandon its vital interests and allies in a region, just kill several thousand Americans and America will withdraw.

As a global power with global interests, the United States cannot afford to send such a damaging, dangerous message. Nevertheless, it would be wise to undertake a regular review of U.S. military posture in the region to ensure that our forces are arrayed in a way that enables them to protect U.S. and allied interests while minimizing the downsides of U.S. military presence for host nations.

Role of the U.S. Military in the Campaign against Terrorism

As Secretary of Defense Rumsfeld and others have made plain, the military will not be the only or even the primary instrument we use in the fight against terrorism. Other instruments such as intelligence, law enforcement, financial measures, foreign assistance, and public diplomacy may ultimately be as or even more important to our long-term success.

Moreover, the military dimension of the campaign against terrorism will not look like any war in recent memory. Rather than a relatively brief, intense assault—like the 100-hour war in the Gulf—it will be a campaign of campaigns involving a widening array of targets and operations over a period of years. Much of the military action may be invisible to the public eye, such as the covert use of special operations forces. And it is unlikely to have a discrete end—a time when we can declare the war on terrorism is over and we have won it.

The campaign will require the proactive use of military forces to seize intelligence opportunities when foreign law enforcement or covert operations are unable to do so. Indeed, when preventive or preemptive action is required, the military may become an instrument of first rather than last resort. The military campaign will also require constant reevaluation and adjustment as a learning adversary changes its mode of operation in response to U.S. actions and as changing circumstances—and possibly unintended consequences—require the United States to adjust its course. Over the life of the campaign, the military may be asked to conduct a range of potential missions:

- **Preventive attacks overseas** to destroy or curtail the ability of terrorist organizations to operate and/or **preemptive attacks overseas** to thwart anticipated terrorist attacks before they occur. Such attacks might involve destroying the operating infrastructure of terrorist organizations (such as operating bases, training camps, and command-and-control assets) or raids aimed at killing or apprehending terrorist leaders and operatives. Under some circumstances, the military may also be authorized to attack third-party financial, surveillance, and communications infrastructures on which terrorists rely;
- **Retaliatory attacks overseas** to punish terrorists and states that harbor or support them. The latter could range from strikes aimed

at destroying a regime's high-value assets (such as military forces, internal security forces, critical infrastructure, leadership, or other targets) to a campaign aimed at removing the regime from power;

■ **Force protection** of U.S. military personnel, dependents, equipment, and bases overseas to ensure freedom of action;

■ **Homeland defense,** which could include a wide variety of tasks, including air defense, missile defense, protection of critical infrastructure, rapid response to chemical or biological terrorism, and support to domestic authorities, among others;[2] and

■ **Military-to-military contacts** to enhance interoperability and coalition capabilities to combat terrorism.

Some of these operations will pose particularly difficult and possibly unique challenges. Chief among them is determining the enemy's center of gravity—what the enemy holds dear—and identifying targets whose destruction would actually change a terrorist organization's behavior or ability to take action against us.

The United States should resist the temptation to focus exclusively or even primarily on targeting individuals like Osama bin Laden. As experience from Central America to Somalia has shown, such manhunts are notoriously difficult and, even if successful, may fall well short of achieving U.S. strategic objectives—in this case, putting terrorist organizations like Al Qaeda out of business.

Instead, the United States should focus on understanding and undermining terrorist networks: how they derive their power, what they value most, their objectives and modes of operation. To be sure, this will require a new approach from intelligence analysts and military planners unaccustomed to dealing with nonstate adversaries. It will also require an unprecedented degree of information sharing and coordination among U.S. and coalition military, intelligence, and law enforcement communities. To be effective, the United States will need to build its own international network to combat international terrorist networks.

As we have seen in combat operations in Iraq and in the Balkans, military targets will frequently be intermingled with civilian populations, heightening the risk of collateral damage if conventional air and missile strikes are employed or the risk to troops if a surgical strike is undertaken. To further complicate matters, terrorist networks often rely on financial, surveillance, and communications infrastructures that are owned and operated by legitimate third-party commercial consortia, some of which involve our closest allies. Attacking assets in these domains presents new and challenging legal and political issues as well as heightened potential for unintended consequences such as fracturing the coalition.

Furthermore, effective military action will be both enabled and constrained by the actions of our coalition partners. The United States will be dependent on certain types of support—intelligence, access to bases and facilities, logistics, overflight rights, and, in a few cases, force contributions—from coalition partners. The precise requirements will vary according to the specific operation, but the decisions of key partners will ultimately create or close options.

Finally, in this type of campaign, tactical military actions can have strategic import. Every potential military operation will have to be assessed not only in terms of immediate costs and benefits but also in the context of its likely impact on our ability to achieve the long-term goals of the campaign. For example, any decision to put large numbers of American troops on the ground in Afghanistan to assist indigenous forces in toppling the Taliban regime could cause instability in neighboring countries like Pakistan and the defection of key partners of the coalition.

Addressing Capability Shortfalls

As Goliath learned when he faced David's slingshot, size and strength get you only so far. Does the U.S. military have the capabilities it needs to successfully support the war on terrorism?

The missions and challenges described above suggest a number of military capabilities that will be critical to the counterterrorism campaign: intelligence, surveillance, and reconnaissance to find a range of ever-changing targets from fixed assets to military forces on the move to individuals and small groups; interoperable and flexible command, control, and communications to ensure that U.S. joint forces can operate effectively together; special operations forces for reconnaissance, target acquisition, search and destroy, and combat search and rescue missions; rapid reaction forces to back up special operations forces in the event that a mission goes awry; linguists, interpreters, and liaison officers who can enable our forces to operate more effectively in distant regions; long- and medium-range precision strike capabilities to ensure that without access to nearby bases we can destroy critical targets with minimal risk of collateral damage; capabilities to enable U.S. forces to project power into a region in the face of an adversary's efforts to deny them access; air and naval supremacy, including suppression of enemy air defenses, to gain freedom to operate; close air support for forces operating on the ground; strategic and theater logistics and mobility for U.S. and coalition forces; force protection against the full range of threats to forces deployed overseas; information operations, both offensive and defensive; and capabilities for seizing or destroying chemical and biological agents in the hands of terrorist groups or hostile regimes.

A number of capability shortfalls are already widely known, ranging from intelligence collection (especially human intelligence) to intelligence fusion and rapid dissemination of intelligence to users; from surveillance to secure wideband communications; from linguists and foreign-area specialists to chemical and biological defense. To fight global terrorist networks effectively, the U.S. military also needs to enhance its own ability to operate as a network. Here the challenge is developing and deploying capabilities that will provide dispersed, mobile forces with a common operational picture, flexible and secure command and control, and networked sensors and shooters. Undoubtedly other shortfalls will be identified as well.

In addition, if the duration of any particular aspect of the military campaign stretches into months, additional shortfalls may arise as forces in the field need to be replaced by others rotating in. Many parts of the force—most notably intelligence, special operations forces, and a number of low density/high demand assets—simply do not have enough people and units to support the rotation base required to sustain lengthy operations. Even forces with a substantial rotation base may feel the pinch over time. If, for example, the president chooses to keep two or three carrier battle groups in one region for an extended period to support the campaign, it will reduce carrier deployments to other regions of interest to the United States.

That said, it is important to remember that much of the U.S. military will not get into this fight unless the administration chooses to launch a large-scale invasion to topple and replace a regime that has sponsored terrorism. In that case, one could expect a campaign on the scale of a major theater war.

In any case, if U.S. military operations in the campaign against terrorism are to succeed in the years ahead, U.S. leaders must do their part on the home front by fully funding the highest-priority forces and by shifting resources to address the most important shortfalls on a priority basis. But both the administration and the Congress must resist the temptation to simply throw money at anything and everything that can be logically associated with counterterrorism and homeland security. Rather, the Department of Defense should undertake a comprehensive and rigorous assessment of the military forces and capabilities required to support the campaign, with the aim of identifying and prioritizing shortfalls. On that basis, the Department of Defense should develop a multiyear program and budget (beginning in fiscal year 2003) to address those shortfalls, in both the near and long term.

This effort should assess the requirements of the campaign against terrorism in the context of other demands that may be placed on the U.S. military at the same time—such as fighting and winning a conventional war abroad and helping to defend Americans at home. Most military forces are likely to be tapped for multiple missions.

Finally, the Department of Defense should make combating terrorism a focus of our security cooperation with other countries. Such an effort should include military-to-military contacts to learn from those who have had experience with this type of war, exercises and security assistance to strengthen the capabilities of those who are willing to fight alongside us, and government-to-government contacts to develop new access arrangements with key countries.

Enhancing U.S. capabilities to combat terrorism will also require continued investment in the U.S. military's transformation—that is, advanced systems, innovative operational concepts, and new organizational arrangements. U.S. defense strategy has long paid homage to the rise of asymmetric threats and the need for the U.S. military to transform to deal with them, but tangible progress in the form of new capabilities, operational concepts, and organizations has been slow. September 11 should serve as a wake-up call to the Department of Defense leadership, the military services, the Congress, and the entire defense community that we must accelerate the transformation process—and fast.

In practice, this means, among other things, improving our ability to protect critical operating bases at home and abroad from attack by weapons of mass destruction, to protect information systems from attack, to project and sustain U.S. forces in environments where an adversary seeks to deny our access, to deny enemies sanctuary, and to develop a common operational picture for forces in the field and flexible command and control.[3] It also means fielding leaner, more agile, mobile, stealthy, and lethal forces that can operate as part of a seamless network. Meeting these operational objectives will require a substantial increase in investment in concept development and experimentation by both the services and Joint Forces Command. It will also require a change in the military's zero-defect culture—that is, the perception that one misstep or mistake will end a promising career—to one that fosters and rewards innovation. More broadly, the Department of Defense will also need to continue to try to free up additional resources for transformation by adopting better business practices, shedding excess infrastructure, and outsourcing and privatization.

Organizing for Success

If one were to take a tabula rasa approach to organizing the Department of Defense for the campaign against terrorism, the current structure—with its regional and functional divisions—is probably the last thing one would design. Fighting a transnational threat like terrorism will require the combined efforts of parts of the Pentagon and the military that rarely work together.

In addition, some key assets, like intelligence and mobility, have been organized around a surge concept, in which assets from other regions are redirected to support the region in crisis. This approach is highly problematic when trying to conduct a global campaign in which action in one region may beget a response in another.

Given the importance and expected duration of the campaign against terrorism, the Department of Defense should consider a number of steps to organize itself for success.

First, increase the number of personnel dedicated to intelligence, planning, operations, and policy oversight of the campaign against terrorism.

Second, create a combined task force of civilian and military personnel from the Office of the Secretary of Defense and the Joint Staff to undertake long-range planning for the military dimensions of the campaign against terrorism. This task force would be charged with thinking over the horizon to develop contingency planning guidance for the regional and functional Commanders in Chief (CINCs). Its focus would be to define the objectives and parameters for future operations in the campaign against terrorism to enable military staffs to begin operational planning and preparation.

Third, in the longer term, the Department of Defense needs to consider changes to its unified command plan that would enhance the military's ability to help defend the U.S. homeland. Specifically, the secretary of defense should create a new CINC for homeland defense. Doing so would put all of the military assets required to support homeland security—air defense forces, missile defense forces, civil support units, and others—under the command of a single four-star general or admiral. It would create a senior, go-to person within the U.S. military whose sole job, day and night, would be to prepare the military for operations to protect against or respond to threats to the U.S. homeland. No such person or focal point currently exists. Historically, assigning responsibility for an area or function to a CINC has been the most effective way to ensure that it receives priority attention in the military's planning, training, and resource allocation. Practically speaking, three principal options should be developed and assessed to create a new unified CINC for homeland defense: reorienting and expanding Joint Forces Command, reorienting and expanding Space Command, or elevating and building on the army's Forces Command.

In addition, homeland defense should be made the primary mission of the National Guard, and elements of the guard and reserves should be reorganized, properly trained, and equipped to undertake this mission. Geographically dispersed with deep ties to their local communities and well-established relationships with state governments, the National Guard is ideally suited to be the military's primary contribution to missions such air defense, consequence management, and backing up civilian law enforcement agencies in crisis.

Specifically, air and missile defense of the United States should be made the primary mission of the Air National Guard. In practice, Air National Guard units would maintain F-15 and F-16 aircraft on day-to-day strip alert at some two dozen bases across the country. Given the Air National Guard's current integration into the rotation base that supports the U.S. Air Force's overseas deployments, this would require some fairly substantial restructuring within the broader air force.

In addition, the Army National Guard should be reoriented to focus on consequence management in the event of a major terrorist attack, especially one involving chemical or biological agents, maintaining civil order, and augmenting civilian capabilities for protecting critical infrastructure. Reorienting the Army National Guard in this way would reorder its current priorities and make acting as a strategic reserve in the event of a long or difficult major war overseas a secondary mission. Over the longer term, the strategic reserve mission might be reassigned to the Army Reserve. Obviously, such a mission shift would have profound implications for the ways in which individual guard units are organized, trained, and equipped.

Conclusion

The U.S. military will have a vital role to play in the campaign against terrorism, and the campaign will present the military with a number of challenges. Meeting these challenges will require rethinking our capabilities, operational concepts, organizations, and ways of cooperating with other key actors in the campaign. But the campaign also offers the military an opportunity that should not be missed: a chance to reconnect with the American people in a powerful and long-lasting way.

Over the past decade, the end of the Cold War, U.S. military downsizing, and a booming economy conspired to distance the American people from the U.S. military as an institution. Fewer people perceived a real threat to the United States or understood why we still need a substantial and expensive military. Fewer people knew someone in their family or community who wore the uniform, and fewer considered entering military service. Now that the threat of terrorism has come home to America, the military has an opportunity to prove itself more relevant to the daily concerns of Americans, to be more appreciated for its contribution to America's security, and to be an attractive form of public service for a generation seeking a way to make a positive difference for their society in the wake of September 11.

Notes

[1] See the U.S. Commission on National Security/21st Century (The Hart-Rudman Commission), the Advisory Panel to Assess Domestic Response Capabilities for Terrorism Involving Weapons of Mass Destruction (The Gilmore Commission), and the Quadrennial Defense Review published in 2001.

[2] Homeland security will be treated in greater depth in chapter 9.

[3] *Quadrennial Defense Review Report,* September 30, 2001, p. 30, www.defenselink.mil/pubs/qdr2001.pdf.

U.S. artilleryman, circa 1945. A coastal artilleryman watching for hostile aircraft that could attack the Chesapeake Bay in Maryland and Virginia in the United States. Photograph: Hulton | Archive/Getty Images.

Chapter 7

Intelligence:
The Long Pole in the Tent

"It's not going to be a cruise missile or a bomber that's going to be the determining factor. It's going to be a scrap of information from some person in some country that is being oppressed by a dictatorial regime . . . that will enable us to pull this network up by its roots."

— *Secretary of Defense Donald H. Rumsfeld*
October 3, 2001

With perfect hindsight, it seems clear that shortfalls in U.S. intelligence information, capabilities, and processes enabled terrorists to strike on September 11, 2001, with surprise and to devastating effect. At the same time, it is clear, as President George W. Bush has said, that the dedicated men and women of the intelligence community are "on the front line of making sure our victory will be secure."

As we consider the long campaign against terrorism before us, and the prospect of additional attacks, intelligence will remain the "long pole in the tent"—the indispensable element of the campaign on which the success of all others will depend.

Unfortunately, given the nature of the adversary, there are no guarantees that the quality of our intelligence on terrorist organizations like Osama bin Laden's Al Qaeda network will substantially improve. Al Qaeda is a flat organization, composed of small cells of individuals in more than 60 countries around the world. It has consistently demonstrated its ability to use a wide range of communications, from low-tech means like face-to face-meetings to high-tech means like encrypted messages embedded in Internet sites. When its communications have been intercepted, it has been extremely agile in changing its modus operandi to evade Western intelligence collection.

Terrorist organizations like Al Qaeda also lack the infrastructure that makes other intelligence targets, like governments, easier to penetrate. Furthermore, the extremist ideology that motivates its recruits and cements an otherwise loose network together makes it extremely difficult—indeed almost impossible—for Western agents to infiltrate. Due to the strength of their convictions, members are unlikely to defect, even if offered substantial incentives. Given these factors, the campaign against terrorism may pose the biggest intelligence challenge for the United States and its allies since the Cold War.

With Good Intelligence, Anything Is Possible; Without It, Nothing Is Possible

Intelligence enables all other components of the campaign against terrorism to be effective, from homeland security to law enforcement, military and covert operations, and coalition building. Decisionmakers in each of these areas must rely on information that is gathered, analyzed, and provided by the intelligence community. Meeting the multifaceted challenges associated with intelligence collection, analysis, and dissemination will be daunting, as each element of the campaign against terrorism poses unique intelligence requirements.

- **Homeland security.** Those responsible for homeland security need to have a general understanding of the threat—that is, the types of attacks that various terrorist organizations are interested in and capable of launching against the United States. If indicators suggest such an attack is imminent, authorities also need specific warning information about the anticipated location and type of attack in order to enhance law enforcement, security, and consequence management efforts. Perhaps the greatest challenge in this area is intelligence sharing and fusion across bureaucratic lines—synthesizing the relevant pieces of information from the overwhelming amount of data collected by a variety of agencies and means into a coherent, timely picture of what is likely to happen. Ultimately, intelligence fusion depends on establishing linkages between disparate bits of information through solid analysis. In an environment in which we are often awash in information, analysis is critical to determining which pieces of information are important and what they mean.

■ **Law enforcement.** In addition to the type of warning information described above, the law enforcement community needs information about individuals who are known or believed to be part of a terrorist organization and who are entering or already have entered the United States, so that domestic surveillance operations can be launched. In short, law enforcement needs both a watch list and some indication of when an individual on the list approaches or enters the United States. Such watch lists existed before September 11, but some agencies lacked the resources to monitor or respond to them effectively. Nor were these lists necessarily shared with state and local law enforcement. In addition, the fact that most of the hijackers involved in the September 11 attacks were not on any watch list and had entered the United States legally suggests, first, that the intelligence community needs to redouble its efforts to identify individuals with connections to terrorist organizations and, second, that the United States needs to rethink aspects of its immigration policy, such as how it keeps tabs on individuals who enter the country on student or other temporary visas.

Inside the United States, law enforcement becomes the chief provider of intelligence that is based on information gleaned from its surveillance and investigation activities. In light of what we now know about the terrorists' activities in the months before September 11, it is clear that domestic surveillance efforts were not as aggressive as they should have been. Did federal law enforcement agencies like the FBI not have a clear enough sense of the people and types of behavior they should have been looking for? Were surveillance efforts thwarted by overly stringent guidelines or judicial constraints? Were technical capabilities for signals intelligence and information management inadequate to the task? Was there a shortage of foreign language speakers to interpret and analyze data in a timely manner? Were there inadequate processes for linking seemingly unrelated activities (a theft of identity papers, a transfer of funds, an enrollment in a flight school, a cash purchase of an airline ticket) into a clear picture of imminent danger? The answers to these questions may suggest important reforms in the law enforcement arena.

■ **Financial operations.** Federal law enforcement and bank regulatory entities attempting to stop the flow of money to terrorists through efforts such as freezing or emptying bank accounts require a different sort of intelligence support. These officials need a clear picture of the financial relationships and modes of operation that characterize a terrorist network—including sources of funding, who in the organization has financial decisionmaking authority, how the money flows into the organization, and how it flows within the organization to operatives in the field. At the tactical level, detailed information on specific contributors, bank accounts, and other holdings becomes critical to effective operations. Here the challenge lies in the simple fact that much of a terrorist organization's financial dealings may be impervious to the kinds of tracking measures used on other targets like organized crime. Terrorist organizations often bank with unregulated institutions that do not meet international standards. They tend to transfer money in amounts small enough to avoid attention and often operate on a cash basis, funneling money illicitly through seemingly legitimate organizations and trusted individuals. These practices make it exceedingly difficult to track, let alone choke off, the money supply.

■ **Military operations.** Decisionmakers in the Department of Defense need a wide variety of intelligence support to conduct military operations. At the strategic level, they need a broad understanding of the intentions and capabilities of terrorist organizations with global reach. At the operational level, they require more detailed information on operating conditions like terrain and weather, as well as the location and nature of terrorist bases, command-and-control facilities, training camps, and other assets to support the development of military plans and target lists. They also require similar information on potentially friendly forces and groups in the region. At the tactical level, the military requires more detailed, often time-sensitive intelligence to support specific operations, from targeting data for precision-guided munitions to information on the exact whereabouts of a particular individual or group targeted for direct action. The challenge associated with the latter is substantial and may effectively limit the extent to which the United States can employ special operations forces in direct action missions to capture or kill individual terrorists.

- **Covert operations.** Covert operations aim to disrupt terrorist operations and, if possible, apprehend terrorists. As in the case of direct action, to be successful, covert operations require reliable, highly detailed, and time-sensitive information on the exact locations, movements, and security arrangements of individuals practiced in the art of deception and evasion. This is a tall order, which usually requires a combination of human intelligence, signals intelligence, constant surveillance, extensive preparation, and a bit of luck to pull off. For good historical reasons, the American intelligence community essentially got out of this business for a time. In light of the new terrorism, however, it needs to get back in, recognizing that there will undoubtedly be some failures on the road to success. This will require reinvigorating a part of the intelligence community that has experienced substantial atrophy while also rethinking the safeguards and oversight procedures that need to be put in place to ensure that covert activity is fully consistent with broader American policy objectives. This will be a long-term effort, requiring years of investment.

- **Sustaining the international coalition.** For years, the centerpiece of U.S. counterterrorism policy has been bilateral intelligence relationships with a number of key countries. In the wake of September 11, these relationships need to be widened and deepened. Central to sustaining the international coalition against terrorism over the long term is finding ways to share important intelligence across national and bureaucratic boundaries in ways that do not compromise sources and methods. This is, of course, a two-way street, as the U.S. intelligence community may sometimes be on the receiving end of such arrangements. When the information is collected through U.S. channels, however, the United States has an overriding interest in ensuring that any information regarding terrorist threats to coalition partners can be shared in a timely manner. The United States also needs to work hard to ensure that allied political leaders have the information they need to make a compelling case to their respective publics that they, too, face a clear and present threat from terrorism. In this arena, the principal challenge is sharing information in enough detail to provide a coalition partner with what it needs to know while protecting U.S. sources, methods, and operational security against compromise.

This is an illustrative rather than a comprehensive picture of the requirements that will be placed on the intelligence community over the course of the campaign against terrorism. But it hints at the wide variety of intelligence operations and products needed to support the various elements of the campaign, as well as the significant challenges the intelligence community will face.

Identifying and Prioritizing Shortfalls

Given the centrality of intelligence to the success of this campaign and the enormity of the intelligence challenge, the U.S. government must take swift action to identify shortfalls in current intelligence capabilities and processes, and develop clear priorities and a comprehensive plan of action for addressing them. As a first step, the executive branch should charter a group that includes both intelligence experts and well-respected outsiders to undertake two assessments.

The first assessment should seek to reconstruct the events leading up to September 11 and the associated intelligence and law enforcement activities to determine what went right, what went wrong, and why. A hard-hitting, government-wide after-action review is imperative if the president and the Congress want to be able to answer the "How did this happen?" question that is on the mind of every American and to take concrete steps to reduce the risks of future attacks. In determining what lessons should be learned, great care must be taken to ensure this assessment does not degenerate into a scapegoating exercise or, conversely, a defensive whitewashing of the facts.

The second assessment should aim to develop a plan of action to address priority shortfalls in the intelligence arena. These may be shortfalls in policy, people, processes, or technology. The assessment would provide a road map for building the capabilities and enhancing the performance of the intelligence community in combating terrorism over the next five to ten years.

Several known shortfalls should be addressed as part of this exercise. The first is a paucity of interpreters and analysts with the language skills, area expertise, and functional expertise needed to sort through and assess the sea of information collected on terrorist organizations and operations around the world. The intelligence community currently lacks an adequate number of people who speak the languages spoken by members of various terrorist organizations and the countries that support them. Most glaring are shortages in speakers of Arabic, Farsi, and a range of Central and South Asian languages.

This shortfall appears to be particularly acute in domestic law enforcement agencies like the FBI, sometimes hampering their ability to keep up with the activities of terrorist cells operating within the United States. Indeed, within a week of the September 11 attacks, FBI Director Robert S. Mueller issued a nationwide appeal for speakers of Arabic, Pashto, and Farsi. The response was overwhelming: By October 1, more than 1,300 individuals—many of them Arab Americans—had flooded the FBI's switchboards and Web site with applications and offers of assistance.

In the short term, bringing hundreds of new linguists into government service may require significant increase in the number of personnel devoted to clearing new hires. In the longer term, the intelligence community needs to devise better ways of drawing on the ethnic diversity of our citizenry that is one of our nation's greatest strengths. Ultimately, addressing this shortfall will be critical to enabling agencies like the FBI to shift from a reactive footing to a more proactive posture.

Another critical shortfall lies in the realm of intelligence sharing, particularly among U.S. intelligence and law enforcement agencies. By all accounts, this has proved to be one of the most vexing challenges for veterans of the fight against terrorism. Even though terrorism was officially identified as a top priority for intelligence and law enforcement before September 11, that alone was not enough to get the right information to the right people at the right time.

Sometimes one agency simply does not recognize that a given piece of data would be of value to another. Too often, however, intelligence information is intentionally held so closely by the agency that collected and analyzed it that it is not shared with all of the parties who have a need to know. This is particularly true in law enforcement agencies like the FBI where a case-file mentality often prevents agents from sharing tactically relevant information within and outside their agency while a case is still being developed. Inadequate information sharing is also a problem among federal, state, and local agencies. Breaking down the bureaucratic barriers to effective intelligence sharing must be one of the highest priorities if we are to succeed in the campaign against terrorism.

Yet, this inevitably raises the specter of intelligence agencies collecting information within U.S. borders, something that has long been seen as a threat to the basic privacy rights of Americans. And it raises one of the greatest challenges the United States faces in the fight against terrorism: How do we create situational awareness—the ability to know what terrorists are doing inside our borders—without becoming a police state?

Being effective in the campaign against terrorism will require us to wrestle this difficult issue to the ground. Creating the situational awareness now deemed essential will require rethinking existing legal authorities that constrain information sharing between intelligence and law enforcement agencies. It will mean developing new methods for lawful surveillance of American citizens and foreigners living in America, while creating adequate oversight to ensure that new methods are not used inappropriately. This might include creating new combined-agency investigation centers, supervised on an ongoing basis by an officer appointed by the court authorized by the Foreign Intelligence Surveillance Act—a real-time privacy ombudsman.

Better analysis and intelligence sharing are both central to addressing a related shortfall: intelligence fusion, or the synthesis of information gleaned from many sources and methods into a larger picture. Intelligence fusion is akin to trying to put together a giant jigsaw puzzle with a diverse group of players, where each must sort through thousands of pieces to find one or two that might contribute to the overall picture. The first challenge is simply to sift through the overwhelming amount of raw intelligence data to pick out the pieces of information that might matter (the analysis challenge). The second is to try to piece together a coherent picture (the fusion challenge), drawing on the contributions of various agencies (the information sharing challenge). Before September 11, players too often failed to put their respective pieces on the table. As a consequence, other players had little or no knowledge of what the overall puzzle might look like, or even what kind of related pieces they should be looking for in their own domains.

The poor state of automation of U.S. intelligence databases further hampers the fusion process. Most of our intelligence data is still in paper files. The extensive databases built by our intelligence and law enforcement communities are woefully out of date because they still require technicians to type in records. The United States needs to invest in real-time, automated introduction of data from the collection source into electronic files.

In addition, the fusion process could benefit enormously from wider use of information gathered from open sources. There is a wealth of open source information, and much of it is more current than our intelligence records. Yet our system has a bias that favors classified information. In a crisis, this tends both to narrow the circle of people who have input into the policymaking process and to lead decisionmakers to place greater weight and certainty on what little intelligence they have than may be justified. If, by contrast, the intelligence community were to use open sources more extensively, we could routinely look at certain issues without necessarily tipping our hand that we were planning operations in an area—and we could make better sense of our classified information by putting it in a much broader context.

Open source information would also undoubtedly be more easily shared between agencies.

The intelligence community also needs to undertake more "red teaming" or "If I were a terrorist…" simulations to better understand the types of attacks terrorist groups might contemplate, and how they might respond. Though imperfect at best, such exercises can be very useful in exposing gaps in thinking and shortcomings in preparation. Both the intelligence and law enforcement communities could use an entity like a federally funded research and development center to analyze terrorist motivations, capabilities, and modus operandi; to help produce search concepts for data fusion; and to think creatively about new operational concepts for fighting terrorism.

Perhaps the most widely discussed intelligence shortfall since September 11 has been the inadequacy of U.S. human intelligence (HUMINT)—that is, intelligence sources or operatives who can penetrate terrorist organizations like Al Qaeda. Since the end of the Cold War, overall funding for intelligence programs has declined by more than 20 percent[1] and HUMINT programs in particular have atrophied.[2] At the same time, the number of potential threats to the United States has skyrocketed. Rather than focus primarily on penetrating the vast infrastructure of one principal enemy, the intelligence community now must cover a diverse set of targets that includes both state and nonstate actors, among them a number of terrorist organizations.

Clearly, this atrophy needs to be addressed, but increasing the number of U.S. operatives may not be the best answer. First, as noted earlier, it is virtually impossible for American operatives to penetrate groups like Al Qaeda due to their ideology, recruiting, and screening methods as well as the compartmented ways in which the cells operate. Second, even if there were reason to believe that our prospects for penetrating these groups would brighten, the development of effective operatives takes years to bear fruit. Developing U.S. agents to penetrate terrorist organizations is simply not the most promising near- or even mid-term solution.

As a result, other approaches for addressing this shortfall must to be given priority consideration. If we cannot penetrate these organizations ourselves, we need to find and work with those who can. This means finding and developing informants with knowledge of the terrorist organizations we seek to target. Dealing with terrorists is, by definition, unsavory business; and combating them effectively may require getting information from some rather unsavory characters. To be effective in this regard, the United States may need to streamline the process for approving the use of such assets.

Perhaps more important, the United States should develop even stronger intelligence-sharing arrangements with those countries that have better HUMINT in areas and on groups of greatest concern. It should also encourage these countries to redouble their own efforts to develop better HUMINT, based on the fact that the new terrorism threatens them as well. One of our central diplomatic goals in the months and years to come should be to broaden and deepen these arrangements as a cornerstone of our bilateral relations with key countries. This should include seeking greater allied cooperation in surveillance and tracking of the financial transactions of various terrorist organizations. If intelligence is the long pole in the combating-terrorism tent, enhanced cooperative relationships with foreign intelligence agencies are the ground lines that will enable it to stand.

The closest cousin to the HUMINT shortfall is that of covert operations, discussed above. In the post–September 11 security environment, we clearly need to reexamine and reinvigorate the American practice of covert operations. But as we do, we must pay proper attention to appropriate guidelines and political oversight.

As noted above, parts of the intelligence community have also lagged behind in technology. The revolution in information and communications technologies has dramatically altered the collection landscape. New modes of communication like the Internet, cable services, and wireless technologies have become commonplace. Encryption technologies, once the purview of governments alone, are widely used in the commercial sector. At the same time, overall funding for intelligence has declined, and the community's investment in research, development, and procurement has simply not been able to keep pace with new technologies. Together, these developments have severely complicated signals intelligence and have left the intelligence community without the technologies it needs to adapt to the new environment.

Recent developments like the creation of In-Q-tel, a unique public–private partnership to provide venture capital to support the development of new technologies that might be of use to the intelligence community, are steps in the right direction. Still, a substantial increase in funding and more aggressive public–private partnerships are needed to identify and adapt cutting-edge technologies to meet the intelligence community's needs. The campaign against terrorism provides an excellent opportunity and catalyst for new approaches.

The sheer numbers of potential intelligence targets in this campaign further suggest that a dramatic increase in the level of resources is required for the intelligence community as a whole. The current community lacks the staff and resources to accomplish all of the missions it is expected to undertake simultaneously. Indeed, as with the military, parts of the community have been organized around a surge concept—the idea that in a crisis, they would be augmented by assets from other regional and functional areas. This concept breaks down when applied in the campaign against terrorism, where U.S. action in one region may prompt a terrorist response in another. We simply cannot afford to go blind in much of the world when there is a crisis in one particular region; nor can we afford to have all eyes trained on only one type of threat—even terrorism—to the exclusion of myriad others.

Many studies have argued that the intelligence community must be completely restructured in order to deal effectively with twenty-first-century threats like terrorism. Few have laid out viable plans for doing so. Some restructuring may well be needed over the long term, but it is unlikely to pay great dividends unless critical shortfalls are addressed on a priority basis. Restructuring should be pursued as a means to address significant problems and shortfalls, but not as an end in itself.

If September 11 changed anything for the intelligence community, it is this: The community is now widely recognized by officials and the public alike as both crucial and in need of additional resources and reform. Nothing will be more important to the success of the campaign against terrorism than meaningfully improving the intelligence community's capabilities and performance.

Notes

[1] Commission on the Roles and Capabilities of the United States Intelligence Community, "Preparing for the 21st Century: An Appraisal of U.S. Intelligence," March 1, 1996.

[2] See, for example, Bobby R. Inman, "Spying for a Long, Hot War," *New York Times*, October 9, 2001, p. 25.

Emergency Call, May 22, 1964. A police officer takes an emergency call from his car on the streets of New York. Photograph: Hulton l Archive/Getty Images.

Chapter 8

Strengthening Law Enforcement Capabilities

"...[W]hile the Constitution protects against invasions of individual rights, it is not a suicide pact."

— Supreme Court Justice Arthur Goldberg
Majority opinion, Kennedy v. Mendoza-Martinez
February 18, 1963

The law enforcement dimensions of the counterterrorism campaign are daunting—both the unraveling of the September 11 network and the detection and elimination of other terrorist cells and plots that put U.S. interests and citizens at risk. Law enforcement agencies have felt beleaguered as global forces and new technologies erode their ability to maintain public safety. The revolution in information technology is the most salient of these forces, but other aspects of economic and political globalization have similar effects. International travel is fast and easy, allowing criminals and terrorists to move about the globe— hidden among tens of thousands of immigrants, students, business travelers, and tourists. Financial and trade networks have experienced a luxuriant proliferation, allowing money and goods to be transferred easily around the planet. Transnational just-in-time manufacturing processes have introduced an urgency in border control that, when combined with government downsizing, has led to minimal inspection of goods coming into the United States. Military and advanced civil technologies are readily accessible in the global marketplace. When exploited in combination and with malevolent purpose, these trends—as we have so painfully learned—can endanger America's safety.

Law enforcement as a counterterrorism tool faces two major challenges: technological change and globalization. These affect national law enforcement across the board. Making law enforcement more effective in meeting these challenges requires taking advantage of new technologies, with adequate legal safeguards for civil liberties; and using globalization as a positive force to build better international law enforcement, through greater information sharing, coordination and cooperation. For the United States, a crucial part of responding to these two challenges will also be to reconsider the constraints placed on law enforcement and intelligence agencies as a result of the political turmoil of the 1970s. The concerns that prompted these constraints have not disappeared, but some limitations on police authorities and cooperation with intelligence agencies need to be reconsidered to better fit the security environment after September 11.

Technological Change and Increased Capability

Communications interception, or wiretapping, has been a powerful tool in the law enforcement arsenal since the early twentieth century. In the past, law enforcement could simply tap a fixed line to eavesdrop on communications—but technological developments from mobile phones to digital telephony have posed new and difficult challenges. In response, law enforcement has sought, with mixed success, to modify some technologies and restrict others. If we do not allow law enforcement agencies to adopt new technologies and procedures to match the changes in commercial communications, wiretap capabilities will continue to decline at the expense of public safety.

The principal challenge to wiretapping comes from the Internet. The Internet uses different communications technologies and protocols than the telephone system, and as more data and voice traffic migrate to the Internet, communications interception will be significantly reduced if law enforcement does not adopt technologies that allow for interception of Internet communications.

Before September 11, public debate focused on the FBI's Carnivore system, which can be installed at Internet service providers (ISPs) to monitor Internet traffic. (The Carnivore system is used mainly with smaller ISPs because large ISPs have proprietary software to perform the collection task.) Once a warrant is obtained, e-mail traffic is examined automatically for messages from a suspect; if a message is found, it is saved for later law enforcement review.

Privacy advocates and some in industry opposed deployment of Carnivore as overly intrusive and are now concerned that the fear and anger generated by the terrorist attack will sweep away opposition to intrusive technologies such as Carnivore. These concerns were unreasonable even before September 11. Greater use of monitoring tools need not be a cause for concern if the appropriate legal safeguards, such as warrant requirements and judicial oversight, remain in place.

New antiterrorism legislation (called the Uniting and Strengthening America Act by Providing Appropriate Tools Required to Intercept and Obstruct Terrorism [USA PATRIOT] Act of 2001), provides a broad range of new authorities, including an expansion of wiretapping and surveillance authorities. This act

- Establishes a nationwide order for pen register (recording telephone numbers dialed from a telephone) and trap and trace (recording the numbers of incoming calls), permitting the interception of communications routed through any jurisdiction in the country. Previously, the law allowed only the placement of interception devices in the jurisdiction where the order is granted. The act also extends pen register and trap-and-trace authority to the address information in the headers of e-mails, which will provide some information about content and Web browsing by revealing Web site names;
- Allows ISPs or other network administrators to authorize surveillance of "computer trespassers";
- Provides authority to compel disclosure of records in connection with an intelligence investigation; and
- Lets law enforcement authorities conduct wiretaps and secret searches in criminal cases under the standards previously applied to the purpose of collecting foreign intelligence, changes search warrant authorities to allow law enforcement agencies to search homes and offices without immediate notification of the owner, and allows sharing information collected in the name of a grand jury with intelligence agencies.

These changes are reasonable adjustments to new technologies if judicial oversight is not diminished. They should probably be continued even after any sunset clause in the new law takes effect. Generally, those sections that respond to terrorism and that retain safeguards (especially judicial oversight) will be beneficial. Those sections that create new authorities for national security or that do not require judicial oversight are problematic. Indeed, these sections may actually work against adoption of technological fixes by calling into question whether safeguards are adequate.

Existing Supreme Court guidelines for wiretapping remain the best guide for any new measure:

- The requesting agency must show probable cause that a particular offense has been or is about to be committed;
- The requesting agency must describe specifically the conversations to be intercepted;
- Surveillance must be for a specific, limited period of time;
- There must be continuing probable cause for surveillance to continue beyond the original end date;
- Surveillance must end once the conversation sought is seized;
- Notice must be given unless there is an adequate showing of exigency; and
- The requesting agency must report back on the warrant so that courts can oversee and limit use of the intercepted conversations.

An even broader challenge to privacy will arise if the U.S. government begins to survey and correlate publicly available information. There are enormous volumes of data on American citizens and the activities of organizations and entities. One of the keys to future counterintelligence could be to do detailed mapping of suspect transactions that are identified through extensive data mining and correlation. Yet, public sources are rarely limited to foreigners only. It is unclear whether existing law governing surveillance applies when law enforcement authorities or intelligence agencies collect and compare such information. Congress and the courts will need to explore this sensitive issue and find a reasonable solution.

The lack of adequate privacy protections for Americans may inadvertently contribute to concerns over increased law enforcement capabilities. As technology reduces anonymity and privacy, Americans might be more comfortable if they knew that data from Internet IDs and surveillance devices like sensors and the global positioning system (GPS) were not being exploited for commercial purposes. Law enforcement must comply with legal constraints and judicial oversight in its use of intrusive technologies. The same constraints, however, do not apply to commercial use of the same technologies. Part of the price for employing more intrusive technologies for public safety might be to limit, through federal legislation, the use of similar technologies for commercial purposes. This would make trade-offs between privacy and security more palatable.

The September 11 tragedy has rightly led the United States to reconsider the balance between law enforcement and new technologies, but restricting encryption—technology that renders stored data and communications unreadable—should not be among the options. Law enforcement officials, already concerned that the Internet and cellular telephony will degrade communications interception capabilities, fear that encryption compounds these challenges. The FBI (and the National Security Agency) fought for a decade to limit encryption's use and to require that encryption products include a backdoor for law enforcement access. These U.S. proposals failed repeatedly because they were expensive, technically difficult to implement, and had little public or allied support.

Without multilateral support from a broad range of countries, U.S. restrictions on encryption would not prevent terrorists from obtaining "unbreakable" products from other sources. Moreover, Al Qaeda has shown flexibility in adjusting its operations to avoid technology that has been compromised—abandoning satellite phones, for example, when it discovered that the United States could listen to messages. We could expect a similar reaction to encryption restrictions, leaving little advantage against the terrorists but real costs for the United States. Backdoors and restrictions on the use of encryption, by making computer networks more vulnerable to cyberattacks, will impose large costs for security and the economy. The benefit of widespread use of encryption outweighs the cost to law enforcement.

Public Surveillance Technologies

Technological changes offer significant increases in the ability of police to monitor public activities. A number of cities already have deployed closed-circuit cameras and automated face-scanning systems to monitor public places. These systems, however, are relatively primitive, require expensive installations, and suffer from an abundance of false positives and misidentifications when the system attempts to match an image to a criminal identity in a database.

Improvements in surveillance will come as new technologies enter the market and are combined into new systems. Cheap, small, unobtrusive portable sensors will collect visual or infrared data. Among them will be disposable sensors—tiny, coin-sized sensors capable of detecting movement or changes in light—and multispectral sensors such as the infrared sensors now found in some cars for night driving. Wireless connectivity will let these sensors link to the Internet through the cellular telephone system, making them easy to deploy and mobile. Inexpensive GPS chips will make it easier to pinpoint the location of the sensors and their targets. Connection to the Internet will allow this sensor data to be matched against large, remotely located databases and analyzed automatically by powerful computing resources.

These networked recognition technologies already exist in prototype form, but improved wireless capabilities (which depend on the United States resolving bandwidth and radio spectrum allocation issues) and improved recognition software need to be developed before they can be widely deployed. In the interim, we will see the piecemeal use of surveillance systems with sophisticated sensors in specific locations like airports or border-crossing points. Using face-scanning systems in well-defined situations (as a mandatory part of the airline check-in process, for example) would overcome many of the shortcomings of today's technology. This system could be based on passport and visa photos (perhaps even drivers license photos). The courts have limited the ability of police to use sensors to look into houses but appear to accept monitoring of public spaces. The basis for this distinction lies in the notion of a "reasonable expectation of privacy" and the Fourth Amendment prohibition against "unreasonable search." It is hard to argue that there is a reasonable expectation of privacy in an airport or a mall.

The benefits of such a system for airport security are unlikely to be challenged, but arguments will come as systems are deployed further afield and as they are combined with GPS or biometric technologies that provide more precise identification and location of individuals. GPS signal processors will continue to shrink in size and cost. When these chips are built into cars, laptops, and cell phones, they will allow authorities to pinpoint location. The result will be a world in which it is much more difficult to hide or be anonymous or lost.

Biometric technologies will link people's legal and physical identities, by using retinal scans, thumbprints, or even voice scans to validate claims to an identity and allow access to systems. Stolen passports would be worthless if they were linked to a retinal scan or digital thumbprint. Multiple identities could be reduced if state and national biometric databases were linked so that part of the application process for a driver's license or passport involved collecting biometric data and checking to see if this data matched a previous application under a different name in a different state or a different country. The United States has already begun to incorporate biometric data into some immigration documents; this could usefully be extended to other forms of legal identification. For biometric technologies to reach their true potential, however, the information they collect must be integrated with the national indices system, the watch lists, and other essential databases. This will require an enormous effort to automate, update, and continually evaluate acquired data.

These new technologies offer improved counterterrorist capabilities but pose difficult legal problems in protecting against misuse. Our legal system has not sorted out the line between private and public for these technologies. The issue lies in defining when law enforcement should collect such data and how that data should be treated (i.e., storage, sharing, and application). Congress and the courts have not dealt with this yet although the laws governing search and seizure or wiretaps offer some precedent. European models of domestic security, where national identification cards and extensive national police powers are routine, do not fit well with America's Constitution and heritage; still, they reflect long experience with terrorism. Some elements of the European approach to counterterrorism can be accommodated to Constitutional safeguards, but others require careful consideration.

International Cooperation

Localized law enforcement is at a disadvantage in an interconnected world. Law enforcement authorities are limited by jurisdiction—the geographical area to which authorities apply—and by sovereignty—the decision of a group of people to govern themselves, without external interference. No government is willing to let another police its citizens.

This is not an insoluble problem. All law enforcement agencies and all governments face the same challenges created by globalization and technological change. At some level, even political opponents are willing to cooperate on issues of law enforcement and public safety; this willingness has been increased (at least temporarily) by the events of September 11. Building cooperative arrangements among national law enforcement agencies that allow for coordinated activities and information sharing can help ensure the forces of globalization work for us, not against us.

The United States has made considerable strides in the past few years, but overcoming sensitivities over sovereignty issues and differences in national laws (even among the United States and its closest allies) will require compromise and delicate work. Domestic security poses a particular problem. France and the United Kingdom, for example, give their domestic security agencies greater authority than does the United States, and these agencies face fewer legal restrictions in wiretapping, warrant requirements, and covert operations. This reflects our very different political cultures—the United States limits the power of the sovereign to a far greater degree than European governments. Major European governments have also faced violent domestic terrorism for a much longer period than the United States has, and they have already made political decisions regarding domestic security that the United States is only beginning to face.

While placing FBI attachés in key countries is an effective tool, much of international law enforcement cooperation is still rooted in the diplomacy of the mid-twentieth century. Most law enforcement cooperation rests on bilateral mutual legal assistance treaties. These treaties differ in scope from country to country. They are difficult to negotiate because they raise complex sovereignty issues like the issue of law enforcement cooperation in general. The September 11 tragedy may offer the United States an opportunity to close some of this distance, both by strengthening existing mutual legal assistance treaties and by seeking broader multilateral arrangements.

The most useful venue for multilateral cooperation has been the G-8—the seven leading industrial economies and Russia. Existing G-8 initiatives on counterterrorism coordination and its Financial Action Task Force for money laundering (which began in the G-7 but has now extended to two dozen countries) form a solid foundation for expanding cooperation in counterterrorism.

Enhanced cooperation and information sharing in border control and immigration should complement these efforts. Immigration is among the most serious vulnerabilities revealed by September 11. The Al Qaeda cell responsible for the suicide-hijackings was recruited in the Middle East, organized in Afghanistan, and managed from Germany. Its members entered the United States from Canada and Europe and did their final planning and deployment from Massachusetts and Virginia, passing undetected through at least three immigration checks. At first glance, this would seem to be a domestic issue, but treating it as a domestic issue will produce inadequate results. Border control is no longer entirely a national problem. The nature of borders has changed extensively in a global economy, and for many the first point of entry into the United States is Canada or Mexico.

Closing our borders is not an option—even the additional checks put in place after September 11 strain the economy. The United States could tighten its visa programs, but we need to recognize that this would contribute relatively little to enhanced security. Potential immigrants have spent years determining the best way to "game" the visa application process, and denying a U.S. visa does little if the option of illegal entry from Mexico or Canada remains open. Few terrorists fly directly to the United States from Afghanistan. Better border security requires both improved immigration procedures in the United States and improved cooperation with other countries in screening entrants.

Improved national immigration procedures have two elements. First, expanded screening at U.S. borders and entry points using information technologies, face scanning against visa and passport databases, biometrics, and other detection systems (such as explosive sniffers) should be a priority. This will make future entries by terrorists more difficult (but not impossible). One unfortunate result of the relaxed immigration restrictions adopted by the United States over the past decade is that it is likely that members and supporters of Al Qaeda are legal residents. Solving this poses political questions that go beyond law enforcement. We do not want to restrict the flow of foreign visitors and students to the United States, but greater care is needed in extending the privileges of residency and citizenship to them.

The United States also needs to complement improved border controls with cooperative immigration efforts. Expanded cooperative immigration efforts among the United States and its allies and neighbors could borrow elements of the Schengen arrangement through which European countries share responsibility for screening foreigners entering Europe.[1] Schengen establishes common entry controls for its members, much the way that a foreigner permitted to enter New York can travel to another state without further screening. The Schengen arrangement is not without flaws, but a similar approach to cooperation in screening entrants to the "West" is necessary.

A cooperative approach to entry would involve greater information sharing, but going beyond that to a degree of coordination poses political problems: Countries would have to agree to deny access to foreigners found undesirable by one, but not all. In the past, the United States has rankled Great Britain by allowing entry to Irish Republican Army members, and Germany has permitted entry to members of terrorist-related groups objectionable to the United States. At a minimum, some sort of restricted entry and notification for individuals on a common control list could address this problem. Further steps would require a willingness to surrender sovereign authorities to some larger consensus.

Law Enforcement and Intelligence Cooperation

An effective response to terrorism will also require a reexamination of the boundary between law enforcement and intelligence. We need to find an approach that allows for effective cooperation between intelligence and law enforcement but maintains their separate roles and responsibilities. The intelligence community has linguistic and analytical skills needed by national law enforcement agencies, and both intelligence and law enforcement communities have unique information that can benefit the mission of the other.

Designing this cooperation presents challenges for both civil liberties and organizational effectiveness. Law enforcement and intelligence operations are fundamentally different. Successful intelligence agencies routinely violate foreign laws. Effective intelligence operations carefully define and limit cooperation with foreign governments in ways contrary to normal law enforcement practices. Respect for due process is essential for law enforcement but not a part of successful intelligence activities. Information collected by law enforcement is ultimately destined for its public use in a trial, whereas the end use for intelligence information is usually a classified report. The more the intelligence function is like law enforcement, the less effective it will be; the more law enforcement operates like an intelligence agency, the greater the concern and the risk to fundamental civil liberties.

Much of the legal structure governing U.S. national law enforcement activities grew out of Watergate-era concerns that the executive branch was using national intelligence and law enforcement assets for domestic political ends. September 11 has led us to reopen the debate over police authorities in a civil state. The politicization of law enforcement in the past few years complicates this issue. Law enforcement at the national level has become a group with its own objectives and priorities, and a willingness to seek them. In classic bureaucratic fashion, it presses to expand its authorities and prerogatives. While this reflects larger trends in the bureaucratization of American government, where large departments have developed rationales and political skills to operate with some independence from elected administrations, it also grows in part from the antagonistic nature of the U.S. legal system and a degree of alienation between police forces and the broader public.

The roots of this problem are complex. The system of federal government relies on the fragmentation of power. The Constitution divides authority among the Congress, the president, and the judiciary, and among the federal government and the states. This division is carried over into agency responsibilities. Fragmented authorities prevent the state from overwhelming democratic government. This approach has served the United States well in many instances, but as new technologies and global networks emerge, the cost of fragmented authorities may outweigh the benefit in some specific areas.

While cooperation with the intelligence community has improved dramatically in recent years—with a jointly staffed counterterrorism center, the exchange of deputies, personnel assigned to each agency's counterterrorism groups, joint meetings, and joint operational and analytical initiatives—bureaucratic competition and legal constraints have sometimes prevented crucial terrorism-related information from being shared in a timely and appropriate manner. Law enforcement and intelligence collection techniques are subject to differing legal authorities, which poses problems for information sharing. Distinguishing between collecting and sharing information can resolve some of these problems. For collection, we would want to preserve the distinction between the

FBI and the intelligence community's authorities. The FBI should not engage in espionage and the intelligence community should not add criminal investigation to its list of collection priorities.

But while collection should remain separate, the United States should remove the barriers to sharing information that bear on criminal investigations or intelligence activities as they relate to terrorism. (Sharing intelligence that bears on other criminal activities is a more complex problem; discussion of it can be separated from counterterrorism.) Concern over misuse of information sharing by the executive branch (or by congressional leadership) is legitimate, but an artificial distinction for information sharing on international terrorism should be eliminated. In particular, the removal of limitations on sharing of information from guidelines for the federal wiretap statute (Title III) or grand jury information will be beneficial for coordinated counterterror efforts.

Yet information sharing will not automatically spring up with the removal of the legal obstacles. The difficulties that law enforcement and intelligence agencies face in coordinating their operations run deeper than policy and procedure, into the very cores of these organizations. Similarly, the fundamental pattern of secrecy protection within the FBI—a case-file security approach—is profoundly counterproductive to developing systematic, analytically based assessments of terrorist network activities. A strategy for promoting effective cooperation—between agencies and within them—must provide both the tools for cooperation and the operational conditions for their use.

Going Forward

The September 11 tragedy may shift the terms of the public debate for issues like privacy, Internet surveillance, and even the allocation of radio spectrum. Security, law enforcement, and homeland defense will be higher priorities than in the past. However, measures that seek to improve law enforcement capabilities by reversing technological change and resisting globalization could involve wrenching changes to the global economy and pose unacceptable risks of economic damage. We have seen globalization derailed before, by the First World War and the Great Depression. One of our goals should be denying Al Qaeda a similar outcome.

How then do we map a course for strengthening law enforcement to combat terror? There are concrete measures at the operational level, but the larger question for effective counterterrorism involves our response to technological change and globalization. As we seek to strengthen law enforcement in democratic societies, four questions should guide our review of any proposed measure:

- Is the measure a necessary response to the technological and global changes of the past decade to prevent the erosion of law enforcement capabilities?
- What is its effect on civil society and the economy?
- Can we take advantage of specific new technologies to make law enforcement more effective?
- Are the necessary legal safeguards and oversights in place to protect civil liberties and economic growth?

Law enforcement authorities are neither a panacea nor a substitute for a comprehensive strategy to eliminate terrorism. Increased police powers pose risks to the fabric of American economy and society. If we are cognizant of these risks and take the necessary steps to safeguard against them, greater international law enforcement cooperation, closer cooperation between law enforcement and intelligence in counterterrorism, and new technologies that restore some law enforcement capabilities can only be beneficial.

Note

[1] The Schengen Agreement came into effect in 1995. It replaced the internal borders of the signatory states with a single external border and created a single set of rules to govern immigration procedures—as well as common rules on visas, asylum rights and checks at external borders. The goal was to enable the free movement of persons within the Schengen area without compromising law and order. Thus the abolishing of internal borders was accompanied by so-called compensatory measures—including improved coordination between the police, customs, and the judiciary and enhanced efforts to combat terrorism and organized crime. At the heart of this effort is the Schengen Information System, through which member states' police stations and consular officials can access and exchange data on specific individuals and descriptions of lost or stolen vehicles or objects.

New York Tank, 1917. One of the first American tanks driving past the "Flatiron" building in New York.
Photograph: Hulton | Archive/Getty Images.

Chapter 9

Strengthening Homeland Security

"The President's executive order states that we must detect, prepare for, prevent, protect against, respond to and recover from terrorist attacks, an extraordinary mission. But we will carry it out . . . . And we will operate from a few basic principles. First, candor. No one should be wary of coming forward when they see a problem. It's the only way to define a solution . . . . The second, cooperation. We must open lines of communication and support like never before, between agencies and departments, between federal and state and local entities, and between the public and private sectors. . . . The only turf we should be worried about protecting is the turf we stand on. . . . Finally, as the President stated, we will continue to secure liberty, as we secure this nation. . . . We will work to ensure that the essential liberty of the American people is protected, that terrorists will not take away our way of life."

— Director Tom Ridge
Office of Homeland Security
Swearing-in Ceremony at the White House
October 8, 2001

In the decades between Pearl Harbor and September 11, 2001, Americans' sense of security at home waxed and waned with the dynamics of the Cold War. In the 1950s, the buildup of Soviet nuclear weapons capable of reaching the United States led to an era of bomb shelters in basements and duck-and-cover drills in U.S. schools. With the arrival of détente and arms control in the 1970s, Americans managed to rekindle a sense that we were safe at home, even as we lived our lives in the shadow of thousands of nuclear weapons aimed at U.S. cities and citizens.

This sense of relative invulnerability was tested in the 1980s when U.S.-Soviet tensions rose but became entrenched in 1989 as the Cold War came to an end. Russia was no longer our enemy, we were the world's sole superpower and our military was unsurpassed—we were a nation at peace. And if the 1991 Gulf War reminded us we still faced threats to our national interests, it also reinforced the sense that America's wars would be fought far from its borders. One Pentagon strategist noted in the early 1990s, "The American military only plays away games."

In the decade following the Gulf War, American national security experts began to worry more about asymmetric threats, including potential threats to the U.S. homeland.[1] Over the same period, the Clinton administration launched a number of initiatives to help federal, state, and local governments enhance their respective capabilities to defend against and respond to potential attacks on U.S. soil, and to better coordinate their efforts. But the American people remained largely unaware or at least incredulous of the threat, even after the first terrorist attack on the World Trade Center in 1993. For many Americans, part of the shock of September 11 was that it seemed so inconceivable.

In the wake of the worst terrorist attacks in history, homeland security has soared to the top of the U.S. agenda. Before September 11, there was a growing commitment among many in government to take prudent steps to guard against potential threats to the United States; since September 11, there has been an urgent public demand and an unprecedented degree of political will to do and spend whatever is necessary, as quickly as possible, to enhance homeland security to the greatest extent we can. Congress's willingness shortly after the September 11 attacks to give the president $40 billion in an emergency supplemental—fully twice what he had requested—was indicative of the country's new mood.

Protecting the U.S. homeland from threats such as terrorism, cyber attack, and weapons of mass destruction will be an extremely challenging task, one rendered more difficult by the open nature of U.S. society, the U.S. economy's reliance on international commerce and trade, and the civil liberties Americans hold dear. Each day approximately 1.3 million people cross U.S. borders. Terrorists have already demonstrated their ability to enter the United States, often legally, and live among us undetected for a period of years. In addition, more than 340,000 vehicles and 58,000 cargo shipments enter the United States on a daily basis, and only 1 or 2 percent of these are currently inspected by customs agents. And each year, there are more than 250,000 attempts to hack into Department of Defense computers, and this represents only a fraction of the attempted intrusions experienced by the U.S. government and industry as a whole.

Enhancing homeland security will be further complicated by the fact that responsibility for dealing with different aspects of these threats cuts across the jurisdictions of more than 40 federal agencies and 14 congressional committees, not to mention countless state and local offices, as well as the private sector. One homeland security expert noted, "We've got great athletes . . . but we don't have a coach, we don't have a game plan, and we're not practicing. How do you think we're going to do in the big game?"[2] Organizing for success will be critical—and also exceedingly hard.

A Three-Pronged Strategy

Homeland security can usefully be defined as the prevention, deterrence, preemption of, and defense against attacks on the United States, and the management of the consequences of any attacks. Inherent in this definition are three broad and enduring objectives that should provide the foundation for a new national strategy for homeland security.[3]

The first objective is to prevent future attacks on the United States. This objective is preeminent, as it is central to the survival of the open, democratic, market-based way of life that distinguishes American society.

Prevention involves stopping threats to the United States before they become manifest, preferably as far away from America's shores and borders as possible. Prevention efforts overseas might include working with allies to roll up terrorist networks abroad, to prevent the proliferation of weapons of mass destruction and long-range delivery systems, or to shut down hackers conspiring to launch attacks against American computer networks. It might also include more immediate actions inside the United States to stop a terrorist from crossing into the country, boarding a flight, or renting a crop duster or commercial truck. Prevention is by its very nature proactive, and often requires taking offensive action to destroy or neutralize a threat before an attack occurs. The U.S. leadership must be prepared to act proactively in concert with established coalitions or alliances—and even unilaterally—to strike against defined, imminent threats to the homeland far from U.S. shores.

Prevention also involves "shaping the security environment to avoid or retard the emergence of threats to the United States," which can only be achieved through American activities overseas.[4] In this regard, the Departments of State and Defense, our allies, and foreign law enforcement agencies all play a significant role in defending the U.S. homeland. Thus prevention may be greatly aided by U.S. engagement abroad. But in the final analysis, the long pole in the prevention tent is the ability to detect threats before they become manifest, and detect them with enough specificity and time to enable preventive action to be taken.

Because it may not be possible to prevent every attack, the goal in practice should be to minimize the likelihood that the most serious attacks on the United States could be mounted successfully. Secretary of Defense Donald Rumsfeld has said, "Our victory will come with Americans living their lives day by day, going to work, raising their children and building their dreams as they always have—a free and great people."[5] The fact that federal law enforcement and intelligence agencies have averted numerous such attacks in the past by acting rapidly on specific indications and warnings is proof that a degree of prevention is possible.

The second objective is to enhance the ability of the United States to protect itself against such attacks. This includes strengthening America's defenses against threats to the U.S. homeland—such as terrorism, cyber attacks, weapons of mass destruction, and air and missile threats—as well as enhancing the security of our borders, territorial waters, airspace, and critical infrastructure.

Essential to the protection of American citizens is an effective capability to defeat or neutralize enemy action once an attack is launched. Whether an immediate, reactive defense against an air or missile attack or a rapidly instigated manhunt to find and foil a terrorist cell or day-to-day security measures to protect our borders and critical infrastructure, a broad range of capabilities—domestic law enforcement, intelligence, military, public health and others—will be needed to mount effective barriers to such attacks. This aspect of homeland security is made particularly complex by the wide variety of acknowledged threats, the increasing sophistication displayed by known terrorists, and their ability to adapt their concepts of operations to take advantage of new technologies and to exploit weaknesses in whatever security measures are in place.

As a result, U.S. efforts to enhance homeland security should not focus only or even primarily on ensuring that terrorists can never again hijack U.S. commercial airlines and fly them into buildings. The United States must anticipate and be able to protect itself against a much broader range of possible threats—for example, terrorist attacks involving airplanes, missiles, trucks, cars, or ships; terrorist attacks involving the release of chemical or biological agents or nuclear materials in major U.S. cities; and both cyber and physical attacks on critical infrastructure. Both lethal, destructive threats and nonlethal, disruptive threats demonstrate the complexity of the problem and the broad range of participants, in both public and private sectors, that must be involved in protecting the United States.

Canada and Mexico have a particularly important role to play in this aspect of U.S. homeland security. The U.S. homeland security may be only as strong as the border and port of entry security of its two neighbors. Conversely, an attack on the United States—especially a chemical or biological attack—might affect their populations as well. This suggests the need to develop even closer bilateral cooperation in law enforcement, border security, intelligence, and other areas.

The third objective is to improve the ability of the United States to respond to and manage the consequences of an attack should it occur. First, the United States must have a robust capability to ensure public safety, continuity of government, command, control, and communications, and the provision of essential services. Effective consequence management is also central to maintaining public confidence and reducing the physical and psychological impacts of terrorism. As we witnessed on September 11, state and local first responders—the local fire fighters, police officers, and emergency medical teams—are often the most important element of effective consequence management, and they must be given the resources, equipment, and training they need to do their jobs well.

Second, the United States must be able to minimize disruption and rapidly restore the functioning of critical infrastructure in the immediate aftermath of an attack. This might involve restoring telecommunications service, repairing energy production and distribution systems, or providing alternative routes and means of transportation. Hardening potential targets, developing contingency plans, and building a degree of redundancy into key systems will be critical to rapid restoration.

Third, the U.S. government must be prepared to take rapid steps to stabilize U.S. financial markets and manage the immediate economic and financial consequences of an attack.

Fourth, federal, state, and local agencies, as well as nongovernmental organizations must be prepared to provide immediate assistance to the victims of an attack, their families, and affected communities.

Central to success in both protection and response are advance planning, exercises and simulations to identify problems and refine plans, and coordination across the federal government and with state, local, and representatives of nongovernmental organizations to prepare for future attacks.

Preparing for the Worst: Bioterrorism and Attacks on Critical Infrastructure

As the United States develops a national strategy for homeland security, particular attention should be paid to two threats that pose the greatest danger to our basic way of life: bioterrorism and attacks on critical infrastructure.

Bioterrorism

Whereas an effective terrorist attack involving chemical agents could produce tens or hundreds of thousands of casualties, an effective attack using biological pathogens could result in millions. It is well established that members of the Al Qaeda organization have sought to obtain biological means of attack and have contacts with states that have biological weapons programs. The anthrax attacks that followed the September 11 attacks effectively ended the debate about whether or not terrorists could access and use biological agents. They have and they will.

The good news is that biological pathogens are generally difficult to weaponize—that is, it is difficult to take them from a laboratory petri dish or vial, produce them in large quantities, and turn them into a form that can be effectively dispersed to cause mass casualties. The bad news is that terrorists would need only a small quantity of a highly contagious pathogen like smallpox to infect enough people to create a mass casualty event. Each infected individual, in effect, would become a walking biological weapon—a danger whose dimensions are magnified in our modern, mobile society. A local bio-attack could quickly become a national crisis with the potential to cripple the country.

The United States should therefore give highest priority to preventing pathogens that could be used in such attacks from falling into the hands of terrorists, and to enhancing our ability to deal with such attacks should they occur.

Today security measures at U.S. and foreign facilities are not adequate to prohibit theft of dangerous pathogens. In the United States, samples of some pathogens like smallpox are kept under very tight security; but samples of others, like anthrax, are housed in research laboratories across the country with only minimal security. Furthermore, literally tons of Cold War–era biological weapons agents remain housed in nonsecure facilities across the former Soviet Union.

In addition, we are ill prepared to prevent the dire consequences of a large-scale bioterrorism attack. The United States currently lacks the stockpiles of vaccines and antibiotics and the means of rapid distribution that would be required for an effective response. We also lack an adequate cadre of first responders who are trained and equipped to deal with such a crisis.

The U.S. government also lacks adequate management strategies, plans, and information systems to cope with a bioterrorism assault. Today senior leaders would simply not receive the intelligence and expert advice they need to make informed decisions. As a result of these shortfalls, state and federal officials could find themselves in the untenable position of having to impose forcible constraints on citizens because they lack other viable tools to contain a crisis. This would pose enormous challenges to civil liberties and horrific choices for decisionmakers. Indeed, the less prepared we are for a bioterrorism event, the greater the panic that will likely ensue, and the more threats there will be to the civil liberties and lives of average Americans.

To address this situation, the president, working with Congress and state and local governments, should launch a major initiative on the scale of the Apollo Project to enhance our nation's capabilities to prevent and respond to biological terrorism. The focus of this project should be fortifying and equipping the public health system to limit bioterrorism's potentially catastrophic effects.

Substantial investments are needed to strengthen public health expertise, infrastructure, and early warning systems. New approaches must be developed to deal with the diseases that might be used as weapons of terror—especially stockpiling vaccines and antibiotics, strengthening regional and national distribution mechanisms, and researching and developing other means of facilitating rapid, effective disease control, such as funding the development of easily deployed diagnostic tools using new biotechnologies. The decision to create a stockpile of 300 million smallpox vaccines was a step in the right direction, but much more needs to be done. Particularly important will be developing an appropriate regulatory process to ensure the safety of new vaccines and antibiotics, as well as providing the medical and pharmaceutical industries with the necessary incentives, such as liability protection, to rise to this national challenge.

This modern-day Apollo Project should also include the development and implementation of an effective security protocol for all U.S. laboratories that store pathogens that could be used effectively in a terrorist attack; an extensive program of analysis, simulations, and exercises to improve our understanding of the challenges we would encounter in the event of such an attack and to identify and prioritize shortfalls that need to be addressed; the development of more detailed plans and decisionmaking protocols for dealing with a bioterrorism event, including clarification of jurisdictional issues between state and federal entities; and procurement at all levels of government of the information systems that would be needed to manage such a crisis.

In addition, the United States must make reducing the biological weapons legacy of the former Soviet Union through cooperative threat reduction programs an even higher priority on the foreign policy agenda. It should also seek to reinvigorate and reorient the process laid out in the Biological Weapons Convention to take the new bioterrorism threats into account. Only in preparing for this worst case can we hope to limit its consequences.

Critical Infrastructure Protection

Enhancing the security of America's critical infrastructure—those physical and cyber-based systems essential to the minimum operations of the economy and the government—is another central challenge in reducing the risks and consequences of future terrorist attacks. One can imagine the disruption and panic that would ensue if an aircraft breached the containment structure of a nuclear power plant, a major city's power supply was shut down, or the New York Stock Exchange's computer system was sabotaged.

Critical infrastructure includes telecommunications, electrical power systems, gas and oil infrastructure, banking and finance, transportation, water systems, and emergency services—80 to 90 percent of which is owned and/or operated by private firms. And with the advent of new information technologies, much of the nation's critical infrastructure has become increasingly automated in recent years— bringing new efficiencies but also new vulnerabilities, including vulnerability to cyber attacks. As in the case of bio defense, an active and sustained partnership between the government and the private sector will be essential to address these problems.

Significant progress has been made in recent years, including the establishment of information-sharing and analysis centers for a number of sectors to address electronic threats, vulnerabilities, incidents and solutions. To date, however, these efforts have focused primarily on cyber rather than physical threats. Given that terrorist organizations like Al Qaeda have demonstrated their interest in producing highly visible mass casualty events, cyber strikes may not be their preferred mode of attack. The Bush administration would be wise to broaden its work on critical infrastructure protection to include a greater emphasis on physical vulnerabilities and threats in various sectors.

This will require not only new threat and vulnerability assessments but also a clearer delineation of who has the responsibility and who has the authority to enhance security measures against physical attacks on various elements of critical infrastructure. For example, who is responsible for providing adequate security at the 103 nuclear power plants operating in the United States? The private utility companies who operate the plants? Local law enforcement? National Guard units under the control of the state governors? These issues need to be urgently addressed.

Organizing for Success

How should the U.S. government be organized for homeland security? This question—at the heart of virtually every policy discussion since September 11—was debated in depth for months and even years before.

Three basic options were discussed most frequently: Give the entire homeland security mission to one existing agency or another, such as the Federal Emergency Management Agency (FEMA) or the Department of Defense; create a new agency by merging elements of existing organizations and missions;[6] or create a strong coordinator in the White House.[7] President Bush seems to have settled the debate, at least for his tenure, by appointing Governor Tom Ridge to be director of the Office of Homeland Security. In essence, the president opted for the third option, a national coordinator in the White House who is charged with bringing together the assembled resources of the entire government. Yet within hours of the announcement, debate resumed over whether Governor Ridge had been given the authorities and institutional standing he needs to be effective in his new post.

President Bush's decision was the correct decision for now—but it is inadequate for the longer term. The precise structure of the long-term organizational solution is probably unknowable at this point. But changes will surely be needed, as will be discussed below.

Designing a long-term, integrated, effective response to the complicated problem of international terrorism waged on American soil requires an understanding of three fault lines that fracture U.S. government at this point in history. The first is divided federal government—the essence of American constitutional democracy. The founders intended a system of checks and balances to produce inefficiencies in decisionmaking that would preclude abuses of power. But they succeeded beyond their wildest dreams. Over time, the U.S. government has evolved to become enormously complex and redundant, with nearly every major department and bureau having some relevant role in homeland security.

The second constitutionally grounded fault line is American federalism—the way in which authorities are divided among the national level and the state and local levels of government. Only the federal government is empowered to wage war or regulate interstate commerce. Generally, state and local governments are responsible for functions such as education, fire protection, emergency response, and local law enforcement. Coordinating a nationwide response to terrorism requires bridging this chasm.

The third fault line is more cultural than constitutional: the separation between our foreign and domestic security apparatus. U.S. political culture has always been wary of excessive government power, and this has limited the role of the military and the intelligence agencies inside the borders of the United States. The military's role within the United States is highly circumscribed by *posse comitatus;* the U.S. intelligence community cannot spy on American citizens; and the domestic surveillance activities of federal law enforcement bodies is constrained by fairly rigid operational restrictions and judicial oversight.

When it comes to fighting terrorism, however, this division between foreign security and domestic security creates a dangerous disconnect. For example, terrorists have used modern communications networks to leap across political jurisdictions, allowing them to operate within the United States in ways that forced law enforcement agencies to abandon the chase. In the past, legal authorities required law enforcement agencies to pursue a complex paper-based process of court orders and warrants. Clearly, this foreign–domestic security fault line creates operational barriers to cooperation among military forces, intelligence, and law enforcement that constantly need to be surmounted—a problem that has been recognized and is being addressed.

As if this picture were not sufficiently bleak, it should be noted that many other democracies are equally fractured in their government structures. The discontinuities on the American scene are replicated among our partner states, complicating the problem of international information sharing and coordination.

A National Coordinator for Homeland Security: The Near-Term Answer

In light of the deep divisions that mark American culture and constitutional governance, a national coordinator is the best and only solution to the current problem of homeland security. Having said that, Tom Ridge has been assigned the most difficult job imaginable: To coordinate a vast and complex government and to instill the focus and agility required to stay ahead of small bands of ruthless terrorists. His task is further complicated by the inherent advantage the terrorists have of hiding inside an America that values its diversity and its openness, and embraces transnational business practices and social interactions.

Given these challenges, Director Ridge should take a strategic approach to his mission. Virtually every major department of the federal government, and certainly the law enforcement and emergency response elements of the state and local governments, all have crucial roles to play in the homeland security mission. Obviously, the national coordinator cannot "run" daily operations of such a vast and disparate array of agencies and bureaus. Instead, he should use his power and influence to shape the priorities, plans, and future competencies of the government to deal with terrorism.

First, we must resist the trap of preparing to fight the last war. It is unlikely terrorists will attempt a strike that resembles the events of September 11, and if they do, we undoubtedly will be better prepared to foil their plans. Instead, terrorists are more likely to attack in unanticipated ways—airplanes one day, anthrax the next. Therefore, the first task of the national coordinator is to think like a terrorist. He should establish a terrorism assessment unit that is specifically designed to strategize as a terrorist would and to research alternative techniques for breaching U.S. security. This should not be an unbounded exercise of human imagination but rather a disciplined review of terrorist doctrine and techniques, intelligence assessments, and a reasoning of goals and effects intended by various terrorist organizations. The terrorist assessment unit should draw widely on the research community in the United States and in other countries as well as less conventional sources such as Hollywood and the broader creative community. Its aim should be to challenge the planning and programming priorities of the various departments and bureaus that share the homeland security task.

Second, the national coordinator should institute an extensive program of war-gaming exercises. For years the Defense Department has conducted so-called tabletop exercises to test assumptions and plans. Other elements of the government have some form of assessment, but usually not with this degree of discipline or sophistication. War games serve five primary purposes. First, they uncover discontinuities in planning for unexpected events. Second, they reveal insights into the complexity of problems that cannot be internalized by reading reports. Experiencing a problem is a far more powerful learning tool than just reading about it. Third, war games establish operational working relationships among participants in peacetime that become crucial for communication and trust in crisis situations. Fourth, war games tend to suspend the typical turf battles when organizations confront just what they can and cannot do, and what other organizations bring to the table in a time of crisis. And finally, they reveal critical shortfalls in processes and capabilities that need to be addressed.

This comprehensive war-gaming program should include periodic training sessions for the president and the cabinet. The war-gaming program needs to contemplate different scenarios and spontaneous developments. The terrorism assessment unit described above would be instrumental in designing the scenarios and identifying the key learning points for each exercise.

Third, the national coordinator should establish an advanced concepts office for homeland security. This office would be chartered to develop new approaches to government operations that would bridge the discontinuities and address the shortfalls identified in the war-gaming process. It would utilize current operations research techniques to identify alternative concepts of operations and help the national coordinator provide guidance to the departments and bureaus to develop new capabilities.

Fourth, Director Ridge should conduct a homeland security strategy review—on the scale of a quadrennial defense review—to define and prioritize objectives, develop a strategy to meet those objectives, and put forward a concept of operations that clearly assigns responsibility for various aspects of the strategy to specific agencies and actors. This planning process should also include a comprehensive assessment of current U.S. capabilities to deal with the full range of threats to the U.S. homeland. The objective should be to identify and prioritize shortfalls in national capabilities that should be addressed on the basis of a combination of the likelihood of the threat and the seriousness of its potential consequences.

Informed by this strategy review, the national coordinator, on behalf of the president, should develop a multiyear, interagency action plan. The plan should specify short-term actions to be taken on a priority basis, long-term investments to be made to enhance capabilities in critical areas, and a clear division of labor, including lead agency responsibility for specific areas and actions. This plan should be issued under the president's signature to guide resource allocation for homeland security across the federal government. It should also be a living document that is reviewed and revised on an annual basis. The process of developing this plan should include every federal agency that will be assigned responsibility for an element of homeland security as well as close consultations with key state and local agencies and actors. Both the assessment and the development of an integrated action plan will be important to ensure that the United States gets the highest possible returns on what is likely to be tens of billions of dollars invested in homeland security over the next several years.

Once this plan is in place, the national coordinator should establish an annual program and budget review process, whereby the activities and expenditures of relevant federal agencies are reviewed in light of the requirements defined in the multiyear plan. This review process would provide a mechanism for ensuring that agency actions are in accordance with the president's guidance and would provide the national coordinator with a critical mechanism for enforcing the president's priorities. Here, consistent and unwavering presidential backing will be essential to the national coordinator's success. The president must effectively communicate to the various agencies that "Tom Ridge's decisions are my decisions, and there will be no appeals."

The national coordinator must also take steps to more fully integrate federal programs and plans with those of state and local governments, and to aid state and local authorities in enhancing their homeland security capabilities. Because state and local governments will likely be the first to respond to an attack, they will bear the lion's share of responsibility in implementing decisions made in Washington. They also will feel the immediate impacts of any attack most acutely. These constituencies will have to be included in discussions and decisions if the United States is to succeed in strengthening security at home.

In the short run, a strong national coordinator for homeland security is the right answer. In the long run, however, we must develop new approaches to government that will bridge these fault lines more effectively. At this stage it is not possible to decide with precision what new structures are required. This should logically emerge after the study-exercise-innovate-review process described above.

Other Organizational Innovations

Given both the importance and likely longevity of homeland security as an issue, the Congress should consider restructuring its committees to deal with it in a more coherent way. The alternative would be to try to provide coherent oversight using a multiplicity of existing committees and subcommittees, each of which would examine only the narrow efforts of the particular agency or agencies it funds. Without a mechanism to provide effective oversight of the homeland security effort as a whole, Congress will have diminished its ability to use its power of the purse and to ensure that the impact of various security measures on our citizens and their basic rights are given due consideration.

Within the Department of Defense, at least two proposals should be considered: the creation of a commander in chief for homeland security and the reorientation of the National Guard to focus on homeland defense as its primary mission.[8]

The administration should also give priority to strengthening FEMA to be the standing interface between the federal government and state and local governments for dealing with the consequences of terrorism on U.S. soil. While FEMA has an excellent track record of coordinating the national response to natural disasters, such as hurricanes and floods, before September 11 it was extremely reluctant to take on post-terrorism consequence management. As a result, it currently lacks personnel with the requisite skills for this mission. Rather than assign the federal coordination role to another agency, FEMA should be strengthened to undertake this task—including considerable investment in new staff and training activities.

Finally, the government should create opportunities for national service in the area of homeland security. The twin attacks on the World Trade Center and the Pentagon have led to an outpouring of national volunteering and participation in the recovery effort. Across the nation, Americans of all ages are looking for ways to help.

The president should create a task force to explore the creation of a homeland security service corps for both young and old Americans who are prepared to give two years to help protect the nation. Volunteers would be trained to serve in a variety of fields, including the Public Health Service, airport security, and the National Guard and Reserve. Modeled after the Peace Corps and AmeriCorps, the new homeland security corps would provide suitable educational and financial benefits to volunteers, and the program would need the strong bipartisan commitment of the president and Congress. The task force could also explore the merits of mandatory national service.

Homeland security is now front and center in America's consciousness, and it is likely to stay there for quite some time, especially if attacks continue. The U.S. government, in partnership with state and local agencies and the private sector, must do everything in its power to enhance our homeland security capabilities, starting by addressing shortfalls in the highest-priority areas and working its way down the list. It also must reorganize to better integrate policies, programs, and budgets across bureaucratic divides.

Making such changes will be painful, but not making them would be worse. Success in bolstering homeland security is essential if we are to preserve our way of life and sustain public support for the campaign against terrorism and for U.S. engagement abroad. From the president to governors, big-city mayors and small-town managers, a commitment to strengthen U.S. homeland security is clear, and it is up to these leaders to continue progress toward an exceedingly challenging goal. But in reaching for it, they—and we—will demonstrate to the rest of the world just how much we value the continuing experiment that is America.

Notes

[1] Most notable are the U.S. Commission on National Security/21st Century (The Hart-Rudman Commission), which has published *Road Map for National Security: Imperative for Change*, www.nssg.gov; and the Advisory Panel to Assess Domestic Response Capabilities for Terrorism Involving Weapons of Mass Destruction (The Gilmore Commission), which has published *Toward a National Strategy for Combating Terrorism*, www.rand.org/nsrd/terrpanel/terror2.pdf; among others. All commissions have reflected detailed consideration of homeland security and have made numerous recommendations.

[2] Randall Larson as quoted in Sydney J. Freedberg Jr., "Shoring Up America," *National Journal*, October 19, 2001.

[3] These objectives were inspired by the three-part framework of prevention, protection, and response that was originally laid out in U.S. Commission on National Security/21st Century, *Road Map for National Security*, Phase III Report, January 31, 2001, 12–14.

[4] Commander Michael Dobbs, U.S. Navy, "Homeland Security: New Challenges for an Old Responsibility," *Journal for Homeland Security* (March 2001).

[5] Donald Rumsfeld, "A New Kind of War," *New York Times*, September 27, 2001.

[6] The U.S. Commission on National Security/21st Century (Hart-Rudman Commission) recommended the creation of a new homeland security agency that would include FEMA, the U.S. Coast Guard, the Border Patrol, and the Customs Service; see *Road Map for National Security*, 15–16, 21.

[7] See, for example, the Advisory Panel to Assess Domestic Response Capabilities for Terrorism Involving Weapons of Mass Destruction (The Gilmore Panel), *Toward a National Strategy for Combating Terrorism*, 7; and Joseph J. Collins and Michael Horowitz, *Homeland Defense: A Strategic Approach* (Washington, D.C.: CSIS, December 2000), 42.

[8] For a discussion of these two proposals, see chapter 6.

Buy War Bonds, circa 1941. An electronic signboard display during a rally at the New York Stock Exchange. Photograph: Hulton | Archive/Getty Images.

Chapter 10

The Economic Dimension: Attack and Defend

> "The uniforms of this conflict will be bankers' pinstripes and pro-grammers' grunge just as assuredly as desert camouflage."
>
> — *Secretary of Defense Donald H. Rumsfeld*
> New York Times
> *September 27, 2001*

From the outset, President George W. Bush made it clear that the struggle against international terrorism would be long and fought on a variety of fronts. That fundamental decision generated two power-ful economic implications. The first was that a strong economy was necessary to support what would undoubtedly be an intensive as well as a long campaign. The second implication was even clearer—eco-nomic institutions would be called on directly to serve as tools in the war against terrorists and terrorism.

Indeed, the first major antiterrorist action taken by the president was on the economic front: On September 24, 2001, he issued an ex-ecutive order blocking property owned by terrorists and prohibiting transactions with persons who "commit, threaten to commit, or sup-port terrorism." The executive order covered 27 specific individuals and organizations. On October 12, 39 additional terrorist organiza-tions were added to the list.

In an age of globalization, the economic aspects of the antiterrorist campaign require the active participation of other nations, in a man-ner analogous to the efforts on the military and diplomatic fronts. And other nations have a clear incentive to help because for nearly a decade, the United States has been the engine of global growth. When terrorists strike at the U.S. economy, the rest of the world feels our pain.

Moreover, the basic task of maintaining a strong economy involves every American citizen—and in a role that runs counter to experience during prior, more conventional conflicts. Especially in World Wars I and II, civilians made a major contribution by consuming less, so that more of the nation's resources could be directed to military production. The current effort is strikingly different: Our mission is to maintain a strong, civilian-oriented economy in the face of a variety of terrorist attacks. It may not feel like an act of personal heroism for a family to go to the ballpark or out to dinner, but maintaining the pace of economic activity is vital in this extended period when the portion of the gross domestic product purchased by the armed services is a fraction of the average Cold War experience.

In a September 24 speech at Chicago's O'Hare Airport, President Bush brought this theme home: "[T]ell the traveling public: Get on board. Do your business around the country. Fly and enjoy America's great destination spots. Get down to Disney World in Florida. Take your families and enjoy life . . . ." And in New York City, which suffered the worst blows of the September 11 attacks, Mayor Rudolph Giuliani made his position clear: "I encourage people from all over the country who want to help . . . come here and spend money. Go to a restaurant, a play . . . the life of the city goes on . . . ."

A sustained campaign against terrorism demands a long-term, comprehensive national economic strategy designed to attack and defend simultaneously—to attack the financial arteries of international terrorism and defend the very productivity and prosperity the terrorists targeted.

First, we must use our powerful economic and financial resources and enlist our economic and financial institutions in an all-out effort to combat and deter terrorist attacks. This involves cutting off financial flows to terrorist groups as well as providing a combination of aid, trade, and investment to countries allied with the United States in combating terrorism. As explored further in other chapters, the effective use of our economic resources also encompasses the U.S. role in alleviating some of the conditions that give rise to terrorism by aiding the reconstruction of failed states and the rebuilding of devastated areas.

Second, we must sustain the growth and productivity of our economy. This objective sounds obvious. However, it becomes much more complicated in the face of further terrorist attacks and as new security procedures designed to mitigate the terrorist threat unintentionally reduce economic efficiency and deter the day-to-day activities of managers, workers, and consumers.

Third, government and industry—in their separate roles—must provide the incentives and financial resources for the research and development of new antiterror technologies and procedures. Examples include sophisticated scanning and identification devices, new-age "nuclear sniffers" that can locate bomb-grade material, and a new generation of drugs to safeguard against chemical and biological attacks. A key related requirement is public–private cooperation to protect the nation's critical infrastructure, which includes a variety of transportation, communication, utility, and energy systems.

In developing and carrying out each of the components of the economic campaign against terrorism, decisionmakers in both the public and private sectors should constantly be aware of the need to strike a balance between strengthening security and weakening the economy. As we have learned in other areas of government regulation of economic activity, there is no benefit in selecting the most costly or disruptive way of achieving important natural objectives (such as a safer workplace or a cleaner environment).

In contrast, public support of a long-term undertaking is enhanced when people believe that the decisions are sensible and effective. The inconvenience and perhaps greater cost of air travel resulting from more rigorous security checks, for example, seems a minor price to pay for a sense of safety.

Economic Impact of the Terrorist Attacks

Before exploring the economic strategy in more detail, it is useful to examine the economic impacts of terrorism—beginning with the September 11 attack and extending to the continuing repercussions. The economic blows associated with September 11 were superimposed on a U.S. economy already on the verge of recession. The negative impacts did not have to be substantial in order to tip the economy over the brink. Consumer spending, the mainstay of the economy before

September 11, was showing significant signs of slowing. The new uncertainties unleashed by the event (over both the U.S. military response as well as terrorist counteractions) resulted in the deferral of enough nonessential consumer purchases to shift the balance toward recession.

Traditionally, the United States embarking on a major military offensive has generated a positive economic response. In the aftermath of Pearl Harbor and the U.S. engagements in Vietnam and Korea, the launch of major military operations provided substantial economic stimulus based on the expectation of new defense production contracts and expansions in the size of the armed services. Yet traditional military forces and equipment will probably play only a complementary role in a sustained antiterrorist campaign. Thus the market response to the struggle against international terrorism is likely to be more complex than during recent historical experience.

Major military engagements also often usher in substantial economic uncertainties. In the early weeks of the Gulf War, for instance, there were major anticipatory increases in the price of oil. Destabilizing uncertainty could prove to be the predominant economic effect of military strikes against targets in nations that harbor terrorists and of the potential counterretaliation. Interruptions of the usual flows of international commerce and investment could well overshadow any positive stimulus resulting from expectations of higher levels of defense orders. The adverse repercussions could even include interruptions in the flow of oil from the Middle East—provoking sharp rises in price as well as substantial reductions in available supply at any point in the future and with little warning.

Some people expect rapid economic recovery from the September 11 terrorist attacks; they base their expectation on an analogy with natural disasters of comparable magnitude such as a major earthquake or hurricane striking a densely populated coastal area. While the immediate impact of such damage to the U.S. capital stock may well be short-lived, that type of analysis discounts the far more important psychological impacts of uncertainty on consumer confidence and spending and on business investment. The United States has not experienced a comparable blow to its sense of national security since at least the Cuban missile crisis and possibly not since Pearl Harbor, with most Americans fearful—and U.S. leaders predicting—that there is more to come.

After a recession of uncertain duration, several sources of stimulus might lead to an upturn in the U.S. economy. These include the repeated reductions in the interest rates by the Federal Reserve System, the substantial sums that Congress has voted to repair and rebuild the damaged areas, special tax cuts to spur business activity and consumer spending, the additional hiring of personnel and procurement of equipment by the federal government for defense and internal security–related matters, lower prices of imported oil because of overall weakness in the global economy, and the need to replenish low business inventories.

When specific sectors and geographic areas are examined, it is clear that the impacts of September 11 and its aftermath are very uneven. The lower part of Manhattan suffered devastating destruction: An estimated 22 buildings were damaged or destroyed. This took out 30 million square feet or 9 percent of the total office space of New York City. Similarly, several industries have been particularly hard hit. The most severe initial effects have been in sectors related to air travel and tourism—the airline companies, makers of jet airplanes, convention centers, hotels, travel agencies, car-rental agencies, and airport-based restaurants. Many companies in these industries are not likely to regain their pre–September 11 market positions for a long time to come.

Some of the most severe negative effects will be felt in the year ahead. As insurance companies sell off their assets and reduce their reserves in order to pay the huge claims they face, there will be a noticeable diminution in their funding of new capital projects, with negative consequences to long-term economic growth. The role of government in underwriting new policies will increase as private carriers become unwilling or unable to include acts of terrorism in the coverage of the new policies that they write—unless government picks up the largest portion of the resulting claims. Although specific legislative details have not yet been worked out, it is realistic to assume that the federal government will cover the costs for a major portion of such risks.

Not all of the post–September 11 economic changes are negative for American business; flag makers, for example, can attest to that. An expansion in the military budget, as discussed above, is now visible and likely to extend for a substantial period. Rising expenditures for diverse missions associated with homeland security can also be anticipated to match the increases in conventional military outlays. The market for antiterrorist equipment and systems (especially high-tech electronics) was already expanding rapidly, both in government and in the private sector, and this growth trend has now intensified.

A new array of growth industries is also in the offing. These include providing early detection of and protection against biological and chemical attacks and guarding basic infrastructure, notably the facilities that produce and distribute electric power as well as telecommunications systems and water supplies. Stepped-up internal security will also mean the purchase of equipment such as face scanners as well as investigative services such as more detailed background reviews of new employees. However, much of this will add to overhead expenses of businesses and therefore will not contribute to real national output. By slowing the pace of production and distribution, new procedures and security technologies may actually reduce national output in the medium term, with uncertain consequences for the long haul.

To a substantial degree, the reduction in travel, especially by air, could prove to be a boon for producers and providers of cell phones and teleconferencing equipment and could also boost employee telecommuting. A substantial percentage of conventional in-person conferences and other meetings will be replaced by virtual meetings in which the participants hear and/or see each other without leaving their localities. Although not a total replacement for face-to-face encounters, these virtual meetings have the added benefit of economizing on people's time and company costs. Simultaneously, longer delays at major airports will reinforce a trend predating September 11, which has seen top management of companies, the entertainment industry, and wealthy customers increasingly bypassing commercial airlines and major airports in favor of more widespread use of company-owned or leased executive aircraft that use smaller, regional airports.

On balance, the cost of doing business in the United States will rise to cover such factors as increased security precautions, higher insurance premiums, and delays in receiving component parts and finished products. Many producers and distributors will have to maintain larger inventories, undermining just-in-time procedures and related business practices that were the bedrock of increased efficiencies that drove productivity upward throughout the past decade.

The campaign against terrorism will also mean reducing the openness of borders and slowing down business and financial activities both within and across national boundaries. On balance, the trend toward increasing the globalization of production will be slowed if not temporarily reversed. (The longer-term consequences of the campaign against international terrorism for the very process of globalization will be taken up in a later chapter.)

Most fundamentally, it will be success in finding and eliminating terrorist networks—more than any economic or financial measures— that will generate the positive attitudes, on the part of business and consumers alike, necessary for sustained economic recovery. It is also true that continued terrorist attacks and the perception of government ineptitude in preventing them—despite substantial financial incentives and economic stimulus to business and consumers—will depress confidence and delay recovery.

Three Elements of a Long-Term Economic Strategy

Combat and Deter Terrorists

The first prong of a long-term, comprehensive strategy is to use economic and financial tools to combat and deter terrorists. In the aftermath of September 11, the United States has worked aggressively to enlist other nations around the world in freezing terrorist assets and, in President Bush's words, to help "starve terrorists of funding." Such actions are an essential component in the economic war against terrorism. At the same time, it is important to note that terrorism is not a particularly capital-intensive enterprise.

The 1993 bombing of the World Trade Center, which killed six people and injured more than 1,000, cost conspirators less than $50,000 for bomb materials and other expenses. Estimates of the costs incurred to launch the September 11 attacks range from $250,000 to $2 million. Those sums, albeit vital to the terrorist organizations, are modest compared with the billions of dollars of direct damage and the even larger losses arising from the repercussions of the attacks. The terrorist attacks on the United States have been, from the terrorists' viewpoint, extremely cost-effective.

Moreover, our responses—such as tracking and stopping the relatively small financial flows—constitute a daunting challenge. With more than a trillion dollars a day moving in financial markets around the world, even the support of all banks in the United States and their foreign branches will not be adequate to significantly restrict the flow of funds to terrorist groups. The cooperation of countries where other money centers such as London, Frankfurt, and Tokyo are located is essential. Yet the individual amounts transferred to terrorists through these marketplaces are miniscule compared with the overall value and number of transactions: a proverbial needle in a haystack.

Cooperation is also needed from the other industrialized countries. Their financial markets may not be as large as those of the major global financial players, but they provide potential cover as well as facilities for making money transfers to terrorists. In addition, the United States will need the help of the Persian Gulf states where individuals with substantial resources have been known to supply funds to terrorists, either out of conviction or out of fear. So far, the success in identifying the charitable organizations funding Al Qaeda has not been matched by the willingness of the Gulf States to freeze their assets.

Similarly, reducing the channels for financial support of terrorism will require increased bank scrutiny of transactions in other countries with large Islamic populations, not only in the Middle East but in Asia—Malaysia and Indonesia, in particular—where others sympathetic to terrorist groups are located. Some countries, such as Switzerland and Singapore, may not participate significantly in any military effort yet should be encouraged, as significant banking centers, to heighten the reviews by their banks to help scour the sources and recipients of terrorist funds.

Just as terrorists based on U.S. soil were able to operate beneath the "radar screen" for months before the September 11 attacks, terrorist groups have learned to collect contributions and make financial transfers outside traditional channels. Examples include networks of friends or relatives abroad, informal brokers unrelated to banks, and special forms of funds transfers developed to avoid Islamic law prohibitions on receiving interest. (Such informal financial and business networks are neither new nor unique to the Middle East.) Human intelligence and other low-tech methods of gathering information about financing should also be strengthened to help identify and then block the flow of funds to terrorist groups. While some of these approaches have been tried before with limited success, the post–September 11 environment is likely to produce a more rigorous response than before.

In these efforts, bank secrecy laws may need to be reviewed and revised to improve the balance between the legitimate rights of individuals to protect confidential information and the need of governments to track and stop the flow of funds to and from terrorist individuals and groups. Care must be taken that such information is provided only to prescribed government agencies for direct use in stopping transfers and not utilized for other purposes. Here again, there will no substitute for a broad, multilateral effort to revise bank secrecy laws. The chain of necessary disclosures will only be as effective as its weakest link: Deposits and withdrawals will quickly migrate from jurisdictions that have updated their bank secrecy laws to those that have not or will not do so.

Tough new anti-money-laundering laws that had languished for years before the September 11 attacks are now in the works, indicating strong U.S. resolve to clamp down on illicit flows of funds. The intent is to make it harder for U.S. banks to do business with shell banks offshore—that is, banks with no physical office, no affiliation with an established bank, and in countries with weak or nonexistent bank regulation. This will also require active monitoring of transactions conducted for wealthy clients (private banking) that can be used to mask movement of funds to and from suspect individuals and organizations.

The legislation would also extend due diligence on suspicious customers to nonbank financial institutions including brokerages, casinos, wire-transfer services, and informal financial intermediaries known as *hawalas*. These nonbank entities would be required to file suspicious activities reports, triggered by movements of more than $10,000 and an enumerated list of other suspect actions—as banks already are required to do.

There can be no assurance the creators of these paperless funds transfers will comply, but the new regulations are nonetheless a step in the right direction. In the current urgent circumstances, consideration should be given to financial rewards for information leading to successful prosecutions for violations of the regulations, provided precautions are taken to avoid unfounded and unwanted vigilantism.

To the extent commercial enterprises at home and abroad can be identified as doing business with terrorist groups and individuals, there is successful precedent in the United States for blacklisting them to prohibit them from doing business with U.S.-based companies and their foreign affiliates. Recent examples include Chinese companies known to have violated the terms of China's agreements with the United States on weapons sales abroad, Indian and Pakistani companies involved in the development of nuclear weapons, and foreign and domestic companies known to have violated U.S. export control laws. Stiff fines (up to $10 million for companies and up to $1 million for individuals with no possibility of reimbursement by employers) have helped make the blacklists effective.

The United States would be wise, however, to avoid trying to impose unilateral and far-reaching sanctions. Such sanctions almost never achieve their objective of changing the behavior of target states; on the contrary, their main effect is to shift the business to our foreign competitors. The more effective way to impose sanctions is to pinpoint them as much as possible to particular offensive actions of governments or companies and to convince our allies and friends to do the same.

Yet another economic tool is for the United States to oppose loans by multilateral development banks and credits from the International Monetary Fund to countries that harbor terrorists—and, conversely, to support providing such monies as incentive for countries to cooperate in the antiterrorist campaign. Again, this approach will only be effective if other major countries support our actions.

Sustain U.S. Growth and Productivity

The second key element of an economic strategy is sustaining U.S. growth and productivity. Stimulating the economy requires an expansionary fiscal policy in the near to medium term, a process already well under way. This calls for a combination of increased spending on productive endeavors and carefully designed tax cuts. Such policies will involve budgetary deficits, but these will do less damage in the short term than a moribund economy. Useful expenditures can finance the fight against terrorism, bolster homeland security, improve the U.S. infrastructure for ground and air transportation, help rebuild New York City, and (within limits) much more.

Tax cuts should be directed at stimulating consumer purchases as soon as possible. One effective approach is to defer payroll tax withholdings for a year or two. Another option is to extend unemployment insurance payments temporarily. Accelerated depreciation would encourage new business investment. While important for addressing immediate recessionary pressures, any short-term financial stimulus should be grounded in long-term economic fundamentals. That means maintaining long-term budget surpluses to finance future Social Security requirements and to support private investment.

Since mid-2001, monetary policy has been appropriately expansionary, and the Federal Reserve System has made it clear that it will continue along this policy path in order to stimulate economic recovery. It is heartening, in the aftermath of September 11, to see the close cooperation that occurred among the major central banks in terms of providing ample liquidity to global financial markets and in lowering interest rates at about the same time.

In terms of fiscal policy, shortly after the September 11 assault, Congress approved a $15 billion support package for the embattled air transport system. A few other sectors—notably insurance—may also need government support. However, too much propping up of weak sectors would end up wasting resources and sending the wrong signal to private enterprises. Even in the face of these unanticipated shocks to the U.S. economy, we should not underestimate the ability of Americans to improvise in the face of challenges. Unless hindered by excessive bureaucratic restrictions, the private sector will have strong incentives to devise innovative responses so that business can effectively operate in the new environment.

Policymakers will need to resist pressure from powerful groups seeking added support for low-priority activities that are of secondary importance—farm subsidies, for example. The aid sought will at times be in the form of import protection. Granting these requests would surely alienate the exporting countries whose cooperation we seek in the antiterrorist struggle and could have the unintended consequence of impeding a return to global growth.

Going beyond the need to reject protectionism, the Bush administration should use this opportunity to push forward with trade negotiations, both at the global level in the World Trade Organization and in the Western Hemisphere. Trade opening would stimulate the U.S. economy, as it would those of cooperating nations. More immediately, international agreement on a new round of trade negotiations would also send the message that the United States is open for business, enhancing confidence both at home and abroad.

Such a message is of particular importance to developing countries, which need more open markets to sustain their export-driven economic growth. From the viewpoint of the United States, more open markets for products from the lesser-developed world would be an off-budget action that would improve the climate for cooperation in the fight against terrorism. Such steps would complement an expanded (and hopefully reformed) U.S. foreign aid program, as well as help developing countries attract needed foreign investment.

The economic consequences of the war on terrorism will likely be particularly damaging to developing nations. Poor countries with weak institutions are often the first to feel the effects of any global economic slowdown as investors seek lower-risk investment environments. Additionally, assistance that may have been coming from developed nations may be curtailed as necessary resources are diverted to more immediate efforts in the fight against terrorists. However, the more fragile their economic and political institutions become, the more vulnerable these countries are as terrorist targets or sanctuaries. The terrorist strikes of September 11 and the subsequent military campaign in Afghanistan underscore that unstable states are not simply humanitarian concerns—they have serious national security implications as well.

One important area for U.S. policymakers who are working to shore up U.S. growth and productivity is energy security. The events of September 11 inevitably call into question American dependence on Persian Gulf oil. The political vulnerability of several key Middle East regimes is all too apparent and may grow worse with the continued application of U.S. military force and diplomatic pressure. Periodic shocks in the Middle East—the fall of the shah of Iran, Arab-Israeli conflicts, the Persian Gulf War—have alerted the American public to the potential instability of both the supply and the sources of crude

oil. In the short term, however, the global economic slowdown is reducing the demand for oil, creating both a substantial production glut
and reducing incentives for the needed long-term diversification of
supply and substantial efforts at conservation.

It remains an open question as to whether one or more oil-produc-
ing nations will seek to use the oil "weapon" to strike against the economic well-being of the United States. Iraq could show its displeasure
with U.S. actions by reducing oil exports although such action would
be costly to Iraq in many ways, including postponing the removal of
sanctions. Unlike other so-called rogue states, Iraq has sufficient funds
at its disposal to take such a measure. Other rogue exporters, such as
Iran and Libya, are more dependent on a steady flow of hard currency
earned by oil exports and would be unlikely to tighten supply unless
targeted militarily.

At present, OPEC possesses sufficient spare capacity, largely in Saudi
Arabia, to offset any Iraqi withdrawal from the market should that
happen. It has been the practice of Saudi Arabia to intervene to keep
the oil market (e.g., prices) stable. But as oil prices decline, market
shares replace prices as the primary goal; and Saudi Arabia, not wish-
ing to improve its position at the expense of other OPEC member-
countries, may be reluctant to cover all of the losses itself. Before September 11, OPEC production quotas were being ignored, with above-
quota output on the order of 1 million barrels a day. With the price of
oil dropping substantially since the attacks, the producers are having
even greater difficulty in coordinating the size of their respective crude
exports. As a consequence, it is difficult to imagine conditions where
cartel discipline would be effective.

In the prolonged struggle against international terrorism, planning
needs to take account of the possibility that at some point the production or distribution of oil from the Middle East would be curtailed
because of terrorist actions. Should oil supplies be disrupted for any
reason, the immediate impact could be quickly mitigated, at least for a
limited time. The U.S. strategic petroleum reserve holds in excess of
540 million barrels, available to offset any serious disruption in imports. Elsewhere, the International Energy Agency has indicated its
intent, should the need arise, to release oil from member-country
stockpiles—possibly as much as 2 million barrels a day, which would
be sufficient to calm the market. Increased cooperation among the

countries in North America would provide more assured sources of supply, even if not enough to resolve the problem. The specific challenge to our oil supply would depend on the nature and extent of the disruption.

Even before the September 11 attacks, there was already a national debate in full swing about reducing American reliance on Middle East energy sources. Arriving at a national consensus on how to secure our energy future has now become much more urgent. Both Republicans and Democrats can use the attacks on New York City and Washington to buttress their respective arguments in favor of new energy policies. Many Republicans advocate a path to energy independence through additions to supply, including exploitation of the resource potential of the Arctic National Wildlife Refuge, plus the opening up of federal lands and offshore areas now out of bounds because of environmental concerns. Proposed oil industry tax breaks and other incentives favored by Republicans, however, could be jeopardized by newly imposed budgetary constraints. Many Democrats will be on the lookout for favoritism to oil interests and will seek to push energy independence through conservation efforts, the more efficient use of energy, and increased reliance on alternative energy sources that are environmentally friendlier.

The vulnerability of our energy supply requires a multifaceted long-term response rather than the selection of either a supply-oriented or demand-oriented approach. Conservation could be promoted by such means as eliminating caps on energy prices and terminating tax subsidies that keep the price of conventional fuels below their true economic costs. Simultaneously, the United States should encourage a greater diversity of the sources and types of fuel available. Specific actions could include reducing regulatory barriers to the production and distribution of energy, promoting the development and use of nonconventional fuel sources, and constructing pipelines to transport natural gas from Canada. Continuing to develop energy resources in the Caucasus would also promote the diversification objective although it would involve more risk than expanding Western Hemisphere sources.

Develop New Technologies and Procedures

The final challenge to government agencies and private enterprises alike is to develop new antiterror technologies and procedures—from hi-tech scanning and identification devices to a new generation of drugs to protect against chemical and biological attacks. One recommendation, discussed more fully in the chapter on homeland defense, is for the president, working with Congress and state and local governments, to launch an initiative on the scale of the Apollo Project to enhance our nation's capabilities to prevent and respond to biological terrorism. Substantial investment should be made in strengthening public health expertise, infrastructure, and early warning systems; and new approaches should be devised to deal with diseases that might be used as weapons of terror. This includes stockpiling vaccines and antibiotics, strengthening regional and national distribution mechanisms, and researching and developing other means of facilitating rapid and effective disease control. A key will be developing an appropriate regulatory process to ensure the safety of new vaccines and antibiotics as well as to provide the medical and pharmaceutical industries with the necessary incentives, such as liability protection and guaranteed returns on their investments, to rise to this national challenge.

Enhancing the security of America's critical infrastructure—such as telecommunications, electrical power systems, gas and oil infrastructure, banking and finance, transportation, water systems, and emergency services—is also central to reducing the threat and damage of future terrorist attacks on the United States. It is not difficult to imagine the pandemonium and loss of life that could occur if a major city's water supply were poisoned, emergency 911 systems were disabled, or a bomb breached the containment structure of a nuclear facility.

The magnitude of the task, however, is daunting. Much of the nation's infrastructure is owned and/or operated by private firms, and much of it remains vulnerable to attack. An early priority, therefore, is to develop adequate stockpiles and protection for those critical assets. The government and the private sector will need to share information on both threats and best security practices. Where necessary, specific public–private initiatives may be required to enhance the security of America's critical infrastructure. However, the effectiveness of private enterprise should not be underestimated, particularly if the public sector provides timely and adequate information on the nature of the possible threats.

Decisions on infrastructure protection will inevitably reduce openness and access. Among the practical actions needed on a priority basis will be a workable legal regime for sharing information between government and business on the operational use of a protected infrastructure.

And because no part of our infrastructure can be fully protected from terrorist attacks, an essential element in a reasonably protected infrastructure is a diagnostic system to determine what is damaged, the extent of the damage, and a means to divert usage to other parts of the infrastructure system for the most essential purposes. The goal should be a U.S. infrastructure that is over time increasingly better protected from terrorism and consistent with a globally competitive American economy.

The Road Ahead: A Balancing Act

One difficulty in waging the economic front of the campaign against terrorism is balancing the demands for greater security against the need to maintain a strong economy. Government leaders and private sector executives need to avoid the mindset that ignores the repercussions of decisions in one category on the performance of the other.

To give one example, the events of September 11 brought home the risks of America's profoundly open nature. There was an almost immediate reaction in the form of tightened border controls and immigration procedures, including more rigorous inspections of trucks and people crossing into the United States from Canada and Mexico. A strong national security justification exists for this because some of the hijackers entered this country from Canada. However, long lines awaiting the inspectors quickly arose—extending at times over several miles.

The result was a very costly impact on the U.S. automobile industry, which needed the Canadian-produced parts coming into the United States on a just-in-time basis in order to maintain production. Inadequate funding apparently limited the ability of federal border control agencies to reduce these delays by expanding their work forces and the amount of overtime their employees could work. This damage to U.S. manufacturing and productivity could be reduced by the adoption of more enlightened regulatory policies.

More basically, homeland security policies and their execution should take account of the need to minimize the adverse impacts on the performance of the national economy. A striking parallel with the conduct of other regulatory activities exists here. Initially, environmental enthusiasts advocated adoption of regulation regardless of cost. In recent years, however, the emphasis has shifted to the adoption of cost-effective strategies that simultaneously clean up environmental pollution and minimize the burdens on the economy.

Americans need to remind themselves that the United States remains the world's economic and financial superpower. Maintaining this nation's unique economic and financial strength is an essential part of a successful long-term struggle against terrorism. Thus, as it proceeds, a comprehensive antiterrorism campaign must fully incorporate the intricate interrelationships between maintaining a strong economy and taking steps against terrorist networks. The challenge to Americans in the years ahead will be to learn how to maintain our civilian institutions and free society in an uncertain environment characterized by unexpected attacks. The flexibility and resourcefulness of our private enterprises will be key assets in this unfolding situation.

Voice of America, November 11, 1918. J. H. Smythe, known as America's "megaphone man," with megaphone and the Stars and Stripes on Armistice Day. Photograph: Hulton I Archive/Getty Images.

Chapter 11

Elevating Public Diplomacy

"How do I respond when I see that in some Islamic countries there is a vitriolic hatred for America? I'll tell you how I respond: I'm amazed. I'm amazed that there is such a misunderstanding of what our country is about that people would hate us .... Like most Americans, I just can't believe it. Because I know how good we are, and we've got to do a better job of making our case."

— *President George W. Bush*
Prime-time press conference
The White House
October 11, 2001

Throughout the Islamic world, America suffers from a bad image. Many Muslims believe that the United States is at best unsympathetic and at worst openly hostile to Islam. They contend that many of its policies are biased against the interests of Arabs and Muslims—including America's alleged unconditional support for Israel, economic sanctions and bombings against Iraq, the stationing of U.S. troops in Saudi Arabia near Islam's holiest sites, and complicity with repressive regimes. They see the attack on Al Qaeda and the Taliban in Afghanistan as an assault on Islam that is precipitating a humanitarian disaster.

These perceptions fuel anti-American frustration among the many and hatred among the few—even as American ideals and America's success remain powerfully attractive. Left unanswered, these perceptions threaten to hinder the U.S. ability to prosecute the war against terror-ism, and, over time, to erode U.S. power and influence in large parts of the world. If the tide of public opinion continues to run strongly against the United States, the leaders of Arab and Muslim countries will find it that much more difficult to join and stay in the coalitions against terrorism. Muslim support for the campaign against terror-ism could collapse entirely. We would risk an anti-American backlash that could destabilize countries like Pakistan, Saudi Arabia, and Egypt. The long-term effort to moderate and modernize Arab and Islamic countries would suffer a serious setback. There also could be a spillover effect that corrodes support from European and other allies for the war against terrorism.

Osama bin Laden and Al Qaeda are competing with the West po-litically and morally, not just violently. They and their terrorist breth-ren are beyond the call of reason. But the people and countries sym-pathetic to their issues if not their means are not beyond reach. A failure to seek these people's and countries' understanding if not en-dorsement will broaden the base from which terrorists can draw sanc-tuary, support, and even successors. Winning the war against terror-ism and securing the resulting peace will be as much an act of persua-sion as of coercion. In that effort, public diplomacy should play a cen-tral role.

The Decline of Public Diplomacy

Portraying the United States as the enemy of Islam and Arabs con-trasts with the picture painted by U.S. foreign policy in the 1990s. The United States intervened in the Persian Gulf, Somalia, Bosnia, and Kosovo for a variety of reasons but with one common result: Hun-dreds of thousands of Muslim lives were saved. The United States pressed the European Union to make Turkey—whose population is more than 90 percent Muslim—a candidate for membership. Succes-sive administrations said they were prepared to recognize a Palestin-ian state and encouraged Israel to forge a lasting peace; in 2000, the United States brokered a historic offer from Israel that would have given Palestinians 95 percent of the occupied territories and domin-ion over East Jerusalem. American troops were deployed to Saudi Arabia at that country's request to protect its people and Islam's holy sites from Iraq. Sanctions were imposed against Iraq by the United Nations, not the United States. Saddam Hussein could end the sanctions by complying with UN resolutions; instead, he has flaunted them and denied his people readily available food and medicine to win a propaganda victory. In Afghanistan, the United States was already the largest food donor before September 11; and long before the U.S. offensive against Al Qaeda, some 4 million people had fled Afghanistan, forced out by civil war and the brutal Taliban regime. Meanwhile, 6.7 million practicing Muslims live and worship in peace in the United States.

America's side of the story is largely unheard in the Arab and Islamic world. One reason is the lack of freely flowing information, plus widespread official censorship and propaganda. Another reason is the failure of American public diplomacy.

During the Cold War, public diplomacy was an effective weapon in the West's arsenal. It gave confidence to dissident groups of politicians, intellectuals, and artists throughout the East bloc. It put a spotlight on the stark differences between capitalism and command economies, between democracy and despotism. It helped provoke the collapse of communism from within.

With the ideological war won, policymakers began to perceive public diplomacy as an expensive anachronism. The spread of and broad access to private media, via satellites and the Internet, would suffice to carry America's message to the world, their argument went; never mind that these media tilt heavily toward materialistic expressions of American success, rarely deal with foreign policy issues, and do not penetrate some critical parts of the world. As a result, the resources devoted to shaping America's image abroad have been in decline. Public diplomacy now accounts for 8 percent of the State Department's total budget.

In 1999, the United States Information Agency was folded into the State Department. The move was born out of a desire to streamline government. Proponents hoped that consolidation would put public diplomacy closer to policymaking. In practice, integration has proved difficult, with public diplomacy officers feeling like second-class citizens and subject to burdensome bureaucratic rules and procedures.

The State Department's culture devalues public diplomacy. Making and executing policy are considered more substantive endeavors.

The most senior officials of the U.S. government rarely grant interviews to foreign media. For foreign policy professionals, there are always more pressing "policy" priorities; for political appointees, such efforts are seen as a waste of time because foreigners do not vote. There is a dearth of senior foreign service officers fluent in difficult languages like Arabic, making them less than effective spokespersons for America.

Particularly in the Arab and Muslim world, American ambassadors who engage actively and frequently with the local media, students, nongovernmental organizations, and religious leaders are the exception, not the rule. Political appointee ambassadors often do not speak the language of the country to which they are assigned. Embassy public affairs teams are understaffed and underfunded. The process of receiving clearance to use policy talking points in public is often so burdensome that the points are moot by the time approval is granted.

The State Department retains important communications assets, including the Voice of America (VOA). At its peak during the Cold War, VOA together with Radio Liberty and Radio Free Europe reached 50 percent of the Soviet populace every week and between 70 and 80 percent of the population of Eastern Europe. Today, VOA is heard by a mere 2 percent of Arabs. It is time for America to rediscover its voice.

Finding America's Voice

Rebuilding public diplomacy will take time and require a sustained effort. The place to start is a clear instruction from the president and the secretary of state that information is a core strategic weapon in America's foreign policy arsenal whose effectiveness must be maximized. The success of our foreign policy in general and the campaign against terrorism in particular is inexorably linked to America's ability to understand, inform, and influence foreign publics.

The president and secretary of state should appoint a bipartisan commission to evaluate the state of public diplomacy and make concrete recommendations for improving its development and delivery—especially to Arab and Islamic audiences. The commission should include experts in communications from the private sector (for example, television programmers, film writers and directors, and advertising specialists) and academics with a deep understanding of the Arab and Islamic worlds. The commission should build on the important work of the U.S. Advisory Commission on Public Diplomacy. It should consider resuscitating a far-sighted presidential decision directive on international public information signed by President Clinton in 1999 but ineffectually executed. The president and secretary of state should promptly review the commission's findings, decide which to accept, and order periodic progress reports on their implementation.

A number of ideas and initiatives are worthy of the commission's consideration:

- **Prioritize public diplomacy in the foreign policy process.** Public diplomacy officials should be included as a matter of course in meetings at which foreign policy is debated and formulated, including at the levels of deputies and principals. This will enable them to inform policymakers of the likely impact of U.S. policies on public opinion abroad and to more effectively communicate government policy. Senior government officials should receive periodic media training and be encouraged to regularly brief foreign media at the Foreign Press Center or in individual interviews. The president and cabinet-level officials should make it a practice to grant interviews to foreign media in advance of and during foreign trips, or when rolling out policy initiatives. Simply including the foreign media in press conferences or pressroom briefings does not suffice; exclusive or limited pool interviews garner significantly more airtime for the interviewee.

- **Strengthen public opinion research.** Public opinion should not dictate foreign policy, but it is vital to helping policymakers shape policy and explain it. Funding for foreign public opinion research remains low—about $5 million a year—and has declined in real terms over the past decade despite new opportunities to do opinion polling in more open societies. The commission should consider increased funding for public opinion research.

- **Develop a rapid response capability.** Technology makes it possible to scour international, national, regional, and local press media; academic publications; and Web sites and chat rooms for critical or erroneous commentary about American policies.

The commission should consider developing a rapid response program. A team of public affairs officers could be tasked to respond full time and in real time to misinformation about American policies. Ideally, no false charge would go unchallenged. The commission also should look carefully at the system for formulating and clearing talking points for senior officials at home and abroad. The United States needs real-time public affairs coordination and dissemination.

- **Empower ambassadors, embassies, and foreign service officers.** In an era of high-speed communications and capital-to-capital contacts, some believe that ambassadors have become obsolete. In fact, their relevance is greater than ever, but their role should be refined to focus more on public diplomacy. In selecting ambassadors and senior embassy officials, greater consideration should be given to language and presentation skills. They should receive regular media training. Senior embassy officials should be encouraged to engage in the public debate in their countries. They should consider it a core function of their job to grant interviews, write opinion pieces and letters to the editor, take part in televised debates and radio call-in shows, and cultivate editorial and opinion writers. Listening is as important as talking: our envoys should spend more time engaging with a broad cross-section of groups and individuals, religious leaders, NGOs, students, professionals, and union members—not just their counterparts in the ministry of foreign affairs. In recruiting and training new foreign service officers, the State Department should focus more on communications skills. It should build and value a public diplomacy career commitment through which it would train a cadre of officers and civil servants in international information and public diplomacy. The commission also should consider whether the U.S. government can improve foreign language training.

- **Create American-presence posts outside of foreign capitals.** In many countries, regional media reaches more people than newspapers, television, and radio programs based in the capital city. American officials rarely are present to engage in the local debate. The commission should consider the creation of regional-presence posts in critical countries, modeled after the program instituted by Ambassador Felix Rohatyn in France in the late 1990s.

- **Take better advantage of media in the Arab and Muslim worlds.** Osama bin Laden scored a propaganda coup when Al-Jazeera, an uncensored satellite network based in Qatar, broadcast his videotaped remarks on October 7. Instead of flooding Al-Jazeera with American officials and American voices to counter bin Laden's hate speech, administration officials initially sought to prevent Al-Jazeera and American networks from broadcasting bin Laden or the Taliban leadership. Although the secretary of state granted Al-Jazeera an interview six days after the September 11 attacks and was followed by the national security adviser, President Bush did not. Al-Jazeera's Washington bureau chief told the press that his network is "desperate to find any [American] officials. We say every day, 'please come talk to us, exploit us.'"

  We need less censorship in the Arab world, not more in the United States or of free media like Al-Jazeera. The administration should develop a proactive outreach program toward media in the Arab world, starting with Al-Jazeera and moderate newspapers like *al-Hayat*.

- **Bolster VOA and create new outlets and media.** VOA broadcasts in the Dari and Pashto languages of Afghanistan are heard by 80 percent of Afghan men. Seventy-two percent say they trust VOA and agree that it provides facts and lets them make up their own minds. But as of October 1, 2001, VOA was broadcasting just 4.5 hours a day into Afghanistan. Its listenership in the broader Arab world is just 2 percent. The commission should consider enhancing the content and quantity of VOA's programming in the Arab and Muslim worlds. Senior U.S. officials and a broad variety of American voices—and particularly Arab and Muslim Americans—should be sought out for interviews. But the commission should guard against VOA becoming a propaganda tool of the U.S. government. The misguided effort to stop

VOA from broadcasting remarks by Osama bin Laden threatened to undermine VOA's widespread credibility.

The commission should assess the effectiveness and penetration of Worldnet, the State Department's global television feed, and recommend whether more resources should be devoted to television broadcasting.

The Internet has become central to global communications. It is especially relevant in countries where the state controls traditional media but not access to the Web. The commission should assess whether the U.S. government is using the Internet as effectively as possible to promote direct communication with foreign publics. For example, the White House and State Department Web sites are highly regarded but passive instruments of public diplomacy—they must be sought out by users. The commission should look at strategies for using the Internet proactively to explain government policy. Also, Internet discussions and video conferencing would allow senior officials to engage in public diplomacy without leaving their desks and help engage outside experts from the United States in public debates and discussions. The commission should consider whether these tools are being used effectively.

- **Develop and support outside validators.** Academics, opinion leaders, former government officials, and prominent Americans in business, the arts and sciences and sports can be important validators for U.S. policy initiatives or for the American way of life. They may possess more credibility than serving government officials. The commission should consider how the U.S. administration can effectively use outside validators. One place to start would be to develop lists of experts for given issues or countries and offer them regular briefings by senior policymakers.

Similarly, foreign government officials can be important validators for U.S. policy. British prime minister Tony Blair has played a lead role in setting out the public case for bin Laden and Al Qaeda's responsibility for the September 11 attacks and in expressing forcefully in Arab media that the war against terrorism is not a war against Islam. American diplomats should consider asking foreign counterparts to take on some of the public diplomacy burden, especially when their credibility is greater.

- **Cultivate foreign opinion leaders.** U.S. government officials at home or abroad rarely approach foreign opinion leaders (columnists, editorial writers, editors, television and radio pundits, former senior officials, academics) or take their calls. The commission should consider developing a system of tracking foreign opinion leaders and proactively engaging American officials with them. Helping inform and shape the opinion of influential foreign voices can be an effective way to get the U.S. message across.

- **Sustain foreign exchange programs.** Student exchanges, visitor programs, and collaboration among universities, foundations, and hospitals open foreign eyes to American values, culture, and society. Some 20,000 Americans and foreigners participate in State Department exchange programs every year. Because participants tend to be or become leading citizens in their countries, the impact of these programs is disproportionate to their size. Nearly 200 current and former heads of state, 1,500 cabinet-level ministers and many private sector leaders have taken part in exchange programs. The commission should consider ways to sustain and expand these programs.

- **Develop message campaigns with the private sector.** The commission should consider whether and how the communications skills of Hollywood and Madison Avenue can be tapped to show America in a better light and to create greater understanding of American policies. For example, advertising campaigns might have been devised to personalize the September 11 tragedy by showing in the Arab media the faces and families of those who lost their lives. A documentary might be developed contrasting the standard of living in northern Iraq (where the UN and local Kurdish officials administer the oil-for-food program) with that of southern Iraq (where the Iraqi government administers the program).

- **Engage Arab and Muslim Americans in communicating America's message.** Arab and Muslim Americans have unique credibility in their countries of origin, an ability to communicate effectively, and an important vantage point from which to explain the United States. Senior administration officials should meet with a broad cross section of this community on a regular basis to explain the rationale for our policies. Individual Muslim and Arab-American leaders might be tapped to play a formal role in overseeing public diplomacy efforts.

- **Undermine censorship and press constraints.** The limits on freedom of the media in much of the Arab and Muslim world will hinder even the most vigorous and sustained public diplomacy campaign. Many people living in target countries have limited access to information from the United States and other democratic countries. Their own media is heavily censored, self-censored by editors, or used as a propaganda tool by governments against the United States to divert attention from their own deficiencies.

As discussed above, the U.S. government should aggressively target influential outlets like Al-Jazeera, bolster our existing ability to broadcast into the Arab and Muslim worlds through VOA and Worldnet, and develop new broadcast outlets and message media like the Internet. Where friendly governments control or exert excessive influence on the media—such as in Egypt and Saudi Arabia—the United States should press for equal time. It also should recognize that cultivating local opinion leaders might be more effective in helping the U.S. message break through than trying to use private media.

The United States also should continue to lead in promoting media reform and supporting independent media around the world. Such efforts might include helping draft media laws and academic curricula; funding—either directly or through nongovernmental organizations—media law and policy organizations, watchdog groups and professional organizations; and providing financial and technical support to independent media.

To prevail in the war against terrorism, and then to secure the peace, the United States must start changing hearts and minds in the Arab and Muslim worlds. A failure to engage on this front would be to sell America short. The information war is less dangerous but probably more difficult than the campaign on the ground in Afghanistan. It will have to be sustained long after American troops return home. But it can be won. America's greatest strength is the ideas that bring us together as a people: freedom, progress, tolerance. The terrorists have nothing to offer but repression, regression, and hate. The war of ideas is America's to win. It is time that we take it seriously.

Refugee Clothing, December 15, 1959. Volunteers of the Women's Voluntary Service Clothing Depot wheel bales of clothing to go to refugees in various countries, as requested by the United Nations Relief and Works Agency (UNRWA). Photograph: Hulton | Archive/Getty Images.

Chapter 12

Reviving Foreign Assistance

"There is no escaping our obligations: our moral obligations as a wise leader and good neighbor in the interdependent community of free nations—our economic obligations as the wealthiest people in a world of largely poor people . . . and our political obligations as the single largest counter to the adversaries of freedom . . . . To fail to meet those obligations now would be disastrous; and, in the long run, more expensive. For widespread poverty and chaos lead to a collapse of existing political and social structures which would inevitably invite the advance of totalitarianism into every weak and unstable area. Thus our own security would be endangered and our own prosperity imperiled. A program of assistance to the underdeveloped nations must continue because the Nation's interest and the cause of political freedom require it."

— President John F. Kennedy
Special Message to Congress on Foreign Aid
March 22, 1961

When terrorists attacked the United States on September 11, 2001, condemnation poured in from all over the globe. While the media focused on expressions of support from the leaders of powerful European and Asian allies, representatives of the developing world were weighing in as well. Leaders from Turkey to Nigeria, Mexico, and Indonesia expressed their condolences to President George W. Bush and offered their support. Officials from developing countries lined up at the United Nations to criticize the terrorist acts, with the representative of Vietnam calling them a "naked insult to the conscience of humankind," and the representative of South Africa noting "the whole world is weeping."[1] The 189 countries at the United Nations passed a strong, unanimous resolution condemning "the heinous acts of terrorism," and calling for "international cooperation to bring to justice the perpetrators, organizers and sponsors of the outrages of 11 September 2001."[2]

At the same time, however, interviews with people on the streets of developing countries around the world revealed a more complex reality. While most people throughout the developing world abhorred the actions of the terrorists, their comments also indicated a distance from the United States. Some claimed that "this is the price that America must pay for its own attitude." Others called for "the Americans to come down from their tower," or noted that "a lot of people feel that the United States couldn't care less about the suffering of three-quarters of mankind."[3]

Far from expressions of support for the terrorists or their political program, these criticisms of the United States were born of people's frustration. Frustration that the richest country in the world, at the pinnacle of its prosperity and power, had seemed to turn away from the acute problems in their countries—from economic stagnation and grinding poverty to a lack of opportunities for people to participate in decisions affecting their lives. Frustration with a United States seemingly impervious to the vicissitudes of the global marketplace. Frustration with perceived American unilateralism. Frustration with the "arrogance" of a country so self-satisfied that it could not pay attention to the problems they faced every day.

In the Arab and Muslim worlds, these concerns were exacerbated by profound frustration with autocratic regimes that failed to meet the aspirations—or even the basic needs—of their populations, by suspicion of American cultural and military presence, and by the perception that the United States has sided with Israel and abandoned the Palestinians in the peace process.

At the start of the new century, more than four-fifths of the Earth's 6.1 billion people live in the developing world. This skewed ratio will continue to rise over the next 50 years because the developing world is expected to add approximately 3.3 billion people even as the industrialized world's population is expected to hold steady or decline.[4]

Simultaneously, an increasingly globalized economy has yet to provide the benefits of economic expansion to many of the world's poor. The number of people living on less than $1 a day has remained relatively constant at about 1.2 billion—or about 1 in 5—over the past decade.[5] At the same time, the gap between rich countries and poor continues to increase, with the average income of the richest 20 countries doubling from 15 times that of the 20 poorest countries in 1960 to more than 30 times today.[6]

The events of September 11 only worsen this bleak picture. The attacks have adversely affected the U.S. economy and prospects for U.S. economic growth—and the shock waves have hit the developing world even harder.[7] In addition, responding to dramatic new foreign assistance needs for the South and Central Asian region threatens to drain already insufficient foreign assistance funding away from many underdeveloped regions. Already, many leaders and analysts in the developing world, assuming that U.S. foreign policy attention and foreign assistance are a zero-sum game as has been the case during past crises, have expressed concerns that the U.S. war on terrorism will cost them dearly. A World Bank official from Africa, speaking to an African audience noted, "Aid flows have halved over the past few years," and, in the wake of attacks on the United States, "we anticipate further cuts."[8]

If the United States expects the world's support in the fight against terrorism, it will need to prove that it stands with the vast majority of the world's population on the things that most concern them—including enhancing developing countries' ability to satisfy their people's social and economic needs as well as addressing some of the political challenges and conflicts that both arise from and exacerbate those needs. As the campaign against terrorism gets under way, a constructive agenda of engagement will be a crucial complement to the agenda of rolling up terrorist networks. And one of the most important tools of that constructive agenda is U.S. foreign assistance.

Foreign Assistance Programs: Not Up to the Challenge

Yet at the start of a new century, U.S. foreign assistance programs are in a state of dysfunction and neglect. The Foreign Assistance Act of

1961, designed to meet the challenges of the Cold War and decolonization, has been amended in piecemeal fashion, creating a patchwork of priorities, authorities, and instrumentalities that are at best incoherent and, in some cases, outright contradictory. Despite numerous attempts to revamp the Foreign Assistance Act, it has not undergone a major revision since 1973.

In 1988–1989, the House Committee on Foreign Affairs undertook a bipartisan, in-depth investigation of foreign assistance and in 1989 produced what became known as the Hamilton-Gilman Report. This report found among other things that, while foreign assistance was a valuable tool in terms of promoting U.S. security and economic interests, the program did not enjoy broad support because it was not seen as effective; had so many objectives that they "cannot provide meaningful direction to be effectively implemented"; and suffered from too many earmarks, reporting requirements, and restrictions. The report also found that there was little coordination of U.S. economic, security, and development policies.

Since 1989, a host of other panels, commissions, reports, and analyses have identified additional deficiencies, including sprawling, disunited programs controlled by multiple agencies without strategic coherence; overcentralization and bureaucratization (with far too many staff in Washington and not enough in the field); and, finally, significant underfunding.

This panoply of problems has led not only to ineffectiveness but also to even further erosion of support for the programs. Only 9 percent of the American public thinks the United States is spending "too little" on foreign aid, while 53 percent think it spends "too much," and 32 percent thinks it spends "the right amount."[9] It should be noted, however, that these views are premised on dramatic overestimations of the amount spent on foreign aid: The average citizen thinks the United States spends 20 percent of its budget on foreign aid, yet the actual figure is less than 1 percent.[10]

Given this situation, the answer today, as identified more than a decade ago by the Hamilton-Gilman Report, is to repeal the Foreign Assistance Act of 1961 as amended and start anew with more focused legislation. In the wake of the terrorist attacks of September 11 and the need for a truly global response, there is no better time to perform a major overhaul of sadly outdated U.S. government machinery.

Designing a New Foreign Assistance Program

One reason the Foreign Assistance Act of 1961 has become so complex is that the reality of being a global power in a time of great needs and great change is not simple. That said, there is absolutely no reason the new foreign assistance act would need to be such a complex or confusing entity. If key actors can agree on a series of principles and follow a disciplined process, a new act could take shape in a relatively short time.

Such a process, to succeed, must begin at the top. The president should commission a small bipartisan group of foreign assistance experts and highly visible political figures to design a new program. This group should consult widely but retain full control of the process so as not to allow it to degenerate into a lowest-common-denominator exercise. While the process should bear the direct stamp of the president, the legitimate powers granted to Congress under the Constitution must be fully respected, and congressional leadership will need to be part of the process every step of the way.

A 10-point agenda could establish the fundamentals of the new approach:

- **Focused and clear objectives.** The new act cannot be all things to all people. The more focused and clear the set of objectives, the more likely they are to be achieved. The more than thirty explicit objectives articulated in the act of 1961 as amended should be reduced to six: (1) transnational threats—using a developmental approach to build international law enforcement capacity and fund specific antiterror, anticrime, and antinarcotics programs to complement traditional security assistance, which would continue through other channels; (2) sustainable development—including a focus on both economic growth and poverty alleviation; (3) humanitarian programs—refugee assistance, disaster assistance, and food assistance; (4) democracy—political pluralism and governance capacity; (5) conflict prevention; and (6) trade and investment programs to build U.S. markets.

  Within each of these areas, specific priorities would have to be set. The new act, however, should avoid codifying a narrow set of priorities based solely on today's needs. Doing so would lead back to the old dynamic of being forced to amend the act every year with a new set of mandates and earmarks. Instead, the new act should serve as a sort of constitution, establishing clear principles based on enduring U.S. interests and ideals and a process for achieving further definition as needs change. This process could be some combination of a set of guidelines along with a defined form of regularized consultation between the administration and key leadership and committees in Congress.

- **Coherence of strategic vision.** The new act not only needs to define priorities; it needs to put forward a coherent strategic vision of how all those priorities are related. Even more important, the act needs to redefine funding and oversight authorities to correspond to that vision. One key change, for example, would be to make sure that all development assistance is provided through the same account and overseen by the same committees in Congress. Multilateral assistance provided through the World Bank, International Monetary Fund, and regional development banks should be examined by the same members of Congress as bilateral assistance. No longer can these accounts be treated as fiefdoms of specific executive branch agencies (i.e., Treasury and USAID) and congressional committees. Rather, a coherent body of people and institutions in both the executive and legislative branches need to sit down together and work out which priorities should be funded bilaterally and which should be funded multilaterally. Until this process is developed, a disconnect between the two will continue. Indeed, working out a clearer division of labor between our own bilateral programs and multilateral programs we support would enhance the U.S. voice in the donor community as well as improve the coherence of operations on the ground.

- **Balancing types of assistance.** The fight against terrorism will confront the United States with a dilemma similar to that experienced during the Cold War—how to use foreign assistance to advance security and other goals simultaneously. This time around, we need to ensure that aid is not simply used to "buy" support of friendly governments, but rather that assistance achieves its goals on the ground in a way that earns local-population support as well. The importance of this issue is illustrated by Egypt, which is simultaneously the recipient of the second-largest U.S. assistance package worldwide and one of the greatest hotbeds of anti-Americanism in the Arab world. This apparent contradiction can be explained at least in part by the fact that many people in Egypt perceive U.S. support as propping up a corrupt and repressive government rather than as a major source of the food they eat, the health care they receive, and the schools they attend.

Egypt is not the only case that highlights the need to find a better balance between security and nonsecurity assistance, and, within the nonsecurity assistance, to establish the right balance between lump-sum program assistance, food aid, and project assistance. Currently, excessively high percentages of American assistance flow through the food aid and program assistance channels at the expense of generally more effective project assistance.

Food aid is an important tool that should focus on disaster relief instead of continuing to be overused as an easy outlet for American agricultural surpluses that distort markets and often do more damage than good. Likewise, program assistance can be useful in helping to shift the political or policy environment, but more of it should be channeled through the multilateral development banks, which have more money and more likelihood of making conditionality stick. This more limited approach for both food aid and program assistance would leave more money for project assistance, the type of assistance that generally provides the biggest bang for the buck in developmental terms.

At the same time, project assistance is not magic. And in order to distribute it more effectively, the U.S. government needs to systematically develop the capacity of local and international nongovernmental organizations to manage larger amounts of development assistance. Working through nongovernmental organizations increases U.S. flexibility, enhances programmatic impact, and helps build a stronger civil society—which has important side benefits for promoting democracy.

■ **Program effectiveness and cost-effectiveness.** A number of practices that have evolved over the past 40 years hobble U.S.

foreign assistance programs' effectiveness on the ground as well as their cost-effectiveness. First and foremost, the practice of excessive earmarking has led to the near breakdown of the entire system. Today's foreign assistance managers have to cobble together a coherent program constrained by more than 120 distinct congressional earmarks—some of which have long outlived their intended purposes.[11] Excessive earmarking not only reduces flexibility to design a program responsive to the needs of a given country; it also distorts the overall shape of the program on a worldwide basis. Because of the constraints on overall amounts of foreign assistance and the tendency for Congress to earmark money for regions such as the Middle East, Africa, and Latin America, other regions such as South and Central Asia have been perennially underfunded. Given recent events, the danger of this approach is evident. The answer, however, is not a new earmark; it is, instead, letting the administration, in consultation with Congress, respond to changing needs. If this is not done, it not only leaves us vulnerable in places like South Asia, it also creates political and economic problems around the globe as resources are siphoned off to address a given crisis—the foreign assistance equivalent of robbing Peter to pay Paul.

A second step toward improving the effectiveness—especially cost-effectiveness—of programs is lifting some of the more rigid buy-American requirements in the contracting process. The legal constraints, combined with the bureaucratic realities of an overly complex contracting process, have led to a scandalous extreme of spending 80 cents of each foreign assistance dollar in the United States, even when the cost of U.S. products is much higher.[12] While helping the American economy is one important result of foreign assistance spending, the United States will benefit much more if its programs are freed to produce cost-effective results in other countries, which ultimately lead to more economic activity with the United States.[13] The current approach is shortsighted in that it not only raises the cost of the programs; it also undermines American credibility with the supposed recipients of foreign assistance. It is time for the buy-American laws to be relaxed and the contracting process streamlined to allow for real competition.

A third proposal to improve program effectiveness is to move from uniform single-year appropriations for foreign assistance programs to a mixture of single-year to multiyear appropriations as needed to correspond with specific programs and funding cycles. This would enhance U.S. leverage with its interlocutors and help to deliver better results less bureaucratically. Congress could and should retain the authority to adjust appropriations as necessary.

■ **Efficiency and timeliness.** In addition to earmarking, a new foreign assistance act will have to address two other problems that impede efficiency—excessive reporting requirements and multiple layers of bureaucracy. All three of these areas will need to be addressed if U.S. programs hope to be efficient, effective, and credible. In any good business, a huge part of a product's value is in having it delivered promptly. Operating U.S. programs more efficiently and implementing them more rapidly will help the United States sustain political commitments, advance U.S. business interests that require a U.S. government partnership, and provide a potentially significant cost savings.[14]

■ **Interagency rationalization and coordination.** Currently, more than 30 U.S. government departments, agencies, and organizations are engaged overseas in development activities of one kind or another. Each of these agencies has its own mandate, priorities, and approach. Any new foreign assistance bill needs to provide a mechanism for coordinating these various agencies, especially in the field. Just as problems in coordinating U.S. government activities in the political, military, and intelligence fields led to reforms designating the ambassador the ultimate authority in-country, so too is there a need for a more rigorous mechanism to authoritatively coordinate developmental efforts.

■ **Leverage investments.** The United States no longer has the luxury of trying to go it alone in pursuing its developmental goals. Through the 1960s, the United States provided more than half the development assistance worldwide. By the end of the 1990s, however, this amount had dropped to 16 percent, or less than one-sixth.[15] Indeed, the size of the U.S. bilateral programs marks the United States as a relatively small player compared with multilateral development banks and other bilateral donors. This means that the United States must seek more opportunities to leverage its limited bilateral monies. Although in some instances this will mean seeking partnerships with other bilateral and multilateral donors, the real challenge will be using foreign assistance to more quickly bring private capital to bear in solving crucial problems. Private monies dwarf official development assistance flows, yet they are not a silver bullet solution. Just as the trade-not-aid mantra had to be converted to trade-and-aid when it met the tough realities of the developing world, so too will the quest to attract private capital need to avoid becoming an either/or proposition. Official development assistance will continue to be needed to address public goods issues, and it will also be crucial to prime the pump of private flows in other areas. This will only occur, however, if more efforts are made to build private sector participation into long-term development initiatives.

- **Presence.** Another important element of the new foreign assistance act will need to address the shrinking U.S. presence overseas. Especially in today's struggle against terrorism, the United States needs allies at the individual level as well as at the governmental level. People throughout the developing world need to see more Americans doing work that directly benefits them. The United States needs a constructive presence to counteract hostile rhetoric that portrays America as nothing more than a soulless capitalist machine. In recent years, however, U.S. presence has declined as USAID has retrenched; and the Peace Corps has dropped from a historic level of 15,000 volunteers in 1966 to a mere 7,300 today. In the case of USAID, more staff needs to be taken from headquarters and deployed in the field, accompanied by increased authority to make decisions once there. The Peace Corps should expand back toward its 1960s highs or, at very least, meet the target of 10,000 set by Congress in 1985.

- **Accountability.** A key component of a new foreign assistance act will be defining and enhancing a rigorous system of accountability for all funds provided. Results-based budgeting should become the norm, with clear lines of authority so that both agencies and individuals can be held accountable for results. If a program performs and meets its identified goals, its budget should reflect that fact. Likewise, if objectives are not met, programs should be reevaluated and potentially discontinued. The U.S. taxpayers' money and trust are far too valuable to be squandered by inefficient, ineffective assistance programs. Where positive results are obtained, proof of the programs' value should be provided not only to Congress but also to the American people. If public opinion polls continue to reveal both ignorance of, and a lack of support for, foreign assistance, then all such programs will be unsustainable over the long run.

- **Resource levels.** While global leadership is not inexpensive, neither is it terribly costly. U.S. development assistance currently totals approximately $11 billion annually.[16] This is a mere 0.1 percent of GNP, significantly down from 0.6 percent of GNP in 1962, after the passage of the most recent foreign assistance act.[17] To pay for the abovementioned changes to foreign assistance programs, the United States should commit itself to immediately funding foreign assistance at no less than 0.2 percent of GNP—the average amount of U.S. foreign assistance during the 1980s. Our medium-term goal should be 0.3 percent of GNP—the amount the United States averaged from 1962 to 1979. If a new foreign assistance act is written, and the abovementioned changes made, the money could be spent both effectively and wisely. In the larger scheme of the struggle against terrorism, this might be one of the most cost-effective investments possible at this time.

Ultimately, the foreign assistance program must change because it does not work. The imperative for a new program is only partially related to the fight against terrorism; most of these modifications are needed regardless. But now that a global threat to U.S. interests and ideals is once again a major part of the equation, it is more important than ever to recognize that promoting development is security by other means.

Writing a new foreign assistance act and reinvigorating development assistance programs would help alleviate real problems in the developing world and address some of the conditions that create the fertile ground in which terrorists take root. It would also help deepen cooperation with the developing world—and, in fact, would likely improve cooperation with other industrialized countries as well, as they have been highly critical of the United States for abdicating its leadership role in this area for far too long. It would put the lie to terrorists' and their supporters' arguments that the United States represents only increasing inequality. And it would be a cost-effective investment in a better, safer world.

By casting our lot with others around the globe, and helping them lift their own lives, the United States will better define who we are as a country—to people, to governments abroad, and to ourselves.

Notes

[1] UN General Assembly debate on resolution A/56/1; Nguyen Thanh Chau speaking for the Asian Group, and Dumisani Kumalo, speaking for the African Group.

[2] UN General Assembly Resolution A/56/1, September 18, 2001.

[3] See, for example: "Muslims world over say US had it coming," Reuters, September 13, 2001; Howard Schneider and Lee Hockstader, "As Mideast Officials Offer Condolences, Some Arabs Rejoice," *Washington Post*, September 12, 2001, p. A-25; and, "While some Arabs rejoice at attack on America, others pause to reflect," Associated Press, September 12, 2001.

[4] *World Population Prospects: The 2000 Revision*, United Nations Population Division, Department of Economic and Social Affairs, ESA/P/WP.165, February 28, 2001, p. v.

[5] According to the World Bank, there were 1.18 billion people making less than $1 in 1987, and 1.17 in 1998. See *Global Economic Prospects and the Developing Countries*, 2001; or see World Bank Poverty Net at www.worldbank.org/poverty/.

[6] World Bank, as posted on World Bank Poverty Net, October 2001, www.worldbank.org/poverty/.

[7] According to the UN, the accelerated U.S. slowdown due to the attacks has reduced 2001 GDP growth projections for South and East Asia from 4.1 percent to 1.7 percent, for Latin America from 3.1 percent to 0.8 percent, for Africa from 4.3 percent to 3.0 percent. See "Following Terrorist Attacks, UN Revises Forecast for World Economic Growth in 2001 to 1.4 per cent; Warns that Long-run growth will be

Adversely Affected," United Nations document ECO/21, PI/1385, October 10, 2001.

[8] Mamphela Ramphele, World Bank managing director for human development, as quoted in James Lamont, "Africa could be worst economic casualty: World Bank war against terrorism and global slowdown may hit continent hard," *Financial Times*, October 23, 2001.

[9] Gallup Poll, conducted February 1–February 4, 2001.

[10] University of Maryland, Program on International Policy Attitudes, February 2, 2001.

[11] Kevin M. Morrison and David Weiner, "Declining Aid Spending Harms U.S. Interests," Overseas Development Council Policy Paper, April 25, 2000.

[12] According to USAID, posted on its Web site in October 2001, "Close to 80 percent of the U.S. Agency for International Development's contracts and grants go directly to American firms," www.usaid.gov/.

[13] One example of the long-term benefit of foreign assistance can be seen in the fact that 43 of today's top 50 importers of American agricultural products were once U.S. foreign assistance recipients. See USAID administrator J. Brady Anderson, "Back to the Drawing Board," *Foreign Affairs* (March–April 2001).

[14] See Henrietta Holsman Fore, "Lean Development and the Privatization of U.S. Foreign Assistance," *Washington Quarterly* 17, no. 1 (Winter 1994).

[15] *Development Co-operation*, 1999 Report (OECD, 2000).

[16] The fiscal year 2002 foreign operations bill provides $9.5 billion for bilateral economic assistance (Title II) and $1.4 billion for multilateral economic assistance (Title IV). In addition, it provides $486 million for export assistance (Title I) and $3.9 billion for military assistance (Title III).

[17] Isaac Shapiro, *Trends in U.S. Development Aid and the Current Budget Debate* (Washington, D.C.: Center on Budget and Policy Priorities, 2000).

Afghan Refugees, August 21, 1980. Afghan refugees cross the Khyber Pass into Pakistan.
Photograph: Hulton | Archive/Getty Images.

Chapter 13

Rebuilding Failed States:
Test Case Afghanistan

"To the Afghan people, we make this commitment: The conflict will not be the end. We will not walk away as the outside world has done so many times before. If the Taliban regime changes, we will work with you to make sure its successor is one that is broad-based, that unites all ethnic groups, and that offers some way out of the miserable poverty that is your present existence . . . . The world community must show as much its capacity for compassion as for force."

— Prime Minister Tony Blair of Great Britain
October 2, 2001

"It would be a useful function for the United Nations to take over the so-called nation-building—I would call it the stabilization of a future government—after our military mission is complete. We'll participate. Other countries will participate. I've talked to many countries that are interested in making sure that the post-operations Afghanistan is one that is stable and one that doesn't become yet again a haven for terrorist criminals."

— President George W. Bush
October 11, 2001

One of the lessons learned on September 11 is that failed states matter—not just in a humanitarian sense, but in national security terms as well. If allowed to fester, such states can become sanctuaries for terrorist networks, not to mention organized criminals and drug traffickers who exploit the dysfunctional environment. As such, they pose a direct threat to the vital interests not only of the United States but to the international community at large.

Afghanistan, torn by decades of war, internal strife, and Taliban repression, exemplifies the danger of failed states. The initial conventional wisdom that reconstructing Afghanistan is "impossible" is giving way to a growing recognition that rebuilding the country will be necessary to permanently destroy terrorist networks from within its borders. Breaking up Al Qaeda and removing the regime that supports it is only the first step. Helping create a set of conditions that will deny opportunities to would-be terrorists is next. And finally, helping put in place political, economic, and social structures to enable the Afghan people to build a better future for themselves will be key to winning the war of ideas. Only if the United States and its allies prove themselves on this front will Muslims around the world believe Western assurances that the struggle against terrorism is not a war against Islam.

Reconstructing Afghanistan will be a monumental task—one that will require broad international support, significant human and material resources, and an unwavering political commitment over time. While some have spoken of the challenge as being comparable to rebuilding Germany or Japan after the Second World War, in fact it will be vastly different. Those countries, despite the destruction they experienced, had strong human and material resource bases to build upon. In addition, the United States enjoyed total control as a military occupation force in those countries, something very unlikely to occur in this case. Nor will rebuilding Afghanistan look much like Bosnia, Haiti, or even Somalia. Indeed, the size of the country, the scope of the human needs, the absolute devastation of any infrastructure, and the loss of most people with education and professional backgrounds combine to make Afghanistan the "mother of all reconstructions."

Given sensitivities surrounding the military campaign, the United States is perhaps not best situated to take an active leadership role on the ground. It can and should, however, lead the political and economic coalition building that will be necessary to sustain the effort.

Under no circumstances can the United States afford to walk away from Afghanistan as it did following the withdrawal of Soviet troops in 1989. Yet, while Afghanistan will be the first big reconstruction test of the war on terrorism, it will not be the last. Similar challenges exist elsewhere, including in the Horn of Africa, where terrorist groups have already exploited the vacuum of state authority and are likely to seek further advantage if Afghanistan ceases to provide them sanctuary. Addressing this challenge will require U.S. government and international capacity that does not currently exist.

Rebuilding Afghanistan or any other nation can neither be solely an American nor an international enterprise. Ultimate responsibility must rest with the people of the country in question. But the United States and the international community have a critical role in providing assistance. Thus the United States and the international community will need to act quickly to build their own capacities for rebuilding failed states and for postconflict reconstruction. The success of a longer-term campaign against terrorism may depend on the test case of Afghanistan.

A Framework for Rebuilding Failed States

In its simplest form, reconstruction efforts need to build state capacity in four key areas: governance and participation, security, economic and social well-being, and justice and reconciliation. In many cases, including Afghanistan, humanitarian needs are so pressing that well-being can be divided into two separate categories: short-term humanitarian crisis needs and longer-term economic and social foundations.

Humanitarian Needs

Even before the fighting stops during a war or period of lawlessness, humanitarian needs push themselves to the fore. Refugee flows to other countries are an inevitable consequence of war and chaos. The number of refugees in the year 2000 grew to 14.5 million worldwide, while an even greater number of people—between 20 and 24 million—were displaced within their own borders.[1] These people suffer from the same vulnerabilities and deprivations as refugees and present an even greater humanitarian challenge for the international community. Not only do they remain closer to the conflict, they lack the protection of international agreements (like the Geneva conventions) and institutions (like the UN High Commissioner for Refugees) to address their manifold needs. In the case of failed states, where central authority has ceased to exist, dealing with internally displaced persons (IDPs) is a special challenge.

Security for humanitarian operations, both inside the country and in neighboring countries, is another increasing concern. While many humanitarian workers can and do work under very difficult circumstances, many operations worldwide are inhibited by a lack of adequate protection for these workers, their supplies, and the populations they are trying to serve. This is a gap that is felt especially acutely in failed states, where there is often no central authority with whom to negotiate for even minimal security.

As in the case of Afghanistan, and previously in Somalia, humanitarian needs are often so pressing that they must be addressed even before the security and political questions have been resolved. After two decades of conflict, Afghanistan has produced almost 4 million refugees, about 1 million IDPs, and millions of people who have remained in place who are vulnerable to starvation and war.[2] Since the beginning of the U.S. bombings, the humanitarian situation has become even more desperate. The United Nations fears that the livelihood of 7.5 million "highly vulnerable" people could be threatened by the lethal combination of conflict, starvation, and the harsh Afghan winter. Before September 11, the survival of 3.8 million Afghan people was dependent on UN and international food supplies. The inability of food convoys to reach the suffering population throughout the country after the onset of the U.S. military strikes and the evacuation of relief personnel has magnified the crisis. To avoid a humanitarian catastrophe, the UN will have to authorize and establish camps and food distribution centers in those parts of Afghanistan where security conditions permit. Waiting until the war is over will risk the lives of millions of people and potentially spark massive refugee flows that could destabilize the region.

The $600 million of relief aid pledged by donor nations ($320 million by the United States) for humanitarian assistance is a good start. Unfortunately, as of this writing, only a minuscule percentage of this money ($35 million) had been received.[3] Significantly more resources from the United States as well as from other wealthy countries will be needed to cope with the dire humanitarian emergency.

Governance and Participation

Establishing a legitimate, coherent central governmental authority is the key to rebuilding a country. Creating a transitional authority to prepare the ground for a government of national unity or other form of indigenous representation often requires considerable international involvement. It is essential to include a broad array of societal elements in the processes leading up to the formation of a government—both to enable power sharing and to prevent alienation that could sow the seeds of renewed conflict.

As an interim authority is established, the international community should assist indigenous efforts to begin rebuilding a viable civil administration and to secure sufficient resources to maintain this governance structure. It should help to launch a process involving both indigenous actors, with popular participation from the grassroots level, and international political and legal experts to review and, if necessary, revise or rewrite the country's constitution.

Once a degree of stability has been achieved, countries should consider means of popular representation. The formation or legalization of multiple political parties and subsequent competitive elections are a way of accomplishing this goal. Dedicated international assistance can often help to attain effective and sustainable democratic progress. Fostering a lively civil society that enables people to participate in as well as to monitor the actions of the government is a key element of any state based on the rule of law. The development of independent nongovernmental organizations and religious institutions, because of their potential to conduct community rebuilding and to engage in a dialogue with the government, is therefore another issue of considerable importance in rebuilding. Finally, the media has an important role to play in the process of rebuilding a governance structure. Truly independent journalists and broadcasters are critical to the fair representation of information and can serve as an important watchdog over the actions of both the government and the international community.

In the case of Afghanistan, the first step in creating a viable state will be to secure some form of basic political agreement among the warring parties and tribes. As in many cases of failed states, the process is less likely to be driven by a formal peace agreement than by a basic power-sharing arrangement among major actors. Lasting peace depends on bringing all factions and interests into the negotiations rather than solely relying on the warring parties to broker a deal. The strategy most likely to produce positive results according to most Afghans is to convene a *loya jirga,* or grand council. This Afghan tradition would allow representatives of the various groups to convene and agree to a future government. Whether or not this process includes the exiled king, Zahir Shah, the selection process for the *loya jirga* must allow for widespread participation. It will be very important that this process involve selecting representation from local *shuras,* or councils, rather than allowing the various warlords to appoint representatives to the grand council. The experience of Somalia is instructive in this regard. Emphasizing the role of the warlords was thought to be the practical solution at the time; instead, it empowered them and led to disaster for Somalia and the international community as well.

The U.S. role in the military campaign will preclude it from playing a central role in crafting a political arrangement in Afghanistan. The United Nations will have to take the lead in Afghanistan, though this may not always be the case with failed states—yet, as UN special envoy Lakhdar Brahimi has repeatedly pointed out, the UN is neither capable of administering the country nor would that be desirable.[4] Nevertheless, the UN must play a central role in political mediation and in coordinating support from the United States and other countries.

Furthermore, a strong friends-of-Afghanistan group should be formed to support the UN's efforts and those of whatever new government emerges. This should be based on the former 6+2 group, composed of neighboring countries Pakistan, Uzbekistan, Tajikistan, Turkmenistan, Iran, and China, plus Russia and the United States, and should expand to include other key players, such as India, and a representative of the European Union. This group would be instrumental in supporting any new government in Afghanistan and would have to ensure that the interests of neighboring states would be addressed without giving any single one of them undue influence in Afghanistan's future.

One of the first needs following a basic political agreement to end the fighting will be to reach agreement on a constitution to serve as the basis for political and legal authority. Afghanistan is fortunate to have a constitution from 1964, which many experts consider a solid foundation. The constitution, drafted under the auspices of the subsequently deposed king, Zahir Shah, provides for a bicameral legislature, one-third appointed by the king, one-third elected by the people, and one-third elected indirectly by regional assemblies.[5] This constitution could either serve as a transitional document or be altered by the *loya jirga* to address today's realities.

A second key issue is empowering participation at the local level. Local *shuras* continue to exist in most parts of the country; they can help to fill the power vacuum of an inherently weak central government and serve as a means to provide much-needed services to the people. Starting in 1997, the United Nations Development Program has run its Poverty Eradication and Community Empowerment (PEACE) program that operates at the subdistrict level through *shuras*. This model would appear to provide a solid base for expanding these types of programs throughout the country.

A third central consideration of governance in Afghanistan is the role of women. The Taliban's extreme subjugation of half of the Afghan population must be reversed by any new government, with the staunch help of the international community. The emancipation of women should in no way be viewed as a culturally insensitive imposition from the outside. Afghanistan has a strong history of women's involvement in society at all levels. Girls have been educated at the primary school level since the 1920s and, according to one estimate, by 1973 there were about 104,000 schoolgirls across the country.[6] Prior to the civil war and Taliban control, 50 percent of the students and 60 percent of the teachers at Kabul University were women; and 70 percent of the schoolteachers, 50 percent of the government civilian workers, and 40 percent of the doctors in Kabul were women.[7] Between 1963 and 1973, women served continuously in the cabinet.[8] This history may help to reestablish rights and central roles for women. At the same time, programs targeting education for women and girls will be necessary to restore this proud history to new generations of Afghans.

Security

Establishing order and security is a fundamental element of rebuilding a country, especially one in which basic institutions have collapsed and a population has been subjected to the ravages of war and chaos. Creating a secure environment involves everything from establishing mechanisms to manage or control belligerent groups, protecting the populace from significant violence, protecting crucial government institutions and infrastructure, and ensuring fundamental territorial integrity (including protection of borders and prevention of illicit weapons flows). While in some cases many of these functions may be performed by either international or local security forces, over the medium run the full burden must be transferred into local hands—in many cases requiring a reform or reestablishment of essential local security institutions.

Few countries currently in turmoil present as difficult or as multi-faceted a set of security challenges as Afghanistan. U.S.-led coalition forces are currently concentrated on fighting the Taliban and destroying the Al Qaeda network. Yet, even assuming a successful campaign against these elements, many aspects of the security dilemma will remain. Creating and maintaining territorial integrity and border controls will coincide with the need to protect hundreds of thousands, if not millions, of IDPs and refugees while providing continued protection for those populations that remained in place throughout the conflict. The rebuilding of infrastructure and the reformation of security institutions, including a complete overhaul of Afghanistan's dispersed military forces, will be essential to crystallizing effective long-term stability.

The dilemma of security in Afghanistan is that despite the large numbers of men under arms, there are no central, national security institutions that can be depended upon to enforce any agreement made among different tribes and factions. Building a national army must thus be a top priority for the new government. Depending upon the various armies and militias of warlords as they now exist would almost certainly result in renewed warfare over the short or medium term.

Before such an army can be built, however, transitional security arrangements will have to be made. Afghanistan is far too large a country with too fierce a tradition of independence to be "occupied" by foreign soldiers. As UN special envoy Brahimi put it: "They don't like being ordered around by foreigners . . . especially in military uniforms."[9] While any transitional security arrangement must thus depend largely on Afghans, there will be a need for an international security presence to maintain stability over the short run. This may involve a small UN force in or around Kabul, or a green-hatted force, likely to be led by a Muslim country, that could play the same role. Depending on the final arrangements arising from the battlefield and political negotiations, the force in or around Kabul may also need to be buttressed by some form of international rapid reaction force to be stationed in-country or very close by.

Another important aspect of security will be obtaining guarantees from all neighboring states to refrain from trying to control or unduly influence events in Afghanistan. UN monitors would be the logical choice to ensure that any agreement struck is implemented by all parties. Some form of political structure like a friends-of-Afghanistan group would be useful in bringing pressure to bear on any neighbor that violates the agreement.

A fourth element in creating a secure environment for the people of Afghanistan will be massive demining efforts. Decades of war have left whole swaths of the country uninhabitable. In fact, with an estimated 724 million square meters of mine-contaminated land in 27 of 29 provinces, Afghanistan has one of the worst mine problems in the world.[10] The threat from land mines will need to be remedied if large numbers of refugees are to return and productive economic activities, including agriculture, resumed on the needed scale.

Finally, special attention must be given to demobilization, disarmament, and reintegration efforts for the tens of thousands of Afghan men and boys whose only occupation for the last decade or more has been "fighter." This may be accomplished through creating opportunities for schooling, farming, or learning a new trade. Ultimately the success of these efforts will depend upon reestablishing an economy capable of providing a significant number of jobs.

Economic and Social Well-Being

Conflict and collapse of state authority lead not only to dramatically high levels of unmet human needs; they also lead to devastated social and economic infrastructure and institutions. Thus reconstruction efforts need to encompass a broad range of social and economic priorities. First and foremost, food security must be ensured for the population. In addition, shelter, health, and education needs must be addressed in the near term, and the seeds of development of these sectors need to be sown. Creating jobs is also essential, not only because it helps personal recovery and provides income to meet other needs, but also because it is essential for social and political stability.

For reconstruction to be sustainable, economic infrastructure and institutions must also be built. This includes everything from physical infrastructure to setting up laws and regulations, a banking system, and institutions to facilitate trade and investment.

In the case of Afghanistan, the legacies of 20 years of continued violent conflict and a three-year drought will continue to hamper food security, creating ripple effects across the health and economic sectors. Concerted efforts from international public health, educational, and agricultural development organizations will be critical to restoring essential public services, generating employment opportunities, and increasing much-needed trade.

In addition, four specific issues must be addressed as priority matters. First, temporary employment generation projects will be needed to start the economy moving again, restore social tranquility, and build political momentum. Drawing on recent experience in East Timor, a similarly structured program in Afghanistan should utilize U.S. resource capacity and UN managerial oversight while encouraging strong local participation in the decisionmaking process.[11]

Second, agricultural markets must be revived. Continued threats of widespread famine may undermine any rebuilding efforts if not adequately addressed. The UN Food and Agriculture Organization warns that the current crisis of population displacement is coinciding with the current planting season, meaning that next year's crop yields will be even lower. While statistics on agriculture in Afghanistan are all but impossible to obtain, surrounding countries provide an adequate assessment of the region's predicament. The production of wheat is 70 percent below the five-year average in neighboring Pakistan, and in Iran acute water shortages for drinking and agricultural use have dramatically affected rural and urban populations. The two main rivers in Tajikistan and Uzbekistan are both far below normal levels, leading to dramatically reduced crop forecasts.[12] Refugee outflows from Afghanistan place undue burdens on surrounding countries' infrastructures that are already at or beyond maximum operating capacity. If the ongoing drought continues into the next two years, the international community may be faced with complete regional destabilization.

In addition, options must be provided in this sector if opium poppies are to be replaced with other crops. Afghanistan remains a major source country for the cultivation, processing, and trafficking of opiate and cannabis products; in 2000, it produced more than 70 percent of the world's supply of opium.[13] The new government in Afghanistan will need to provide an ironclad guarantee to help eradicate opium poppy fields. The agriculture sector in Afghanistan contributes 53 percent of the gross domestic product and employs an estimated 67.2 percent of labor.[14] The international community, for its part, will have to provide a great deal of assistance, not only for eradication efforts but also for alternative development projects, most of which will be in the agricultural field.

Third, transportation networks must be revived, especially those linking the northern and southern parts of the country. This will be essential to food security and peace because most of the country's food must pass this way. With a geographical area slightly smaller than the state of Texas, Afghanistan has just over 15 miles of railway and 13,125 miles of highway, with only 1,745 of those being paved.[15] Compare this with Texas's 31,000 miles of paved highways, and it is not difficult to envision the logistical barriers that will face the United States and the international community.[16] Moreover, due to the military campaign, the current situation is probably much worse than indicated by these statistics. Both because of the importance of infrastructure in the rebuilding process and because of the optics of the world's superpower having destroyed some of the little infrastructure that existed, the United States should consider leading an effort to directly address needs in this area.

Fourth, education must be made a top priority, with focus in three key areas. First, school opportunities must be made available to women and girls to reestablish their role in Afghan society. Afghanistan, a country whose academia was dominated by women (nearly a 3 to 1 ratio) before the Taliban takeover in 1996, is now faced with nine illiterate women out of every ten, and only 3 percent of girls are receiving primary education.[17] Second, educational opportunities need to be provided as an option to help demobilize and reintegrate young combatants. Third, special attention should be paid to Kabul University. The Taliban closed this once proud center of learning and social dynamism. Reopening the university might help to attract some Afghans back and provide a locus for the Afghan intelligentsia to help address the many reconstruction needs of the country.

In addition to these four immediate priorities, the international community should assist the new Afghan government in two areas for progress over the long term. First, Afghanistan, for many years the heart of trade throughout Central Asia, should make investments to revive that role. Second, the UN could help Afghanistan negotiate an oil pipeline deal (similar to what it did for East Timor), which would provide much-needed funds to support a nascent state. To date, companies have invested $30 billion in developing oil and gas fields in Kazakhstan, Turkmenistan, Uzbekistan, and Azerbaijan, but exportation of this resource to the West involves expensive and lengthy pipelines. Recently, Washington has proposed a $3 billion pipeline from Azerbaijan, on the Caspian Sea, through Georgia, to Turkey's Mediterranean coast. A shorter pipeline would be much less costly (roughly half the cost of the longer version), and if the next government in Afghanistan is able to guarantee internal security, the country could reap enormous economic benefits.

Justice and Reconciliation

The related yet distinct challenges of justice and reconciliation represent another central aspect of rebuilding failed states. Arguably, none of the three other pillars can function positively without the initiation of effective justice and reconciliation mechanisms. Without the resolution of basic questions of justice and injustice, governance will lack credibility and fairness, the economy will remain corrupt and nontransparent, and security will be impossible to maintain as unresolved grievances and conflicts will find violent expression.

Justice is the more traditional, formal process of determining guilt or innocence through the fair application of existing laws and rules. Often those who have committed the worst atrocities must be handled through this system. Reconciliation efforts can provide a complementary process, often using time-tested local mechanisms, to shed light on wrongs committed and to pass judgment in a way that allows both victims and perpetrators to coexist in the community.

The challenges in building a system of justice range from creating effective law enforcement capacity to establishing an impartial justice system, drafting new legal codes, and ensuring the system complies with international humanitarian law. Experience in recent post-conflict cases has demonstrated the importance and difficulty of developing indigenous law enforcement capabilities. The significance of proper institutionalization of a fair and transparent judicial system and corresponding legal codes cannot be overstated.

Reconciliation processes are at least as multifaceted and essential to rebuilding a country as reforms in the justice sector. Whether community conflict resolution takes the form of truth-and-reconciliation commissions, as most prominently seen in post-apartheid South Africa, or whether other avenues for dealing with past wrongs are chosen, broad participation is essential if a bitter page in a country's history is to be turned. Individual empowerment through counseling, confidence-building measures that build trust between former opponents, and the initiation of broader community dialogues are just as much part of reconciliation as the challenges of building civil society actors that promote such aims as religious freedom and the emancipation of women.

In the case of Afghanistan, justice and reconciliation will play out on two totally separate levels, one relating to Al Qaeda terrorists and those who have supported them, and another dealing with intra-Afghan conflicts.

In his speech to the Congress on September 20, 2001, President George W. Bush predicted that "whether we bring our enemies to justice or bring justice to our enemies, justice will be done."[18] If key members of Al Qaeda are indeed apprehended, there are three major options for trying them: trials in the U.S. court system or that of another country whose nationals have been killed, trial in a secret military tribunal, or establishment of an ad hoc international war crimes court under Chapter VII of the UN charter.

While some have expressed concern about classified information being divulged during trials, the military tribunal option is a non-starter if the United States hopes to use trials to help defeat Al Qaeda politically and undermine their support worldwide. Trials in the U.S. court system, on the other hand, are a distinct possibility. This option could showcase the American justice system and prove that it can work even under the most extreme circumstances. At the same time, any trials in the United States may not be perceived as "fair" in many parts of the world, and may do more harm than good in terms of undermining support for Al Qaeda. Perhaps the best option of the three would be to create an ad hoc war crimes tribunal for the perpetrators of September 11, and all those members of Al Qaeda and the Taliban who could be linked to that or previous terrorist attacks. While the United States would not "control" the outcome, it could work with other members of the Security Council to establish firm ground rules for the court that would ensure that justice is done. In this way, the cause of justice and that of political defeat of Al Qaeda could be advanced simultaneously.

Regardless of which course of action is eventually followed, one thing remains clear: Any future Afghan government will have to collaborate closely with the law enforcement and legal authorities of the international community to ensure the permanent dissolution of the Al Qaeda network and committed cooperation to deliver its members to court.

Aside from the question of Al Qaeda, Afghanistan will require support to establish its own justice system and its own reconciliation processes for intra-Afghan wrongs committed. This will be a challenge, as there are few functioning justice mechanisms in the country, and supporting the creation of a system that looks very different from Western systems could be difficult for the United States and its allies. Ultimately, the UN and other Muslim countries may be of most help.

Beyond justice, there is a great need for reconciliation mechanisms. Years of civil war and ethnic conflict have left deep psychological as well as physical scars. It will be up to the people of Afghanistan themselves to decide how to utilize the various options that reconciliation mechanisms offer. Yet, in order to empower such processes to take root, the international community should provide considerable support to the new central government, to local authorities, and to newly formed civil society actors to promote intra-Afghan reconciliation.

An Agenda for the United States

As difficult as reconstruction in Afghanistan will be, there will be other needs to follow. Specifically, if Al Qaeda is ejected from Afghanistan, other soft spots in the international system may come under pressure to serve as a basis for terrorist operations. The most likely candidates range from Somalia to the Caucasus, Yemen, Sudan, or parts of the Philippine or Indonesian archipelagos.

Obviously the United States and its allies cannot and should not try to rebuild all weak or failing states. At the same time, where we pursue concerted military operations in the future, we will need to follow them with a serious program to reconstruct a central authority with the capability and the inclination to deny terrorists future use of their territory. Otherwise, our military efforts will be in vain. In other cases, we may want to support reconstruction or stabilizing efforts so as to avoid having to use our military at all.

Addressing the challenges of failed states in the fight against terrorism will be even more challenging than attempts at post-conflict reconstruction undertaken over the past decade. Unlike Bosnia and Kosovo, none of the likely scenarios will play out on the doorstep of Europe, and thus mobilizing Europeans' long-term support may be more difficult. Unlike in East Timor, there are few likely candidates among regional powers to lead a military coalition willing to address problems "in the neighborhood." Unlike the case with Haiti, the United States is unlikely to have the motivation and the leverage provided by proximity. Of all the cases, Somalia—notably the least successful of all interventions in the 1990s—may provide the closest analog in terms of future challenges we are likely to face.

With fundamental security interests at stake, the United States may be better able to garner sustained bipartisan support to pursue these kinds of activities than in the past. At the same time, however, the mixing of security interests with humanitarian interests may make it more difficult to engage international partners in these long-term, expensive enterprises especially if future attacks continue to single out American interests.

Dealing with totally failed states like Afghanistan, as opposed to some of the post-conflict reconstruction cases of the 1990s where there may have been at least something to build on, will also entail greater needs, higher costs, and longer time horizons. Because many of the likely candidates for intervention are in the Muslim world, an additional challenge will be to find acceptable ways to intervene that do not further the terrorists' aims of splitting the United States from the Muslim world. This will require mobilizing Muslim allies and finding Muslim interlocutors to undertake many of the sensitive political and military missions.

All this is to say that establishing a fundamental division of labor between the United States, other countries, international, and non-governmental organizations will be all the more important. The United States, for its part, will have to define where it can best take the lead and where it should play a supporting role. In many cases, the United States will have to use its significant leverage to build the political and economic coalitions necessary to follow through. In addition, there is little doubt that the UN will need to be involved in many of these cases. Full and unwavering financial and political support for the United Nations will be called for in the coming years. This will need to involve tough-love efforts to ensure that the UN is up to the tasks it is assigned.

Because of the likely need for ongoing U.S. military operations to protect American citizens and interests, and the potential sensitivities this may elicit, the United States may need to turn to others to undertake the fundamental security aspects of reconstruction efforts. It will certainly not be sufficient to throw a Hail Mary pass in the direction of the United Nations every time a security presence is needed. The United States cannot afford to opt out entirely. To succeed in securing a country, whatever forces are there—whether a green-hatted multi-national coalition of the willing or a blue-hatted UN force—might need a strong military alliance backing them up, outside the country if necessary. The United States will have to play a key role in this regard.

Justice concerns are another area where the United States might appear less able to play a lead role in Muslim countries. In fact, the

United States could play an important role in establishing ad hoc international war crimes courts where they may be called for. As for support for internal justice systems in the countries in question, the United States is home to a number of notable Muslim legal scholars and could reach out to recruit other region-specific and language-capable experts here and around the world.

One area in which the United States can and should continue to play a preeminent role is on the humanitarian side. In addition, the United States has great experience with promoting democratic governance and participation as well as long-term social and economic development. In these areas, however, the United States has a great deal of work to do to build up rapidly deployable, effective civilian capacity sufficient to the needs in post-conflict countries and failed states.

In addition to improving capacity in each of these specific substantive areas, the United States government will need to improve its ability across the board to do effective interagency planning, training, and coordination. And, of course, we will need to address long-standing problems with both funding mechanisms and funding levels for these types of activities.

American leadership in post-conflict reconstruction will take many forms. Sometimes the United States will need to lead boldly and overtly; other times it will need to provide quiet but firm support for the efforts of others. In any case, in order to mobilize the international resources necessary, the United States will need to demonstrate its unequivocal commitment not only to filling "holes" in the international system but to helping local residents address their own long-term economic, political, and security needs in these saddest of places on Earth.

Notes

[1] U.S. Committee for Refugees (USCR), *World Refugee Survey 2001* (Washington, D.C.: USCR, 2001); see http://www.refugees.org/news/press_releases/2001/global061901.cfm.

[2] The U.S. Committee for Refugees estimated approximately 2 million refugees in Pakistan at the end of 2000, 1.5 million in Iran, and 400,000 in other countries. The USCR estimated 900,000 "internally displaced" existed before September 11. During 2000, the UN High

Commissioner for Refugees, using narrower criteria for refugees, revised its estimate of the "official" refugee population to 2 million, of whom 1.2 million lived in refugee villages.

[3] "Refugees Find Little Comfort in Pakistan," *Christian Science Monitor,* October 11, 2001, p. 6.

[4] Karen DeYoung and Vernon Loeb, "Land-Based Fighter Bombers Join Airstrikes in Afghanistan," *Washington Post,* October 18, 2001, p. 1.

[5] See www.afghan-politics.org/Reference/Constitution/1964/Afghan Constitution.htm.

[6] Nasrine Abou-Bakre Gross, compiler/editor of *Qassarikh-e Malalay: Memories of the First Girls High School in Afghanistan* (Falls Church, Va.: Kabultec-Amdam, 1998).

[7] Associated Press, March 10, 1997, and http://www.feminist.org/afghan/facts.html.

[8] Ashraf Ghani, lead social scientist, Social Development Department, World Bank, on National Public Radio, October 22, 2001.

[9] DeYoung and Loeb, "Land-Based Fighter Bombers Join Airstrikes."

[10] Human Rights Watch, "Human Rights Backgrounder: Landmines in Afghanistan," October 2001.

[11] In a collaborative effort, the Office of Transition Initiatives (OTI) and the UN were able to address the basic employment needs of all 13 districts within East Timor. Approximately 50,000 men and women were employed as a result, with OTI providing the bulk of the capital, tools, and labor costs while UN administrators implemented and managed the projects. In other parts of East Timor the program expanded to include the resources of OTI, UN Transitional Administration in East Timor (UNTAET), UNDP, UN Peacekeeping Forces, and local East Timorese leadership. See http://www.usaid.gov/hum_response/oti/country/timor/etim2000.html, October 26, 2001.

[12] See http://www.usaid.gov/hum_response/ofda/centralasia_sr4_fy02.html, October 26, 2001.

[13] See U.S. Drug Enforcement Administration, Intelligence Division, Europe, Asia, Africa Strategic Unit (NIBE), *Afghanistan Country Brief: Drug Situation Report,* September 2001, http://www.dea.gov/pubs/intel/intel0901.html, accessed October 26, 2001. According to the official U.S. government estimate for 2001, Afghanistan produced an estimated 74 metric tons of opium from 1,685 hectares of land under opium poppy cultivation. This is a significant decrease from

the 3,656 metric tons of opium produced from 64,510 hectares of land under opium poppy cultivation in 2000. Important to note, however, is that the UN International Drug Control Program (UNDCP) estimates levels at 185 metric tons. (The reason for the disparity can be attributed to collection gathering. While the U.S. government relies primarily on image-based survey assessments, the UNDCP utilizes ground-based surveys.) This would suggest a reduction in opium production of 94 percent from the 2000 total of 3,276 metric tons and a reduction of 96 percent from the record high of 4,581 metric tons reported by the 1999 survey. Regardless, a mean of 129.5 metric tons in the midst of a three-year drought still provides enough to cause alarm. See UNDCP, *Afghanistan Annual Opium Poppy Survey 2001*, www.undcp.org/pakistan/publications.html.

[14] See CountryWatch, *Country Review: Afghanistan*, http://www.countrywatch.com/files/001/cw_topic.asp?vcountry=001&tp=ag, accessed November 8, 2001.

[15] Central Intelligence Agency, *World Factbook 2001*, www.odci.gov/cia/publications/factbook/index.html.

[16] Texas Department of Transportation, September 2001.

[17] *Human Rights Watch* 13, no. 5 (C) (October 2001). See UN Special Rapporteur of the Commission of Human Rights, "Question of the Violation of Human Rights and Fundamental Freedoms in Any Part of the World: Report on the situation of human rights in Afghanistan submitted by Mr. Kamal Hossain, Special Rapporteur, in accordance with Commission resolution 1999/9," E/CN.4/2001/43, March 9, 2001, para. 46.

[18] President George W. Bush, speech to the U.S. Congress, September 20, 2001.

Children at Open Air School, June 30, 1939. Children use a 10-foot-high geographical globe constructed from weather resistant material during geography lesson. Photograph: Hulton I Archive/ Getty Images.

Chapter 14

Regional Strategies

This chapter examines policy choices tailored to specific regions around the world. The observations are structured around four basic questions: What is the regional context in which the September 11 attacks occurred? What is the threat of terrorism in the region? What is the United States likely to ask of the leading states in the region over the long term? And, how is the region likely to respond to such requests? Each section seeks to point out new opportunities for strategic cooperation while raising red flags over the difficult compromises that might be required to sustain that cooperation—and the unintended consequences the United States may be forced to confront down the line.

In the earliest stage of the campaign against terrorism, South Asia is the obvious focus of military action. Yet every region has an important role to play throughout the various stages of the campaign. Some regions already confront terrorist groups within their borders. Others may become likely destinations for terrorists who seek sanctuary. The Americas have special significance for U.S. homeland defense, whereas Europe and East Asia, as key financial centers, are crucial for halting the flow of terrorist funding. Indeed, the threat of global terrorism demands a global response.

South Asia

"Pakistan is facing a very critical situation. The decision we take to-day can have far-reaching and wide-ranging consequences. The crises are too strong and too widespread. If we take the wrong decision in this crisis it can lead to even worse consequences. On the other hand, if we take the right decision, its results will be good."

> — *General Pervez Musharraf*
> *in a televised address to the people of Pakistan*
> *September 19, 2001*

In November 1999, candidate George W. Bush was subjected to a television interviewer's pop quiz, in which he was asked to name the leaders of four international hot spots. Pakistan and India were both on the list. Bush did not know either.

Yet no one could have predicted then that, less than two years later, terrorist strikes on American soil would catapult South Asia to the top of U.S. priorities. In the aftermath of September 11, not only U.S. leaders but also many ordinary Americans know General Pervez Musharraf's name, and they will ultimately need to know much more about the tangled issues that engage the United States with the surrounding region.

The repercussions of the September 11 attacks upset the regional agenda. A major effort to strengthen relations with India, started in the Clinton administration and continued by its successor, had been the centerpiece of U.S. regional policy. Suddenly, Afghanistan is at the eye of the storm and Pakistan the key coalition partner. Meanwhile, Sri Lanka waits in the wings, hoping the antiterrorism campaign will generate new assistance against its terrorism-prone adversaries, the Liberation Tigers of Tamil Eelam (LTTE).

The renewed attention to Pakistan will have lasting consequences. The interests underlying the U.S. approach to India are still important—such as expanding economic relations and the need for a broader network of strong bilateral relationships in Asia at a time when the region is changing rapidly. But the United States will need to place increased importance on encouraging a peace process in Kashmir, where India and Pakistan have been locked in a stubborn dispute over the area's ownership and future since 1947.

The United States and Pakistan will soon face diverging goals in Afghanistan and Kashmir. The longer-term U.S. antiterrorism agenda will make Pakistan's stability much more important than it was before the September 11 attacks. High-profile U.S. military operations in Afghanistan have triggered a reaction that strains that stability, and the effort to keep General Musharraf's government on an even keel may once again inhibit the rebuilding of political institutions that Pakistan so badly needs. Stability in Afghanistan will also be far higher on the U.S. agenda than previously, although America's ability to achieve that objective is limited. An increase in violence in Kashmir, whether or not the government of Pakistan is directly complicit, could lead to an India-Pakistan confrontation, vastly complicating both regional security and the U.S. agenda.

Pakistan: On the High Wire

Pakistan is of primary importance not only because of the vast border it shares with Afghanistan, but also because of its controversial political and intelligence ties there.

Pakistan's internal political weakness and institutional decay, coming on top of the long Pakistan-U.S. involvement in Afghanistan during the Soviet occupation, sowed the seeds of today's problems. When the United States and the Soviet Union ended arms supplies to their respective Afghan associates in 1991, Afghanistan and Pakistan were already awash in arms, with guerrilla groups that had fought the Red Army contending for power in Afghanistan. With the fall of the Afghan Communist government in 1992, Pakistan saw an opportunity to achieve its long-standing goal of installing a friendly government in Kabul. The first government that achieved international recognition was never able to consolidate its control. Out of this power vacuum, the Taliban arose, with financial and other support from Pakistan's Inter-Services Intelligence (ISI) and from Osama bin Laden.

Afghanistan continued to attract fighters from all over the Muslim world. Their agenda went beyond Afghanistan, to include spreading their harsh interpretation of Islam within Pakistan and carrying the same agenda into Kashmir. They made common cause with like-minded groups in Pakistan, including adherents of the fundamentalist Deobandi Muslim schools in several parts of the country.

The collapse of the regular school system had made religious schools, or *madrassas,* run by these groups into an attractive option for villagers.

The products of these *madrassas*, often trained in military skills as well as religious studies, pursued a brutal sectarian agenda within Pakistan, sparking violence between Shi'a and Sunni. In addition, they became the spearhead of Pakistan's efforts to keep alive the insurgency that started in Kashmir in the late 1980s. Several successive Pakistan governments, despite their concern about these groups' domestic activities, shied away from confronting them. The Kashmiri cause is popular in Pakistan, and government policy remains strongly committed to the cause as well. The militants' Islamic credentials and Kashmir activities, as well as the progressively weakening institutions of the Pakistani state, meant that governments feared an upheaval if they came down on the militants too firmly.

As the campaign against terrorism got under way, the initial U.S. approach to Pakistan focused on four main requests: intelligence on Afghanistan and on bin Laden, use of Pakistani airspace, logistical support, and use of Pakistan's full relationship with the Taliban as leverage in conveying U.S. demands. Pakistani president, General Pervez Musharraf did not agree until he had held an all-day meeting with the army and received its support.

Musharraf recognized the risk he was taking in siding with the United States. In explaining his action to the nation, he couched his decision in terms of the Indian threat. India, he argued, wanted Pakistan to be branded a terrorist state, and he was not going to fall into that trap. He also listed four key national interests that Pakistan would defend at all costs. These included its nuclear arsenal and its "sacred cause in Kashmir."

Musharraf's decision was popular with the more prosperous and better-educated groups in Pakistan, who saw it as an opportunity to restore a modernizing momentum to Pakistan's development. The initial reaction from the militants and the religious political parties was verbally harsh, but their demonstrations were relatively small (thanks in part, no doubt, to the efforts of military and police groups to suppress turnout). The disturbances that followed the start of military operations in Afghanistan were larger and were most severe in Quetta, a city with an unusually large concentration of pro-Taliban Afghans. Continued high-profile U.S. military action will probably increase the discontent. Many Pakistanis are skeptical about helping the United States, which they feel has repeatedly betrayed them. The

U.S. aid cutoff in 1990 and more recently the expansion of U.S. ties with India left Pakistanis feeling they had been used and discarded. Future Pakistani policy will be colored by this experience.

The story of U.S.-Pakistan relations is one of competing agendas. Over the coming months, the United States will be pressing Pakistan for cooperation in two new areas, both of them more difficult to implement and more complicated for Musharraf's political future. The first has to do with the next government in Afghanistan, the second with Kashmir.

American military action in Afghanistan is intended to dislodge the Taliban government. For the United States, stable leadership in Afghanistan is the key postwar objective. Pakistan wants a dominant part in filling the resulting power vacuum. Pakistani efforts to pick a favorite may well undercut this goal. Pakistan's hostility to the Northern Alliance and the reservations about Pakistan among a variety of other non-Taliban groups are signs of the thorniness of this issue.

Kashmir presents two problems. The first concerns Pakistan-based groups that are using violence in Kashmir. Several such organizations figured on the Bush administration's list of organizations whose assets were frozen in the United States. For the Pakistan government, U.S. attention to these organizations threatens the fire wall Pakistan wants to keep between the antiterrorism campaign and militant activities in Kashmir. The Pakistan government is unlikely to be strong enough to eliminate the militant groups in the near future.

The second and more acute problem is the risk that violence in Kashmir—whether or not it fits the definition of terrorism—will spark an India-Pakistan military clash. The October 1, 2001, suicide bombing and gun battle at the state assembly building in Srinagar, in the part of Kashmir held by India, is an ominous sign. The organization that claimed credit, Jaish-e-Muhammad, has had a mercurial relationship with the Pakistan government but had not been the object of a government crackdown. Such an incident could escalate into an India-Pakistan confrontation, destabilizing Pakistan and dragging the United States into a crisis management operation under very unfavorable circumstances. This argues for a diplomatic approach designed to encourage a peace process. However, increased violence in Kashmir makes such an approach vastly more difficult.

Despite these likely policy conflicts, the U.S. interest in Pakistan's own stability is if anything stronger than ever. A split in the army or a radical shift in government policy could lead to the export of nuclear materials or know-how. A weaker Pakistani state is more likely to be a haven—wittingly or not—for future terrorists with global ambitions.

The two principal threats to the current government are a popular upheaval, which becomes more of a risk if military action in Afghanistan is prolonged, and disagreements within the army, which are more likely to be sparked by differences of view over forming a successor Afghan government or over Kashmir. A long-term program aimed at rebuilding institutions and continued, steady dialogue with Pakistan's political and military leaders are critical tools in helping Pakistanis to strengthen their battered state.

The United States may well downplay its traditional push for restoring democracy. Ultimately, however, creating healthy political institutions in Pakistan is an essential part of making Pakistan a healthier presence in the region. The United States will also need to move away from sanctions, which only result in removing the tools needed to manage a very messy postwar situation in Pakistan.

India: Star Player Sidelined . . . for Now

India made an unprecedented offer of military cooperation to the United States after the terrorist attacks. It wants to strengthen relations with the United States, to prevent Pakistan from becoming the driver of U.S. regional policy, and to make Kashmiri militant groups into objects of the American antiterrorist campaign.

The most important part of India's terrorism problem is Kashmir—the main source of its dispute with Pakistan, the centerpiece of two wars, and the object of competing claims by both countries. India's political mismanagement of the parts of Kashmir it controls has left the population rebellious and sullen. Pakistani support, directly and indirectly, has intensified a 10-year insurgency. Some of the Kashmiri militant groups have engaged in terrorism; others have abandoned terrorism for nonviolent methods; still others now focus more on military targets.

Besides Kashmir, India faces armed insurgencies that occasionally resort to terrorism in several parts of its troubled Northeast. India is also convinced that the government of Pakistan is behind a number of attacks on civilian targets in different parts of India, the most dramatic of which was a series of murderous bombings in Mumbai (then Bombay) in 1993. India has sought extradition of the chief suspect in these bombings from Pakistan.

The United States has relatively few direct requests of India at this stage—chiefly sharing intelligence and strengthening existing antiterrorism cooperation. Visible Indo-U.S. cooperation will make Pakistan very uneasy. The United States would also greatly welcome a cooling of tempers and rhetoric between India and Pakistan. The early indications are not encouraging.

India's interest in minimizing the U.S. relationship with Pakistan will probably continue, and therein lies the main policy conflict the United States is likely to face with India. For the United States, this is clearly a time to pursue a relationship with both countries and stay away from the zero-sum mentality that both relentlessly try to impose on their ties with the United States. Major military supply for Pakistan is the greatest Indian sensitivity.

There is a substantial risk of an India-Pakistan crisis, perhaps even before the Afghan military operations are over, if violence in Kashmir continues to mount. The United States should launch a serious diplomatic effort to bring India, Pakistan, and the Kashmiris into a peace process once the immediate Afghan military operations are concluded. Recognizing that this will not bear fruit quickly, the United States needs to be quietly, creatively, and persistently involved over an extended period. India has strongly resisted third-party involvement in Kashmir for the past 30 years, but its improved relations with the United States make possible a more active diplomacy, provided it remains discreet.

Promoting peace in Kashmir is distinct from the antiterrorism campaign. But as long as the Kashmir issue festers, it will feed India-Pakistan hostility and create a potential new nest from which global terrorists will hatch and take flight.

Afghanistan—What Comes Next?

The short-term goal for the United States in Afghanistan is to hunt down Osama bin Laden and disband his Taliban hosts.

The long-term U.S. goal is the stability of the region. This requires a two-pronged approach. Politically, the power vacuum will need to be filled with a government that has a base broad enough to survive in the turbulent atmosphere of Afghanistan; economically, reconstructing the country after two decades of war will be a task of Herculean proportions. The track record of foreigners in bringing about constructive change in Afghanistan is poor. Without it, however, the chaos and breakdown in authority that made Afghanistan an exporter of terrorism in the past will reassert themselves.

The U.S. coalition-building efforts and military operations shook up the political system in Afghanistan and rocked the Taliban's power base among Pashtun tribal leaders. This political upheaval is almost certain to lead to formation of a new government, whether or not regime change is officially part of the U.S. agenda. This process will be messy and may take substantially longer than initial estimates suggest.

The key contenders for power include the following:

- Taliban leaders, who will probably have some guerrilla support and may have extensive help from Pakistan. Taliban leaders are almost exclusively Pashtun Sunnis. They are likely to split, but members of the group could turn up in alliance with other players.
- The Northern Alliance, a loosely tied organization of tribal groups, chiefly Hazaras, Uzbeks and Tajiks, that has support from Russia and India. Its leaders figured prominently in the first post-Soviet Afghan government but never consolidated their control, and their virtual absence of Pashtun allies is a critical weakness. They have never made peace with the Taliban.
- Other guerrilla commanders prominent in the anti-Soviet campaign, some of whom have been living outside Afghanistan (including Pakistan's former favorite, Gulbuddin Hekmatyar).
- Pashtun tribal leaders who had an arrangement with the Taliban but who may now have changed sides.
- The former king, Zahir Shah, who may have an important role as a traditional authority figure. His age (86) and his 30-year exile from Afghanistan make it unlikely that he can play a long-

term role. He has called for the summoning of a *loya jirga,* a traditional assembly of tribal chiefs.

Pashtuns are Afghanistan's largest ethnic group, at close to 40 percent of the population; others include Tajiks, Uzbeks, and Hazaras, and a significant Shi'a minority. Historically, no one has been able to rule Afghanistan without creating an ethnically diverse power base and working out understandings—including subsidies—with a sufficient network of tribal and clan leaders around the country. All governments for the past couple of centuries have been dominated by Pashtuns.

Outsiders with an interest in the outcome include Russia, China, India, Pakistan, Iran, and Afghanistan's Central Asian neighbors. But the stronger the outside role in selecting a government, the less stable that government is likely to be. Dissuading outside powers from trying to meddle will be a tall order, especially since all of them have a legitimate stake in the outcome and will claim to understand the situation better than the United States.

Afghanistan has never had a strong central government, and past governments have ruled on the basis of a complicated internal balance of power. Against this background, it is almost certain that a new government too would have a weak center, with most power remaining in the hands of local leaders. These in turn will probably fight out their differences on the battlefield, at least until a clearer pecking order stabilizes. The international community may be able to shorten this process and reduce the amount of violence involved by providing early support to a leader who emerges from a *loya jirga* or other internal consensus process. Access to relief supplies coupled with a requirement to use them all over the country to meet urgent humanitarian needs could help elevate a consensus leader to a steadier position of primus inter pares.

But this can only work if the interested countries agree on stability as the overriding goal and are willing to avoid pursuing their own preferences beyond the point where they offend other important players. It follows that maintaining contact among the outside powers with the greatest interest in stabilizing Afghanistan will be key to the long-term U.S. approach. The 6+2 group comprising Afghanistan's neighbors plus the United States and Russia has been the key group thus far, but the inclusion of anyone with the potential to become a spoiler should be considered—India, for example.

Economically, Afghanistan is one of the poorest countries in the world, with a subsistence agricultural economy and no industrial base. It is currently suffering from two decades of civil war; the death, exile, or displacement of close to half its population; a complete absence of normal government services (even by its own low standards); and a devastating drought. A massive humanitarian relief and reconstruction effort will be an essential part of U.S. strategy. Indeed, that process has already begun with the Bush administration's pledge in October 2001 of $320 million in aid.

Three key ingredients make up the relief effort. The first and most basic is food distribution. Second comes refugee relief, both for those displaced within Afghanistan and for those who have managed to leave the country. Before the latest crisis erupted, an estimated 2 million refugees lived in Pakistan, and that number could easily double. Iran also has a significant refugee population. Finally, Afghanistan's infrastructure, never very extensive, needs to be completely rebuilt and a foundation laid for resuming normal agricultural production. Before the crisis, the United Nations and nonofficial aid groups were undertaking the task of distributing relief supplies. They will need to resume a quasi-governmental role in that regard.

In Afghanistan as in the rest of the region, one of the real dangers for the United States is unintended consequences. Military operations and political upheavals in Afghanistan could lead to upheavals in Pakistan, India-Pakistan clashes, and agonizing and complex clashes in priorities between the United States and all three of these countries. Crises drive governments toward short-term thinking to deal with the emergency at hand. In this case, however, a long-term perspective needs to be factored in from the start, or the United States is likely to reap a whirlwind.

■ ■ ■ ■ ■

The Middle East

"It is the duty of every Palestinian to support bin Laden because he's backing our cause."

— Twenty-two-year-old art student at al-Najah University
in the West Bank city of Nablus
"Palestinian Police Open Fire on Rally for Bin Laden"
washingtonpost.com
October 9, 2001

"We assert our utter rejection of these attacks and assert that confronting them must not touch innocent civilians and must not extend beyond those who carried out those attacks."

— Emir Sheikh Hamad bin Khalifa al-Thani of Qatar
President, Organization of the Islamic Conference
October 10, 2001

It is both easy and dangerous to stereotype the problem of fighting terrorism in the Middle East. The only way that the United States can hope to approach the struggle successfully is to understand its complexity and deal with it accordingly.

There are some 21 to 23 countries in the Middle East, depending upon how states wish to align themselves at any given time. They sweep across North Africa from Morocco to Egypt, cover the Levant, and then cover the Arabian peninsula and the Northern Gulf, ending in Iran.

All of the Middle Eastern states do have much in common. All but one—Israel—are principally Islamic. All but two—Israel and Iran— are primarily Arab. All have lagged behind most regions of the world in development, including the most wealthy oil states whose oil income is not a substitute for a balanced and diversified economy. Most have experienced massive population growth. The population of the Middle East doubled from 1950 to 1980, rose from 174 million in

1980 to 290 million in 1999, and is projected to rise to 390 million in 2015. The net result is negligible real growth in per capita income from 1965 to the present, with the World Bank estimating an average real growth of only 0.1 percent over a 35-year period.

All have seen massive social upheavals, as largely agricultural states have become urbanized, breaking down the traditional economic structures, and forcing massive changes in family, clan, tribal, and community life. In the period from 1950 to 1980, the urbanized population grew from roughly 27 percent to 48 percent. Between 1980 and 1999 alone, the urban population grew from 84 to 169 million and from 48 to 58 percent of the total population.

Most Middle Eastern states also have very young populations. Roughly four out of ten Middle Easterners are 14 years old or younger. The result is a flood of young men and women entering the labor market, most with limited educational preparation for competing in a modern economy and who are pouring into labor markets that are already saturated owing to a lack of broad economic development. In many countries, formal and disguised unemployment for young men between 18 and 25 equals or surpasses 30 percent.

In many states, women face serious barriers to full participation in society. Statistics on migration outside the region do not measure the number of young men and women who wish to leave or are frustrated. In 2000, however, a poll of the male students in a Moroccan university indicated that some 70 percent replied they would emigrate to the West if they were guaranteed a decent job.

This failure to develop, as well as active structural social turmoil, are compounded by the failure of secular ideologies to offer either economic or political success. Pan-Arabism, socialism, communism, secular nationalism, and capitalism have all failed in most of the Middle East. There has been no successor to Nasser in the Arab world, and no leader to compensate for defeat in the Arab-Israeli conflict, failed national economies, and a steady loss of status. The Iranian revolution became a symbol of conflict between the region's people and U.S.-backed oppressive leaders but has ended in a popular backlash, symbolized by the election of President Khatami and paralyzed by power struggles between the Khatami and hard-line factions.

Other wars and civil conflicts have compounded the problem. The Arab-Israeli wars still go on in the form of a Second Intifada, and the images of Israeli tanks attacking Palestinian youths and of Arab funerals have come to be seen as symbols of U.S. support for an oppressive Israel. The Iran-Iraq conflict and the Gulf War have left a lasting legacy: first, the large-scale use of weapons of mass destruction and, second, policies that many Arabs see as a U.S.-led impoverishment of the Iraqi people.

In some areas—most notably North Africa, Bahrain, Iraq, Lebanon, Saudi Arabia, and Yemen—these pressures have also increased ethnic and religious tensions. In North Africa, tribal and community feuds and rivalries have become steadily worse, as has the tension between Arab and Berber. Algeria has had a brutal and enduring civil war between its corrupt ruling junta and violent Islamic extremists, but all of the Northern African states have had at least some serious internal security problems. Similar problems have created new tensions between the majority Sunni sect of Islam and various other sects, particularly the Shi'a of Bahrain, Saudi Arabia, and Iraq. This, in turn, has added to tensions between Iran—the one Shi'a-dominated state—and those states with Shi'a minorities. In the case of Yemen, religious tension interacts with tribal tension, a history of decades of civil war, and the legacy of Marxist radicalism imported into Aden in the 1930s.

Given this background, it is hardly surprising that many of the region's people have turned back to religion for security and hope. In broad terms, this shift has been stabilizing, allowing people throughout the region to cope with economic and social pressures within the traditional tenets of Islam. The failure of secularism and the rise of Islam have, however, led to the rise of a wide range of extremist movements within virtually every state in the region that advocates violence, regime overthrow, and terrorist opposition to secularism and the West. While these movements represent a small minority in every country, they are a key source of terrorism and they interact with the various civil wars and tensions or conflicts between states.

These movements are constantly evolving in character, strength, ideology, and the level of violence they are prepared to use inside and outside of the region. So far, only Al Qaeda and its closest associates have become global terrorists in the sense of focusing on targets outside the Middle East. Nevertheless, the U.S. State Department's list of known and well-established movements is still a warning that the United States and its allies may face a wide range of threats in the future and that a number of Middle East–based organizations have links to groups in Central and South Asia.

The rise of Osama bin Laden, Al Qaeda, and many other violent movements that cloak themselves in the mantle of Islam is a natural result of the social, political, and economic forces described above and of a "clash within a civilization" that has spilled over into attacks on the United States, the West, and secular forces from outside the region. At the same time, nothing could be more dangerous in shaping a counterterrorism strategy than to lump together the different movements and terrorist groups, or to limit any U.S. strategy to dealing with regional terrorism rather than include the threat of asymmetric warfare by regional states against the United States and its allies. There is probably no other region in the world with so many states that might conduct covert or proxy operations against the United States, possibly with weapons of mass destruction.

A Tour of a Troubled Region

A successful counterterrorism strategy tailored to the Middle East must consider a host of problems and threats as well as the interactions among them.

In Morocco, growing economic and demographic problems threaten the mid- and long-term stability of the regime. The country's economy is heavily dependent on drugs; migration problems affect labor; tensions exist between Arab and Berber; and the regime has continuing problems with its Islamists.

Algeria is still involved in a decade-long war that pits Islamic extremists against a corrupt military junta. While the struggle has been largely localized, there have been episodes of Islamic extremist violence in France. Some members of the most extreme groups have been affiliated with Al Qaeda, other terrorist groups, and operations against the United States.

Tunisia has been relatively peaceful but only because of the government's systematic suppression of its Islamic extremists.

Libya has been a source of support for terrorism, has conducted covert and proxy operations against U.S. and French targets, has some chemical weapons, and has explored the acquisition of biological weapons. This active support for terrorism has diminished sharply over the past two years, but General Mu'ammar Qadhafi is having his own problems with Islamic extremists and hostile tribal groups in the Green Mountain area and has been extremely volatile in his political alignments.

Egypt has fought its own war against terrorism for more than a decade. Some elements of its Muslim Brotherhood support violence, and the al-Jihad (a.k.a. Jihad Group, Islamic Jihad, Vanguards of Conquest, Talaa' al-Fateh) is closely associated with bin Laden. Like Islamic extremists in Algeria, these movements have broad links to terrorism outside Egypt. Al-Jihad has been associated with bin Laden's attacks on the United States and has murdered Western tourists as well as many Egyptians. Other Egyptian terrorists have operated in the United States and have served as volunteers for the Taliban and Al Qaeda.

While Egypt has succeeded in containing the domestic manifestations of terrorism, the basic social, economic, and political problems that have generated an Islamic extremist reaction remain. Egypt is experiencing steadily greater problems in terms of public resentment of U.S. ties to Israel and popular blame of the United States for the plight of the Iraqi people.

Israel and the Occupied Territories are the scene of what may be a prolonged low-intensity conflict between Israel and the Palestinians. Islamic extremist movements like the Palestinian Islamic Jihad and Hamas have long committed violent acts of terrorism against Israeli civilians. The Second Intifada is, however, generating equally extreme elements within the militias of the Palestinian Authority; and the Hizballah of Lebanon has strengthened its ties to extremist groups in the West Bank and Gaza. These groups have concentrated largely on Israeli targets in the past but have had elements associated with broader terrorist groups like Al Qaeda. They blame the United States for much of Israel's conduct and present a growing risk that the Intifada could turn on U.S. targets as well as Israeli ones. More generally, the Arab and Islamic worlds blame the United States for much of the Second Intifada and Israel's ability to maintain its occupation of the West Bank and Gaza. Bin Laden has used television coverage of the Second Intifada as a key element in his propaganda and training films, and Arab and Islamic media routinely blame the United States in their coverage, exacerbating the resentment felt by Islamic extremists throughout the Arab and Islamic worlds.

Lebanon is no longer occupied by Israel, but it does have large Palestinian refugee camps, and the Hizballah and Amal Shi'a forces that drove Israel out of Southern Lebanon are seen by many in the Islamic and Arab worlds as models of how asymmetric warfare can defeat modern Western powers as well as Israel. The various Syrian, Hizballah, and Hamas training camps for Islamic extremists in the Bekaa Valley have provided paramilitary and terrorist training for a broad range of groups from other countries, and some have been led by members of the Iranian Revolutionary Guards and Iranian intelligence. Syria is also able to allow Iranian operations to take place on foreign soil, while Iran can use the Hizballah and Amal as cover. Such movements have not played a major role in global terrorism, but these camps helped train some of the Saudi terrorists associated with the attacks on the National Guard Training Center and the Khobar Towers.

Syria, and particularly Syrian air force intelligence, played at least some role in encouraging the attacks on the U.S. Marine Corps barracks in Beirut in 1982. Syria has also long supported a range of Palestinian extremist and antipeace groups and has hosted them in Syria as long as they do not conduct operations from within the country. Syria has a history of using proxy groups in violent attacks and has worked closely with Iranian hard-liners in supporting the Hizballah and violent Palestinian groups involved in the Second Intifada. It has at least tolerated the training of gulf terrorist groups on Lebanese soil. It has extensive chemical weapons stocks, and probably some biological weapons.

Jordan has fought terrorism for decades and has generally managed to halt the launch of terrorist operations from its soil. It does, however, have strong Islamist parties and is forced to allow some extremist groups to operate on its soil until they can be proven to be violent. Its economy was crippled before the Second Intifada and has grown steadily weaker, while its heavily Palestinian population has become increasingly anti-Israeli and anti-American. Jordan's midterm stability is increasingly uncertain, and its problems are compounded by the steady flow of arms across its borders with Iraq, some of which do reach the West Bank and Gaza.

Experts disagree sharply about Iraq's role in terrorism. The best evidence is that Iraq routinely uses violence against its opposition overseas, but such activity has been limited in recent years—probably both out of fear of U.S. action and the fact that most Iraqi opposition groups in the West and Middle East are heavily penetrated by Iraqi intelligence. Iraq does not have a proven history of making extensive use of proxy movements to attack the United States and other targets. Some believe that Iraq was involved in both attacks on the World Trade Center, but the evidence is limited and U.S. intelligence does not agree. Iraq does have a long history of supporting violent anti-Iranian terrorist movements like the People's Mujahhedin—which systematically attacked and sometimes killed U.S. military and officials in Iran before the fall of the shah. Iraq has significant stocks of chemical and biological weapons and its leadership has sometimes taken extreme military risks. Iraq has also actively supported efforts to smuggle arms into Jordan, many of which are intended to go to the West Bank and Gaza. The Iraqi government's largely successful effort to blame the United States for the suffering of the Iraqi people as a result of UN sanctions has been a major factor in increasing Arab and Islamic extremist opposition to the United States.

Iran is a Shi'a nation that has often had tense relations with the Sunni ruling elites of its neighbors. It has supported Shi'a extremists and terrorists from Bahrain and Saudi Arabia, and experts like former FBI director Louis Freeh and former head of the U.S. Central Command Anthony Zinni believe the previous leadership of the Iranian government had knowledge of, and supported, the attacks on the Khobar Towers. Iran has a long history of recruiting, training, and arming the Hizballah in Lebanon and did the same with the Hazaras in Afghanistan. The Khatami government has sharply reduced Iran's activity as it affects the gulf states, but not in terms of the Arab-Israeli confrontation or Afghanistan. The government is also deeply divided, with far more hard-line elements in charge of the military and intelligence branches, and the most prominent mullah, known as the supreme leader, has repeatedly condemned the United States. Iran has chemical and biological weapons and is seeking nuclear weapons.

Saudi Arabia has fought its own internal battles against Islamic extremism. At the same time, its oil wealth has declined by nearly 60 percent in per capita terms since the peak oil revenues of the early

1990s, and it has failed to diversify its economy or rapidly reduce its dependence on foreign labor. Real and disguised unemployment among young Saudi males approaches 30 percent. Saudi Arabia also allowed its Islamists to contribute to Islamic charities associated with terrorism and to dominate its education system—much of which is taught by expatriate teachers, some of whom support violent Islamic extremism.

The Saudi royal intelligence service has estimated that some 12,000–25,000 young Saudis have had some kind of training or experience with paramilitary groups and Islamist extremist groups since the Soviet invasion of Afghanistan. Some Saudi Shi'a have also been trained in Iranian paramilitary and terrorist training camps in Lebanon and Iran. While these pressures do not threaten the regime in the near term, they help explain why Saudi Arabia has been a source of volunteers for terrorist acts and has played a major role in Al Qaeda. The Saudi regime does not seem to face any near-term threat of overthrow, and it is tightening its restrictions on Saudi extremists. At the same time, its five year plan projects a continued deterioration in the economic conditions that help breed terrorism, and Saudi extremists have used attacks on the United States and the West as a proxy for attacks on the Saudi regime since the days of Nasser.

Bahrain, Kuwait, Oman, Qatar, and the United Arab Emirates (UAE) have their own problems and instabilities, and the Omani government has had to take increasingly strong measures against a small group of Islamic extremists. Bahrain's Sunni ruling elite is making progress in dealing with its Shi'a community, however, and Qatar and the UAE are more concerned about the problems of controlling a foreign labor force that approaches 60 percent of the population than terrorism per se.

Yemen has made faltering but important strides toward the rule of law and a more democratic government since South Yemen disintegrated following decades of civil war between various Marxist extremists in 1990. Its present regime did, however, use Islamic extremists in its battle against South Yemeni secessionists in the mid-1990s, and Yemen has a long history of hosting extreme Arab national movements and of tolerating extremists that do not conduct antiregime operations on Yemeni soil. It has deported many non-Yemeni extremists since the bombings of the U.S. embassies in Kenya and Tanzania and the attack on the USS *Cole*, but many Yemeni extremists can still operate from its soil.

A Successful U.S. Strategy: No Generalizations, No Illusions

This capsule survey of the Middle East necessarily ignores many of the complexities in each country. It also cannot begin to survey all of the extremist and terrorist groups that operate in each country or across national lines. One key problem is that extremist groups are constantly changing their leaders, names, and methods. Opportunistic coalitions and cooperation come and go with little or no warning. This why umbrella groups like Al Qaeda can have ties to so many groups, even Shi'a and semisecular groups with which it shares little in common in terms of religion or ideology.

At the same time, this survey should make several things clear about a U.S. strategy for dealing with terrorism.

First, no strategy that attempts to generalize across the entire Middle East can have any hope of success. The United States must tailor its strategy to specific countries and movements, and the strength of its bilateral efforts will largely determine its success. Moreover, it must deal with individual terrorist groups separately and not in terms of broad labels that ignore the specific character and objectives of individual movements.

This will require a large, nuanced, tailored, and dedicated counterterrorist effort, one that looks beyond known terrorist threats to monitor developments in each country and each extremist group. The United States cannot count on predicting future terrorist groups before they begin to act, their degree of support from regional governments, or their means of attack. The best it can do is create dedicated interagency teams that focus on the different national threats and groups, pull together all of the necessary skills and expertise, and strengthen the teams it deploys in each country.

There are no near-term prospects that international or regional programs and agreements will be substitutes for strong bilateral, in-country counterterrorism programs. Each U.S. ambassador in the Middle East should be supported by a fully staffed counterterrorism team—including all of the assets needed to create a strong human intelligence program and an integrated CIA, FBI, and attaché effort. These counterterror programs need to be supported with equally determined efforts to identify and deal with the risks of asymmetric warfare. This will require much stronger political-military teams and attaché staffs that can concentrate on their substantive mission and not representational duties. It will also require longer tours of duty, tours with family dependents resident at post—even if this sometimes means added risk to U.S. civilian and military personnel—and proactive and constant contact with the nationals of the country involved instead of a fortress mentality.

Second, nothing could be worse than a clash-of-civilizations approach that broadly focuses on Islam and/or the Arab world. All of our major allies in the region are already fighting their own battle against the "clash within civilizations," and any approach that deals with terrorism in terms of labels like "Islam" and "Arab" will simply strengthen the hand of the extremists we seek to defeat.

There are severe limits to regional cooperation that grow as much out of the differences between Arab states as from tensions with Israel and the West. The United States should, however, seek to create a regional forum for counterterrorism that includes representation from the United States, Europe, Russia, and Israel and that deliberately cuts across cultural differences. One key aspect of this effort must be to come to grips with the problem of legal and illegal immigration from the region—not only from the security perspective but also to ensure that legal Arab and Iranian visitors and immigrants get the rights and respect they deserve. Such a forum could also help to reduce the growing cultural backlash and anti-immigrant fear in Europe—and thereby help to mitigate corresponding regional resentment and extremism.

Third, a strategy that deals with terrorism without considering the risk of proxy attacks by states, some with weapons of mass destruction, ignores the highest level of risk to the United States and its allies. Counterterrorism is not an answer to the problems of the Middle East unless it is tied to a strategy for strengthening U.S. capabilities to fight asymmetric warfare and to a broadly based and intensive counterproliferation effort that mixes defense, offense, and arms control. As may be the case in Afghanistan, this means preparing for regime change and major regional wars, although it does not mean acting preemptively or escalating without clear cause.

One critical aspect of this effort must be to encourage the engagement programs and counterproliferation efforts of U.S. Central Command and the efforts of the U.S. military to deal with chemical, biological, radiological, and nuclear (CBRN) threats not just as a matter of homeland defense but as regional security concerns. This too requires longer tours of duty, and more specialized training and language skills. It also means more tours accompanied by dependents and deeper involvement with foreign nationals, even if this means added risk to U.S. personnel. The United States needs a proactive military commitment to full-time partnership with the military and national security forces of friendly states in the region. The United States also needs to support its commanders in taking the necessary risk of exposing Americans to terrorism rather than make every terrorist success an exercise in blaming the regional commander most directly involved.

At the same time, the United States should consider developing a more clearly defined policy for the region—or even the world—that declares the United States will use military force in response to any act of asymmetric warfare by a state or state-sponsored mass terrorism that involves the use of CBRN weapons. This policy should further state the United States will not only defend its own territory by destroying the regime involved, but will also come to the aid of any state that comes under such attack. Such a strategy might be expanded to take the form of a UN Security Council resolution although the support of the council is now uncertain. There is, however, a need for a stronger and better-defined level of deterrence to such attacks, particularly in the Middle East. A clear policy would not only put extremist regimes on notice and reassure our allies, it would serve as a justification for prompt and decisive action if further attacks occur.

Fourth, the United States cannot impose an Arab-Israeli peace, nor should it ever try to do so purely on Palestinian or expedient terms. But a highly visible U.S. peace effort that goes on in spite of all the frustrations involved is absolutely vital to minimizing the impact of extremism and terrorism. There is also a clear need for presidential and congressional leadership that puts open pressure on Israel in areas where its conduct is clearly unfair, such as the settlements issue. The United States should never abandon or weaken an ally, but domestic political expediency is a recipe for future terrorist attacks on the United States.

Fifth, the United States must alter the perception that it is responsible for the plight of the Iraqi people by undertaking a major information campaign and making sanctions humane in ways that focus on limiting Saddam Hussein's military buildup and capability to proliferate without crippling Iraq's economy and development. Although as of this writing Iraq does not seem to have played a role in the attacks on the World Trade Center and the Pentagon, that possibility exists—as does the risk of future Iraqi attacks on the United States and its regional friends using terrorist proxies or covert asymmetric warfare. The United States must prepare for such contingencies and make it clear to both Iraq and the world that any such aggression— particularly using CBRN weapons—will result in a war that will bring an end to Saddam Hussein's regime. At the same time, the United States must recognize that some states that encourage terrorism are far worse than others; make it clear that it will not tolerate military encroachments on the Kurdish security zone or Iraqi conventional military action outside its borders; and quietly work to remove Saddam's regime while finding ways to use the UN's control over much of Iraq's oil wealth to channel the flow of investment, goods, and services to aid the Iraqi people.

Sixth, the United States needs to clearly recognize that measures like the Iran-Libya Sanctions Act that was renewed in the summer of 2001 are not helping the United States to deal with Iran or to moderate its conduct. The United States needs to establish economic ties to Iran's moderates and do what it can to move toward an official dialogue. This does not mean appeasement or tolerance of Iran's treatment of Israel and proliferation, but it does mean the kind of engagement pioneered by our southern gulf allies and that the United States found successful in dealing with the former Soviet Union and China. The United States should end its sanctions policy, with the exception of its efforts to halt the flow of arms and the equipment and technology to make weapons of mass destruction. It should adopt a policy of sustained informal and formal engagement with Iran, conduct as much dialogue with Iran's government as is possible, and make efforts to use targeted and well-defined forms of trade and investment to reach out to Iran's people. At the same time, it must make constantly clear that the United States opposes any Iranian support of terrorism and violent extremism, that Israel has a right to exist in peace and security, and that proliferation is a threat to the region and ultimately to Iran itself.

Seventh, counterterrorism is as much a war of ideas as a struggle for security.[1] The United States needs to create an ongoing public information campaign targeted at the Arab world and Iran with ample radio, television, Internet, and print resources. This program should include a major effort to ensure that U.S. views are readily available in Arabic and Farsi, but it should also include a strong Voice of America program focused on objective reporting. It should fully engage nations like Iraq with efforts that counter lies and propaganda. And it should repeatedly underscore, through rhetoric and reporting, that the United States supports the values of Islam—contrary to the lies and distortions spread by Islamic extremists and terrorists.

Eighth, the United States should create large-scale cooperative programs for training regional experts in counterterrorism, and it should restructure and expand programs like the International Military Education and Training program to help train friendly experts in both the military and paramilitary aspects of counterterrorism and to cope with the regional threat of asymmetric warfare.

Ninth, the United States should develop both regional and bilateral programs designed to help deal with the region's need for economic reform. There are serious limits to what the United States can do that market forces and internal pressures for reform cannot. Middle East states and peoples must see, however, that the United States both cares about regional development and seeks to use its own aid programs and role in international organizations to achieve it. This may well mean a more proactive role in encouraging the entry of regional states into the World Trade Organization and working with the private sector and regional governments to ease the barriers to private investment and the expansion of trade.

Tenth, the United States needs to create both regional and bilateral programs to deal with the special problems of energy security from the wellhead to U.S. ports. The Saudi concept of a permanent regional organization to maintain an importer-exporter dialogue is one way to deal with the economic and political side of the issue. More broadly, however, the United States needs to systematically examine the vulnerability of the region's energy production and export facilities, assess the need for improved defenses against terrorism and asymmetric warfare, and work with nations to reduce key vulnerabilities and weaknesses.

More broadly, the United States cannot afford a strategy of illusions. No Middle East Marshall Plan or any amount of U.S. aid can fully solve the region's underlying economic problems. Only a few countries like Jordan can actually absorb economic aid efficiently and honestly, and the most unsuccessful regimes are not only the worst potential threats, they are also least able to use aid. Strongly encouraging economic reform and diversification is a different story, however. Targeted aid, trade agreements, and similar measures focused on building up the private sector and encouraging international investment can be successful if they are tailored to help those regimes that will allow their nations to help themselves.

The same is true of well-meaning slogans about democratization. The United States can and has encouraged nongovernmental organizations to help in this regard, but U.S. government efforts to try to impose U.S. values and norms on virtually all of the states in this region will simply increase anti-American, anti-Western, and anti-secular resentments. The United States must move carefully and cautiously to seek to improve the rule of law and the level of representative government, but there are severe real-world limits to what it can do to address the structural causes of terrorism. In most countries, it will take more than a decade before major progress can occur that will significantly reduce the present level of economic, demographic, and social problems.

This confronts the United States with the reality that it can only succeed in the near and medium term by addressing "easy" problems like an Arab-Israeli peace settlement and the plight of the Iraqi people. Every other regional step will be in the medium to long term at best.

In the interim, the United States will also have to live with the fact that many countries in the region conduct their own internal security and counterterrorism operations in ways that violate human rights and target peaceful political opposition as well as extremists. Here the United States should continue its human rights efforts but have no illusions about the prospects for sudden change.

President Bush has emphasized that the United States will fight against terrorism for as long as it takes. When it comes to our strategy in the Middle East, that will be a very long time indeed.

■ ■ ■ ■ ■

Europe

"The Parties agree that an armed attack against one or more of them in Europe or North America shall be considered an attack against them all and consequently they agree that, if such an armed attack occurs, each of them, in exercise of the right of individual or collective self-defence recognised by Article 51 of the Charter of the United Nations, will assist the Party or Parties so attacked by taking forthwith, individually and in concert with the other Parties, such action as it deems necessary, including the use of armed force, to restore and maintain the security of the North Atlantic area."

— Article 5, The North Atlantic Treaty
April 4, 1949

"We were with you at the first. We will stay with you to the last."

— Prime Minister Tony Blair of Great Britain
October 2, 2001

In the immediate aftermath of September 11, Europe's response to the pain of American citizens was spontaneous and genuine, and its official support for the Bush administration was unanimous and real. From the mountains of flowers that appeared before U.S. embassies from Brussels to Bratislava, to the moment of silence observed by citizens across the continent, to the presence of British prime minister

Tony Blair during President Bush's September 20 speech before the U.S. Congress, in countless ways and venues, Europe said, "We stand with you."

Whatever transatlantic tensions there may have been during the previous nine months, the horrific events of September 11 are a reminder that in moments of crisis, the United States and Europe still look to each other before they look to anyone else. In building a coalition against terrorism, the Bush administration rightly began by securing its European base rather than focusing on Asia or Latin America, the purported beneficiaries of a reoriented American foreign policy. This reflex confirmed that the states of Europe and the United States form a community of values that can become a community of action when these values are at risk. Such solidarity will be a powerful political and practical weapon in the campaign that lies ahead.

Keeping the alliance together will not be effortless, however. While the United States and Europe share common goals, there are significant differences over policies that could be exacerbated as the campaign unfolds.

During earlier post–Cold War military campaigns, from the Persian Gulf to the Balkans, such differences were contained because the enemy and the interest were clearly identifiable and common, and military action was kept short and—for the allies—fundamentally painless. That will not be the case this time: the enemy is elusive; the campaign, open-ended. Even as the U.S. administration must show visionary strategic leadership in waging "the first war of the twenty-first century," it will have to work hard to sustain vigorous European cooperation on the nonmilitary fronts of the war on terrorism and actual participation on the military front itself.

The Terrorist Threat in Europe

Over the past three decades, periodic waves of terrorism have threatened civil order within most European countries. A number of the most infamous terrorist groups were defeated—for example, the Red Brigades in Italy and Baader-Meinhof in Germany—and some of their leaders (and many of their followers) ultimately co-opted by the state. Some of these indigenous groups have endured, however, and their actions have served as a constant reminder of the country's vulnerability to violence—groups such as the Basque Fatherland and Liberty (ETA) in Spain, the Real Irish Republican Army (RIRA) in Ireland and the United Kingdom, and the Kurdistan Workers Party (PKK) in Turkey.

Some in Europe may be tempted to equate the terrorism they have experienced with the threat posed by Al Qaeda and Osama bin Laden. In fact, there are important differences. First, terrorism in Europe is mainly local. Moreover, it tends (though not always visibly) to pursue a clear and limited political agenda, to target officials of the state (politicians, police, military) and not civilians, and to limit destruction instead of seeking maximum civilian casualties. As a result, Europeans have sometimes found negotiated political solutions with their terrorist groups—even in such seemingly intractable conflicts as those in Northern Ireland and Corsica.

That said, Europeans have tended not to seek negotiations in response to foreign-induced terror—such as France faced in the mid-1980s and, again, in the mid-1990s. Partly motivated by fear that terrorist cells could spread among the millions of Muslim citizens living in France and elsewhere in Europe, the French government's response was brutal (and occasionally oblivious to fundamental civil liberties) but effective.

In the current campaign, negotiations are not an option. The perpetrators of the September 11 attacks were not interested in any plausible, identifiable goal that might serve as a focus for negotiations, however defined.

In recent years, the discovery and dismantling of Al Qaeda cells in nearly a dozen European countries probably helped prevent terrorist plots and save untold innocent lives. Yet it is tragically clear that some cells have eluded detection: Several of the individuals responsible for, and connected to, the September 11 attack lived, worked, and were educated in Germany or, allegedly, Britain.

The presence of Al Qaeda in Europe, combined with Europe's identity as a wellspring of Western values and culture and its role as America's ally, suggest that European interests will become targets for attack. As French president Jacques Chirac said September 18, after meeting with President Bush, "This time, it was New York; next time, it could be Paris, Berlin, or London."

Such an outcome will be even more likely if the United States hardens its potential targets and Europe does not. Even if future terrorist strikes are "limited" to U.S. interests in Europe, collateral damage to Europeans could also be significant. In most European capitals, U.S. embassies and corporate flagships are centrally located; their reinforced protection will leave them less vulnerable than their neighborhoods. Moreover, the close relationship between the United States and Europe means that even a terrorist strike on the U.S. mainland sends waves across the Atlantic: The September 11 assault was the worst terrorist attack on British citizens in that country's history.

U.S. Requests from Europe: Stand by Me

For the alliance between the United States and European states to be sustainable and effective, two cautions are in order.

First, 100 percent followership from all the allies will not be possible. It is therefore a given that not everything will be done together, but so is the expectation that nothing be done by any partner that is incompatible with the strategy and aims of the campaign.

Second, the U.S. administration will have to consult closely with its European partners—whether for actions that would be undertaken in common or for complementary actions that can be pursued separately. While it will not be possible to do everything together, it will be imperative to ensure that together the members of the alliance (and the various coalitions) do everything necessary to prevail in the campaign against terrorism.

Military support. A mere 24 hours after the attack on America, NATO invoked the collective defense clause of its founding treaty for the first time in the alliance's 52-year history. "An armed attack" against one ally, reads Article 5, "shall be considered an attack against them all."

NATO's action was an important declaration of political solidarity. It underscored that while the United States was the immediate victim of aggression, the values it shares with allies and friends (and even rivals)—democracy, openness, tolerance—were targeted beyond continental America. It also served as a potent reminder that even a nation without peers cannot be a nation without allies for long.

As a practical matter, NATO's expression of support is more ambiguous. The NATO treaty itself is vague about actual obligations of NATO members. Each member has leeway to decide for itself its appropriate response, including the use of armed force. It has always been understood that different members will contribute differently to NATO operations depending on their capabilities and circumstances.

While military action with NATO members and their assets will obviously be desirable and is likely to occur, such action should not be developed and pursued within NATO—as was the case for the Kosovo war. To launch the campaign as NATO's "second war" would require the United States to cede some political and operational authority to the North Atlantic Council and to European generals, thus making it more difficult to act quickly and stealthily. Other than command and control and AWACS aircraft, NATO has few assets of its own to engage in any conflict; most belong to its individual members. Moreover, a NATO label on the "war of 911" would resurrect the sad crusading image of the last millennium—not a war for civilization but a war among civilizations led by a mostly Christian West against the infidels of Muslim fundamentalism.

Nonetheless, individual NATO members remain the hard core of the grand coalition being formed; their contributions will be diverse and substantial. The political support extended by the allies will be needed "to restore peace and stability," as written into Article 5. Individual allies—along with NATO partner countries and aspiring members—can also be called upon to take part in special operations; join coalitions-of-the-willing on the ground; permit access to critical military facilities; grant overflight privileges; share intelligence; and crack down on terrorist access to safe houses, financial services, and technical training on allied soil. While some of these requests proved problematic during the Gulf War, the swift invocation of Article 5 suggests that cooperation from NATO countries will be smoother than in the past. As German chancellor Gerhard Schröder pledged on October 4, "If there were a concrete request, there would be unlimited cooperation. And by unlimited, I mean unlimited."

Within such a cooperative context, individual NATO countries can bring important capabilities to the table. The British, for example, have highly trained special forces that can take part in commando operations. So do the French and the Germans. Turkish air bases may be critical to specific military missions. The U.S. administration should seek to create as much European buy-in to the campaign against terrorism as possible by including as many Europeans as possible in its prosecution.

One potential obstacle to European support for and participation in military action may be the absence of a legal basis. Throughout the Balkan conflicts of the 1990s and during the debate about revising NATO's strategic concept, various European governments insisted on the need for a legal basis for military action, ideally from the United Nations. Arguably, such a basis already exists in Chapter VII of the UN Charter, especially after the 18 other NATO countries acknowledged the events of September 11 as an armed attack against the United States. That basis was extended globally after the UN Security Council adopted unanimously an extraordinary and unprecedented resolution presented by the United States. The European Union turned this into an institutional triple play at its summit of September 22, when the 15 EU members—decidedly more outspoken under the institutional cover provided by their partners—pledged their "unlimited solidarity" for the campaign against the "barbaric acts" of September 11 and cited Chapter 7 of the UN Charter as a basis for military action.

Still, as the antiterror campaign expands beyond bin Laden and Afghanistan, some European nations may insist on a legal basis for using military force.

Political support. France and Britain will be critical allies to the extent the United States continues to seek UN Security Council approval for any specific actions. And as support is needed and sought for parallel initiatives in other international organizations (including the Organization for Economic Cooperation and Development, the Organization for Security and Cooperation in Europe, the International Civil Aviation Organization, and others), European allies and friends can provide a core base of votes and lobbying power.

European countries can also play important roles as intermediaries to the Arab world. Already, the EU troika and Britain have made significant overtures to Iran. France and Spain have close ties to Algeria, Morocco, and Tunisia; Italy has economic ties to Libya. France has political ties with such sensitive countries as Lebanon and Syria; Britain does with Egypt. The European tradition of support for the Palestine Liberation Organization as well as the reality of EU "constructive engagement" with Iraq, could be effectively leveraged for support. Finally, Turkey's role as a bridge between Europe and Asia, between the Islamic and Judeo-Christian worlds, and between Israelis and Palestinians, could pay invaluable political dividends even as it causes political strains within Turkey.

Intelligence and law enforcement cooperation. In the areas of intelligence and law enforcement, coordination within Europe will be just as important as cooperation with the United States. Even now, only Britain, France, Germany, Italy, Portugal, and Spain have specific antiterrorist legislation in effect. That legislation differs widely from one country to the next, and none seems to offer a precise definition of its aim. Each country protects itself against its own variety of terror but displays indifference about its neighbor's. There is no single EU arrest warrant; extradition procedures remain slow and tedious; information is not always shared. Europol—the European police office established in 1992 to combat international organized crime—is supposed to support domestic law enforcement agencies, but data and assets are not properly integrated and organized for collective action.

In short, while the countries of Europe have waged many wars on terrorism over the past decades, they have not waged these wars in common, and even less have they attempted to wage a single war. September 11 may be the needed catalyst for an effective integration of the current mosaic.

The United States also will depend heavily on individual European countries for leadership on the various fronts of the antiterror campaign. Britain and Germany, for example, will be indispensable for unraveling the financial network that feeds terrorist groups with funds. The discovery that some of the money that sustained the 19 hijackers passed through German, British, and Swiss banks has awakened Europe to the fact that, in the words of an EU official, it has become "a sieve for dirty money." As a result, Germany and Britain announced they would adopt new laws to obstruct the flow of funds to terrorist organizations—including the creation of financial intelligence units and the relaxation of bank secrecy rules. Switzerland and France have expanded their investigations of suspicious accounts.

Enhanced coordination could pay substantial dividends on the intelligence and law enforcement fronts. For example, French intelligence has effectively penetrated the Islamic world in its midst. The EU is considering the creation of a common border police or, at the least, the adoption of common standards. And cooperation everywhere will be at premium for quick police interventions resulting from tips and other intelligence information originating elsewhere.

Europe's Response: You've Got a Friend

The United States will likely ask Europeans for the kind of help they should be able to give: intense and sustained cooperation on the non-military fronts (diplomatic, intelligence, financial, law enforcement); and limited participation in the military sphere (overflight, basing, logistics, and intelligence). However, political and tactical fault lines could emerge that threaten European cooperation and participation. The burden will be on diplomats to prevent them from opening or to breach them if they do.

Unity versus criticism. In Washington, praise for NATO's historic invocation of Article 5 quickly became concern that the allies were hedging their commitments.

Leading figures in Europe publicly urged caution, warning that their expressions of support were not blank checks for American military action. And not only could there be no blank check, neither was there a war, as repeatedly emphasized by European defense ministers in Germany, France, and Italy. "We do not face a war," stated Rudolf Scharping. Rather, added Chirac, this would be a "conflict" that transcended any known label because it was "of a completely new nature."

To be fair, cautionary notes have been the exception, not the rule. Political support for America has been wide and deep, ranging from the extraordinary pace of NATO decisions, to the overwhelming Bundestag vote supporting possible German participation in military action, to the unprecedented ease with which the European Union displayed its commitment to wage the campaign with and in support of the United States. In addition, allies have an obligation to state their limits to Washington.

Put another way, a diversity of views is the essence of a democracy—and of relations among them. But the expression of views will inevitably strain the transatlantic link. Thus, to the extent possible, the allies should keep their criticism moderate and behind closed doors. Nor is this the time to debate each other's policies in the past tense—

what should have been done but was not in the Middle East, for example, or in the gulf.

In return for solidarity, Washington owes its allies no surprises. Especially under conditions when the risks of failure may be borne most directly by the allies, ongoing, real-time consultations are a reasonable quid pro quo for unity. Moreover, these consultations must be a genuine exchange. Over the past 20 years, European countries have built a long list of instances when "consultation" mostly amounted to a one-sided U.S. briefing.

Rhetoric will play an important role, as words can create unwanted and unnecessary fissures. President Bush's September 20 call for Osama bin Laden "dead or alive" awakened European fears, including Blair's, of a shoot-from-the-hip sheriff in Washington. While the image catered to domestic constituencies, it hurt the president's own interest in coalition building. Similarly, the president's reference to the nation's new "crusade" was not helpful in the cultural context within which the campaign will be waged.

In Europe, the word "war" awakens memories of large-scale mobilization, invasion, and occupation—actions and events that shaped the continent's darkest hours throughout the first half of the past century. These images, however, are likely to bear little resemblance to the reality of the war against terrorism. To help avoid confusion and sustain solidarity within the Euro-Atlantic community, U.S. leaders should constantly and clearly communicate America's goals and means to allies as well as to the American people.

States of concern. The most significant threat to transatlantic cohesion is policy toward the many countries suspected of, or known as, harboring terrorists: Iraq, Iran, Syria, Sudan, Somalia, Yemen, and Libya.

If Washington pursues military action beyond Afghanistan, it could cause real tension with the allies and potentially undermine their participation in the broader antiterrorism campaign. Europeans will support exerting political pressure on these countries to get out of the terror business, but in the absence of compelling evidence linking these countries to global terrorism, they are unlikely to support military action in the event political pressure fails—with the exception of Britain in the case of Iraq. However, if Europeans, along with the Russians and Chinese, apply that pressure vigorously—as they failed to do in the case of sanctions on and arms inspectors in Iraq—they may have some success in changing the behavior of these states.

Conversely, some in Europe may seize the moment to try to bring countries like Iran and Syria more fully into the community of nations and enlist them in the war against terrorism. This was the objective of a highly publicized visit by British foreign secretary Jack Straw to Iran, shortly after September 11. Meanwhile, the EU Troika is likely to engage in similar missions. Absent coordination with and support from Washington, such overtures could become irritants to alliance solidarity. This is especially true if the U.S. administration interprets such overtures as efforts to increase economic engagement with these states at a time when the United States may be seeking to sanction them economically.

Some Europeans are also likely to return to an alleged connection between U.S. support for Israel and terrorism. As a matter of principle, no political grievance, no matter how just, can ever justify terror. In fact, even if Israel and the Palestinians were to make peace tomorrow, the terror attacks would continue because their ultimate aim is to undermine Western values and turn the clock back a thousand years. Everything else is peripheral. Of course, Americans and Europeans should focus on pursuing peace in the Middle East for its own sake. Doing so is vital to enlisting and sustaining the participation of Muslim countries in the various coalitions against terrorism.

The transatlantic agenda. Although transatlantic relations will now focus intensively on the new conflict, the agenda that existed prior to September 11 has not disappeared.

If the Bush administration expects the Europeans to be there for a U.S.-led multilateral coalition, it must also be willing to address multilaterally issues of European concern. This will mean, for example, that the United States will have to continue to provide support for a robust NATO protection force for the EU and OSCE monitors in Macedonia. It may also mean that the Bush administration will want to revisit its opposition to the climate change treaty, biological weapons protocol, the Anti-Ballistic Missile (ABM) Treaty, the International Criminal Court, and other issues that Europe had viewed as demonstrations of a new U.S. unilateralism since January 2001. This does not mean acceding to European positions in order to buy their participation in the war against terrorism. It does mean proposing alternatives and negotiating compromises.

During the first half of 2001, much was written and said about the United States and Europe diverging over ideals and interests. The events of September 11, 2001, were a powerful reminder that we remain the best of foul-weather friends. The community of values protected by NATO and the community of interests built within the EU must now merge into a community of action. This is not a new ambition; it is the realization of a vision forged more than 50 years ago after the dehumanizing brutality of two world wars. As another wave of brutality builds, the challenge for European and American policymakers will be to show themselves worthy of the determination and statesmanship of their predecessors.

■ ■ ■ ■ ■

Russia

"The Russian Federation has been fighting international terrorism for a long time now, relying exclusively on its own resources, and it has repeatedly urged the international community to join efforts. Russia's position is unchanged: We, naturally, are still ready to make a contribution to the struggle against terror."

— *President Vladimir Putin of Russia*
announcing support for the U.S. military operation in Afghanistan
September 24, 2001

"President Bush appreciated very much President Putin's offer of concrete cooperation in the common fight against international terrorism . . . . [T]he President also wants to note particularly President Putin's remarks about the situation in Chechnya in which President Putin called on Chechen insurgents to disassociate themselves immediately from the international terrorist networks, and meet for discussions to resolve the crisis in Chechnya. The Chechnya leadership, like all responsible political leaders in the world, must immediately and unconditionally cut all contacts with international terrorist groups, such as Osama bin Laden and the Al Qaeda organization."

— *Ari Fleischer*
White House Press Secretary
September 25, 2001

In the months prior to September 11, 2001, the U.S.-Russia relationship had become stuck somewhere between friend and foe. President George W. Bush had come to office promising a qualitatively different relationship with Russia that finally transcended Cold War–era suspicions and rivalry. Yet, aside from some sweet murmurings by each president to the other at their first meeting, two years after NATO's use of force in Kosovo—to which the Russians had vociferously objected—a chill was still in the air. Among many contentious issues still crowding the agenda were the Bush administration's pursuit of missile defense and the intended abrogation of the ABM Treaty and questions about the future direction of NATO enlargement. In addition to these vexing matters, some fairly substantial divisions at the uppermost levels of the U.S. government were leaving some doubt about what the goals of the relationship with Russia were supposed to be.

Has all that changed since September 11? Has the United States finally entered a dramatically new era of cooperation with Russia— particularly between both militaries—that has been an objective since the end of the Cold War? Ten years after the collapse of the Soviet Union, could terrorism be the enemy that makes Russia and the United States, if not exactly friends and not exactly allies either, coalition partners then against a pernicious global challenge?

The Terrorist Threat through Russian Eyes

Throughout the 1990s, Russia was engaged in debates about its national interests, foreign policy priorities, and the nature of the security threats it confronted. Under the leadership of President Vladimir Putin, Russia's foreign policy and security policy has generally demonstrated a greater clarity than under his predecessor. Internal economic weakness consistently tops the list of threats to national security; international terrorism just as consistently has followed among the most important external sources of threat.

Leading government officials, including Putin himself, have argued for U.S.-Russian cooperation against international terrorism, suggesting that no one state acting alone can defeat the many networks that wind through porous borders, exporting fanatic terrorists who freely kill civilians as well as themselves. After September 11, many in Russia and at least some in the United States have argued that Washington now understands what Moscow has confronted in Chechnya all these years and what Russians experienced in 1999 when several apartment buildings were blown up, killing more than 300 citizens.

For Russia, the threat of terrorism manifests itself in conflicts and instability from the mountains of Tajikistan to the waters of the Black Sea, encompassing the countries of Central Asia and the Caucasus in a common arc of instability that arises from Russian weakness and Islamic fundamentalism. Members of Al Qaeda have been in Chechnya for several years, and Russia has had a serious and sustained encounter with radical Arab extremists on its territory. Although exact numbers have been very difficult to establish authoritatively, these networks appear to have come to Russia in the period between the end of the first Chechnya war in 1996 and the beginning of the second war in October 1999. They increased their presence during the second war and have since been able to find recruits and funnel money into Chechnya, sometimes with the help of powerful elements in the gulf.

Russia's leaders and public were quick and sincere in expressing condolences to the United States after the September 11 attack. But the Russian government went far beyond well wishes, providing intelligence about bin Laden connections and activities as well as detailed information about the situation inside Afghanistan pertaining to future military options. These behind-the-scenes actions were extremely well received in Washington and thought to represent more than token gestures of cooperation.

Yet public Russian commentary has also been tinged with a tone of self-satisfaction and self-righteousness for having fought in the front lines and borne the brunt of international terror largely alone while warning a complacent and misdirected West to heed the growing danger. There is also some grumbling in quarters of the general staff about U.S. military forces, like those in Bosnia and Kosovo, operating with live ordnance so close to Russian territory.

Now as the international campaign focuses on Afghanistan, the scene of terrible trials and past failures during the Soviet era, Russia must be prepared to cope with the potential for greater instability, Islamic radicalism, and refugee pressures in Central Asia. It is not a frontline country to conflict in Afghanistan, but its former bases are integral to the prosecution of the war and, given Russia's proximity and recent history, will not be immune to these risks.

Fifteen percent of the Russian population is Islamic and, as the birth rate of the Slavic population declines, that proportion will increase substantially. Despite its brutal war against Chechen separatists and its labeling of international terrorism as the root cause of that conflict, Russia claims not to be threatened by Islam itself—only extremism. Russia has tried for years to strike similar definitions and distinctions in its war against fundamentalist Islam–inspired terrorism that the United States is now seeking to finesse in its campaign. Yet an international conflict that sets the advanced world against poor Islamic countries and societies risks further activating an already alienated Islamic identity against Slavic, Orthodox, and European Russians. Russia's already troubled relations between the central government and ethnic regions could be complicated even more by a rise in Islamic identity. In Tatarstan, for example, both official and public concerns have been voiced about Russian support for U.S. military operations in Afghanistan that are killing innocent Muslims.

Layered over these regional concerns of poverty, religious extremism, political repression, and internal instability is a very problematic geopolitical situation. The post-Soviet territories—from Abkhazia to Kyrgyzstan—across Russia's southern borders hold critical resources and also the potential for spreading instability. Much of that landmass contains what little fertile agricultural land the country possesses and substantial portions of its industrial base. More critically, the Caspian and Central Asia are important sources of Russian, Kazakh, Turkmen, and Azerbaijani oil and gas wealth and hold the potential for other countries in the region to profit from transport routes as well. Although Russia is not as dependent on energy exports as are some of its other post-Soviet neighbors, its economic future turns on its energy exports and trade. The Russian economy cannot realistically expect growth, reform, and development over the next decade without healthy global energy prices and the ability to sell large quantities of crude on world markets.

Russia thus has a vital national security and central economic interest in both regional stability and continued access. Russia is drawn to the idea of U.S. help to eradicate the terrorist threat but not at the expense of being challenged in the region by American political, economic, and military presence. Russia needs the United States to hunt bin Laden and Al Qaeda, but to do so in a way that does not contribute to the instability and extremism already present. Russia seeks not only cooperation in achieving U.S. objectives, but partnership in defining and executing them.

This will prove very difficult, for despite the apparent commonality of U.S. and Russian interests against terrorism and the real links between bin Laden, Afghanistan, transnational terrorism, and Chechnya, there are important differences too—not least of which is an understanding of exactly who should be labeled a terrorist. Furthermore, the United States and Russia have not spent the 1990s investing in mechanisms for security cooperation outside U.S. programs to help in dismantling and securing Soviet nuclear weapons and materials. Important voices in the Russian security and military elites strongly suspect that the United States wants access to Central Asia on a permanent basis and wants to ease Russia out.

For now, these Moscow elites have lost the policy debate. President Putin's September 24 announcement that Russia would grant overflight rights for humanitarian missions in the operation in Afghanistan, and not rule out more substantial support, was a significant step. Russia will try neither to exclude the United States nor to thwart the counterterrorist mission, and it did not try to pressure its southern neighbors to refuse cooperation to the United States in terms of access and bases to prosecute its military efforts in Afghanistan. It is crucial to note, however, that the support was measured and carefully calibrated. It did not open Russia and Central Asian airspace to unlimited U.S. missions, nor did it publicly commit Russian forces to the campaign.

Finally, over the longer term, Russia and the other post-Soviet states in the region are concerned about China's role. In recent years, China has joined with Russia, Kazakhstan, Tajikistan, Uzbekistan, and Kyrgyzstan to form the Shanghai Cooperation Organization in a joint effort to combat "terrorism, separatism, and extremism" in the Central Asian region. Despite this collaboration, Russia and the Central Asian states are keeping a close watch on China's regional policy and presence. As China looks to Central Asia as a potential solution to its growing energy demand, it may become a more involved regional actor. There are clear suspicions about a rising China and what that would mean for potential competition for influence in Central Asia.

In economic terms, insofar as China becomes a market for Central Asian produce and raw materials, other states in the region, including Russia, would stand to benefit. But Russian strategists are also worried about China's contributing to the problem of Islamic fervor in Central Asia. China's Xinjiang province is viewed as a potential source of regional instability that could worsen the tendency for cross-border movements of armed groupings and opposition forces, and the Russian political elite remains ambivalent about China's regional role. An active China creates opportunities for cooperation and trade, but it also creates an increasingly powerful competitor in a region where Russia is weak. Putin's decision to cooperate with the United States was also inspired by determination to play a role in the conduct of the war and potentially balance China's rising profile—in order for Russia to have a say in regional security arrangements in the medium to long term.

The Promise and Limits of U.S.-Russian Cooperation

In the short term, the United States has received support for various limited forms of overflight and basing rights from Russia and the Central Asian countries. If U.S. operations against bin Laden and Al Qaeda remain targeted and limited, it is likely that this support will continue and even be incrementally expanded for conducting effective combat operations. Russia has also taken an active role in the resupply of the Northern Alliance. Russian reinforcement of its forces in Tajikistan is probably more related to concerns about security of the Afghan-Tajik border than to actual Russian military support in Afghanistan (and the Russian government has been consistent in at least publicly ruling out a role for Russian military forces in Afghanistan).

Basing and support for U.S. forces over the medium term will also be crucial for dealing effectively with the armed forces supporting, and supported by, bin Laden and his network. As U.S. leaders have suggested, the military campaign in Afghanistan will last for months, perhaps even years. Bases in nearby countries, from which to operate mobile forces to enter Afghan territory, will be essential. Russia itself is probably too far removed to be of effective support (though Russian bases and facilities might provide backup), but direct Russian assistance will be necessary in Tajikistan because that government is dependent on Russia. Russia's support in continuing overflight rights and a general level of political support for regional efforts will also be essential to the conduct of an effective campaign.

The second primary asset Russia can provide in the medium to long term is intelligence. Its military has long and bitter experience fighting in Afghanistan's hostile terrain, as well as ties with the Northern Alliance, which itself has fought in Afghanistan for 20 years. Closer intelligence cooperation was one of the immediate benefits of September 11; yet, the United States needs to be aware of the limits of Russian intelligence, which is not necessarily comprehensive, unbiased, or unprocessed. Russian intelligence for fighting in Chechnya, for example, has proved to be quite inadequate despite the cooperation of elements of the Chechen leadership with the government. Russian forces in Chechnya are often surprised on the battlefield, and their inability to effectively identify actual combat personnel is a contributing factor to its indiscriminate use of force and its "cleansing" operations that terrorize and kill civilians as much if not more than combatants. Thus U.S. intelligence cooperation with Russia must be careful and focused.

Issues between the United States and Russia

President Putin's September 24 statement of support for the U.S. war against international terrorism came in the face of strong objections from the military elite. His decision to embrace common interests with the United States in defeating terrorist networks was neither altruistic nor without foundation. It was, however, rooted in self-interest and in foreign policy trends developing over the past two years.

Russian foreign policy has been building cooperative relations in Europe for some time. In addition, for months before September 11, the Putin government had been pursuing membership in the World Trade Organization, a negotiated agreement on missile defense, and deep cuts in strategic nuclear forces. Putin's more pragmatic tone on NATO was apparent during the summer, when it was part of official and unofficial speculation on Russian membership as well.

If the attack on the United States and common interests in combating terrorism crystallized and gave new impetus to these trends, they did not create them from scratch. For the medium and long term, it is important to understand that the choice against competitive, zero-sum calculations was not a sudden about-face on Putin's part. Thus the bases of cooperation are more reliable than would be the case if it were merely the latest whim of Russia's leader.

At the same time, the fact that cooperation is genuinely in Russia's interest means that as the relationship develops—whether it proves to be a partnership, alliance, or the coalition of the moment—the principle supporting U.S. policy should not be paying Russia for its support but finding areas where working together can be mutually beneficial. The good news is that in several important areas cooperation with Russia can support not only the fight against terrorism but also the long-term goal of increasing Russia's integration with the West. These include economic issues, Russian relations with NATO, working to end the war in Chechnya, stemming proliferation of dangerous weapons materials, and promoting the rule of law.

Economic issues and WTO prospects. Putin's main international economic priority has been Russian accession to the World Trade Organization. Many in the Russian leadership already suggested before September 11 that, given Russia's importance to international stability, its economic dislocation following the Cold War's peaceful end and the USSR's demise, and the importance of Russia's continuing integration into the world economy, Russia should not be held to the highest standards as it negotiates accession. Although Putin has not explicitly suggested a WTO quid pro quo for Russian support for antiterrorism, he has repeatedly raised the centrality of WTO membership to his policy in speeches and meetings with foreign leaders. At a strategic level, these test balloons are to be welcomed even if the actual economic and financial details of accession will require intensive negotiations. Even with all the economic and political challenges they face, it will be better to have both China and Russia in the WTO than outside the organization feeling alienated and angry at those within.

There have been subtle signals about a further price tag for Russian support for the campaign against terrorism, and these have focused on several potential areas for greater economic relief. The Russian government has made clear that the looming humanitarian crisis around Afghanistan will overwhelm Russia's ability to cope and that it will be necessary for Russia to receive international resources for refugee relief. Russia has also increased its military support for the Northern Alliance in Afghanistan, but Putin has noted that given Russia's limited economic capacities, it would be helpful if the country received financial support for its increased efforts to bring down the Taliban. Putin has explicitly said that Russia does not expect debt relief, but if it has difficulties over the next two years in meeting its obligations to the Paris Club, he will likely expect greater flexibility in rescheduling Russia's substantial debt to international creditors.

Russia-NATO relations. Immediately after the September attacks, analysts speculated that Putin might demand a halt to NATO enlargement as a price for Russian counterterrorist cooperation. However, Putin has surprised international opinion by, if anything, softening his government's position and attitudes about expansion. Clearly, concern about NATO still lingers and plays a role in Russian calculations, and Moscow has invariably tried to steer the international action into councils where it has more sway. Russian officials have called for UN and UN Security Council approval for all operations from current military strikes to subsequent efforts at humanitarian relief and nation building. Needless to say, UN oversight would give Russia a veto. Russia proved willing, however, to work within the Permanent Joint Council to issue a message of support for a war against terrorism.

It is interesting that Russian officials for some time have reminded the West that NATO should focus on terrorism as a threat. Putin himself said that events have shown that NATO's mission should be combating international terrorism, not bombing in Kosovo. Defense

Minister Sergei Ivanov and Putin attended NATO meetings in Brussels, in a display of consultation and cooperation that starkly contrasted with Russia's cold shoulder to NATO following the Kosovo campaign.

While in Germany in late September 2001, Putin refrained from denouncing NATO enlargement plans and instead called for NATO to focus on the broadest possible enlargement as part of its evolution to the new security environment. Although he did not explicitly call for NATO to welcome Russia as a member, his choice of emphasis on encouraging broader NATO enlargement comes after many influential voices in Russia, Europe, and the United States have raised the prospect of Russia's joining the alliance.

Most dramatically, in late October 2001, the Russian government raised with NATO the idea of NATO assistance in Russian military restructuring. The dismal shape of Russia's military establishment has been one of the major factors distorting its foreign policy away from the real security challenges the country faces. The military has also persisted in focusing on the United States as a threat in Cold War terms and has been a major obstacle to military cooperation programs. Russian willingness to engage with NATO on military restructuring would be an extraordinary opportunity to overcome a major hurdle in Russia's overall cooperation and integration with the West.

Given Russia's simmering concerns that the United States will eclipse Russian influence in Central Asia, it is plausible that Putin has concluded that the way for Russia to join the United States effectively in a counterterrorist mission is by bringing Russia closer to NATO. This suggests that Russia may ultimately be more concerned about NATO's missions than its borders.

Help in ending the war in Chechnya. In September 2001, in the wake of the terror attacks, the Bush administration found itself scrambling to assemble a new, more flexible position on the Chechen war to signal its appreciation and newfound understanding for at least aspects of Russia's plight. Concurrently, Russia still finds itself stuck in a quagmire, no closer to tracking down the terrorists than it was two years ago, when the "counterterrorism" war began.

The second Russian war in Chechnya, like the first, has led to thousands of Russian military fatalities and tens of thousands of civilian deaths. The war has created large refugee populations and the type of desperate environment ideal for recruiting terrorists, and the brutal prosecution of the conflict has damaged nearly every fragile democratic institution that had developed in post-Soviet Russia. Russian and Western nongovernmental organizations have documented Russian military atrocities against civilians in Chechnya and the involvement of Russian troops in various forms of corruption. The Russian government has sought to suppress reporting that portrays the savageness of its campaign and to instead depict life there as returning to normal, never mind the rubble of what remains.

Cooperation with Russia against terrorism and concern over human rights abuses in the conduct of the war need not be mutually exclusive. The way in which the Russian military forces have conducted the current war has done more to incite extremism and terrorism than it has done to quell it. The United States should make clear that stopping the kinds of wholesale human rights abuses seen in Chechnya is part of the counterterrorism strategy.

Seeking a reasonable resolution of the conflict in negotiation with moderate Chechen nationalists could help stabilize the situation sufficiently to allow the return of refugees and relative normality. Russia should be encouraged to allow for greater international mediation efforts to help seek an end to the long-running war. Moreover, a political solution would help isolate extremist-terrorist groups that are much more militant than the overall Chechen population. This new environment would require the deployment of a small, professional antiterrorist force as opposed to the current 80,000 unpaid, untrained Russian troops.

The U.S. government and international organizations should also have a role in making sure that assistance to the region is substantial and immediately forthcoming. Chechens will have good reason not to believe assurances by the Russian government that assistance will rebuild Chechnya; very little reached Chechnya in the interwar period, and even less has reached the region since 1999. Refugees will not return unless the fighting stops and rebuilding begins, with schools, hospitals, water supplies, and other basic functions restored.

Promoting the rule of law. The international community and the United States have been permissive of Russia's noncompliance with a variety of international norms, from looking the other way on money laundering to the involvement of Russian peacekeepers in Bosnia in illicit trafficking. Yet, the corruption that runs through most public institutions in Russia makes it an ideal territory for terrorist networks. The United States should help to strengthen the rule of law in Russia—an effort that would not only combat terror but also bolster Russian democracy, enhance public safety, help steady the climate for business investment, and further the prospects for Russia's integration with the West. To pursue this goal effectively, the Bush administration should work with Congress to reverse the trend of shrinking assistance budgets for democracy promotion and institution-building initiatives for Russia.

Keeping weapons of mass destruction from falling into terrorists' hands. Part of the U.S. effort to prevent future—and potentially more devastating—terrorist strikes must be to bolster international nonproliferation and counterproliferation efforts, especially in Russia, where the largest source of dangerous nuclear, chemical, and biological weapons materials and know-how is found. This enduring threat must be tackled with newfound zeal and a sense of mutual threat to both the United States and Russia.

Specifically, the United States should work with Russia and key allies to broaden and deepen cooperation on nonproliferation and Nunn-Lugar-type programs. When looking to revitalize Nunn-Lugar and other threat reduction programs, the United States must take into account what has transpired in the past—what has worked, what has not, and why. It must also seek to expand these programs in light of September 11 and the subsequent anthrax attacks in the United States and the fears that even deadlier pathogens could find their way into terrorist hands. Specifically, U.S. leaders should urge Russia to fully disclose the size and composition of its Cold War stockpiles of chemical and biological agents—something Moscow has been loath to do for some time. The United States and others must examine ways to assist Russia in accelerating the destruction of vast stockpiles of excess biological agents, enhancing the security of stockpiles and facilities that remain, and restoring the security of Russia's borders and its export control system. The United States should also explore ways of expanding ongoing cooperation with Russia on the safety, security, and disposal of nuclear materials.

In addition, the United States should work with its European allies and Japan to increase their financial support for expanded threat reduction programs aimed at reducing the chances that chemical, biological, and nuclear weapons materials could fall into the hands of terrorist organizations or the states that sponsor them.

The debate over missile defense. Finally, although the Putin leadership remains concerned about U.S. missile defenses, American missile defense policy itself is unlikely to be a major roadblock to counterterror cooperation. The Putin leadership has long understood that Russia has little leverage over the decision. The Russian strategy has been to argue for the United States to pursue limited defenses in cooperation with other states (including Russia, but also Europe) and to move quickly on a new agreement to reduce offensive nuclear weapons. This strategy is unlikely to change. The Bush administration seeks mutual withdrawal from the treaty, and Russia has some small measure of leverage here. The Russian government will press for joint decisions on defensive and offensive arms and will seek to link them as closely as possible, and this policy objective is likely to transcend the new political realities post–September 11. Ultimately, however, cooperation over terrorism in its broadest meaning trumps the ballistic missile defense concerns. The geopolitics of Eurasia, Eurasian stability, and the challenge of terrorism are simply a higher priority than seeking to prevent the United States from freeing itself to develop an antimissile capability that is not likely to be fully realized for some time.

The post–terror agenda in U.S.-Russia relations holds out the potential of substantial strategic realignment. Rivalries and suspicions will surely continue, but aspects of the current arena, as described above, now hold the greatest prospect for true collaboration and cooperation in recent history. The urgency of the terrorist challenge and the intensified potential for partnership carry with them the distant prospect of a fundamental transformation in relations.

Looking Ahead

On October 4, 2001, the *Washington Post* reported that in the first confusing hours after the September 11 attacks, President Putin was the first foreign leader to speak with President Bush. The American president had put U.S. military forces on high alert. Putin wanted to let Bush know that Russian troops, for their part, had been ordered to stand down, avoiding a further increase of tension on an already alarming day. According to the *Post,* President Bush later recalled, "It was a moment where it clearly said to me that he understands the Cold War is over."

Bush's sentiment captured a hopeful sense that not only had one era in U.S.-Russia relations ended, but a new one might begin. It is too early to tell whether an entirely new framework for bilateral relations will bear fruit, and it is worth recalling that the expectations of policymakers in the mid-1990s never quite matched the realities of the militaries' work together. Even with Putin and Bush making the most reassuring pronouncements supporting joint efforts to combat terrorism, in the day-to-day grind, both militaries are likely to lag in their enthusiasm for each side's proposals, as they have in the very recent past. It is also important to recognize the serious differences between the two countries on issues as fundamental as who is a terrorist and how to fight such an enemy.

But whether or not the Cold War is over, clearly a new war has begun and, this time, Russia and United States—although uncertain what to call their newfound status—agree that they are on the same side.

■ ■ ■ ■ ■

Central Asia

"As far as Uzbekistan and its fight against terrorism are concerned, I would like to tell you the following. The first point is Uzbekistan grants its airspace to American aircraft and helicopters. The second point is Uzbekistan is ready to upgrade and step up cooperation between special services for the exchange of intelligence information. Uzbekistan gives its permission and gives use of one of its airfields and its facilities for the United States' aircraft and helicopters as well as for personnel employed in search and rescue opera-

tions. At the moment there is work going on on the legal document, which will formulate the mutual commitments, and obligations, and guarantees. And I would like to use this opportunity to
say that we have no secret deals, no covert negotiations with the
United States."

— *President Islam Karimov of Uzbekistan*
Press Conference with Secretary of Defense Donald H. Rumsfeld
October 5, 2001

"It is a great thing for us that we have a pact with America to fight
the terrorists . . . . The terrorists should not be allowed to exist at
all. It is time to finish them, and to bring them to ruins."

— *Ashud Otamuradov, citizen of Uzbekistan,*
as quoted in the New York Times
October 18, 2001

Before September 11, 2001, U.S. officials viewed Central Asia largely
as a potential source of new energy resources at the fracture line between Russia and the West. The region's internal tensions were seen as
being of only peripheral interest, and its ongoing struggles with Islamic extremists and various ethnic activists were perceived more
through the prism of human rights than as problems of international
terrorism.

While U.S. officials monitored the interaction among extremist and
terrorist activity in Central Asia, violent Islamic movements in Afghanistan, the Russian problem in Chechnya, and Uighur and Kazak
groups in China, such connections were given low priority. The tensions between Uzbekistan and Tajikistan on the one hand and Pakistan on the other were generally seen in terms of Afghanistan's internal problems; the fact that Pakistan was using the Taliban, Osama bin
Laden, and Al Qaeda to create a Pakistan-influenced Afghanistan and
to obtain "freedom fighters" it could use against India was not viewed
as a development that was helping to create a sanctuary for global
terrorism.

The United States did openly link bin Laden and the Taliban to the Islamic extremist threat in Kashmir and to the tensions between India and Pakistan. It also noted that terrorists trained in Afghanistan attempted to assassinate the prime minister of Bangladesh in August 2000—but again, it addressed these issues largely as regional problems and not as part of a global network. And although U.S. intelligence recognized that the Taliban and bin Laden actively supported Islamic terrorist groups in Central Asia, and the U.S. State Department—especially after 1998—provided clear and repeated warnings about the impact the Taliban and bin Laden were having on the region, the connection between bin Laden's influence in Central Asia and the threat he posed to the United States was not emphatically drawn.

It is now all too clear that the United States needs a new strategy in dealing with Central Asia—one that takes into account how terrorism in Central Asia interacts with terrorism in Russia, China, South Asia, and the Middle East. The United States must do more to ensure that regional and internal tensions in Central Asia do not create new terrorist movements that link together to become global threats. Preventing post-conflict Afghanistan from reemerging as a source of regional terrorism will be a crucial part of that effort. A careful balance will need to be struck in pursuing cooperation with Central Asian states, without condoning the repressive policies of those states against their citizens. Finally, the United States must work with key states—like Russia, China, and Pakistan—on the periphery of Central Asia to help create and maintain stability in this troubled part of the world.

The Threat of Terrorism in Central Asia

Internal problems in Central Asia are the rule rather than the exception. The collapse of the former Soviet Union resulted in relatively weak and divided states, often facing a deep schism between secular governments and resurgent Islam. Although some have the ability to exploit their energy wealth, none enjoys a modern economy or infrastructure. Their agricultural sectors are weak while their industrial sectors—many of which were tied to Soviet military production—are overspecialized.

Central Asia's governments are largely autocratic, showing little toleration of dissent, and so far have failed to shape effective programs for economic reform and growth. Strong elements, if not all, of the political oppositions in these countries have arisen from their societies' Islamic awareness, so the fight for regime control has also taken on the character of anti-Islamic repression. This, coupled with high population growth rates, exacerbates ethnic and religious tensions and is a potent recipe for the emergence of terrorist and extremist movements.

These problems have been compounded by feuding among the Central Asian states and their competitive quest for external sources of aid and power. Rivalry has been particularly intense among the states near Afghanistan. Tajikistan's mistrust and animosity toward Uzbekistan has deep historic and ethnic roots—exacerbated by Uzbek president Islam Karimov's policy of destabilizing Tajikistan and repressing Uzbekistan's Tajik minority. Kyrgyzstan resents the Uzbeks' claim to leadership of Central Asia and worries about potential manipulation of its substantial Uzbek minority.

At least at present, Central Asian terrorism and violent extremism are largely national or regional, rather than international, although terrorism in the Central Asian states has been a major issue for Russia.

Russia and Regional Counterterror Cooperation

The ongoing conflict between Russia and Chechnya has been the source of broad tensions in Central Asia and in the Islamic world—increasing the radicalization of internal Islamic populations and encouraging violence and spreading instability throughout Central Asia and the Caucasus.

At the same time, it also has helped spur regional efforts to combat terrorism that may be a basis for improved cooperation with U.S. antiterrorism programs. Russia has provided steadily increasing counterterrorism and counterinsurgency warfare aid and equipment to the Central Asian states. It also led the members of the Commonwealth of Independent States (CIS) in creating a CIS-wide counterterrorism center in Bishkek in December 2000, directed by General Boris Mylnikov, the former first deputy director of the Russian federal security services department for combating terrorism. The center has begun developing a CIS-wide database on terrorism.

Through the Shanghai Forum, Kyrgyzstan, Kazakhstan, Tajikistan, Russia, and China have also cooperated in antiterrorist activities. Kazakhstan and Kyrgyzstan reached separate bilateral agreements on counterterrorism with China in June 2000, and Uzbekistan signed bilateral agreements with Turkey, China, and Italy in October and November 2000. Uzbekistan decided to formally join the Shanghai Five in June 2001, and the group then changed its name to the Shanghai Cooperation Organization.

Kazakhstan

Kazakhstan has not been the scene of extensive terrorism. It remains under the tight control of President Nursultan Nazarbeyev—although he has tolerated some peaceful political opposition and dissent. There has been tension between Kazak and Slav, however, and clashes with violent elements in the minority Uighur community. Troubles with the Uighurs have led Kazakhstan to cooperate with China in suppressing Uighur nationalists and extremists and possibly have led it to largely ignore China's treatment of its Kazak minority.

The spread of Islamic sects has been a subject of increasing concern to the government, although it has blocked the creation of terrorist cells. The radical Islamic Hezb-e Tahrir Party active in Kyrgyzstan and Uzbekistan also has a presence in southern Kazakhstan. This helped spur Kazakhstan to join the Shanghai Cooperation Organization and to support the creation of a joint Central Asian rapid reaction force to deal with armed Islamist extremists.

Kyrgyzstan

Kyrgyzstan's relatively tolerant approach to moderate Islamic groups has helped to limit the emergence of more militant factions. A major regional crisis erupted in Kyrgyzstan in August 1999, however, when members of the Islamic Movement of Uzbekistan (IMU) crossed the border from Tajikistan and took four hostages. The militants released their captives without incident and retreated to Tajikistan but returned in a larger force later that month and seized 13 more hostages, including four Japanese geologists, their interpreter, a Kyrgyz Interior Ministry general, and several Kyrgyz soldiers. IMU militants continued to arrive in subsequent weeks, numbering as many as 1,000 at the incursion's peak.

The State Department estimates that the IMU's goal was to infiltrate Uzbekistan and destabilize the government. The militants first demanded safe passage to Uzbekistan; additional demands called for money and a prisoner exchange. Uzbekistan refused to allow them to enter, leaving Kyrgyzstan's ill-prepared security forces to combat the terrorists with Uzbek military assistance, Russian logistic support, and negotiation assistance from other governments. The militants' guerrilla tactics enabled them to maintain their position in difficult mountainous terrain, frustrating the Kyrgyz military's attempts to dislodge them. Observers speculated that only the approach of winter forced the militants to retreat into Tajikistan, where negotiators were able to facilitate an agreement between the IMU and Kyrgyz representatives.

The militants on October 25 finally released all hostages except a Kyrgyz soldier they had executed. Kyrgyzstan released an IMU prisoner, but Kyrgyz and Japanese officials denied Japanese press reports that they had paid a monetary ransom for the hostages' release. Although an agreement stipulated that all IMU militants would leave Tajikistan after the hostage crisis, some IMU militants remained in the region—and further hostage incidents have taken place involving foreign nationals.

Tajikistan

Tajikistan in the 1990s was mired in a bloody civil war that killed tens of thousands and shattered its already weak economy. Only with Russian military support was the regime of President Emomali Rahmonov able to prevail in 1997. He then created a coalition government with his former Islamic opponents.

Russia controls the Tajik-Afghan border, and Russia's 201st Motorized Rifle Division patrols the border and provides frontline defense against incursions and infiltration from Afghanistan. Russia and Tajikistan jointly operate the Dushanbe airport, and Russia controls the military base and Kulyab 30 miles from the Afghan border. The Tajik government has resisted Taliban and extremist Islamic penetration of its territory, but because it is in a coalition with the former

Islamic opposition, its room for action or alignment against Islamic groups is constrained.

Despite Russian military presence, much of the country is not under government control and harbors myriad clan-based, Islamic militant and drug-trade groupings that compete, coexist, and overlap. A new movement called the Islamic Movement of Tajikistan (IMT) was formed in mid-2000. Some fear an alliance between the IMU, the IMT, and the United Tajik Opposition (UTO) has planned to try to take control of the strategic Ferghana valley. There were a number of clashes between government and rebel forces in the summer of 2001, and arms caches were found that belonged to these three groups.

The Russian forces—some 25,000 altogether—are themselves reported to be corrupt and facilitate the drug trade from Afghanistan that has been a major resource for the Taliban. (Afghanistan's opium crop totaled 3,656 metric tons in 2000 and accounted for 72 percent of the world's illicit opium. Since 1997, more than 96 percent of the Afghan opium-poppy crop has been cultivated in Taliban-controlled areas.)

Turkmenistan

Turkmenistan has not been the scene of major terrorist activities, possibly because it did more than any other regional state to create good relations with the Taliban. It has made some efforts to limit Taliban and other extremist movement through the country, but its neighbors have still accused it of being a sanctuary for the Afghan regime. Ironically, it may be the most vulnerable to the effects of U.S. military operations in Afghanistan because its long border with Afghanistan is a relatively level desert, in contrast with the mountainous terrain on the Uzbek-Afghan and Tajik-Afghan borders. This has meant that extremist fighters cannot use the territory for cover and protection, but it also means that Turkmenistan is likely to be the easiest destination for refugees.

Turkmenistan has cooperated with Russia, the CIS, and China in dealing with known Islamic extremists, but Russian border troops left the country in 1999, and Turkmenistan did little at first to create effective border controls. It has since cooperated with Uzbekistan in controlling its borders and strengthened the controls on its border with Afghanistan in 2000. Nevertheless, its weak armed forces and internal security forces did not pose a major barrier to movement across its borders before September 2001.

Uzbekistan

Uzbekistan has a largely secular, autocratic government that has had serious problems with Islamist extremists while having to deal with some 250,000 Afghan refugees of Uzbek ethnicity on its soil. The main source of violent opposition and terrorism is the Islamic Movement of Uzbekistan (IMU)—a coalition of Islamic militants from Uzbekistan and other Central Asian states opposed to Uzbek president Islam Karimov's regime. Its goal is the establishment of an Islamic state in Uzbekistan. Its recent propaganda includes anti-Western and anti-Israeli rhetoric.

The IMU has operated out of major camps in Afghanistan near Kunduz and Mazaar-e Sharif and in Tajikistan. It is believed to be responsible for five car bombs in Tashkent in February 1999 that killed 16 persons and wounded more than 100 others. The government arrested or questioned hundreds of suspects about their possible involvement in the bombings. Ultimately the government condemned 11 suspects to death and sentenced more than 120 others to prison terms.

The IMU also instigated two hostage crises in Kyrgyzstan in the fall of 1999. The State Department reports that its militants probably number in the thousands. Most are believed to be in Afghanistan, though some may have remained in Tajikistan. The IMU receives support from other Islamic extremist groups in Central Asia, and its leadership broadcasts statements over Iranian radio.

Uzbekistan expelled IMU leaders such as Tahir Yoldash and Jumma Namangani to neighboring countries in 1999. However, its crackdown against extremism has punished hundreds of Uzbek Muslims whose only "crime" is to worship outside the control of the state. Since 1998, Uzbek authorities have sentenced large numbers of young men to prison for being Islamic extremists—often without connecting them to any violent acts. It did offer an amnesty against what it called Wahhabism in April 1999, but required young men to admit their guilt in studying "nontraditional Islam" abroad.

Uzbekistan has accused its neighbors, especially Tajikistan, of helping extremists and of allowing the IMU to operate on its territory. It
has accused Kyrgyzstan of leniency toward Islamist groups. These ac-
cusations have uncertain validity, however. The IMU has been closely
connected with the Taliban, which has actively opposed the Tajik government because of its support of the Northern Alliance in Afghanistan. Northern Alliance leader Ahmed Shah Massoud—murdered by
suicide bombers shortly before September 11—was a Tajik hero.

During 2000, IMU forces infiltrated its fighters into the mountains
of the Surkhandar'inskaya Oblast in the south, which led to clashes
with Uzbek military forces that drove them into Tajikistan. Tahir
Yoldash and Jumma Namangani were sentenced to death in absentia.
The IMU's continuing military infiltration and attacks helped lead
the United States to designate the IMU as a foreign terrorist organization on September 25, 2000.

These factors also prompted Uzbekistan to obtain extensive Russian aid in improving its security forces and training its troops for
mountain warfare. It joined the Shanghai Cooperation Organization
in mid-2001.

U.S. Requests and the Likely Regional Response

In the short term, the United States has received support for various
forms of overflight and basing rights from the Central Asian countries. A joint U.S.-Uzbek statement released October 12 underscores
that cooperation "includes the need to consult on an urgent basis about
appropriate steps to address the situation in the event of a direct threat
to the security or territorial integrity of the Republic of Uzbekistan."
The joint statement also says that the two countries "commit ourselves
to eliminate international terrorism and its infrastructure."

Basing rights in Central Asia could prove essential as the campaign
progresses. U.S. officials have emphasized repeatedly that the United
States is not going to be able to eliminate Al Qaeda's training bases,
support camps, and personnel by bombing alone. They have also made
clear that the United States has no interest in occupying Afghanistan.
Thus the United States will need bases in nearby countries from which
to operate mobile forces that will, over a period of months and maybe
years, enter Afghan territory in a sustained effort to destroy the ter-

rorist network's resources and infrastructure. Pakistan may be the primary location for such bases, but Central Asian states can be valuable as well—and Russian support and assistance will be necessary both directly (as in Tajikistan) and indirectly.

An important component of the regional strategy will have to be restricting, if not ending, the drug trade that has helped finance the Taliban and bin Laden's network. The countries in the region have not been effective toward this end, but they lack the resources to more capably police their borders and to provide incentives for the professionalization of Russian and local border guards. The United States will need to work with Central Asia to end its role in the terrorists' drug trade.

The other major asset Central Asia can provide to the campaign against terrorism is intelligence. The military forces of all the countries in the region have long and unhappy experience with combat in Central Asian terrain—not only as a result of the Soviet Union's war in Afghanistan but in coping with the conflicts of the 1990s. In addition, the countries in the region have close ties and long experience with the Northern Alliance, which itself has fought in Afghanistan for 20 years.

A necessary caution is in order, however. Although Russia and the Central Asian countries may currently have better human intelligence in the region than the United States, that intelligence is not necessarily comprehensive, unbiased, or unprocessed. Thus the value of intelligence cooperation for the United States is conditioned by two factors: the more primary the intelligence, the better; and effective human intelligence will depend not only on Russian sources but on Uzbek, Tajik, Turkmen, Pashtun, and other local residents who have joined the battle against extremists. If the operation becomes perceived as the West against all Islam, this crucial support from secular, moderate citizens may erode.

Indeed, one of the concerns expressed by many countries, particularly those in the Islamic world, is that U.S. military operations in the region will stir up greater instability and misery for the people who live there. Effective humanitarian assistance will be crucial for sustaining broad support for the U.S. campaign. The United States must negotiate now with the states of Central Asia to provide them the resources and support they need to welcome and provide for refugees—

and to distinguish legitimate refugees from terrorist infiltration. Large relief efforts in Turkmenistan, Uzbekistan, and Tajikistan are likely to be as important to the campaign's success as military assets per se.

Beyond this short-term support to cope with the effect of military operations, Central Asian governments are already beginning to talk about the need for substantial development and financial assistance to cope with the conditions of backwardness and poverty that help to fuel extremism. Given the authoritarian cast of the governments, they will also seek to minimize political or economic conditions on such assistance.

Certain countries in the region may also seek military assistance. Uzbekistan has been pressing the United States for modern equipment to deal with the IMU and to distance itself from reliance on Soviet military stocks. It is unlikely that Tajikistan or Kazakhstan will move as strongly to obtain U.S. military assistance, given their closer ties to Russia, but they may argue for limited materials related to border security (Tajikistan) and air support (both Tajikistan and Kazakhstan). And if indeed the Turkmen border becomes flooded with refugees, that country will need substantial support as well.

Other areas for cooperation may emerge as time goes on—for example, the agreement reached in October 2001 for the United States to help Uzbekistan remove large quantities of anthrax from a Soviet-era germ-warfare test site on its territory.

Key Areas for Attention and Action

There are no magic solutions to the internal tensions in the region, or to the problems raised by the tensions between many regional regimes and Islamic activists. There are, however, two keys to U.S. success in fighting terrorism in Central Asia.

The first is an engagement strategy with each country that not only creates a strong counterterrorism team in each U.S. embassy, but that also focuses on the long-term political and economic development of each state and demonstrates an active American concern for the welfare of Central Asia's people. The United States cannot "fix" Central Asia, any more than it can "fix" the structural causes of terrorism in any other part of the world. Nor can it avoid, as the sole superpower and leading secular economic power in the world, becoming the inevitable target of extremists and ultraconservatives. The United States can, however, prove that it cares—by making visible efforts to help Central Asia progress and working to lift the lives of the people of each state even as it strives to crush terrorism.

The second key is to avoid creating any form of a new Great Game in Central Asia. Difficult as it will be to juggle the different interests involved, the United States must work with China, Russia, India, Pakistan, and the Islamic nations of the Middle East to create a common effort to bring regional stability. This will mean recognizing Russian and Chinese interests in the region, and sometimes it will involve difficult trade-offs between counterterrorism and human rights issues in these countries that will be a continuing test of American diplomacy. Regardless, there will be no simple way to deal with these issues, and this is a matter of sustaining a U.S. effort over decades, not years.

There are eight other areas where the United States needs to take action to shape an effective regional strategy toward counterterrorism.

First, Russia will be key to any successful coordinated regional counterterrorism effort. The United States must seriously rethink its past emphasis on low-level competition and trying to create Central Asian buffer states in the former Soviet Union. It may be possible to develop a far more cooperative effort in dealing with extremism without sacrificing U.S. interests. This could involve U.S. support of the CIS counterterrorism initiative—perhaps U.S. observer status in this organization—and even finding some way to create a bridge between the United States, Russia, China, and the Central Asian states that links the CIS and the Shanghai Cooperation Organization.

Second, the United States must recognize that success will depend heavily on the stability of post-conflict Afghanistan, the influence of Iranian hard-liners' interest in Central Asia, and relations between India and Pakistan. The roles of Iran, Pakistan, and India will be as important in ensuring that Central Asia does not become locked into some new form of Great Game as those of Russia and China.

Third, the United States should reevaluate its present energy and pipeline policies to see if they can be recast in terms of regional cooperation that involves China and Russia while still providing commercial opportunities to U.S. and other Western firms. Creating a common interest in what may be the region's key near- to medium-term source of income and in overall energy infrastructure, can both tighten

U.S.-Russian-Chinese cooperation in counterterrorism and focus on an important area of regional development.

Fourth, the United States needs to create both regional and bilateral programs to deal with the special problems of energy security from the wellhead to U.S. ports. One possibility to deal with the economic and political side of the issue is the Saudi concept of a permanent organization in the region to maintain an importer-exporter dialogue. More broadly, however, the United States must systematically examine the vulnerability of the region's energy production and export facilities and the need for improved defenses against terrorism and asymmetric warfare; and the United States must work with nations to reduce key vulnerabilities and weaknesses.

Fifth, as in virtually every other part of the developing world, the United States should review both its own foreign aid program and its approach to shaping the aid policies of international organizations and should work to link its aid policies in Central Asia to its efforts on counterterrorism and extremism. There is a clear need for a new focus in aid efforts and for giving them new visibility. More effective, more visible development assistance can help counter the ideas that the United States and the West are hostile to Islam and that they do not care about the future of the peoples in the region.

Sixth, the United States should build on the work already accomplished by USCENTCOM and U.S. Central Command and U.S. European Command to provide stronger military assistance efforts focused on the military aspects of counterterrorism. Greatly expanding the International Military Education and Training (IMET) program would be cost-effective for reaching large numbers of regional military personnel. As in other parts of the world, the United States should also explore whether new forms of IMET and other training programs are needed to develop regional counterterrorism expertise.

Seventh, the United States should explore where such cooperation in Central Asia can be expanded to include a larger role for NATO European states. If the struggle in Afghanistan creates a better climate of cooperation—as it may well do—the United States should treat such cooperation as a potential bridge to more lasting action. It should also be said in this context that the United States need not always take the lead. Supporting European and Russian efforts as partner, not as leader, might do much to improve relations and defuse charges of American arrogance.

Eighth, the United States should pay careful attention to linking its counterterrorism and counterproliferation efforts in the region. The flow of technology and expertise out of Russia through Central Asia presents a constant low-level risk that will require continuing attention.

More broadly, the United States cannot afford a strategy of illusions in Central Asia any more than it can in the Middle East. Throwing money at the region will not address its underlying economic problems. Trying to impose U.S. values and norms on Central Asia will at best founder and at worst create an anti-American, anti-Western, and anti-secular backlash. The United States should encourage economic reform, along with targeted aid, trade agreements, and other measures designed to build up the private sector and spur international investment. It should continue to work, along with nongovernmental organizations, to strengthen the rule of law and democratic institutions. But it should also accept that the economic, political, and social problems the region confronts will take at least a decade to remedy— and that the will to change must come from within Central Asian societies themselves.

■ ■ ■ ■ ■

The Caucasus

"The unremitting defamatory campaign that has been mounting in the Russian media for several years now . . . is clearly designed to trigger the spread of military hostilities onto Georgian territory and to apply blunt pressure on our government and change the course of our independent foreign policy."

— *President Eduard Shevardnadze of Georgia*
Harvard University
October 3, 2001

"It is becoming absolutely clear that either the Georgian leadership does not control the situation on its own territory, or that it is manipulating terrorists to its own ends."

— Defense Minister Sergei Ivanov of Russia
October 9, 2001

The Caucasus region—surrounded by Iran, Russia, Turkey, and the Caspian Sea—is a strategic transit corridor from Central Asia to Europe. Since the fall of the Soviet Union, the United States and Russia have vied for influence over this region and its vast energy resources— oil reserves that could be as high as 200 billion barrels. The countries of the Caucasus region have grown used to relying on the United States to protect them against Russian aggression. But now, with the possibility of U.S.-Russia rapprochement in the common fight against terrorism, some in the Caucasus fear their region's interests will be superseded.

At the same time, the Caucasus states may find an increased opportunity to cooperate with the United States. In addition to providing their airspace for potential overflights, they can provide critical intelligence on the ground. Hence, in addition to being energy-producing and -transit countries, the countries of the Caucasus have a chance to become relevant in enhancing regional security.

Stability in the Caucasus will continue to be critical for U.S. interests. First, uninterrupted transport of Caspian oil and gas will be increasingly relevant—especially given uncertainty over the reliability of Persian Gulf supplies as the campaign against terror unfolds. Second, the region is crucial for military communication lines from Central Asia to Europe. And third, instability in the Caucasus could permit the mountainous and conflict-ridden territory to become a preferred hideout for terrorists, posing a huge risk to the whole region.

Yet the United States must confront the worrisome, growing anti-American tendencies in the Caucasus. The governments of the Caucasus have little legitimacy owing to rampant corruption, including at the top levels of the government. Average people, who had hoped to enjoy the benefits of their countries' "joining the West," have observed instead increased poverty and injustice. Although citizens blame the governments for their deepening misfortune, they are infuriated by the perception of close U.S. ties to their leaders. Saudi Arabia's radical Wahhabis have increased their activity in the Caucasus over the past several years, often exploiting these feelings of frustration, injustice, and even hopelessness. Crime, kidnappings, and attacks against Westerners have been on the rise, especially in Georgia.

Clearly there is tremendous tension among these dynamics, and tough compromises will need to be made. The challenge for the United States over the next year will be management of its potentially conflicting relations with Russia and the Caucasus region. The challenge for the Caucasus region will be to maintain the delicate balance in its relations with its giant neighbor to the North as well as internally.

The Terrorist Threat in the Caucasus

The people of the Caucasus have for decades, time and again, rebelled against Russian authority. In the 10 years since independence, several rebel groups of different ethnic and religious backgrounds have carried out operations not only against Russia but also against each other. And although Russia characterizes the threat it perceives as tied to Islamic fundamentalism, Russian policy has directly contributed to the growth of radicalism, and possibly even terrorism, in this region.

The rebellious Chechens are the chief targets of Russian anger and antiterrorist efforts. Russia has twice waged war against the Chechens to prevent them from seceding from the Russian federation. Chechens humiliated the Russian military in the first war, which ran from 1994 to 1996. So far, Russia has been unable to declare success in the second war, which began in 1999.

Although Chechens are regarded by some in the Caucasus as brutal for their methods, they also have garnered sympathy for having taken on the Russians for so long. They enjoy strong financial backing from some radical Islamist groups from the Middle East, with the bulk of the money coming from Saudi Arabia. Russians claim that Osama bin Laden's network trains and finances some of the Chechen rebels. Following September 11, Russia has been using the term "international terrorists" in reference to Chechens—a clear attempt to build a case for the international coalition to go after the Chechen rebels.

Of the three Caucasus countries, only Georgia has borders with Chechnya. Georgia also has had the most problems with controlling its borders and preventing the penetration of Chechen rebels, Islamic mujahhedin, and possible terrorists. Chechen rebels have found refuge on the Georgian side of the Russian-Georgian border—the Pankisi gorge. A September 18, 2001, Russian Foreign Ministry note, or rather ultimatum, to Georgia described Pankisi gorge as a "logistical base of support for international terrorists," and on October 11, the Russian Duma passed a resolution condemning Georgia for harboring Chechen terrorists.

At the beginning of the second Russian-Chechen war in 1999, Georgia took in thousands of Chechen refugees and placed them at the border region, where thousands of Kists—Georgian citizens of Chechen origin—already lived. Consequently, when then-president Boris Yeltsin asked Georgian president Shevardnadze to use bases in Georgia to mount attacks against the Chechens, Shevardnadze did not agree for fear of being dragged into a war. Now that Moscow has decided to target the Chechens, Georgia is at the center of Moscow's antiterrorism efforts.

Georgia also lacks control over Abkhazia, the separatist region in Georgia's northwestern corner, bordering Russia. It is believed that Russia trained and sent some Chechens to fight against Georgians in Abkhazia during the 1992–1993 war. One of the Chechen fighters was Shamil Basayev, who later became one of the leaders of Chechen rebels fighting against the Russians.

In fact, after September 11, some in Georgia may have helped about 300 Chechens to move from the Pankisi gorge to Abkhazia to help fight against Abkhaz separatists. In early October 2001, a UN helicopter was shot down over Abkhazia, local clashes resumed, and Russia and Georgia started accusing each other of fomenting instability. The Georgian parliament passed a resolution to get rid of the Russian peacekeepers in Abkhazia but, given that the Georgian army is not strong, it is unclear who might replace the Russian forces to maintain relative stability there. The challenge for Georgia is to restrain emotions and not provoke a Russian reaction.

Unlike Georgia, Armenia has military cooperation with Russia and also has had the fewest problems internally with terrorists. Oil-rich Azerbaijan, for its part, faced the risk of several bin Laden associates trying to operate on its territory and recruit Azeri locals in 1998. With cooperation from the CIA and FBI, the Azeri leadership managed to extradite these terrorists. Since President Putin took office in Russia, Azerbaijan has even extradited Chechen rebels in order to show Russia its cooperation on antiterrorism.

U.S.-Caucasus Cooperation in the Antiterrorism Campaign

The Caucasus region offers the United States some important strategic assets—in particular, overflight access for Afghanistan-bound warplanes taking off from the Incirlik air base in Turkey. The United States asked Armenia for, and was granted, permission to use its airspace in retaliation against Afghanistan. Azerbaijan has offered its territory for refueling and landing of American jets. Georgia has also offered the United States full use of its airspace and military bases in the campaign against terrorism.

Yet the significance of the Caucasus region in the months ahead is not so much how it can help the United States, but whether it will become the "price" for Russia's own cooperation. Since the United States declared war against global terrorism, Russia has built a case that Georgia needs to cooperate with Russia to ensure tighter border security and to stop harboring Chechen terrorists, especially those who may have links to Osama bin Laden's network. Failing that, Russia, as some there have indicated, might enter Georgian territory to go after these men, who are part of the "global terrorism" problem. The growing concern is that no matter what the Georgians do now, Russia may use going after terrorists as a pretext to exert more military and political pressure on Georgia and eventually the entire Caucasus region.

Even worse, individual military commanders at the Russian-Georgian border may take matters into their own hands—with or without permission from Moscow. Some of the hard-liners still have not forgiven President Shevardnadze, who was a key player in both the demise of the Soviet Union and the reunification of Germany. There have been several assassination attempts. Hard-line elements resent Georgia's close relations with the West and are always on the lookout for opportunities to destabilize Georgia. Now they may have found one.

In the weeks immediately following September 11, Georgia tried to secure unequivocal U.S. support against potential Russian aggression, which President Shevardnadze received during his trip to Washington in early October. The danger is that some in Georgia may try to exploit U.S. support and use deniable cooperation with the Chechens to challenge the Abkhaz, which would inevitably draw in the Russians. Such a gamble would only lead to further conflicts throughout the region.

The Road Ahead

There are a number of steps the United States should take to enhance cooperation and promote stability in the Caucasus—in support of the ongoing campaign against global terrorism and as part of broader U.S. strategic concerns.

First, U.S. authorities must continue stressing a clear red line to Russia. Although sustaining Russian cooperation in the war against terrorism will require a degree of U.S. flexibility and compromise, the price of that cooperation cannot be a free hand in Georgia. Moreover, Georgia should not become an excuse for Russian military failure in Chechnya. The U.S. administration needs to continue sending firm signals to Russia at the highest levels that antiterrorism cooperation in Central Asia and against the Taliban by no means translates into a free pass for Russian actions in Georgia and the broader Caucasus. President Bush needs to outline clearly to President Putin the international political and economic costs of aggression in the Caucasus. U.S. leaders should also engage European allies in furthering stability in the Caucasus.

Second, the United States must impress on President Shevardnadze the urgency of containing the Chechens in Georgia. To succeed, he needs to make an immediate and serious effort to combat corruption as well as improve socioeconomic conditions and the rule of law in Georgia. Clear progress is needed to strengthen the country internally and to prevent terrorists with religious, ethnic, or ideological messages from gaining adherents. The challenges Shevardnadze faces are daunting—but the dangers of inaction are worse. A weak Georgia will leave itself, and by extension the whole Caucasus, extremely vulnerable to being dragged into a terrible regional conflict.

Third, the United States should provide increased border security assistance to the Caucasus region, especially Georgia. For its part, Georgia needs to explore new options, ranging from asking for help from the United States, Turkey, or NATO under the Partnership for Peace program, to finding new ways to cooperate with Russia on combating terrorism.

Fourth, for the United States to be effective in helping to enhance stability and security in the Caucasus, section 907 of the Freedom Support Act needs to be repealed. Section 907 limits the type of support that can be provided to Azerbaijan for securing its oil and gas pipelines that transport oil produced by American companies. Because of section 907, the United States cannot undertake many security-enhancing operations in Azerbaijan and Armenia that are essential in the long-term fight against terrorism.

Fifth, the United States should provide increased regional assistance for combating organized crime and corruption. The FBI center that will start operating in Georgia in 2001 could function as a regional clearinghouse—focusing on, among other things, tracking down and choking off international financing for terrorists in the Caucasus region.

Sixth, the United States and Russia should work together on promoting stability in the Caucasus. There is a possibility that terrorists, bombed out of Afghanistan, would try to make their way into the rugged mountains of the Caucasus. The implications are terrifying: resumption of regional conflicts on ethnic or religious grounds and attacks on oil and gas pipelines. Given the high stakes Russia and the United States share in preventing such developments, leaders should seize opportunities to enhance cooperation in a number of areas, such as a renewed commitment to the resolution of regional conflicts.

Finally, all governments with a stake in this region, corporations that are making long-term investment decisions, and the people of the region need clear signs from U.S. leaders that the United States will help maintain stability in the Caucasus. A new initiative to include Armenia into the east-west energy corridor would also help reduce some tensions by giving Armenia a stake in regional stability and moving it closer to the West. Given its stated goal of a long-term fight against global terrorism, the United States also needs to rethink the type of military, economic, and political engagement it is willing to support in the Caucasus.

In March 1998, Deputy Secretary of State Strobe Talbott testified before Congress: "In our view, the South Caucasus has the potential to become one of the real success stories of the next century. The area is blessed with both human and natural resources. History, however, has not been so kind." As the new century begins, the future of the Caucasus remains uncertain. It is fair to say that U.S. policies in the coming months and years will play a major role in determining whether the Caucasus region emerges as a stable, pro-U.S. ally or sinks into further chaos, with implications far beyond its boundaries.

■ ■ ■ ■ ■

Africa

"The worst hit area will be Africa, where in addition to the possible increases in poverty of 2–3 million people as a result of lower growth and incomes, a further 2 million people may be condemned to living below $1 a day due to the effects of falling commodity prices. Commodity prices were forecast to fall 7.4 percent on average this year, and are likely to fall even more as a result of the events of September 11. Farmers, rural laborers, and others tied to agriculture will bear a major portion of the burden. Travel and tourism represent almost 10 percent of merchandise export for the region and are also likely to be disrupted. The 300 million poor in Sub-Saharan Africa are particularly vulnerable because most countries have little or no safety nets, and poor households have minimal savings to cushion bad times. About half the additional child deaths worldwide are likely to be in Africa."

— *"Poverty to Rise in Wake of Terrorist Attacks in U.S."*
World Bank News Release
October 1, 2001

"On September 11, I shook my head . . . . Where have you people [the U.S. government] been? We've been chasing these people for years, but were we really listening? Were we paying attention? We were asleep, we were sleepwalking. Why weren't we better prepared? . . . I very sincerely believe that the bombings in Nairobi and Dar es Salaam were in training for what happened at the World Trade Center."

> — *Unidentified juror*
> *at the trial of four terrorists convicted of bombing*
> *the U.S. embassies in Kenya and Tanzania in 1998*
> *"Morning Edition," National Public Radio*
> *October 19, 2001*

Africa's Apprehensive Friends and Skeptics

Fully one-third of Africa's 700 million citizens are Muslim. Yet, for the vast majority, radical Islam has had minimal resonance. Indeed, Africa is replete with enduring traditions of tolerance and coexistence among Muslim and non-Muslim communities, most notably in Ethiopia, Ivory Coast, Senegal, Kenya, Mozambique, and South Africa. There are stark exceptions: Militant variants of Islam have taken root in Sudan under the National Islamic Front (NIF), Somalia, the breakaway Shari`a states of northern Nigeria (Nigeria's Muslim population comprises half of its 120 million citizens), and communities in South Africa's Cape Town and Durban. But Africa's chronic wars and broken states have thus far not been associated with political Islam.

Nonetheless, most of Africa's Muslims, like their non-Muslim African brethren, are impoverished global have-nots who live in acute— and worsening—marginality that invites local sectarian and interethnic strife, despair, and anti-Western resentment.

During the past decade, frustrated Muslims living under corrupt, malfunctioning governments across the Horn of Africa, West Africa's Sahel zone, and areas of southern Africa have looked increasingly to Islamic agencies funded by Saudi and other Persian Gulf donors to provide education, health, social welfare, and security. This weakly

understood phenomenon has often stabilized communities and enhanced the local legitimacy of Muslim social activism. At the same
time, it has provided the means to mobilize anti-U.S. and anti-Western sentiment and has created havens for militant actors who endeavor
to act in solidarity with Al Qaeda. From the outside, differentiating
among legitimate social welfare action, rhetorical posturing, and support for international terrorism is a formidable challenge.

Although in the immediate aftermath of September 11 many African leaders expressed heartfelt sympathies and condolences, the reaction in many African states was strikingly muted and ambivalent. Some
feared that the inexorable U.S. military campaign might harm Muslim civilians (and outrage domestic constituencies), invite further attacks on U.S. facilities in Africa that would wound and kill many Africans, and, reminiscent of the Gulf War a decade earlier, set back the
continent economically and trigger cuts in international development
assistance.

The toned-down reaction also reflected a skepticism of America, if
not outright anti-Americanism in some corners, that follows from
America's swift disengagement in 1993–1994 from Somalia and pas-
sivity in early 1994 in the face of the Rwanda genocide; a perception
of U.S. detachment from Africa's profound needs (many in Africa continue to argue that the Bush administration is woefully indifferent to
Africa, contrary indications notwithstanding); and the perceived U.S.
bias in favor of Israel in the Middle East crisis. As U.S. military action
commenced in early October 2001, virulent anti-U.S. sentiment surfaced in select hot spots—including from Muslim cleric leaders in
coastal Kenya, religious leaders and official media in Khartoum, and
rioters in Kano in northern Nigeria who played upon acute, preexisting sectarian tensions and whose violence quickly left more than 120
dead and threatened to spread to several major urban centers.

A notable exception to Africa's muted response was the reaction of
a small set of powerful African leaders with comparatively strong, established ties to the United States. Nigerian president Olusegun
Obasanjo swiftly backed U.S. and British operations against Al Qaeda
and the Taliban regime. South Africa, Ethiopia, Kenya, Uganda, and
Angola, among others, soon followed, with frequent emphasis on the
need for hard evidence and targeted retaliation. Most significant,
Senegalese president Abdoulaye Wade, whose country is 95 percent

Muslim, rallied the leaders of Nigeria, South Africa, Botswana, Ghana, Mozambique, and Tanzania to issue a joint statement on September 18 in London condemning the September 11 attacks as "monstrous and demented" and pledging "to work tirelessly with all relevant international forums to strengthen international cooperation, cut off financial support to terrorists, and dismantle terrorist networks wherever they exist."

Interestingly, though, when Wade hosted a summit in Dakar in mid-October, the results fell far short of his original ambitions and reaffirmed Africa's fundamental hesitancy about identifying too overtly with the U.S. antiterrorism campaign. Only ten African heads of state appeared (of whom the majority did not represent regional powers). Instead of endorsing a major new pact on terrorism, participants temporized—issuing a declaration calling for a meeting of the Organization of Africa Unity (soon to be transformed into the African Union) to monitor developments and evaluate implementation of the existing African Convention against Terrorism. That desultory initiative was adopted in 1999 following the bombings of the U.S. embassies in Dar es Salaam and Nairobi, signed by 36 of Africa's 53 states, and subsequently ratified by only 3.

The hope of Wade and others for a fresh African pact that expressly aided the U.S. campaign was prompted in part by fear that the emerging war in Afghanistan would lay waste to their New African Initiative (NAI), adopted by the Organization of African Unity and praised by the G-8 summit in Italy in July 2001. The NAI seeks a "new global partnership" to end Africa's marginal position in the world economy, spur trade, and reduce poverty. African political and economic reforms would be reciprocated by increased external developmental and financial flows from the West along with expanded debt relief and trade and investment opportunities.

To some degree, an unspoken quid pro quo underlay Wade's antiterrorism initiative: African leaders would actively endorse the United States and United Kingdom in the international antiterrorist campaign and, in return, would expect substantial American and British support of the NAI at the G-8 summit in Calgary in July 2002. The message to U.S. policymakers is clear: Robust U.S. support for the elements of the NAI, tailored to bring substantial benefits to Senegal, Nigeria, and the other core states overtly willing to pledge their partnership with the United States in battling international terrorism, will be essential to building an enduring coalition within Africa.

The September 11 Shift

Before September 11, the U.S. administration's priorities in Africa were HIV/AIDS; trade and investment; conflict resolution in Sudan, Zimbabwe, and the Democratic Republic of the Congo; and building bilateral ties with regional powerhouses Nigeria and South Africa. The centrist, pragmatic policy featured much continuity with the Clinton administration and built self-consciously on bipartisan congressional initiatives.

After September 11, a new element was added as the U.S. focus swung dramatically onto unfinished business in the Horn of Africa. Overnight the possibility arose that the full roster of U.S. terrorist concerns with Sudan might be resolved and that the newly appointed U.S. envoy, former senator John Danforth, might emerge an authoritative and influential force in the quest for a negotiated peace settlement to end Sudan's 18-year internal war.

Suddenly, too, the United States had to think anew about long-forgotten Somalia and the vast empty spaces of its interior that provide haven to the armed Islamic militants known as Al-Itihaad. The United States had to quickly weigh what unilateral actions it might take in the future to contain and eliminate Al-Itihaad's terrorist practices and how this new imperative might redefine the bilateral U.S. ties with Somalia's neighbors, most notably Kenya and Ethiopia. The latter might involve new forms of intelligence and military collaboration, joint efforts to upgrade frontier security, and improved controls over banking systems. Kenya and Ethiopia were quick to register their sympathies and commitment to cooperate extensively with the United States, although the specifics are still to be defined. Each harbors hopes of closer security ties and future favorable action by the United States in granting debt relief and supporting new funding facilities from the World Bank and International Monetary Fund.

Nigeria and South Africa are vital to U.S. interests in Africa. Each is a populous, regional hegemon that in the 1990s shed dangerously repressive forms of rule to embrace new democratic forms of governance. Each has massive sway, in economic and security terms, upon its surrounding neighborhood. The leaders of both nations play a prominent role globally in rallying developing states for better terms of trade, debt relief, and enhanced political authority in international forums. Not surprisingly, each is at the forefront of the NAI.

Yet, post–September 11, the United States has had to begin acknowledging that both of these nations contain an implicit terrorist threat that will figure more prominently in bilateral relations over time. In Nigeria, the United States will have to confront the reality that President Olusegun Obasango's rule, two-and-a-half years after the return of democracy, has failed to curb gross corruption and bring about any new national dialogue to mitigate acute regional, religious, and ethnic tensions. One result is Christian-Muslim polarization that has inspired 11 breakaway Islamist republics in the North and, just prior to September 11, violence that left more than 2,300 dead in the major northern city of Jos alone. In South Africa, Washington will have to engage gingerly with Pretoria to deal more frontally and effectively with Al Qaeda cells.

U.S. diplomatic and intelligence capacities in Africa have been steadily depleted over the past decade and indeed have been further degraded since September 11 as substantial personnel and resources have been diverted. Diplomatic personnel dedicated to Africa were slashed by 15 percent in the mid-1990s, at the same time that intelligence personnel were cut back more than one third, and fully a dozen aid missions were shuttered. These developments predictably translate into a weakened grasp of quickly evolving trends on the ground (the United States currently has at best weak insight into northern Sudan, northern Nigeria, and central and southern Somalia) and create acute vulnerabilities that can be brutally exploited—as was seen in the August 1998 bombings of the U.S. embassies in Dar es Salaam and Nairobi that left 224 dead and more than 4,000 (the vast majority Kenyans) seriously injured.

In this context, as the U.S.-led war against terrorism unfolds, U.S. citizens and embassies, along with innocent Africans, could easily be the targets of new violence. Both Secretary of State Colin Powell and Assistant Secretary for African Affairs Walter Kansteiner have called attention to weak U.S. capacities in Africa and the imperative to redress them. Progress thus far has been slow. Future results will require sustained, high-level attention.

The Terrorist Threat in Africa

A few select places in Africa potentially offer refuge and popular support for radical Islam: Sudan, central and southern Somalia, northern Nigeria, and South Africa—most important, Cape Town. These are sites where one may see violent anti-U.S. reaction as the United States moves against Al Qaeda and the Taliban. They are also locales where Al Qaeda operatives in flight may attempt to relocate. Anti-U.S. violence may also flare in Kenya, Mali, Ivory Coast, and Tanzania (especially Zanzibar). Libyan ruler Mu'ammar Qadhafi has a history of terrorist activities in Africa that has been in remission in recent years, at the same time that he has launched an expansive campaign to win political allegiances across Africa. With the exception of his efforts to influence the Sudanese government, Qadhafi's actions have seldom intersected with actions by radical Islamist elements.

The most serious and complex challenge lies in the Horn of Africa. Sudan is one of seven countries on the State Department's list of state sponsors of terrorism and since 1989 has been a self-proclaimed Islamic republic. Twelve years hence, its Islamic revolution is exhausted and widely discredited, internally and externally. From 1991 until early 1996, Khartoum provided a home to Osama bin Laden; it may still provide a haven to members of the Al Qaeda network. Al Qaeda business linkages reportedly persist in the banking sector and export-import and agricultural commodity enterprises. Al Qaeda enjoys an unknown level of popular support within northern Sudanese society. The radical Islamist leader, Hassan Turabi, who sought for himself and the National Islamic Front government a leading international role on behalf of political Islam, has been detained for most of 2001, and demonstrations of support in northern Sudan on his behalf have been modest but persistent.

Since first moving against Turabi at the end of 2000, President Umar Al-Bashir has attempted to moderate his external image and rehabilitate his external linkages. Internally, he has shown no proof of willingness to pursue a negotiated peace settlement to Sudan's 18-year internal war and has persisted in aerial bombardments of civilian humanitarian sites in southern opposition areas and in egregious human rights abuses.

Al-Itihaad, the radical Islamist movement assembled out of mujahhedin veterans, operates in the stateless space of central Somalia, in the midst of other Muslim charities that enjoy considerable popular legitimacy for the social welfare they have created. Supported by wealthy Saudi elements, Al-Itihaad was named in September 2001 by the Bush administration as one of the 27 entities supporting Al Qaeda. Its banking net extends into Kenya and the Persian Gulf and relies extensively upon the *hawala* system. In the early 1990s, Al-Itahaad dominated the port of Merca and the inland center of Luc. At its peak, it has been able to muster upward of 3,000 armed fighters, has staged operations in Ethiopia and Kenya, and has coordinated activities with terrorist entities operating out of Khartoum. Its power and personnel have declined significantly at each of the three points during the past five years when Ethiopian forces have intervened massively inside Somalia.

Sudan and Somalia's neighbors will be essential to consolidating gains and containing persistent threats. However, before September 11 the Horn of Africa had entered a period of heightened instability that easily could worsen.

The highly lethal Eritrea-Ethiopia border war (more than 100,000 dead during 1998–2000) ended in December 2000 with the Algiers accord and the subsequent insertion of 4,000 UN blue helmets. Yet, in 2001, Ethiopia and Eritrea both entered a period of unprecedented instability within their respective ruling cliques. An internal putsch almost overturned Ethiopian president Meles Zenawi in the first half of 2001; a hard-line reaction against the Algiers accord left the authoritarian Eritrean government of Isaias Afewerki in place. Most recent and alarming was the arrest, in mid-September, by the Eritrean government of 11 senior Eritrean officials on charges of treason along with a continued crackdown on students and journalists. Since then, Eritrean president Afewerki has also threatened to pull out from joint UN peacekeeping mechanisms.

Kenya is essentially bankrupt and warily edging toward national elections at the end of 2002 that may replace President Daniel arap Moi (in power since 1978). The most recent IMF/World Bank mission to Kenya refused to resume any funding facilities. Djibouti could be easily overwhelmed by violent developments in Somalia.

Nigeria, where 50 percent of the 120 million citizens are Muslim, could see a deepening rift along ethno-religious lines. In the 11 self-proclaimed Islamic states of northern Nigeria, authority rests with governors linked to the northern military power base that plundered Nigeria under Sani Abacha and saw its influence collapse, much to its surprise, with Obasanjo's electoral triumph in 1999. These governors have successfully consolidated their positions through an aggressive critique of Obasanjo's failure to curb corruption and decentralize authority as well as his close alliance with the West. There is a great deal of favorable sentiment toward Al Qaeda in the North and easy, unregulated flows of finance, people, and commodities linked to external Islamic networks.

Al Qaeda cells exist in Cape Town and Durban, and Al Qaeda has been affiliated with two Cape Town movements—People against Gangsterism and Drugs (Pagad) and its associate, Qibla. Pagad launched a bombing campaign in Cape Town in 1998 that included American targets. Both Pagad and Qibla are on the official U.S. list of terrorist organizations. Although only an estimated 2 percent of South Africa's population is Muslim, that figure is growing as proselytizing efforts reach beyond the Asian population to the mixed race and black African communities. The South African government has been too ill-informed and ill-equipped to bring effective controls upon radical Islam within its borders.

In sum, as the campaign against global terrorism unfolds, several flash points in Africa will merit special attention. First, Al Qaeda elements and sympathizers may seek refuge in central or northern Somalia, in league with Al-Itihaad. That could invite a strong U.S. military response and possibly new cross-border interventions by Ethiopia. Second, there is a risk of a violent anti-U.S. reaction in northern Sudan that could derail the ongoing U.S.-Sudan dialogue on terrorism. Third, Al Qaeda's influence could expand in northern Nigeria, possibly contribute to a violent anti-U.S. reaction there, and potentially create a crisis of governance for President Obasanjo. A fourth threat, perhaps more modest than the others, would be terrorist assaults on U.S. interests and others in Cape Town and Durban, which would test the mettle of President Thabo Mbeki and reshape the contours of U.S.-South African relations.

U.S. Approach to the Region: Spotlight Sudan

Sudan has been and will remain center stage in the post–September 11 campaign against terrorism. First, Sudan's special knowledge of Osama bin Laden's operations is of urgent importance to Washington. Indeed, Sudan and the United States have been in a bilateral dialogue on terrorism since the spring of 2000. But Sudan also has fresh experience of being on the wrong side of the U.S. antiterror equation—with the U.S. cruise missile strike against the El-Shifa pharmaceutical plant following the August 1998 bombings of U.S. embassies in Nairobi and Dar es Salaam.

In this context, it is hardly surprising that Sudan swiftly became a priority focus of U.S. investigators immediately after September 11— or that the Sudanese foreign minister lost no time in expressing condolences and Sudanese president Al-Bashir announced that Sudan had broken all links to bin Laden and would cooperate fully in identifying those responsible for the attacks. If Washington concludes that Sudan deserves to be placed in the "enemy" box, Khartoum would suddenly find itself locked into a new and dangerous pariah status, an outcome it understandably fears.

In the first week following the September 11 attacks, Khartoum worked assiduously to avoid this outcome. In fact, Sudan may be the most dramatic example of U.S. pressure and dialogue producing a major turnaround and a singular success in forging a new international coalition against terrorism. According to U.S. officials, Sudan has responded cooperatively "across the board" to U.S. requests for specific information and actions, making an "implicit" offer of access to military bases and overflight rights and providing names and locations of individuals in the Al Qaeda network as well as access to Sudan's banking system.

The United States, for its part, has been quick to respond. Khartoum's newfound willingness to cooperate has drawn an overt acknowledgment from Secretary of State Colin Powell and other U.S. officials. Senior Republicans in the House of Representatives, under pressure from the White House, have postponed indefinitely debate on the Sudan Peace Act, a bill that would have bolstered support to the southern rebels in Sudan and punished foreign companies doing business in the country. And, on September 28, the United States acquiesced to a UN Security Council decision to lift sanctions on Sudan that were imposed in April 1996 after an assassination attempt on Egyptian president Hosni Mubarak.

Nonetheless, these developments represent only the opening phase of a new and urgent U.S.-Sudan dialogue on terrorism. More probing requests will come from Washington, and new, disturbing information on past and present practices may surface, strengthening the ever-louder argument of hard-line U.S. activists that Khartoum shares an enduring commonality of purpose with bin Laden and should there-fore be in the first tier of target states. Within Sudan, there is also the risk of a violent radical Islamic reaction to increasing cooperation with Washington, which might erode President Al-Bashir's room for maneuver.

The United States will almost certainly push for further measures, including expanded efforts to identify and renounce all remaining ter-rorist ties, a willingness to ship known terrorists abroad to face justice, and enduring cooperation in international intelligence and law en-forcement efforts. Beyond terrorism, it will be critically important that Washington not ease pressure on Khartoum to improve its deplorable human rights record, enhance humanitarian access, cease aerial bom-bardment of civilian sites, and return in earnest to the negotiating table to seek a just peace settlement to Sudan's war. There is a clear risk that Khartoum may conclude that cooperation on international terrorist issues has won it space on internal war issues and that Wash-ington will be distracted by other, more pressing matters in South Asia.

Outside of Sudan, U.S.-African bilateral dialogues on terrorism have been minimal. In the wake of the 1998 bombings, there was enhanced U.S. cooperation with Kenyan investigators and law enforcement offi-cials. There has been some modest progress on anticrime collabora-tion in South Africa, such as FBI training of a special new anticrime unit, the Scorpions, but there has been little focus on the common threat of terrorism, except with regard to individual violent incidents. South African intelligence services remain hostile to collaboration with the United States; both apartheid-era holdovers and veterans of the African National Congress who were trained and assisted by the So-viet Union remain suspicious of U.S. intentions.

U.S. counterterrorist activities in Nigeria and other West African states have been negligible. American disengagement from Somalia, dating from the spring of 1994, has been virtually complete. The United States has been largely reliant in this period on intermittent monitoring conducted by its embassies in Addis Ababa and Nairobi.

The Road Ahead

Post–September 11, Africa matters to U.S. interests in significant new ways, both good and bad. The challenge now is to manage this new dimension of U.S. foreign policy—identifying programs, resources, and people to handle its requirements and integrating it effectively with inherited policy priorities.

There is now greater recognition in the United States that Africa's institutional weaknesses, autocratic governance, and economic marginality pose serious threats to U.S. security interests. In the near to medium term, these vexing factors are only expected to worsen; in the midst of a global economic downturn aggravated by the aftermath of September 11, the World Bank predicts the worst impact will be felt in Africa. Africa's exceptional circumstances give rise to porous borders; places to hide; opportunity for bribery; and a ready, aggrieved audience—all of which could significantly benefit a terrorist network seeking advantage in Africa. Openings already exist in Sudan, Somalia, northern Nigeria, and South Africa that must be addressed systematically. Other openings could appear in several other African settings and quickly merit priority attention.

At the same time, an important subset of Africa's leaders appears genuinely ready to work with the United States in the battle against international terrorism. Their commitment is linked—in a direct and timely way—to their quest to reverse Africa's decline through new reciprocal partnerships with Western powers. If managed carefully and aggressively, so that credible new U.S. commitments are put in place and African partners show tangible progress in economic and political reform, including respect for human rights, the United States may realize genuine gains in the next five years and consolidate ties with an enduring, core African coalition. Where this opportunity is mishandled, the United States could easily find itself in intimate alliances—reminiscent of the Cold War—with unsavory and ultimately unreliable partners.

The aftermath of September 11 also brings greater recognition that Africa matters to the United States as an important and growing source of nongulf oil. Currently, the Central/West African basin accounts for 17 percent of U.S. oil imports and more than 80 percent of U.S. trade and investment in Africa. In coming years, U.S. investment, production, and imports in and from this region are expected to rise steadily. This factor has its most powerful impact on U.S. bilateral ties with Nigeria and Angola; in these two instances, future debate over U.S. policy will continue to center on the best means to curb corruption, promote tolerance, broaden developmental benefits from oil, respect human rights, and resolve long-standing internal armed conflicts. The challenge will be to balance U.S. policy on the difficult internal reforms required of Nigeria and Angola with the short-term goals of securing new oil flows and expressions of political allegiance.

Looking ahead, several key actions will be critical to an effective U.S. counterterrorism policy in and with Africa.

A first priority will be to demonstrate U.S. resolve in bringing multiple enhanced benefits to those states that are both reliable antiterrorist partners and credible economic and political reformers. That will mean overt, strong U.S. diplomatic leadership to support the NAI. It will mean deepening and broadening the trade and investment opportunities of the Africa Growth and Opportunity Act (AGOA); increasing debt relief and facilities through the IMF and World Bank; steadily enlarging U.S. commitments to battle HIV/AIDS so that they surpass $1 billion within a year; and otherwise doubling bilateral assistance in support of economic growth, conflict reconciliation, and the rule of law. It will also mean elaborating a serious energy strategy for Africa, one that focuses on building management capacity, transparency and accountability, power generation, and regional integration of energy grids. It is less important, post–September 11, that the United States embark on wholly new initiatives than that it bring to scale existing policy priorities that require substantially higher commitments to be effective and earn credibility and leverage in Africa.

A related second priority will be to elaborate a Horn of Africa strategy that better engages the Horn's Muslim communities; consolidates recent gains in bilateral terrorism cooperation with Khartoum; effectively contains and reduces Al-Itihaad's influence in central and southern Somalia; clarifies strategy vis-à-vis the Somaliland government in northern Somalia and the fledgling Transitional National Government in Mogadishu; and spells out how the United States will pursue—versus compromise—its enduring interests in democracy, respect for human rights, economic reform, and just peace settlements to the region's internal wars.

The latter considerations will be especially important in the U.S. strategy to end Sudan's war and in U.S. relations with regional partners such as Kenya and Ethiopia. As Ethiopia and Kenya inevitably turn to the United States for new forms of security cooperation to address threats in Somalia (and perhaps also assist with ending Sudan's war), the United States should have a medium-term strategy at hand. Washington should not desist, for example, from pressing aggressively for curbs on Kenyan governmental corruption and for an orderly and transparent national electoral transition into the post-Moi future. Nor should it shy away from engaging Addis Ababa on full implementation of the Algiers peace accord (ending Ethiopia's interstate war with Eritrea) and genuine democratic and economic liberalization. At all points, Washington will need discipline and caution in addressing the threat of instability in Asmara and Addis Ababa and the breakdown of the Algiers accord—and Washington will have to be realistic in judging what Kenya and Ethiopia are capable of delivering in their dangerous neighborhoods.

A key element to the U.S. Horn strategy will be accelerating administration efforts, led by former senator John Danforth, to bring the Saudis, Egypt, Kenya, and key Europeans behind a concerted multilateral effort to achieve a just negotiated peace settlement in Sudan. The United States should also expedite the restaffing of the U.S. embassy in Khartoum (suspended since early 1996).

A third priority will be defining a strategy for effectively incorporating U.S. counterterrorism concerns into bilateral relations with Nigeria and South Africa. Corruption and sectarian violence in Nigeria, along with uncontrolled movement of people, goods, and finances into the North, remain complex, volatile issues. The same can be said of Pagad and Qibla—two antigovernment, anti-Western organizations in South Africa. These are subjects that U.S. diplomacy will have to approach gingerly and flexibly, and where new forms of outreach and leverage will be essential. As in the case of the Horn, a challenge will be to integrate this new dimension of U.S. foreign policy with preexisting priorities.

A fourth priority is bolstering U.S. human capital and resources—significantly strengthening U.S. intelligence, diplomatic, and foreign assistance capacities in the Horn and West Africa, the latter with special reference to northern Nigeria. Much more effort will also be needed to understand Libyan president Qadhafi's expansive policies in Africa. Overall, this effort will require a multiyear strategy to recruit and train additional career personnel.

Fifth, the Bush administration will need to accelerate its planned review of U.S. security assistance to Africa—for example, the Africa Crisis Response Initiative and Operation Focused Relief—to configure these programs to strengthen military counterterrorist capacities in Kenya, Ethiopia, Nigeria, and South Africa. These programs will need to incorporate substantial nonmilitary assistance to strengthen border controls, law enforcement, and financial controls. There will be a need for substantial increases in flexible economic support funds to at least $300 million a year.

All these measures can muster bipartisan support from Congress if the administration extends itself in a concerted fashion. All can win support in Africa if U.S. policies meaningfully and powerfully answer the needs of serious African reformers and if they are accompanied by systematic, early consultations. The challenge for U.S. leaders is to summon sufficient political will to back good intentions with the resources necessary for success. Half-hearted or cheap measures will be a formula for policy failure and erosion of U.S. credibility—an outcome that could potentially be more costly down the road.

■ ■ ■ ■ ■

East Asia

"I told [President Bush] what I wish to tell you tonight: that we mourn with America, that we share your grief and outrage, and that we strongly condemn terrorism in all its forms and manifestations.

Indonesia is ready to cooperate with the United States and other civilized countries on counter terrorism."

> — *President H. E. Megawati Soekarnoputri of Indonesia*
> *U.S.-Indonesia Society, Washington D.C.*
> *September 19, 2001*

"The United States is a terrorist nation. They are terrorists who must be driven from the face of the earth."

> — *Al-Habib Muhammad Rizieq bin Hussein Syihab*
> *leader of the Islamic Defenders Front*
> *during a protest at the U.S. embassy in Indonesia*
> *October 9, 2001*

Before September 11, 2001, East Asia was ready for the spotlight, preparing to take center stage in U.S. strategic calculations and focus. President Bush's first visit to Asia was on track for late October, including an Asia-Pacific Economic Cooperation (APEC) meeting in Shanghai and subsequent summits with China, Japan, and South Korea. The 2001 Department of Defense Quadrennial Defense Review to be released at the end of September was to call for an enhanced focus on Asian security, reflecting recognition that it was the site of the three most serious strategic challenges in the world—on the Korean Peninsula, across the Taiwan Strait, and in nearby South Asia (India and Pakistan). Regional allies and friends warmly anticipated this new wave of serious U.S. attention and broad implicit support.

Following September 11, East Asian nations now rightly expect that the spotlight will be diverted—and East Asia's growing political, economic, and military challenges once again pushed to the wings. President Bush canceled his summit meetings in Beijing, Tokyo, and Seoul although he proceeded with APEC. And, while East Asian leaders understood these cancellations, the symbolism of the U.S. president's accelerated departure and his single-minded attention to the counterterror campaign at the economic forum underscored their concerns over America's shift of focus.

Sustained U.S. engagement in the region is critical to the confidence of allies and friends and to the success of regional initiatives—from economic recovery to the challenges of Korea and Taiwan. Now, East Asians fear, the United States will direct the bulk of its resources to the counterterrorism campaign and its political, emotional, and intellectual energies to the clear and present challenge to the U.S. homeland.

Still worse for East Asia, U.S. attention is wavering even as the events of September 11 exacerbate regional economic troubles. East Asia's export-driven economies rely heavily on the U.S. market. The loss of consumer confidence in the United States and the expected rise of buy-American patriotism in the aftermath of September 11 will further depress East Asian economies and worsen internal conditions in countries already weakened by Japan's stagnation.

Finally, East Asian leaders are wary about how the United States will conduct its counterterrorism operation. Many have their own restive Islamic communities with local grievances and sympathies for suffering Islamic brethren in Afghanistan and elsewhere. Others provide open support for the United States and may become targets for terrorism should the United States misstep. These leaders recognize the critical role the United States plays in the stability and security of the region but now, in an increasingly volatile international environment, fear a backlash both externally and internally for their associations with the United States.

Threat of Terrorism in East Asia

East Asia is not considered the front lines of international terrorism. Yet it is surely in the wings. On the one hand, East Asia offers some of the world's most advanced societies and steadfast U.S. alliances. On the other, the region could be the next seedbed for the growth of radical Islam.

The most sensitive area is maritime Southeast Asia, where Islamic identity is an essential part of the political establishment in key countries. More than one in five of the world's Muslims live in the region. Indonesia boasts the world's largest Islamic population, and Malaysia has taken a leading role internationally in promoting Muslim interests. Although largely secular political societies, Southeast Asian nations are particularly concerned about the growing radicalization of Islamic political identity, potentially upsetting delicate internal racial and ethnic balances and threatening social cohesion.

Cells of militants trained and financed by Osama bin Laden have already appeared in the region, making Southeast Asian leaders increasingly anxious about the growth of radical Islamic political movements inside and across their borders. Although not created by bin Laden, these radicals have benefited from his assistance to pursue agendas of secession and instability.

In the Philippines, for example, funds from bin Laden have been linked with the Abu Sayyaf group, an armed radical Muslim movement that has perpetrated kidnappings in seeking an independent Islamic state in the southern province of Mindanao. Ramzi Yousef, mastermind of the 1993 World Trade Center bombing, had ties to the group, whose members have reportedly trained with the Taliban.

In China's western province of Xinjiang, a series of violent Uighur separatist groups, some with links to Afghanistan, have been seeking to carve out an Islamic state of East Turkestan, causing the Chinese government to elevate terrorism to the top of its security agenda. China attributes bus explosions in Beijing and bomb attacks in Xinjiang to these groups.

In Indonesia, the Free Aceh Movement, dedicated to establishing a strict Islamic state in the Indonesian province at the archipelago's northwest tip, has been associated with veterans of the Afghan struggle. The Lashkar Jihad, which some have linked with Osama bin Laden, has recruited several thousand volunteers in the Moluccas to join in a bloody Muslim-Christian war during the past three years.

So far, militant Islamic groups in Indonesia and elsewhere have been linked only to local objectives. The degree to which they are coordinated is uncertain. However, many governments that in the past turned a blind eye to some of the commercial activity and money laundering of extremist Islamic groups, including bin Laden's organizations, are taking a second look. The use of Islamic charities and Islamic banks in such nations as Singapore and Malaysia to funnel terrorist financing is receiving fresh attention as a key aspect of an international terrorist network.

Even if they are localized, violent Islamic movements pose profound challenges to the political and economic stability of nations and the region. The political, economic, and social transition occurring in Southeast Asia—particularly in Indonesia where instability is rife and police control negligible—make the region a serious potential breeding ground for radical Islam.

Priorities, Partners, and Pitfalls

The United States should conduct its antiterrorism campaign in East Asia with an eye toward long-term sustenance of its overall strategic approach to the region: maintenance of strong bilateral alliances; robust military presence; management of tensions, particularly on the Korean peninsula and across the Taiwan Strait; sustainable economic development; and democratization.

First, the United States should press for practical and concrete support from its regional allies. Japan in particular must play a visible role to avoid the damage caused to the alliance during the Persian Gulf War, when Japan's reluctance to assist the U.S.-led coalition with anything but money raised serious concerns among the U.S. policy elite and public alike about the relevance of the alliance to core U.S. security interests. Japan's prime minister has led his legislature to make bold reforms in Japan's domestic law to allow for Japanese military support in intelligence sharing, mine clearing, refugee assistance, and other logistical and financial aid. Although the law places a one-year time limit on authorizing this assistance, the United States should not underestimate the exceptional commitment it represents, the precedent it sets, and the contribution it makes to the sustainability of the alliance in the long term.

Japan should also be encouraged strongly to serve as a close partner in addressing defense against other nontraditional security challenges of the future—particularly cyber security and theater missile defense. Heightened cooperation to address attacks on an increasingly digitalized domestic infrastructure and on research and development for missile defense will play a central role in shaping the U.S.-Japan alliance in a new age of international vulnerability.

South Korea and Australia have offered armed forces, airports, seaports, and military bases to the campaign. It is likely that both nations will provide all requested assistance to the U.S.-led effort. From South Korea the United States may request relatively little—possibly medi-

cal and transportation assets—but the symbolism of such contributions should be welcomed as testaments of allied solidarity and moral
support.

Soon after September 11, Australia invoked the mutual defense
clause in the ANZUS treaty, akin to NATO's invocation of Article 5.
Australia has authorized use of its military personnel and equipment
for counterterror operations. In addition to its contributions to the
antiterrorism campaign, Australia may help fill key gaps in U.S. military roles internationally should U.S. armed forces be diverted elsewhere. Australia has fought shoulder-to-shoulder with the United
States in every war over the past century, and its well-equipped military forces are highly trained as U.S. partners.

China

The fight against terrorism presents new opportunities for and challenges to U.S. relations with China. The United States and China have
a common interest in fighting Islamic extremism and international
terrorism, given recent national experiences. Over the past several years,
China has joined with Russia, Kazakhstan, Tajikistan, Uzbekistan, and
Kyrgyzstan to form the Shanghai Cooperation Organization in a joint
effort to combat "terrorism, separatism, and extremism" in the Central Asian region—focusing on the Taliban and, by extension, Osama
bin Laden.

As a member of the UN Security Council and a major regional
political force, China's active participation is an important factor in
the effectiveness of any international effort. The United States should
certainly solicit Chinese cooperation in diplomatic initiatives, international law enforcement, and intelligence sharing. China should also
be encouraged to provide monetary support for refugee and other
humanitarian assistance in South Asia, as needed.

In pursuing the antiterrorism campaign over time, China will likely
consult closely with the Shanghai Cooperation Organization—but will
follow the lead of Pakistan, with which it has developed a deep political, economic, and military relationship. China's long-term strategic
interests lie in maintaining strong relations with Pakistan—to both
counterbalance Indian influence in South Asia and safeguard its relationship with the Muslim world. As long as Pakistan remains on board

the U.S.-led effort, China will not make waves. But should Pakistan come to oppose U.S. initiatives, China will likely jump ship as well.

China has indicated its interest in leveraging its antiterrorism assistance against support for its own fight against internal "separatists." The Chinese government will insist that the United States at least look the other way in its fight against the Uighurs of Xinjiang. As time passes, China may also seek to apply the term separatists to Tibet and Taiwan.

Although every reasonable effort should be made to minimize disagreement between the United States and China, the U.S. government should be careful not to sacrifice other core interests, such as Taiwan security and human rights, at the altar of antiterrorism. China has as much to gain from combating terrorism as does the United States. The United States should support Beijing's fight against Muslim extremism. However, the United States should be careful to distinguish its support so as not to endorse indiscriminate abuses of China's Muslims or other minorities in this campaign. Opposing such abuses and promoting Chinese tolerance of Islam (and other religions) overall would serve as further evidence that the international campaign is not a war against Islam. The United States should balance these sensibilities as integral elements of a nuanced and comprehensive long-term counterterrorism campaign.

Southeast Asia

Leaders in Indonesia, Malaysia, and the Philippines have tried in the past, with only modest success, to combat the rise of radical Islamic groups through a range of political, economic, and military means. Following September 11, the United States will require increased intelligence and surveillance cooperation throughout Southeast Asia as well as the development of effective internal security organs to monitor the potential growth of radical networks.

It is crucial that the United States promote the establishment of new financial transparency measures to root out funding of terrorist networks among Muslim banks in Malaysia and Singapore and selected Islamic charities. Failure to help detect and destroy these suspected financial links should result in sanctions against those institutions and public condemnation of those nations.

The United States should also reinforce to Singapore and Thailand the importance of continued access and other military support functions as the campaign against terror proceeds. Singapore has agreed to provide unqualified assistance despite concerns about its Muslim minority and neighbors with large Muslim populations. Longtime ally Thailand, with similar concerns including a violent Muslim-led movement on its southern border, nonetheless has expressed its strong support for the U.S.-led counterterrorism campaign—reaffirming it is prepared to render "all possible assistance" to the effort, including military facilities upon request.

The United States should be particularly sensitive to Indonesia's and Malaysia's delicate internal situations. Although Indonesian president Megawati courageously expressed her country's support for the international campaign against terrorism, she will continue to be politically vulnerable to domestic Islamic opposition and to other radical factions that will seek to gain adherents as the campaign unfolds. The negative reactions of the Indonesian and Malaysian governments to the U.S. military campaign in Afghanistan in fall 2001 illustrate the limits to public support from those countries. The United States should not be surprised if Indonesia and Malaysia continue to avoid public association with visible U.S. military action. Nonetheless, the United States should still demand quiet, substantive support behind the scenes.

The United States will need to tread carefully, however, in the event it reengages the Indonesian military in the antiterrorist effort. Lingering resentment over the perceived connection between U.S. military assistance to Indonesia and past abuses of the military under former president Suharto may ultimately exacerbate Indonesian anger toward the United States—especially in the absence of real efforts to bring Indonesian officers to account for their past.

Of all Southeast Asian nations, the Philippine government has responded perhaps most dramatically by offering not only impassioned verbal support but also U.S. military access to the former U.S. bases at Subic Bay and Clark—an extraordinary turnaround a decade after the Philippines drove the U.S. military from its soil. The United States should pursue such offers, not only in the interest of the antiterrorism effort but also to promote further military reengagement with the Philippines and facilitate America's military reach in the region over the longer term. U.S. intelligence agencies should also work more closely with their Filipino counterparts to learn more about the extent and nature of Abu Sayyaf's association with bin Laden. The two governments should also coordinate their responses to any terrorist threats from the group.

As it engages Southeast Asian governments, the United States must take pains not to be seen as serving any particular political faction or opposing the growth of legitimate Islamic political parties that are functioning within the democratic process. The more the United States can demonstrate that it is committed to democratic processes and norms as a legitimate channel for the expression of moderate, popular Islam, the more it can defuse the perception of U.S. meddling in domestic affairs and of a war against Islam itself.

Five Areas for Attention and Action

Going forward in East Asia, the United States needs to pay attention to and act in five key areas. First, the United States should press for all available assistance, particularly from allies, as substantive and symbolic reflections of broad support for the antiterrorism campaign. It should require robust intelligence cooperation and law enforcement from all nations, as well as logistical support for U.S.-led operations from regional allies in particular. All nations must be pressured strongly to maintain international efforts to freeze assets and to take other actions stanching financial flows to terrorist organizations. The United States should also request financial support from the more advanced nations of the region, particularly Japan, Australia, South Korea, Singapore, China, and Taiwan. That said, U.S. requests for support should recognize the different levels of assistance nations may in practice provide.

Second, Indonesia and Malaysia should be included in any international antiterrorism campaign. The involvement of the two leading Islamic nations of East Asia will bolster credibility for the cause, particularly among East Asian countries. Overall, the United States should recognize that the ability of Indonesia and Malaysia to openly support U.S.-led actions will depend on the nature of those activities and whether they are perceived as opposing Islam or exacerbating political tensions within their societies.

Third, the United States should pay priority attention to helping Indonesia secure internal stability. The success of moderate political Islam will ultimately prove the best antidote to radical Islam. Massive corruption, collapse of government institutions, ethnic conflict, and lack of effective internal policing are only some of the challenges facing President Megawati's new government as she sets out to rehabilitate Indonesian society. The United States should lead an emergency assistance initiative, employing international financial institutions and others, to help alleviate conditions in the country.

In addition, the United States should promote a constructive political settlement in Aceh, professionalization of the Indonesian armed forces, and law enforcement training to help address lingering irritants within Indonesian society that undermine stability.

Fourth, the United States should press the Association of Southeast Asian Nations (ASEAN) and the ASEAN Regional Forum (ARF) to focus on terrorism. Asian multilateralism on security issues has traditionally been weak. In the aftermath of the Cold War and the regional financial crisis, the 10-member ASEAN lost its cohesion and direction. Combating terrorist networks that may be developing within their societies could serve as a unifying mission.

Likewise, the 23-member ARF, heretofore an unwieldy and impractical vehicle for addressing regional security matters, is nonetheless an appropriate venue for a regional approach to terrorism. The United States should promote establishment of a special ARF subcommittee on terrorism that would facilitate information sharing and other relevant cooperation. The ARF chair should serve as a more assertive and sustained public voice in East Asia for focusing and sustaining attention on counterterrorism. The United States should also urge the ARF to revise its consensus requirement for taking action, which has led to stasis in ARF decisionmaking. And the United States should reinforce prior initiatives from Thailand and the Philippines that sought to soften the prohibition against "intervention" in other countries' internal affairs.

Finally, the United States should make special efforts to reassure the region in word and deed that the U.S. strategic approach and commitment to East Asia remain unchanged. Given the continuing questions surrounding Korea, the Taiwan Strait, the rise of China, regional economic development, and other matters, East Asia's fundamental importance to the United States is as critical as ever. U.S. leaders must proceed with plans to focus greater attention and resources on East Asia. And the United States must take a proactive role in addressing the region's economic challenges through active bilateral engagement with Japan, China, and others, as well as multilateral engagement in forums such as APEC.

In the end, the United States will require the assistance of all East Asian nations in the campaign to fight global terrorism. These nations in turn will continue to look to the United States to maintain its essential commitment to the security of an Asia-Pacific region that remains among the most dynamic and potentially unstable in the world.

■ ■ ■ ■ ■

The Americas

"[B]oth our governments share a great project, a fully democratic Western Hemisphere that grows in prosperity and trades in freedom. Some have described the century that just passed as the American century. Now we look forward. We have a chance to build a century of the Americas . . . ."

— President George W. Bush
Remarks at arrival ceremony
honoring President Vicente Fox of Mexico
September 5, 2001

"Century of the Americas: Missing in Action?"

— Headline
washingtonpost.com
September 27, 2001

On September 5, 2001, a relaxed, upbeat President George W. Bush welcomed Mexican president Vicente Fox to the White House. The friendship and genuine, easy rapport between the two former governors seemed to reflect a new era in U.S. relations with the Americas. President Bush had come to office pledging to put the Western Hemisphere front and center in his foreign policy. His first foreign trip had been to Mexico, where he visited Fox at his ranch. His first multilateral meeting was in Quebec City, at the Summit of the Americas. He has supported the Colombian government in its difficult struggle for peace. He has been committed to opening and expanding trade from Alaska to Argentina. He and Fox have launched unprecedented negotiations on border and immigration reform.

Yet, just days after the Mexican state visit ended, the Twin Towers crashed to the ground. And, just as abruptly, the momentum of U.S. hemispheric relations stalled. Suddenly issues that had once seemed so promising, like immigration reform, seemed perilous. Suddenly the openness we in the United States valued at our border with Canada seemed to make us vulnerable. Economic integration, which for much of the 1990s had been vigorously pursued, now showed its downside as U.S. trading partners felt the pain of American recession. With Washington's attention and resources suddenly focused on fighting terrorism, many in the hemisphere wondered where they would rank on the new U.S. agenda.

The Threat of Terror in the Region

Cuba features on the U.S. government list of state sponsors of international terrorism, and a number of countries in the Americas have experienced terrorism on their soil. The U.S. State Department's *Patterns of Global Terrorism 2000* lists terrorist groups in Colombia, Ecuador, Peru, and the South American triborder region where Argentina, Brazil, and Paraguay meet. Most of these are indigenous organizations that use terrorist means for political ends—such as Sendero Luminoso (Shining Path) in Peru and the Revolutionary Armed Forces of Colombia (FARC).

The triborder area, however, is a focal point for Islamic extremism—primarily Hizballah and to a lesser extent Hamas and Gamaat i-Islami (Egyptian Islamic Group). According to the State Department's counterterrorism coordinator, Francis X. Taylor, "These organizations engage in document forgery, money laundering, contraband smuggling, and weapons and drug trafficking."[2] And offshoots of some nonindigenous terrorist groups operate closer to U.S. soil: In Canada, operatives of some 50 such groups, including Al Qaeda, Hamas, and Hizballah, engage in fund raising, money laundering, and related activities. In December 1999, the arrest of an Algerian, Ahmed Ressam, as he attempted to cross into the United States near Blaine, Washington, led to a joint U.S.-Canadian investigation of a Montreal cell of the Armed Islamic Group (GIA) that is connected with Al Qaeda. This investigation revealed that many terrorist groups with small operations in Canada were in fact linked to one another through Al Qaeda. There is also evidence that Hizballah has a presence near the U.S. border with Mexico.

The problem of terrorist activity in Latin America is compounded by powerful drug cartels in a number of countries, particularly Colombia. The lucrative drug trade, and the violence and corruption it engenders, create a climate of instability that terrorists can exploit. Moreover, there is evidence of cooperation between traffickers and terrorists—a deadly nexus that has nearly torn Colombia apart.

What the United States Needs from the Americas

Although the United States is unlikely to ask for military contributions from any of its neighbors—save NATO ally Canada—there are a number of areas in which support and cooperation will be essential.

At the broadest level, solidarity among the hemisphere's 34 democracies bolsters President Bush's assertion that "this is not just America's fight . . . . This is the fight of all who believe in progress and pluralism, tolerance and freedom."

On September 21, two resolutions to that end were approved in the Organization of American States (OAS). The first, invoked at a plenary session of ministers of foreign affairs of the Rio Treaty (Inter-American Treaty of Reciprocal Assistance of 1947), activated a provision that labeled the terrorist attacks against the United States as an attack against all. Then, in a separate resolution, the ministers in their OAS capacity (not all OAS members are parties to the Rio Treaty) reaffirmed the first. The resolutions refer to cooperation to deny terrorist groups the ability to operate in their territories; to pursue, capture, prosecute, and extradite terrorists; to exchange information; and to ask all states to ratify the international convention for the suppression of financing terrorism. They provide a constructive backdrop to specific requests the United States may make of individual countries.

In particular, the United States will need enhanced assistance from Canada and Mexico along the more than 7,500 miles of mutual land borders, where U.S. homeland defense and foreign policy converge. Facial recognition systems and the sharing of data for background checks could help prevent a terrorist from slipping across our northern or southern border. But the challenges are daunting: Each year, some 7 million trucks, 1.5 million railcars, 35 million personal vehicles, close to 200,000 buses, and 95 million people cross from Canada into the United States; and some 4.2 million trucks, 500,000 railcars, 90 million personal vehicles, 300,000 buses, and 300 million people legally cross the U.S. border from Mexico. (In addition, hazardous waste material regularly comes into the United States from Mexico, a procedure that is required under the provisions by which U.S.-owned *maquiladora* plants are permitted to operate. This needs rethinking, which would require more secure hazardous waste dumps in Mexico.)

Tightening security at the border will have major economic repercussions for the more than $400 billion in bilateral trade between Canada and the United States. There is substantial coproduction of goods involving Canadian and U.S.-based firms, much of it on a just-in-time basis, and random security delays at the border could wreak havoc with supply chain management supporting industrial production in both countries. To avoid damaging the economy, the two countries will have to make security measures uniform and constant along the border, as it is not the delay that is most costly, but its unpredictability. Since 1989, Canada and the United States have invested millions of dollars in modernizing the border for commercial traffic; after September 11, the priority must be to extend the use of technology to improve and hasten inspections of individual border crossers as well.

Canada and Mexico have a powerful incentive to work with the United States on border security and other fronts in the fight against terrorism. A number of Mexicans and Canadians perished in the World Trade Center attack. Tomorrow's terrorist, armed with a biological weapon, could launch an assault in Buffalo or El Paso that infects our neighbors as well. And both countries offer myriad U.S. targets that will become attractive alternatives for terrorists as countermeasures taken by the United States limit access to targets here.

A second key area for inter-American cooperation against terrorism is immigration. Again, this will be especially salient for Canada and Mexico, which are the first points of entry for many people into the United States. Canada should be urged to pass pending immigration and refugee laws that will add resources and procedures for better applicant screening and monitoring and for the enforcement of deportation orders. The United States and Canada should also consider, as Canada has proposed, a system of perimeter screening of people patterned on the European Union's Schengen Agreement, in which the two nations would have a common standard for permitting entry to foreigners. In time, Mexico could be incorporated into the security perimeter; but the need to act quickly means that Canada and the United States should move forward bilaterally for now.

Before September 11, President Fox had been urging regularization (amnesty) for undocumented Mexican immigrants and expanded opportunities for Mexican temporary workers in the United States. The sympathetic reception those proposals received appears to have cooled. As Washington rethinks U.S. immigration requirements, Mexico should be asked to strengthen its own—and to crack down harder on the *polleros* who facilitate illegal crossings across the border. Terrorists in the past have preferred to enter the United States with phony papers, but this may change if document examination becomes more rigorous. Mexico should also be urged to suppress the sophisticated manufacturing of false documents that occurs within its territory.

Finally, both Canada and Mexico will have to strengthen airport security. A plane leaving Toronto or Ciudad Juarez is in easy striking distance of U.S. soil. Both countries are now screening departing air passengers more rigorously than before. Mexico should be asked to implement a system of marshals on flights destined for the United States—as Canada has already done on key U.S.-bound flights.

A third area for hemispheric cooperation against terrorism is in choking off the money supply on which Al Qaeda and other networks depend. This will require particular cooperation from a number of

Caribbean island nations, where underregulated banking systems are vulnerable to criminal network abuse. The United States should seek better money laundering intelligence as well as an end to tax havens.

Caribbean island nations that have promoted themselves as tax havens were under pressure before September 11 to alter their status, but then received some support from Secretary of the Treasury Paul O'Neill regarding respect of their sovereign rights to have their own tax structures. Not only has the Treasury Department changed its position, but the islands may now have to cooperate in tracing fund flows more than they had anticipated so as to retain their tax-haven status.

The Road Ahead

In the immediate aftermath of September 11, it is not surprising that the spotlight of U.S. attention has swung to Afghanistan and its neighbors. But it would be a mistake if, over the long term, the Americas were kept backstage. As the United States launches a campaign in which close collaboration with other nations will be essential, it should not abandon the important progress of recent years in building a closer, more cooperative partnership with the nations of the Western Hemisphere.

Moreover, the regional challenges that existed before September 11 remain. Turning our back on the Americas now could mean instability—and perhaps hostility—on our doorstep in the future.

As the United States considers its national security in the long term, a number of hemispheric issues deserve ongoing priority.

First, the region's economy—already in a slump—has been adversely affected by the September 11 shock. Latin America's economic growth forecast for 2001 has been slashed. Argentina is still in financial crisis. Growth of Mexican gross domestic product—heavily dependent on exports to the United States—was expected to be about 4 percent in 2001; instead, it will be close to zero. Given the size of the U.S. economy, economic weakness in Latin America will not have a major effect on the United States, but the economic health of U.S. neighbors will have important security implications in the near term.

One economic issue that may get a boost from September 11 is President Bush's pursuit of trade promotion authority (TPA). The Bush administration, with only modest Democratic congressional support, is pushing ahead on TPA, using the argument that free trade will stimulate the U.S. economy. Securing TPA would create the possibility for real progress toward a free trade area of the Americas—something most of our hemispheric neighbors want. Not only would a free trade area be in the U.S. economic interest, it also would improve the atmosphere for hemispheric cooperation overall.

Second, the U.S. policy response to September 11—in terms of both the economy and homeland security—must also include an element of diplomacy to engage Mexico and Canada across a range of issues where U.S. goals require particular cooperation from our immediate neighbors. Both the Fox administration in Mexico and the Chrétien government in Canada have pledged their unconditional support for the United States in this crisis, but Fox must deal with a governing coalition and Chrétien with a party caucus that may hinder each leader's ability to react favorably to U.S. requests. In addition, President Fox faces strong nationalist sentiment in Mexico, where a majority of the public does not favor unconditional support for the U.S. effort. The United States will need to exert clear leadership and concerted pressure on Mexico to ensure that it follows through on promises of support.

Third, the United States should be attentive to the further deterioration of order in Colombia and Venezuela. Together with Canada and our European allies, we should continue to support the Colombian government but forcefully oppose the continuation of demilitarized zones within Colombia. These zones, where Colombia has chosen not to deploy its army, have become fertile ground for Colombia's FARC guerillas—and FARC has used them to harbor international terrorist groups such as the IRA. In Venezuela, President Hugo Chávez heads an increasingly unstable and radical government that has cultivated ties to the FARC, Fidel Castro in Cuba, and even Iraq's Saddam Hussein. Chávez has declared his support for the United States and offered intelligence help after September 11, but the United States must hold him to account for any ties that he maintains with international terrorism and its state sponsors.

Fourth, the United States should continue working with hemispheric partners to combat drug trafficking and crack down on other criminal syndicates with international reach. From Afghanistan to Colombia, drug trafficking is an important source of funding for terrorist groups, and smuggling operations are useful to terrorists who would ship individuals and biological and chemical weapons into the United States. Efforts to halt this traffic should include continued emphasis on judicial and law enforcement cooperation, which should be made a precondition for U.S. foreign aid.

Finally, as we in the United States seek support and cooperation from our neighbors in the campaign against terrorism, we will further our cause if we keep in mind the aspirations of these countries. Canada will cooperate eagerly on security but will fight to maintain the openness of borders that sustains the Canadian economy. The Caribbean financial centers will want to remain in existence. Mexico will want to return at some point to the issue of immigration. Brazil is deeply interested in moving ahead with global negotiations in the World Trade Organization. The more the United States can be a partner to our neighbors on issues that matter to them, the more we can expect their partnership on what matters most to us.

Notes

[1] For a more in-depth discussion of public diplomacy, see chapter 11.

[2] Anthony Faiola, "U.S. Terrorist Search Reaches Paraguay," *Washington Post*, October 13, 2001.

King of the World, circa 1965. Image of a businessman carrying a briefcase superimposed on top of a globe. Photograph: Hulton | Archive/Getty Images.

Chapter 15

Globalization Goes to War

"The issue is not how to stop globalization. The issue is how we use the power of community to combine it with justice. If globalization works only for the benefit of the few, then it will fail and will deserve to fail. But if we follow the principles that have served us so well at home—that power, wealth and opportunity must be in the hands of the many, not the few—if we make that our guiding light for the global economy, then it will be a force for good and an international movement that we should take pride in leading. Because the alternative to globalization is isolation."

> — *Prime Minister Tony Blair of Great Britain*
> *Labour Party Conference*
> *Brighton, England*
> *October 2, 2001*

Much has been written about how the forces of globalization—the relentless expansion of market forces, the breakneck speed with which capital moves around the globe, rapid technological innovation, the transmission of Western cultural values and images globally, and the constant search for realizing greater economic efficiencies—influence everything from indigenous cultures and environmental and labor standards to productivity patterns. Yet, remarkably little attention has been given to how globalization might impact global conflict and vice versa.

Perhaps we bought into the excessive optimism of the prophets of globalization who either implied or stated outright that conditions of globalization made a major, sustained conflict unlikely, or that the process itself was irreversible. Yet September 11 has altered those comfortably held assumptions. We have come to understand globalization as an inexorable economic force, an inescapable wave that alters everything in its path. If that is true, what will happen when the logic of globalization collides with the consuming passions of a global conflict? Is the relentless march of market liberalization and global optimism over? Can globalization and a lengthy and expensive campaign against global terrorism coexist?

The Tools of Globalization, Wielded against the Toolmakers

Globalization has been variously portrayed as a target, a transmission mechanism, a casualty, and a survivor of the recent terrorism. Certainly, globalization's fingerprints are all over the September 11 attacks. The September 11 assailants struck at obvious symbols of America's global power projection, both military and economic. Subsequent anthrax attacks, whether perpetrated by Al Qaeda or not, targeted influential political and media headquarters using the U.S. mail service—all of them seen as instruments of America's international influence and reach. The tentacles of Al Qaeda's network stretch from Afghan caves to Hamburg hostels, Indonesian islands, and Florida flight schools, and many of its operatives hide in plain sight among Muslim communities in the industrialized democracies. Secretary of State Colin Powell invoked a corporate metaphor when he described the Al Qaeda network as a holding company for international terrorism. Others have described Osama bin Laden as the CEO of terror. There is even speculation that bin Laden associates sought to play the stock and options markets in anticipation of the attacks.

The technological innovations touted as the handmaidens of globalization—the Internet, globalized financial networks, the expansion of commercial aviation—proved their moral indifference by enabling terrorists to wreak havoc on a catastrophic scale. Now, the realization that the vast connections created by globalization have also empowered some bad neighborhoods in the global village has provoked a disquieting query: Terrorists used the tools of globalization against us; must we now dismantle or retard parts of globalization in order to defeat them?

To its fiercest critics, globalization represents a vehicle for repression, exploitation, and injustice, virtually synonymous with American power and (as they perceive it) arrogance. The rage that incited Islamic fanatics to drive planes into buildings, it is argued, is in part a response to the belief that globalization begets poverty and cultural contamination. These misguided acts, the analysis continues, must be interpreted as vengeful strikes by groups either oppressed or marginalized by the global economy. There have been long-running complaints about how multinational corporations have led to the polluting of local cultures and the Coca-Colonization of the planet. Now, however, and in the Middle East especially, the concept of globalization carrying with it—like a virus—dominant American culture and values has become entwined with the most volatile local issues: religion and politics.

This critique fundamentally equates globalization with a host of other phenomena, including the encroachment of world capitalism on local economies, the perception of American hegemony in all its manifestations, and spreading signs of modernity. Terrible conditions of poverty and ignorance are important in explaining the failed states that litter the world's landscape and the resonance of Al Qaeda's appeal for many from Central Asia to Somalia. Ironically, most of these countries have been spurned rather than split by globalization, but the outward manifestation of disaffection by the dispossessed is still often directed at foreign forces rather than ruling regimes. The regimes and dominant power groups inside these societies have generally been content to let the supposedly pernicious forces of the United States and the harshness of global capitalism take the rap for local conditions that owe themselves more to poor governance and endemic corruption.

To many in the West, the gorgelike rifts within these societies can be explained without any fundamental reference to the global marketplace: Surely the events of September 11 have far more in common with the Iranian hostage crisis of 1979 than with the Asian financial crisis of 1998. And the debates within Saudi Arabia, Egypt, and Algeria are centered only in the most trivial way on whether to ban Western television and video games. The real fight is over who wields power and how dissent is manifested. Indeed, the rebuttal goes, far from being the primary cause of poverty, globalization represents the best chance to cure the global conditions of inequality and injustice across the globe, including in the Middle East. How ironic, then, if globalization were to become one of the casualties of the terrorist attacks and the subsequent retaliation and response.

In most respects this is a dialogue of the deaf. The ardent advocates of globalization who see it as a means to alleviate poverty rarely have the chance to interact with the mobs that stoned the Islamabad McDonald's restaurant in the hours after American warplanes first hammered Taliban positions in Afghanistan. And community representatives in the underdeveloped world have little opportunity to explain to Western financial leaders or big-business executives how the march toward globalization has marginalized some, left many behind, and alienated others. The G-8 demonstrators and Al Qaeda have radically different political agendas, and while there is virtually no comparison between the two groups, they do represent the opposite ends of the anti-globalization spectrum.

Several vital questions associated with globalization have been triggered by the September 11 attacks: Can the process and power of globalization be in any important way disassociated from America's global omnipresence? Can the process of globalization be reconciled with local dissatisfaction over the intrusion of what are to some unwanted images and values? Is there something fundamentally incompatible between globalization and a conservative interpretation and practice of Islam? Can detractors ever be convinced of globalization's potential for raising the quality of life for the poor and healing societal rifts? And will major multinational firms—fearful of resentment and retaliation—continue to see globalization as the best growth strategy in the face of growing local opposition to global brands?

These are all enormously important issues to explore, most of which lie beyond the scope of this particular inquiry. Questions about the complex relationship between the manifestations of globalization and the changing attitudes of the dispossessed in the world community in the wake of September 11 will be taken up elsewhere by sociologists, economists, and even anthropologists. The primary subject for this examination is: How will the economic dimensions of globalization survive the first wave of terrorist attacks and the subsequent efforts by the United States and others to target the terrorists themselves?

The Damage Done

Before considering the implications of the counterterror campaign for globalization's future, one must appreciate September 11's impact on and damage to the state of the global economy. A previous chapter already explored the consequences of the attacks for the U.S. economy—the direct destruction of capital and the necessary costs to rebuild, the high toll on consumer confidence, the damage and subsequent impact on specific sectors, and the initial steps taken to stem the damage. This chapter will consider the implications for the global economy and the associated risks for the continued path and pace of globalization.

It is already clear that September 11 has led to the worst U.S. economic dive in more than a decade, and the global economy—already weakened by slowing demand—is now reeling as well. The direct hits, literally, on Wall Street sent tremors through financial markets around the world. With the United States in contraction, Japan mired in a decade-long slump, and European countries squabbling over competing political agendas (one calling for managing deficit requirements, the other arguing for the need for economic stimulus), the world economy is poised on the brink of a financial "perfect storm." That is a combination of economic, financial, and trade dynamics that act and interact together in ways that magnify and increase the overall damage done.

Financial policymakers and political leaders in the major economies are scrambling for ways to prevent the storm clouds from breaking, but the prospects are growing darker. Layoffs are mounting from first world to third, from old-economy industries to new-information-technology firms. The stakes for the global marketplace and the dynamism of the world economy could not be higher: A 1 percent drop in U.S. gross national product would equal a decline of about $100 billion; a 1 percent drop in global gross national product represents a reduction of nearly $350 billion.

The sectors hit hardest by the disaster—airlines, the travel and leisure industry, insurance and reinsurance firms, and emerging new technologies—are the very linchpins of an interconnected world and, taken together, have been the driving forces of the globalization process over the past decade. For the technology sector, September 11 confirmed what many had already feared: Recovery in this highly globalized industry will not come any time soon. The long-term direction of the oil sector is difficult to predict; right now demand-side weakness is dominant, but a supply disruption associated with continuing military operations in the Middle East would quickly add to a growing list of global economic worries. World trade growth could very well slow to zero next year for the first time in decades; and the secondary implications in terms of depressed U.S. capacity to absorb imports, particularly from Latin America and East Asia, are also likely to be substantial.

Although many of the economic indicators are troubling indeed, the outlook for globalization is not all bleak. Correlated recessions in the developed economies, contraction in emerging-market finance associated with the flight to safety, tight linkage across borders in highly internationalized sectors, and oil market shocks are not new phenomena. And although history is replete with examples of these types of developments dealing harsh blows to increases in trade and national development, none has proved fatal. Moreover, the U.S. policy response has been swift and sure thus far. Not since the 1960s have interest rates been at this level, and not since 1975 has there been a bigger one-year boost in fiscal stimulus.

On its own, the process of globalization, though badly shaken, would be expected to recover over time despite a shaky short-term prognosis. The question remains, however, as to how well the industries, financial practices, and technologies that have driven global growth and productivity will fare while governments and businesses clamp down on these very efficiencies in the name of antiterrorism. Simply stated for globalization, will the cure turn out to be even worse than the disease?

Whither Globalization?

Western societies have become vulnerable to terrorist attacks because of efficiencies by persons, companies, and countries in their quest to maximize productivity. Curbside check-in, e-tickets, streamlined procedures for border crossings, freer immigration procedures in industrialized societies, and just-in-time delivery of international packages and shipping were all introduced to improve productivity and advance competitiveness. Now, several of these globalization-era efficiencies have either been temporarily discontinued or curtailed—and some may ultimately be sacrificed in the name of national security or, more precisely, homeland security.

Concerns are already being raised in the business community in the United States and abroad that a sustained campaign against terrorism could have cataclysmic short-term consequences for global growth and could potentially undermine the very process of globalization. And if the Gulf War came to be known as the "CNN war" because of the newly acquired capability to conduct bomb damage assessments via cable, in the war against terrorism, we will be able to track how the conflict is affecting financial portfolios around the clock and across the world's many stock markets, currency trading desks, Web sites, and cable stations.

In some respects, the current risks to globalization are not unique. The world experienced an earlier period of global integration prior to 1914, only to find these advances rolled back by the onset of World War I. While pre–World War I connectivity was based more on trade and access to resources than on global communications, the global economic rupture that resulted from war set back the cause of open markets and free movement of capital for generations.

So, how is the collision between American hard power in the struggle with international terrorism and globalization's quest for greater efficiency and the breaking down of barriers likely to come out? There are essentially three scenarios that warrant scrutiny:

The best revenge is living well. First is the possibility that the domestic and international forces that favor the continuation of unfettered globalization will prevail. Indications of this outcome will be a short military campaign; a discernible shift in political rhetoric to "the best revenge is living well"; and Governor Ridge's return to Pennsylvania after a frustrating stint in Washington trying to institute tighter border controls, more intensive airline security procedures, and serious business support for heightened homeland security.

America already has a powerful yearning for a return to the familiar patterns of domestic life associated with September 10, and indeed there is a global and national desire to return to business as usual. Yet the terrorists may have other plans. Another cataclysmic act of international terrorism perpetrated against the American homeland would make a return to an era of unfettered freedoms impossible. A handy shorthand formula is that American impatience with security-related inefficiencies will vary directly with the elapsed time between terror-ist episodes. The longer the lapse, the greater the impulse will be to streamline procedures and improve efficiency once again.

Adaptation and globalization can coexist. Second, the United States and the international agents and institutions of globalization could adapt to heightened security measures and the inevitable dis-ruptions brought on by war. In this scenario, the process of greater global integration, trade, and communication will continue unabated with some modifications. Whole new lines of business innovation will spring up around security services and technologies. Although this added cost on business interaction would be in many senses unwel-come, there would be some offsetting benefits from a vibrant new security-related sector that is already showing signs of robust invest-ment and growth. Electronic scanners and chemical sniffers will find new markets. Pharmaceutical companies working to develop vaccines against biological and chemical warfare agents will see their stocks skyrocket. Tele-video services and remote conferencing capabilities will take the place of frequent business trips. These may not fully compen-sate for significant losses and lack of forward momentum elsewhere, but globalization's potential to adapt with an appropriate incentive structure should not be underestimated.

This process would be similar in many ways to the fundamental structural adjustments in the U.S. economy that were spurred by the 1973 oil shocks, such as the rapid move toward greater fuel efficien-cies, better insulation technologies, and the development of alternate sources of supply. Ultimately these steps to heighten security can only be effective and competitive if they are adopted relatively uniformly throughout the G-8 and the other industrialized democracies. U.S. competitiveness would be sorely tested if its reforms were not matched by other major states in the international economy and if the United States were forced to carry the burden alone.

You can't go home again. The third possibility is that the 1990s era of go-go globalization will be one of the first casualties in this sus-tained campaign against global terrorism. And a tragic lesson of 1914 is that, once lost, the advances of globalization—free and unfettered trade, rising productivity, open and optimistic mindsets, ease of travel, and global trust and confidence—are extraordinarily difficult to regain. Signs of this troubling outcome might be an increase of xeno-phobia in leading states; trade protectionist forces on the rise, par-ticularly in industrialized countries; and the substantial reduction of foreign direct investment as well as cross-border remittances. The cul-tural and communications interconnectivity now taken for granted would be strained or curtailed, with an associated rise in nationalism and perhaps militarism as well.

Any hint of a rise in these indicators of protectionism, isolationism, or a stirring for a fight is always cause for concern, but is even more worri-some during a period of simultaneous global economic downturn.

It is too early to tell which is the most likely outcome in this process of struggle and reconciliation, adaptation and innovation. It is not too early, however, to work toward fashioning a consensus around the need to simultaneously adapt to new security challenges and sustain the process of globalization.

The drive to increase the security of U.S. borders undeniably runs counter to the very forces that propel globalization. Some have re-ferred to the new transactions costs as a terrorism tax, and at least initially, the surcharge associated with new security measures may prove to be significant, even exorbitant. It will be impossible to address the demands for greater security and scrutiny of cross-border move-ments—of goods, people, information, financial capital, even mail—without some setbacks to the market-imposed demands of faster, cheaper, and less bureaucratic. At a minimum, there will be a tempo-rary setback to just-in-time operations across borders, fewer flights, and greater scrutiny for work and student visas. And certainly, if ter-ror strikes again with the scale and precision witnessed on September 11, there could be a significant chilling effect in the overseas opera-tions of multinationals, mounting turmoil in financial markets, and the slowing of trade flows to a trickle.

But short of a cataclysm, new patterns will likely emerge, like water rushing around new rocks in a stream. There may even come a time when corporations look back upon reliance on face-to-face meetings as profoundly inefficient; when the age of the business class, global fre-quent flyer seems oddly clumsy and quaint. New technologies will emerge, new practices will take hold, new ways of doing business will take root.

Globalization, in short, will adapt.

Flag Cutter, circa 1955. A factory worker cutting out flags as they come off the production line at the Abacrome Company, United States. Photograph: Hulton | Archive/Getty Images.

Chapter 16

To Prevail:
Key Findings and
Recommendations

Findings

As the United States seeks to chart its course in the world post–September 11 and to devise its strategy for the long-term campaign against terrorism, what assumptions and judgments should guide the thinking of Americans? What factors should we have in mind? On what should we be focused? This section attempts to answer these questions by laying out a series of findings that describe what has changed in the world, what the United States should look for or expect in the months and years to come, and what we should guard against. Many of these findings identify new opportunities to advance U.S. interests; others highlight pitfalls to be avoided and risks to be managed. Taken together, they embody the authors' best judgments as to what will be critical to success in the campaign against global terrorism and what key challenges we must address along the way.

1. The New Terrorism

Many Americans, and much of the world, got a first stark glimpse of the new face of terrorism on September 11, 2001. Yet, the reality is that international terrorism has been changing dramatically over the past 10 years—in its motivations and aspirations, its organization, and its reach. September 11, for all its uniqueness, was not without precedent or warning: Earlier plots, from the first World Trade Center bombing in 1993 to the thwarted conspiracy around the time of the millennium celebrations, also sought horrific levels of carnage.

The determining difference between the older forms of terrorism and the new lies in the realm of motivation. Specifically, the key characteristics of the new terrorism derive from the explicitly religious terms in which grievances and goals are expressed. Thus Osama bin Laden's message comes first and foremost in the form of his *fatwas,* or religious rulings. An example is his 1998 *fatwa* demanding that "all those who believe in Allah and his prophet Muhammad must kill Americans wherever they find them." Many argue that the goals in all terrorism are ultimately political, but it is important to note that a core belief of most extreme Islamists is that the categorical division between politics and religion is a false one. The West must take them at their word and recognize that, at least on the side of our opponents, religious beliefs are central to how they conceptualize the conflict and its resolution.

The belief that violent struggle is divinely mandated underlies the defining characteristic of the new terror—the effort to create massive, history-changing bloodshed. Because the new terrorists do not seek to be brought to the table for political negotiations, they are not inhibited by the risk of popular revulsion at their acts. Because they believe their attacks to be justified by God, they are not constrained by earthly morality. They explicitly target civilians, not representatives or symbols of the state. Suicide strikes are part of their training regime; self-sacrifice for the cause is glorified. And in lashing out at the United States and the West, they seek not just maximum destruction of lives, but destruction of a way of life. As such, they pose a threat unlike any terrorist group we have ever seen.

Although the media has fixated on the role of bin Laden as the head of the Al Qaeda network, it is probably more accurate to portray Al Qaeda as a multiheaded hydra with only loose central control. The organization does not appear to have any direct state sponsors, but its ability to tap deep reservoirs of sympathy in many Muslim societies has enabled it to gain power, garner finances, and attract supporters. Western intelligence agencies have had little success with infiltrating and tracking Al Qaeda cells. Their very nature makes them exceedingly difficult to penetrate, and their tradecraft has been demonstrated to be creative and effective when it matters.

The Al Qaeda network spans dozens of countries, with perhaps thousands of trained and dedicated operatives working as part of per-

haps hundreds of cells scattered around the globe. Its commercial activities, both legitimate and illegal, include heroin distribution, dia-
mond sales, honey production and marketing, pharmaceutical facto-
ries, fishing fleets, and basic manufacturing. The organization maintains accounts and conducts sophisticated financial transactions
through banks from Switzerland and Sudan to Singapore. Although
Afghanistan has served as a headquarters of sorts for Al Qaeda, destroying or disrupting the organization there will not necessarily eliminate the group's global reach.

Thus, the threat posed by Al Qaeda is different and more dangerous than other terrorist groups, past or present. The United States
must assume that these terrorists' pursuit of destruction is limited
only by their abilities. Indeed, there is a great deal of evidence to suggest that the Al Qaeda organization has sought to acquire chemical
agents, nuclear weapons components, and perhaps biological pathogens for use in terrorist attacks. The large-scale use of such weapons
of mass destruction would potentially produce even more catastrophic
results than the September 11 attacks.

As of now, Al Qaeda is the first and only group that combines religious motivation with a desire to cause maximum bloodshed to demonstrate international capabilities. Nonetheless, the appearance of violent groups in many religious traditions and among recently created
cults suggests that Al Qaeda may not be the last new terrorist group
with global reach. There is also the real danger that smaller organizations, or even malevolent individuals acting alone, may seek to piggy-
back on Al Qaeda's attacks with smaller assaults that fuel a sense of
vulnerability and play into Al Qaeda's objectives.

At least two other major terrorist groups merit further consideration. Hamas and Hizballah both seem to fall in a nether zone between old-style political terrorism and religiously motivated terror.
Both groups have conducted relentless campaigns of violence against
Israel. But neither has thus far managed attacks that left anything like
the toll of September 11, nor do these two groups have a demonstrated
ability to conduct large-scale operations outside of the Middle East.
As a matter of political consistency, the persistent, high-profile threat
these groups represent must be countered in the course of any war on
terrorism. In addition to the crimes these groups have already perpetrated, a question for the future will be whether the success of bin

Laden's organization will lead these and others to attempt more violent attacks as a way of showing their capability and the determination of both their operatives and supporters.

2. The Imperative to Prevail

The United States and its international partners must prevail in the campaign against global terrorism; we have no choice given the nature of the threat we now face. But the victory we seek is difficult to define. Unlike the 100-hour Gulf War and even the nearly half-century long Cold War, this war has no clear finish line. In this sense, it is more like the "wars" the United States has waged on crime or drugs or poverty. Like these threats, terrorism will never be completely eradicated from Earth. But the risks of terrorism can be substantially reduced. Therefore, success or victory in the war against terrorism must first be defined in terms of reducing both the probability and the consequences of further attacks.

Victory in this campaign will also be piecemeal and incremental, and many triumphs will be invisible to the public eye—a plot foiled, a cell infiltrated, a line of financing severed. For the public, then, benchmarks of success will not always be quantifiable. The value of assets frozen, number of training camps destroyed, or names of terrorists captured can be added to the U.S. side of the scorecard—and indeed, there should be a concerted public information effort to make such triumphs visible and thus bolster confidence in the campaign. But perhaps the truest measure of victory will be our sense of national safety, and our ability, as Secretary Rumsfeld put it, to live our lives in relative freedom.

We cannot go back to life as it was on September 10—innocence lost can never be regained. But we can set our sights on a future in which the sense of freedom, optimism, and boundless possibility that defines us as a nation is restored. To prevail in this struggle, Americans will have to be even more determined and patient than the terrorists themselves.

What lies directly ahead will be a decisive chapter in America's story that will demand an unusual degree of focus and sustained commitment. Prevailing in the war on terrorism must indeed be Americans' primary, immediate priority. It must be "our calling," as President Bush has said—not in a religious sense, but in the sense of meeting a challenge that will define this moment in the history of our nation and of the civilized world. Nevertheless, even in the face of a continuing threat, the campaign against terrorism should not be made the sole organizing concept for the totality of U.S. foreign and domestic policy. It should not trump indefinitely, or negate, the rest of our national agenda.

Indeed, it must be weighed and balanced against the other priorities that will continue to affect the vital interests and character of the nation. For example, problems that existed on September 10 still existed on September 12—from nuclear proliferation to global economic downturn to the spread of HIV/AIDS. And important opportunities, from reducing barriers to free trade around the world to laying the foundations for a durable peace in places like the Balkans, Northern Ireland, and the Korean peninsula will be lost without sustained U.S. engagement. Similarly, on the domestic front, improving homeland security will not fix the U.S. health care crisis, improve education, or alter the fact that one in six American children lives in poverty; however, it could, if pursued without adequate reflection and debate, erode civil liberties.

The strategic mantra during the Cold War was the maintenance of the balance of power. In this new campaign against international terrorism, a better mantra may well turn out to be the power of balance, where the ultimate effectiveness of the U.S. national effort will require balancing many competing demands and priorities.

Achieving this balance will be very difficult if the nation continues to feel under attack. But, as Americans conduct the long campaign against global terrorism, there is good reason to resist the sort of all-consuming national passion that characterized the early Cold War era. McCarthyism and covertly staging coups against democratically elected governments in the name of anticommunism were not high points in recent U.S. history. In the final analysis, it is hard to imagine much domestic tranquility or the pursuit of other worthy foreign policy or domestic priorities without advances in the war against terrorism. But in making the campaign a national priority, we must take care not to neglect or abandon all other foreign and domestic policy objectives—or to disregard the values for which this nation stands.

3. The New Response

The necessity of defeating international terrorism cannot be overstated. Meeting this challenge will require the United States and its coalition partners to mount a long-term campaign on a broad range of fronts. The overarching goals of the United States in the campaign should be to reduce the threat of global terrorism, to enhance the security of Americans at home and abroad, and to sustain the resoluteness of U.S. and international purpose. The specific objectives of the campaign are clear: To attack and destroy global terrorist networks; to punish states sponsoring terrorism until they stop; to build stronger capabilities to combat terrorism and secure the U.S. homeland; to strengthen international norms and actions against terrorism; and, over time, to ameliorate the conditions that provide fertile ground for terrorists.

Success will require a fundamentally new approach on the part of the United States and its coalition partners around the world. One of best ways to fight a network is to create a network of our own. The United States and its international partners must build their own global network of intelligence, law enforcement, military, financial, diplomatic, and other instruments to successfully take on global terrorist organizations like Al Qaeda.

This will require a new vision of cooperation—domestically and internationally. At home, hitherto fierce bureaucratic competitors—both within the federal government and among federal, state, and local agencies—must learn to work together. Our goal must be an unprecedented degree of coordination among a wide variety of communities, including intelligence, law enforcement, military, diplomatic, finance, emergency response, public health, private sector, and so on. Internationally, the United States must rally and sustain a coalition of coalitions, each responsible for tackling a different part of the broad campaign. Independently and collectively, these coalitions must work to wipe out any global terrorist networks that exist and render inhospitable the terrain for future ones to take root.

This campaign will also require an unprecedented degree of staying power from the American people, for it is likely to be—to partially paraphrase Hobbes—nasty, brutish, and *long*. Sustained presidential leadership and focus will be critical to keeping Congress and the American people on board. This will be particularly important when the campaign experiences setbacks—unintended, negative consequences; an unsuccessful operation; and, worst of all, more terrorist attacks— as it inevitably will. As in past "wars," we will lose some battles in this one, especially given that we face a thinking, agile, determined, and patient foe. In the end, victory will require that we sustain American purpose and resolve in the face of repeated unthinkable attacks, or in the absence of them, possibly for years to come.

The United States did not choose this conflict, but the country cannot choose not to fight. The costs of a failure of persistence and resolve are too great to contemplate, however hard and long the campaign. At the time of the Cuban Missile Crisis, President Kennedy said, "The costs of freedom are high, but Americans have always paid it." Once again, our nation will have to rise to the challenge—until we have prevailed.

4. The New Politics

President Bush came to office pledging to change the tone of political discourse in Washington. His first months in office belied that goal; in the space of a day, however, the events of and national response to September 11 achieved it. The lawmakers who gathered on the steps of the Capitol to pledge their unity and sing "God Bless America" became one of the earliest symbols of a new national solidarity and resolve. A bipartisan spirit has largely prevailed since then, with political disagreements mostly civil and within the confines of seeking to do the best for the country. The challenge will be to preserve the unanimity of purpose essential to prevail, while neither making unquestioning support for administration policy a test of patriotism nor eroding the system of checks and balances.

Both parties have already learned important lessons from the September 11 tragedy and its aftermath, sometimes coming at the expense of party orthodoxy. For Democrats, the priority of defense, intelligence, and other security issues has been reinforced. For Republicans, the government's role and relevance in American citizens' daily lives has been elevated. These new alignments have already resulted in some surprising common ground; for example, members from both the Right and the Left have raised profound concerns about the potential long-term implication for civil rights of various proposals designed to combat terrorism at home. The tragedy also appears to have energized the vital center in American politics, at least in the Senate, with key leaders like Senator John McCain and Senator Joe Lieberman transcending party labels to work together to get things done.

There is broad support in both parties for extensive fiscal stimulus, even if it means substantial increases in government expenditures in the short run. To some degree, we are all Keynesians now in our support for federal stimulus and spending. We are also likely to see virtually every major initiative in Congress—from enhanced trade authorities to new minimum-wage laws—described by its proponents as an essential tool in the fight against terrorism. This propensity to get on board the antiterrorism spending wagon is not a new phenomenon. After all, one of the primary rationales for the Federal Highway Act in the 1950s was that better roads were said to be essential in the event of a major conflict with the Soviet Union. In congressional debates, increased continental travel, transport, business, and tourism were cited only as incidental benefits.

On some issues, however, partisanship has survived the September 11 attacks. For example, the question of federalizing the airport security function caused concern in Republican ranks about the potential for a large new organization with ties to organized labor, and Democrats railed against Republican plans in the House of Representatives to give the majority of post–September 11 financial relief to corporations rather than individuals. And, inevitably, there will be a return to more partisan politics in time, but the hope is that future dialogue and debate will be characterized by civility instead of the rancorous point scoring that set the tone in the 1990s. The real enemy does not sit across the aisle but is making preparation to attack America again.

5. The Need for International Engagement

In the wake of September 11, the Bush administration has moved decisively to reach out to other states worldwide for support and cooperation. So far, Americans have solidly backed this outward-looking approach. Indeed, public opinion polls have shown strong levels of American support for U.S. engagement in the world. Yet, as the campaign against terrorism progresses, public support for engagement may wane. U.S. leaders must be alert for—and must seek to reverse—signs of public disenchantment with American engagement abroad.

Over time, especially when we experience setbacks, some Americans may conclude that our engagement abroad simply aggravates resentment of the United States and offers targets for terrorists to strike. They may ask why the U.S. military is stationed in places like Saudi Arabia and Korea, believing that the greater defense requirements are here at home. They may question whether U.S. support for Israel is exacting too high a toll. They may balk at providing development and other assistance to foreign nations when millions of Americans are out of work and struggling to support their families.

It would be a tragedy for our nation and the world—and a victory for the terrorists—if American leadership and engagement in the world became a casualty of September 11. Stronger homeland defense must be an essential element of a sustained U.S. strategy against global terrorism; but it need not, and must not, substitute for or supersede America's robust international presence and priorities. Indeed, if September 11 has taught us anything, it is that security and prosperity at home are directly affected by forces far beyond U.S. borders. Americans cannot escape the world. But we can, and must, work to shape it. Sixty years ago, World War II invalidated the premise of America's historical isolationism. Now our political leadership must work to ensure that the destruction we endured on our soil on September 11 does not demolish our engagement and leadership in the world.

6. The Potential for Strategic Realignment

The aftermath of the September 11 terror attacks has created the most fertile environment for strategic realignment and diplomatic initiative since the fall of the Berlin Wall. At least five potential U.S. initiatives—all unlikely before September 11—are now conceivable given the transformation of the international environment:

- **Refocus on building alliances.** The aftermath of the crisis has validated those who favor a strong focus on alliance relationships in the formulation and execution of U.S. foreign policy. Long-standing security ties, such as the NATO alliance and our bilateral alliances with countries like Japan, are serving as the building blocks for the various antiterror coalitions. The strong support from our allies in the struggle against terrorism raises the prospect of a spillover effect in which alliances can be used for other important purposes, such as reinvigorating efforts to deal with the proliferation of weapons of mass destruction.

- **Be open to potential realignment of relations with Russia and China.** Many believe the campaign against terrorism has the potential to dramatically reorient the U.S.-Russia and NATO-Russia agendas. Indeed, Russia could prove to be an indispensable partner in this fight. Enduring problems in the relationship, however, will likely have an impact on cooperation—such as Russian mistrust over NATO expansion and different approaches to countering terrorism, as crystallized in Chechnya. Similarly, the United States and China share a common interest in combating Islamic extremism. This could form the basis for closer cooperation in other areas as well. But the United States must not permit counterterror collaboration to trump the rest of our agenda with China—especially on contentious issues like Taiwan and human rights.
- **Reevaluate dual containment.** Dual containment is no longer likely to produce positive results for the United States in the Persian Gulf, but a successor policy has yet to be identified. The support from Tehran in the early phases of building the coalition against international terrorism was most welcome and opened the door for reevaluating the broader U.S.-Iran relationship. Although there are still dangerous elements inside Iran's government, there is also an enhanced desire for a better relationship with the United States. This could open the way for greater cooperation in a host of areas, including energy. Better relations with Tehran could also be useful as part of a renewed effort to dislodge Saddam Hussein in Iraq and to bring a degree of stability to neighboring Afghanistan.
- **Restore dual engagement toward India and Pakistan.** The Bush administration's initial strategic orientation had focused a great deal of attention on India, continuing a trend initiated in the last part of the Clinton administration. The intense U.S. focus on the Taliban and the Al Qaeda organization in Afghanistan has now moved Pakistan to the forefront of the U.S. agenda.

This raises two questions: First, is the relationship with Pakistan sustainable in light of Pakistan's internal sources of instability and the differences between Pakistani and U.S. agendas in Afghanistan and Kashmir? Second, how can the United States continue to deepen its relationship with India, which is important both for the antiterrorism campaign and for overall U.S. goals in Asia? If the U.S. objective is a stable and peaceful South Asia, the United States cannot and should not lean toward one at the expense of the other. The United States now has an opportunity to reinstate a deeper and more evenhanded approach to India and Pakistan that would better serve U.S. interests and enhance stability in the region.

- **Reassert leadership in the Middle East peace process.** The escalating violence between Israel and the Palestinians underscores the need for outside assistance in helping to restart and frame negotiations and to play the honest broker. The United States is uniquely suited to play this role. Seeking a peaceful settlement between Israelis and Palestinians is important on its own merits, not as a response to the terrorist attacks. Yet it is also clear that continued Israeli-Palestinian strife fuels resentment of the United States in the region and enables extremist forces to exploit broader discontent. Greater security and stability for Israel and the Palestinians would improve the climate for political dialogue and regional integration in the larger Middle East.

7. Quid Pro Quos

Some of those who are cooperating with the United States in the fight against terrorism have agendas we do not share. Some have come to the table requesting unpalatable quid pro quos for their support. We need to be clear-eyed and pragmatic in determining, on a case-by-case basis and as the situation evolves, how far our need for counterterrorism cooperation should take us with nations whose domestic policies we may not like, whose positions on other issues we may not support, or who may have antagonistic relationships with other important U.S. partners.

To raise just a few of the challenges ahead:

- The early phases of the war against terrorism have already seen increased U.S. communication and some cooperation with regimes such as Iran, Sudan, and Syria, all of which have been state sponsors of terrorism. How will we reconcile this with a policy of zero tolerance for state sponsors of terrorism?
- India and Pakistan both have offered strong support to the struggle against terrorism. India has sought U.S. support in branding as terrorists the militants that conduct attacks in Kashmir. Pakistan supports some of these Kashmiri groups and wants to keep a fire wall between Kashmir and the terrorism issue. The United States will not be able to satisfy both.
- Russia has offered solid support for the U.S. campaign against terror. Yet the indiscriminate and disproportionate use of force by Russian troops in Chechnya has done more to inflame terrorism than to extinguish it.
- Uzbekistan won U.S. favor early in the campaign for its willingness to host U.S. military forces involved in the mission in Afghanistan. But because Uzbekistan faces a threat of its own from a violent Islamic group with ties to bin Laden, its response has been to crack down on independent Muslims overall—that is, Muslims who practice their religion outside the control of the state. In the process, Uzbek authorities have imprisoned and tortured numerous innocent Muslims. This may cause some in the region to question the U.S. assertion that the war against terrorism is not a war against Islam.
- China has hinted that the price for greater cooperation in the war on terrorism may be a more sympathetic U.S. stance when it comes to Tibet and Taiwan.

The United States will need to make some hard choices and possibly compromises as it prosecutes the campaign against terrorism, but it should always balance its near-term actions against the long-term implications and consequences.

8. An International Coalition of Coalitions

The September 11 hijackers carried passports from Saudi Arabia, the United Arab Emirates, and Lebanon. Their apparent ringleader was

Egyptian. In the months and years before they launched their attack, some of them had lived or traveled in Germany, Spain, the Czech Republic, Malaysia, Canada, and a host of other countries. Their suicidal strikes on the World Trade Center and the Pentagon claimed victims from more than 60 countries. The September 11 attack may have been directed at Americans, but it was international in both its inception and implications.

Such a global threat demands a global response; and the long-term, multifaceted campaign against global terrorism will require constant international coalition building and maintenance. Yet there is no single, monolithic coalition or grouping of nations that can fulfill all U.S. objectives. Rather, the United States will have to build and sustain a series of interconnected coalitions around each key aspect of the campaign. Each coalition will comprise distinct actors, though memberships may overlap. As with a suit of armor, the ultimate ability of these various coalitions to help protect the United States and the civilized world more broadly will depend not only on each individual coalition but also on how the coalitions are fused together and how the seams are reinforced. The coalitions will need to be engaged at varying levels of intensity over different time periods—with activities sequenced carefully—and they all will need to evolve as circumstances change.

The United States will need to balance carefully the various coalitions throughout this process. Although some coalitions will be mutually reinforcing, especially if their actions are sequenced properly, action by some of the coalitions on certain issues will inevitably increase tensions in other coalitions and restrict options in other spheres. This will be most true of military action, especially if undertaken on a largely unilateral basis.

The United States has a right and a duty to protect its citizens, including through unilateral action when necessary. Indeed, effective military action that achieves broadly accepted objectives and limits collateral damage has the potential to enhance U.S. credibility and leadership in other areas as well. That said, military action, especially when undertaken unilaterally to achieve objectives not widely shared among coalition partners, might severely restrict the U.S. ability to mobilize key countries to support other priority fronts in the fight against terrorism.

The campaign against terrorism clearly will call for greater multi-layered, multilateral cooperation than the United States has ever engaged in to date. In the weeks following the September 11 attacks, the Bush administration has recognized the importance of coalition building—using multilateral forums including the United Nations, NATO, and more than 40 other international organizations to create a sense of common purpose. Maintaining this shared sense of purpose as well as credibility in the eyes of the international community will be critical to success over the long term, and international organizations like the United Nations can play a key role as a touchstone of international legitimacy. The real challenge, however, will come as the searing memory of September 11 recedes and the fight against terrorism expands to directly affect more countries.

Maintaining the broad range of coalitions required—to destroy terrorist networks directly linked to September 11, to dismantle other terrorist networks, to broaden and deepen a clear set of international norms against terrorism, to sustain global economic growth and development, to provide humanitarian relief, to rebuild failed states, and to support moderate Islam—will require monumental effort. The United States cannot and should not aspire to lead them all. Although U.S. participation is necessary across the board, the Bush administration should actively recruit countries and international organizations like the United Nations to take the lead on some of the coalitions at the earliest possible stages of the campaigns. In fact, the success of some of these coalitions may depend on a low U.S. profile.

To maintain broad-based international support over time, the U.S. government will need to prove consistently its collaborative, multilateral bona fides. The campaign against terrorism will suffer if it is the only foreign policy priority that the United States handles in this fashion. The more the United States can participate in collaborative efforts on issues of concern to other countries, such as missile defense, the International Criminal Court, and even climate change, the more partners the United States will have in its struggle against global terrorism.

9. The Value and the Limits of Military Operations

The U.S. military has a vital role to play in the campaign against global terrorism, from launching attacks to destroy the terrorist networks responsible for the unspeakable death and destruction of September 11 to preventive actions that curtail the ability of terrorist organizations to conduct future attacks; from operations to depose a regime that directly supported or provided sanctuary to terrorists with global reach to contributing to the defense of the American homeland.

Americans' willingness to use the U.S. military, particularly our willingness to put American soldiers on the ground in battle repeatedly and in the most adverse conditions, also signals the depth of our national resolve and commitment to this campaign. This is a war for which we are willing to sacrifice, if sacrifice we must, to win. And the military operations we conduct are the most visible sign of our national will.

Nevertheless, the utility of military operations can be extremely limited against a loose, global network of small cells of terrorists with little infrastructure, especially when they go to ground. The more Al Qaeda operates like a virtual network—with little communication that can be intercepted, no visible infrastructure, and highly decentralized leadership—the less relevant the military will be as an instrument in the campaign against it. Indeed, less visible activities in the intelligence, law enforcement, and financial arenas may have much more powerful effects on the ultimate success of the campaign than the military actions we more often see reported in the media. The same may be true of longer-term efforts to ameliorate the conditions that create fertile ground for global terrorism, such as foreign assistance, economic development, democratization, and the rebuilding of failed states. This should be kept in mind if and when the requirements of the military elements of the campaign come into conflict with those in other domains.

10. Intelligence Is the Long Pole in the Tent

With hindsight, it seems clear that shortfalls in U.S. intelligence information, capabilities, and processes enabled terrorists to strike on September 11 with surprise and to devastating effect. At the same time, it is clear, as President Bush has said, that the dedicated men and women of the intelligence community are "on the front line of making sure our victory will be secure."

As we consider the long campaign against terrorism before us, and the prospect of additional attacks, intelligence will remain the long pole in the tent—the indispensable element of the campaign on which the success of all others will depend. With good intelligence, anything is possible; without it, nothing is possible.

Indeed, intelligence enables all other components of the campaign against terrorism to be effective, from homeland security to law enforcement, military and covert operations, and coalition building. Decisionmakers in each of these areas must rely on information that is gathered, analyzed, and provided by the intelligence community. Meeting the multifaceted challenges associated with intelligence collection, analysis, and dissemination will be daunting because each element of the campaign against terrorism poses unique intelligence requirements.

Unfortunately, given the nature of the adversary, there are no guarantees that the quality of U.S. intelligence on terrorist organizations like bin Laden's Al Qaeda network will substantially improve without significant operational changes and sustained effort by the intelligence community. As a flat organization that comprises small cells of individuals in more than 60 countries around the world, Al Qaeda has consistently demonstrated its ability to use a wide range of communications, from low-tech means like face-to-face meetings to high-tech means like encrypted messages. When its communications have been intercepted, it has been extremely agile in changing its modus operandi to evade Western intelligence collection.

Terrorist organizations like Al Qaeda also lack the infrastructure that makes other intelligence targets, like governments, easier to penetrate. Under these circumstances, national technical means of collection are less effective. Furthermore, the extremist ideology that motivates its recruits and cements an otherwise loose network together makes it extremely difficult—indeed almost impossible—for Western agents to infiltrate. Owing to the strength of their convictions, members are unlikely to defect, even if offered substantial incentives. Given these factors, the campaign against terrorism may pose the biggest intelligence challenge for the United States and its allies since the Cold War.

11. Enhancing Situational Awareness without Becoming a Police State

One of the greatest challenges the United States faces in the fight against terrorism is how to create situational awareness—the ability to know what terrorists are doing inside U.S. borders—without becoming a police state.

The planners and perpetrators of the September 11 attacks lived, prepared, and hid among us for several years, and yet we were largely unaware of their activities. Indeed, one of the things that stands out about the September 11 episode is how little actionable intelligence was available prior to that date and how much various intelligence and law enforcement agencies have gathered since then. How could this have happened?

One answer is that the system was not tuned to collect the right data and to evaluate that data properly. This suggests the need to redesign data collection and analysis priorities and strategies for the intelligence and law enforcement communities. Another answer is that relevant bits of information were available within various agency files, but remained unfound needles in the enormous haystack of intelligence data. This suggests the need for new technologies to organize, store, and retrieve information that the U.S. government already collects. A third answer is that individual agencies may have identified key pieces of information, but failed to share and correlate the data in a way that enabled them to put all the pieces together and see the larger picture. This suggests the need to enhance data sharing and correlation across agency lines. But this inevitably raises the specter of intelligence agencies collecting information within U.S. borders—something that has long been seen as a threat to the basic privacy and political rights of Americans.

Being effective in the campaign against terrorism will require us to wrestle this difficult issue to the ground. Creating the situational awareness now deemed essential will require us to develop new methods for lawful surveillance of American citizens and foreigners living in America while we create adequate oversight mechanisms to ensure that new methods are not used inappropriately. In short, in the future we must do better at finding and tracking terrorists on American soil while also protecting the civil liberties that are essential in our society.

12. Preparedness for Dealing with Bioterrorism and Attacks on Critical Infrastructure

The United States is ill prepared to deal with the worst threats to its homeland: bioterrorism and attacks on critical infrastructure. Whereas an effective terrorist attack involving chemical agents could produce tens or hundreds of thousands of casualties, an effective attack using biological pathogens could result in millions. It is well established that members of the Al Qaeda organization have shown interest in biological means of attack and have contacts with states that have biological weapons programs. The anthrax attacks that followed September 11 effectively ended the debate about whether terrorists could access and use biological agents. They have and they will.

Fortunately, biological pathogens are generally difficult to weaponize—that is, it is difficult to take them from a laboratory petri dish or vial, produce them in large quantities, and turn them into a form that can be effectively dispersed to cause mass casualties. Unfortunately, terrorists would need only a small quantity of a highly contagious pathogen like smallpox to infect enough people to create a mass casualty event. Each infected individual, in effect, would become a walking biological weapon—a danger whose dimensions are magnified in our modern, mobile society. A local bio-attack could quickly become a national crisis with the potential to cripple the country.

Today, security measures at U.S. and foreign laboratories are not adequate to prohibit theft of dangerous biological samples. In the United States, samples of some pathogens like smallpox are kept under very tight security; but samples of others, like anthrax, are housed in research laboratories across the country with only minimal safeguards. Furthermore, literally tons of Cold War–era biological weapons agents remain housed in nonsecure facilities across the former Soviet Union.

In addition, we are ill prepared to prevent the dire consequences of a large-scale bioterrorism attack. The United States currently lacks the stockpiles of vaccines and antibiotics and the means of rapid distribution that would be required for an effective response. Also lacking is an adequate cadre of first responders who are trained and equipped to deal with such a crisis. The U.S. public health system is not prepared to meet this challenge.

Nor does the U.S. government have adequate management strategies, plans, and information systems to cope with a major bioterrorism assault. Today, senior leaders would simply not receive the intelligence and expert advice they need in time to make informed decisions. As a result of these shortfalls, state and federal officials could find themselves in the untenable position of having to impose forcible constraints on citizens because they lack other viable tools to contain a crisis. This would pose enormous challenges to civil liberties and horrific choices for decisionmakers. Indeed, the less prepared we are for a bioterrorism event, the greater the panic that will likely ensue and the more threats there will be to civil liberties—and to the lives—of average Americans.

The United States should therefore give highest priority to preventing pathogens that could be used in such attacks from falling into the hands of terrorists, and to enhancing the U.S. ability to deal with such attacks should they occur.

In addition, the United States should give even greater attention to preparing for devastating cyber and physical attacks on the nation's critical infrastructure. Although some progress has been made on this front over the past several years, effective attacks on our country's power grids, telecommunications and information systems, or transportation system could be truly devastating. Bolstering our ability to defend against and manage the consequences of such attacks should be a high priority for the United States.

13. Winning Hearts and Minds

Throughout the Islamic world, America suffers from a bad image. Many Muslims believe that the United States is at best unsympathetic and at worst openly hostile to Islam. They contend that many of its policies are biased against the interests of Arabs and Muslims—including America's alleged unconditional support for Israel, economic sanctions and bombings against Iraq, stationing of American troops in the same country as Islam's holiest sites, and complicity with repressive regimes. They see the attack on Al Qaeda and the Taliban in Afghanistan as an assault on Islam that is precipitating a humanitarian disaster.

America has also become a symbol of the profoundly disquieting threat that modernization poses to individuals and institutions in traditional societies and a target of the frustrations many in Arab society feel toward their own regimes, which have often failed to meet their citizens' political, economic, and social needs yet are the recipients of U.S. support.

These perceptions fuel anti-American frustration among the many and hatred among the few—even as American ideals and America's success remain powerfully attractive. Left unanswered, these perceptions threaten to hinder the U.S. ability to prosecute the war against terrorism and, over time, to erode U.S. power and influence in a large swath of the world. If the tide of public opinion continues to run strongly against America, the leaders of Arab and Muslim countries will find it that much more difficult to join and stay in the coalitions against terrorism. Muslim support for the campaign against terrorism could collapse entirely. The United States would risk an anti-American backlash that could destabilize countries like Pakistan, Saudi Arabia, and Egypt. The long-term effort to moderate and modernize Arab and Islamic countries would suffer a serious setback. There also could be a spillover effect that erodes support from European and other allies for the war against terrorism.

Osama bin Laden and Al Qaeda are competing with the West politically and morally, not just violently—and if the terrorists themselves are beyond the call of reason, the people and countries sympathetic to their issues if not their means are not beyond reach. A failure to seek their understanding if not endorsement will broaden the base from which terrorists can draw sanctuary, support, and even successors. Winning the war against terrorism and securing the resulting peace will be as much an act of persuasion as of coercion.

Portraying the United States as the enemy of Islam and of Arabs contrasts with the picture painted by U.S. foreign policy in the 1990s. The United States intervened in the Persian Gulf, Somalia, Bosnia, and Kosovo for a variety of reasons but with one common result: hundreds of thousands of Muslim lives were saved. The United States pressed the European Union to make Turkey—whose population is more than 90 percent Muslim—a candidate for membership. Successive administrations said they were prepared to recognize a Palestinian state and encouraged Israel to forge a lasting peace; in 2000, the United States brokered a historic offer from Israel that would have given Palestinians 95 percent of the occupied territories and dominion over East Jerusalem. American troops were deployed to Saudi

Arabia at that country's request to protect its people and Islam's holy sites from Iraqi aggression. Sanctions were imposed against Iraq by the United Nations, not the United States. Saddam Hussein could end the sanctions by complying with UN resolutions; instead, he has flaunted them and denied his people readily available food and medicine to win a propaganda victory. In Afghanistan, before September 11, the United States was already the largest food donor; some 4 million people were forced out of Afghanistan by civil war and the Taliban regime, long before the U.S. offensive against Al Qaeda. Meanwhile, millions of Muslims live and worship in peace in the United States.

America's side of the story is largely unheard in the Arab and Islamic worlds. One reason is the lack of freely flowing information and widespread official censorship and propaganda. Another reason is the failure of public diplomacy, which has been in decline since the end of the Cold War. Still another is the perception of those in many parts of the world that the world's richest country, at the pinnacle of its prosperity and power, has turned away from the acute problems in their countries—from economic stagnation and grinding poverty to a lack of opportunities for people to participate in decisions affecting their lives.

To prevail in the war against terrorism, and then to secure the peace, the United States must start changing hearts and minds in the Arab and Muslim worlds. By its actions, it must prove that it stands with the vast majority of the world's population on the things of most concern to them—including enhancing developing countries' ability to satisfy their people's social and economic needs, as well as addressing some of the political challenges and conflicts that both arise from and exacerbate those needs. Through its words, the United States must communicate the U.S. side of the story more effectively. It must also listen. After all, effective public diplomacy is not just about good public relations or selling America's side of the story; it is also about real dialogue.

The information war is less dangerous but probably as or more difficult than the campaign on the ground in Afghanistan. It will have to be sustained long after American troops return home. But it can be won. America's greatest strength is the ideas that bring us together as a people: freedom, progress, and tolerance. The terrorists have nothing to offer but repression, regression, and hate. The war of ideas is America's to win. It is time that we take it seriously.

14. Why Failed States Matter

One of the lessons learned on September 11 is that failed states matter—not just in the humanitarian sense, but in national security terms as well. If allowed to fester, such states can become sanctuaries for terrorist networks, not to mention organized criminals and drug traffickers who exploit the dysfunctional environment. As such, they pose a direct threat to the vital interests of not only the United States, but the international community at large.

Afghanistan, torn by decades of war, internal strife, and Taliban repression, exemplifies the dangers of failed states. The initial conventional wisdom that reconstructing Afghanistan is impossible is giving way to a growing recognition that rebuilding the country will be necessary to permanently root out terrorist networks from within its borders. Breaking up Al Qaeda and removing the regime that supports it is only the first step. Helping create a set of conditions that will deny opportunities to would-be terrorists is next. And finally, helping put in place political, economic, and social structures to enable the Afghan people to build a better future for themselves will be key to winning the war of ideas. Only if the United States and its allies prove themselves on this front will Muslims around the world believe Western assurances that the struggle against terrorism is not a war against Islam.

Reconstructing Afghanistan will be a monumental task—one that will require broad international support, significant human and material resources, and an unwavering political commitment over time. Although some have spoken of the challenge as being comparable with rebuilding Germany or Japan after World War II, in fact it will be vastly different. Those countries, despite the destruction they experienced, had strong human and material resource bases to build upon. In addition, the United States enjoyed total control as a military occupation force in these countries—something very unlikely to occur in this case. Nor will rebuilding Afghanistan look much like Bosnia, Haiti, or even Somalia. Indeed, the size of the country, the scope of human needs, the absolute devastation of any infrastructure, and the loss of most people with higher education and professional backgrounds combine to make Afghanistan the "mother of all reconstructions."

Given sensitivities surrounding the military campaign, the United States is perhaps not best situated to take an active leadership role on the ground. It can and should, however, lead the political and economic coalition building that will be necessary to sustain the effort. Under no circumstances can the United States afford to walk away from Afghanistan as it did following the withdrawal of Soviet troops in 1989.

Although Afghanistan will be the first big reconstruction test of the war on terrorism, it will not be the last. Similar challenges exist elsewhere, including in the Horn of Africa, where terrorist groups have already exploited the vacuum of state authority and are likely to seek further advantage if Afghanistan ceases to provide them sanctuary. Addressing this challenge will require U.S. government and international capacity that does not currently exist.

Rebuilding Afghanistan or any other nation cannot be solely an American or an international enterprise. Primary responsibility must rest with the people of the country in question. But the United States and the international community have a critical role to play in providing assistance. Thus the United States and the international community will need to act quickly to build their own capacities for rebuilding failed states and for postconflict reconstruction. The success of a longer-term campaign against terrorism may depend on the test case of Afghanistan.

15. Root Causes

Nothing—neither the culture of grievance, nor the sense of Palestinian abandonment, nor the resentment of American policies or preeminence—can justify or excuse the September 11 attacks. Any search for root causes must keep that reality foremost in mind. At the same time, if Americans hope to succeed in diminishing and defeating global terrorism over time, we must try to identify and mitigate the conditions that have permitted terrorists like bin Laden to recruit young men to become willing suicide bombers and have spawned deep-seated hatred of the United States and the West in some parts of the world.

In the Middle East and Persian Gulf, a number of Arab states, many of them friendly toward or aligned with the United States, have played an undeniable role in the formation of fanatical Islamic groups like Al Qaeda now waging a terrorist campaign against America. The debate about the root causes of Islamic terrorism continues to swirl in Arab intellectual circles, with the familiar culprits represented as U.S. support for Israel and abandonment of the Palestinians or the presence of U.S. military facilities in close proximity to Islam's holiest places.

Yet, the single most important driver of Islamic rage is the failure of many "moderate" Islamic states to create modern governments responsive to the needs of their people and viable civil societies where even minimal levels of debate and democracy are tolerated. A number of these regimes risk being failures in progress, with governing structures that are fundamentally unrepresentative and corrupt and economies that do not meet the basic needs of their growing populations. Saudi Arabia and Egypt—one rich, one poor—have both failed to provide a modern political program or a compelling vision of progress to compete with dark forces in their societies seeking to sustain the cult of Muslim victimology at the hands of Western infidels. Numerous moderate or democratic voices in many Middle Eastern states have been imprisoned or silenced.

Instead, many regimes have tolerated fundamentalist clerics preaching an antimodern credo that endorses violence, as long as it is directed at others. Many Middle Eastern schools, mosques, universities, and discussion groups favor a form of rarefied militant theology that might prompt the politically disaffected or religiously zealous alike to leave for the fight abroad. Numerous Islamic states have inadvertently helped to create Al Qaeda, either by failing to address the societal conditions that make fertile recruiting grounds for terrorists, by providing financial support to the organization, or by simply looking the other way. The support provided by many Islamic states to extremists extends well beyond simple training camps in Afghanistan to an entire fabric of public acceptance and private support throughout the Middle East and its environs.

The United States has tolerated these regional dynamics for years for several reasons ranging from Cold War necessities and the prospect of progress in the Middle East peace process to the long-standing need for a reliable flow of petroleum products from the gulf. However, the propensity of Middle Eastern leaders, seeking to find an accommodation with extremist and violent elements of Islamic society, to subtly side with the forces of political regression has backfired badly. Ironically, one of the only political leaders to openly challenge extremists in his society in favor of a more tolerant, benevolent interpretation of Islam is President Khatami of Iran, a country that still has strong elements of its society that are implacably opposed to the United States. There are, however, some trends to be encouraged. Bahrain, for example, has taken steps to increase tolerance, pluralism, and political participation.

If the United States prevails in its quest to make attitudes toward international terrorism a defining litmus test in international politics, then the practices of buying off extremists, suffocating legitimate voices of opposition, and seeking to export the violence outside national borders must cease. Aid and comfort to terrorists comes in myriad forms in the Middle East, and U.S. intolerance must extend well beyond the provision of training bases, money laundering, and political safe passage. Ultimately, the United States must begin to prepare for the possibility that unless ruling regimes in Saudi Arabia, Egypt, and elsewhere can embrace new policies that combine zero tolerance for terrorists, greater liberty and economic opportunities for their citizens, and ultimately more political participation, they may end up as casualties in this international campaign over the long term.

The conditions that allowed bin Laden's brand of global terrorism to take root and grow, and to find sympathy or at least tolerance in many quarters across the Middle East and other regions, must be addressed. The United States needs a new strategy toward the Middle East that recognizes these realities. Admittedly, this would be a radical departure from decades of U.S. policies that have consistently traded off democratization in favor of stability. Nor would it be a change without substantial risks. If reform is pursued too quickly, it could potentially destabilize a number of regimes in the Middle East, disrupt the flow of oil supplies, and even create governments who are openly supportive of terrorist organizations like Al Qaeda.

On the other hand, failure to pursue reform quickly enough could doom us to the same fate. Demographics in the region suggest that sitting regimes do not have a great deal of time to create nonviolent outlets for rising popular discontent. Coming up in these societies is a generation of angry young people who have no voice and few prospects. Seen in this light, creating more opportunities for economic development and political participation is a much more appealing alternative than violent overthrow at the hands of extremists who have gained the support of a deeply disaffected population.

In the wake of September 11, U.S. strategy in the Middle East must change. The top U.S. priorities must be assisting—if necessary, pressuring—various regimes to create more modern governments responsive to the needs of their people as well as more pluralistic civil societies in which the average citizen has greater opportunities for political participation and fostering economic development that provides an alternative to violence, especially for younger generations.

16. The Rediscovery of America by Americans

One of the most important impacts of September 11 is also one of the most obvious. One sees it in the American flags that grace everything from homes to cars to overpasses to office buildings to lapels. One sees it in the outpouring of donations and condolences to the families of the victims of the September 11 attacks, in the lines around the block to give blood at local Red Cross centers, in the flood of calls received by government switchboards from people who want to volunteer to do something, anything, to help. Americans—young and old, rich and poor, white and black, urban and rural—have been reawakened to what is right and noble and good about the land we love. We have rediscovered the idea and the ideal that is America. We have rediscovered what we have to lose.

Leaders at all levels of American society have an obligation to ensure that our outpourings of patriotism are accompanied by adequate reflection about our national choices and policies, both at home and abroad. Is American society what we want it to be? Is our role and impact in the world what we want it to be? Does what we do reflect what we believe? These leaders also have an opportunity to help channel American patriotism into paths that make a difference—such as volunteering, public service, and supporting the war on terrorism in any way that we can—and away from paths such as racism, vigilantism, and national arrogance that could destroy the very essence of what we hold dear.

One measure of victory in the campaign against terrorism will be Americans' ability to hold on to what distinguishes us as a nation—the openness of our society, the optimism of our national character, the fundamental freedoms we experience in our everyday lives—even as we adopt new security measures to protect them.

Recommendations

This section highlights for U.S. decisionmakers a number of high-level, actionable recommendations that flow from this volume's analysis and findings. This is not a comprehensive summary of all the recommendations made throughout the book; rather, it is a compilation of some of the most important concrete steps that should be taken in the campaign against global terrorism. A number of these recommendations focus on ways to strengthen U.S. homeland security, addressing particular areas of vulnerability, enhancing the government's capacity and performance, and seeking ways to harness the talent and energy of broader American society in service of this goal. Several of the recommendations propose concrete steps that should be taken to deny global terrorists support, sanctuary, and access to more devastating means of attack. Still others seek to address some of the underlying conditions that have created fertile soil in which the new terrorism has been allowed to take root and grow. Taken together, these proposals offer the United States a forward-looking agenda for action in the war on global terrorism.

1. The United States, working with the United Nations, other countries, and international relief organizations, should immediately launch an international emergency program to avert a humanitarian disaster in Afghanistan this winter.

After two decades of conflict, Afghanistan has produced almost 4 million refugees, about 1 million internally displaced people, and millions of people vulnerable to starvation and war who are still in place. Since the beginning of U.S. military operations and the resulting suspension of much of the international aid effort inside the country, the humanitarian situation has become even more desperate. The United Nations fears that the livelihood of 7.5 million "highly vulnerable" people in Afghanistan could be threatened by the lethal combination of conflict, starvation, and the harsh weather this winter.

Before September 11, the survival of 3.8 million Afghan people was dependent on UN and international food supplies. The inability of food convoys to reach the suffering population throughout the country after the onset of the U.S. military strikes and the evacuation of relief personnel has magnified the crisis. Consequently, if there is a humanitarian disaster in Afghanistan this winter, the United States will likely be blamed for it in many parts of the world. It would be hard to imagine a more tragic unintended consequence of this campaign, or a more divisive event for the coalition, than millions of innocent Afghan lives lost. Clearly, the United States and the broader international community should be doing everything in their power to avert such a disaster.

To avoid a humanitarian catastrophe, several steps need to be taken on an urgent basis:

- First, the United States should advocate a strategy of doing everything possible to sustain Afghans where they currently are, so as to avoid massive refugee flows that would cause immense suffering and potentially destabilize the region. In the first instance, the U.S. military, working with opposition forces on the ground, should conduct a coordinated campaign to consolidate their control over parts of the country and secure key lines of communication for the delivery of humanitarian relief supplies.

- Second, the United States should strongly urge the UN to authorize and set up camps and food distribution centers in those parts of Afghanistan where security conditions permit. Waiting until the war is over would risk the lives of millions of people and potentially spark even more massive refugee flows that could destabilize the region. In areas where there is no opposition military presence, the UN should seek to negotiate access to set up camps and relief distribution centers within Afghanistan as necessary.

- Third, the United States should press the countries surrounding Afghanistan to accept additional refugees should it become necessary and should provide significant support to the UN and host nations to set up additional camps in the region.

- Fourth, the Red Crescent, the Islamic counterpart to the Red Cross, should be urged to take a lead role in the relief operation on the ground, and the United States should staunchly support the international effort to raise and deliver additional resources. The $600 million of relief aid pledged by donor nations ($320 million by the United States) for humanitarian assistance is a good start. Unfortunately, as of this writing, only a minuscule percentage of this money ($35 million) had been received. Significantly more resources from the United States as well as from other wealthy countries will be needed to cope with the dire humanitarian emergency. In particular, the United States should work with its European, Asian, and Middle Eastern friends and allies to take leadership roles in this effort, both financially and politically.

- Fifth, the United States should offer to airlift relief supplies to the region for distribution by the UN and nongovernmental organizations on the ground and should dramatically increase its own airdrops of relief supplies inside Afghanistan.

Millions of innocent Afghan lives hang in the balance, and the United States and the international community should do everything in their power to save them. Failing to do so would mean not only a tragic loss of life but also a loss of moral leadership and, as a result, much dimmer prospects for the long-term success of the campaign against terrorism.

2. The president should launch a national, public-private initiative on a grand scale to minimize the risks posed by bioterrorism to the United States.

In the 1940s, President Roosevelt launched the Manhattan Project to ensure that the United States and its allies would develop atomic weapons before the Axis powers did; in the 1960s, President Kennedy initiated the Apollo Project to make America the first country on Earth to put a man on the moon; in the 1980s, President Reagan began funding the historic effort to map the human genome. In the first decade of the twenty-first century, a comparable challenge and opportunity looms before us—to neutralize the threat of bioterrorism. Working with Congress, state and local governments, and private industry, the president should mobilize the best and brightest minds in America to undertake an urgent, intensive program to develop a national arsenal of vaccines, antibiotics, and other means of disease control for every biological pathogen that could be used in terrorist attacks on the United States.

The focus of this modern-day Apollo Project would be to dramatically strengthen the U.S. public health system—its expertise, infrastructure, early warning systems, and pharmaceutical arsenal—to minimize and contain the effects of any bioterrorism attack on U.S. soil. This should include developing new approaches to deal with diseases that might be used as weapons of terror—especially stockpiling vaccines and antibiotics, strengthening regional and national distribution mechanisms, and researching and developing other means of facilitating rapid, effective disease control, such as funding the development of easily deployed diagnostic tools that make use of new biotechnologies. The decision to create a stockpile of 300 million smallpox vaccines was a step in the right direction, but much more needs to be done.

Particularly important will be mobilizing the scientific, medical, and pharmaceutical sectors to fully support this effort and providing them with the necessary incentives, such as liability protection, to rise to this national challenge. The federal government will also have to take the lead in developing an appropriate regulatory process to ensure the safety of new vaccines, antibiotics, and antiviral drugs.

This initiative should also include the development and implementation of new security protocols for all U.S. laboratories that store pathogens that could be used effectively in a terrorist attack; an extensive program of analysis, simulations, and exercises to improve Americans' understanding of the challenges we would encounter in the event of such an attack and to identify and prioritize shortfalls that need to be addressed; the development of more detailed plans and decisionmaking protocols for dealing with a bioterrorism event, including clarification of jurisdictional issues among local, state, and federal entities; and procurement at all levels of government of the information systems that would be needed to manage such a crisis.

America has risen to such historic challenges before. It is time to do so again.

3. The president and the Congress should significantly enhance U.S. intelligence capabilities for the campaign against terrorism.

If intelligence is indeed the long pole in the tent of the campaign against terrorism, it is imperative that the United States act quickly and wisely to identify and address the most serious intelligence problems in the counterterrorism campaign. For starters, the president should call for a comprehensive assessment to identify shortfalls in intelligence policy, capabilities, practices, and resources that could hamper the future effectiveness of the campaign. On the basis of these assessments, the administration should then develop a multiyear action plan to address priority issues and shortfalls.

Second, the president should give high priority to strengthening U.S. bilateral intelligence sharing and cooperation with countries that have the most to offer the United States on the terrorist organizations of greatest concern. After September 11, all such intelligence arrangements are now defining political issues in U.S. relations with many other countries. One of the central U.S. diplomatic goals in the months and years to come should be to broaden and deepen these arrangements as a cornerstone of U.S. bilateral relations with key countries. This should include seeking greater international cooperation in surveillance and tracking of the financial transactions of various terrorist organizations.

Third, the Congress should substantially increase the level of resources devoted to the intelligence community in general and the campaign against terrorism in particular. This will be essential to address critical shortfalls in a timely manner in areas such as HUMINT, covert operations, analysts, linguists, and area specialists, and in the integration of new technologies.

Fourth, the guidelines and processes for intelligence sharing within the United States need to be overhauled to enable more rapid and effective intelligence fusion and ensure adequate situational awareness. This needs to occur not only at the federal level but also among federal, state, and local agencies. American lives are now on the line, and there is simply no excuse for bureaucratic infighting that compromises America's ability to exploit the intelligence it has.

This will be no small challenge. It will require a shift in focus from a case-file approach to more fundamental and proactive data analysis.

Where are the terrorists likely to be hiding among us and how will we find them? How can we distinguish suspicious activities in a complex and dynamic society like America? It will also require substantial investment in data correlation and analysis capabilities as well as a new willingness to share data across bureaucratic lines. Improving our ability to correlate data will inevitably require us to reevaluate the rules and procedures governing the gathering of intelligence on American citizens and others living in the United States. We must develop new methods for lawful surveillance of American citizens and foreigners living in America. Specifically, the United States should create new combined-agency investigation centers that are supervised on an ongoing basis by an officer appointed by the court authorized by the Federal Intelligence Surveillance Act; this officer would essentially serve as a real-time privacy ombudsman to ensure that there is no inappropriate use of new investigative techniques.

Fifth, the intelligence and law enforcement communities need to undertake more red teaming or if-I-were-a-terrorist simulations to develop a better understanding of the types of attacks terrorist groups might be willing to contemplate and how they might respond in various situations. Though imperfect, at best, such exercises can be useful in exposing gaps in our thinking and shortcomings in preparation.

Finally, the intelligence community cannot and should not be expected to solve all of its problems on its own. It should pursue new public-private partnerships to engage the best technologists in the country to help it surmount its most substantial technological hurdles. Particular emphasis should be placed on investment in new technologies to organize, store, and retrieve information. After September 11, it should not be difficult to find private sector partners. More broadly, the intelligence community should seek to leverage America's diversity and openness at every opportunity, engaging experts and linguists outside the narrow confines of the federal government through a combination of outreach and outsourcing.

If September 11 changed anything for the intelligence community, it is this: The community is now recognized as both crucial and in need of additional resources and reform. Nothing will be more important to the success of the campaign against terrorism than meaningfully improving the capabilities and performance of the intelligence community.

4. Congress should refrain, in the near term, from passing legislation that would make the new Office of Homeland Security a cabinet-level department or fundamentally reorganize the U.S. government for homeland security.

A number of recent studies and legislative initiatives on homeland security have recommended sweeping institutional changes to the U.S. government, ranging from establishing a cabinet-level homeland security agency to passing a new homeland security act comparable in scope and import to the National Security Act of 1947. But if history is any guide, such fundamental organizational change would be, at this time, both unnecessary and premature. Lessons from World War II and since suggest that the keys to success in organizing the U.S. government for any sustained and complex campaign or effort—in this case, sustained homeland security operations—are full presidential empowerment of one person under the chief executive to drive the train as well as institutional flexibility to adapt and change as the operations unfold. Success also depends on ensuring that the empowered individual is focused on setting priorities, determining who should be responsible for what, and applying pressure where necessary to make sure that the president's priorities are actually implemented—not on conducting day-to-day operations. President Bush's conception of Governor Ridge's role as director of the Office of Homeland Security appears to be consistent with this model; establishing a new cabinet-level homeland security agency would not be.

In addition, going down the path of major institutional change at this stage in the campaign would risk diverting the attention and energy of both leaders and operators from the task at hand—taking concrete steps to improve the immediate U.S. capacity to deal with further terrorist attacks at home—to fighting rearguard actions to protect agency turf from encroachment by a new department. An ongoing crisis is not the best time to undertake a fundamental reorganization. Furthermore, we should not commit ourselves to legislated institutional change before we have enough experience to know what we really need to meet the new challenges we face.

In time, a reorganization may be necessary; if so, the Congress and the executive branch would need to work in partnership to define the best course of action. But it is simply too early to know what form such change should take. For now, Congress should give the president the time and discretion to try organizational and process innovations within the White House and departments. As the results come in, Congress and the executive branch should open a dialogue on whether and how the U.S. government should be fundamentally reorganized for homeland security missions over the long haul.

5. The president should empower the new director of the Office of Homeland Security to undertake a number of organizational and process innovations to fulfill his charter.

Although major legislation is not warranted at this time, there are several important steps the president and the director of homeland security should take to meaningfully improve the performance of the executive branch in the homeland security arena. Specifically, the director should

- Establish a terrorism assessment unit that thinks like a terrorist and researches alternative techniques for breaching U.S. security, with the aim of shedding new light on the planning and programming priorities of the various agencies that share the homeland security mission;
- Institute an extensive program of war gaming, including periodic exercises for the president and the cabinet, to uncover discontinuities in planning, enable senior officials to experience the complexity of "real" events, establish working relationships among participants who would operate together in crisis, transcend organizational turf battles, and highlight critical shortfalls in processes and capabilities that need to be addressed;
- Establish an advanced-concepts office to develop new approaches to government operations that would bridge the discontinuities and address the shortfalls identified in the war-gaming process;
- Create a planning staff to work with other agencies to develop a national homeland security strategy; assess current U.S. capabilities to carry out that strategy; and develop a multiyear, interagency plan of action, to be signed by the president, to guide resource allocation for homeland security across the federal government;

- Establish an annual program and budget review process, whereby the activities and expenditures of relevant federal agencies are reviewed in light of the requirements defined in the multiyear plan and the president's priorities enforced; and
- Take a number of concrete steps to more fully integrate federal programs and plans with those of state and local governments and to aid state and local authorities in enhancing their homeland security capabilities.

The president should also strengthen FEMA's capacity to deal with the consequences of terrorist attacks on U.S. soil, particularly those involving biological, chemical, or nuclear weapons or materials. This will require considerable investment in new staff and training activities.

The president should also demonstrate to his cabinet early on that, when it comes to homeland security, the director of the Office of Homeland Security speaks for him and there will be no appeals. This, more than any other factor, may determine the director's ability to succeed.

6. The congressional leadership should convene a panel of members to evaluate and recommend options for reorganizing congressional committees to enable more effective oversight of crosscutting issues like homeland security.

Some 14 congressional committees currently claim jurisdiction over some aspect of homeland security. In practice, this means Congress is essentially trying to provide oversight by looking at the problem vertically through 14 different soda straws. Given its power of the purse and its last word on how resources are actually expended by the federal government, Congress can have an enormous impact—positive or negative—on the coherence of an area of activity.

After September 11 and the subsequent anthrax attacks, the stakes involved in homeland security are as high as they can be, and they are likely to remain so indefinitely. There is no issue more important for Congress to engage on at this time in our nation's history. And there is no activity of the federal government in greater need of additional integration and synchronization. Providing this will require both the executive branch and the Congress to look horizontally across all dimensions of homeland security, something that the Congress is not currently organized to do.

Therefore, the leadership of the Senate and the House of Representatives should jointly establish a panel of members to review and assess options for reorganizing the congressional committee structure with a view toward increasing Congress's ability to provide effective oversight on, and bring greater coherence to, issues like homeland security that cut across traditional departmental and jurisdictional boundaries. This panel should make its recommendations to the congressional leadership within one year.

Congress has a key integrating role to play and an invaluable contribution to make to strengthening the security of Americans at home. But it may need to change its committee structure to do so effectively.

7. Congress should consider the creation of a homeland security service corps.

The twin attacks on the World Trade Center and the Pentagon have led to an outpouring of national volunteering and participation in the recovery effort. Across the nation, Americans are looking for ways to contribute to the campaign more directly and meaningfully. One of the ways to help sustain this sense of national purpose over time will be to create opportunities for national service in the area of homeland security. Indeed, this initiative serves two essential functions; it helps create more human capacity to deal with a daunting challenge, and it helps to connect people to the national effort at hand. The president should create a task force to explore the creation of a Homeland Security Service Corps for young and old Americans alike, who are prepared to give two years to help serve and protect the nation. Volunteers would be trained to serve in a variety of fields, including the Public Health Service, Airport Security, and the National Guard and Reserve. Modeled after the Peace Corps and AmeriCorps, suitable educational and financial benefits would be made available to volunteers, and the program would need the strong bipartisan commitment of the president and Congress. The task force could also explore the merits of mandatory national service given the challenges of a new age.

8. The secretary of defense should accelerate the U.S. military's transformation to deal with terrorism and other asymmetric threats.

We now understand, all too painfully, the lesson that many of our adversaries, and would-be adversaries, took home from the 1991 Gulf War: If you are going to challenge the United States, do not take on the conventional might of the U.S. military; rather, use asymmetric means like terrorism, cyberwar, or weapons of mass destruction to exploit America's vulnerabilities and avoid its strengths. Indeed, the fact that asymmetric threats were on the rise had become a common refrain among U.S. national security experts over the past decade, but it did not sink into the public consciousness or fundamentally change our defense spending priorities—until now.

After September 11, it seems clear that enhancing U.S. military capabilities to combat terrorism, defend the U.S. homeland, and deal with asymmetric threats more broadly will require significant changes in the U.S. military—how it fights, how it is equipped, and how it is organized. U.S. defense strategy has long paid homage to the rise of asymmetric threats and the need for the U.S. military to transform to deal with them, but tangible progress in new operational concepts, advanced systems, and organizations has been slow. September 11 should serve as a wake up call to the Department of Defense leadership, the military services, the Congress, and the entire defense community that we must accelerate the transformation process—and fast. The future is now here.

In more operational terms, transformation means meaningfully improving the military's ability to undertake a number of key tasks, like protecting critical operating bases at home and abroad from an attack with weapons of mass destruction. The secretary of defense should increase investment in better systems to detect chemical agents and biological pathogens, active and passive defenses to protect forces and populations from their devastating effects, and capabilities to contain and minimize the consequences of an attack with weapons of mass destruction should one occur.

Another key task is being able to protect information systems from cyber attack. Here, greater investment should be made in strengthening our computer network defenses and in developing counterhacker units that seek to turn the tables on any cyber intruders and put them on the defensive.

One of the greatest challenges the U.S. military is likely to face in the future is projecting and sustaining U.S. forces in environments where an adversary seeks to deny our access or where access is otherwise restricted, as in Afghanistan. This particular challenge argues in favor of increasing the Defense Department's investment in longer-range systems such as strategic bombers and long-range unmanned aerial vehicles and unmanned combat aerial vehicles relative to investing in shorter-range systems such as tactical strike aircraft. It also argues for an emphasis on stealthy systems—be they aircraft or submarines that can deliver needed firepower while evading detection—as well as forces that can forcibly gain access when it has been denied, such as Marines, specially trained Army units, and special operations forces capable of conducting quick in-and-out raids behind enemy lines.

More broadly, transformation means fielding leaner, more agile, mobile, and lethal forces that can operate as part of a seamless network to combat terrorists and other threats. Here, the long pole in the tent is adequate investment in the command, control, communications, computers, intelligence, surveillance, and reconnaissance (C4ISR) capabilities essential to achieving an all-seeing picture of the battlefield and a flexible and dynamic system of command and control.

Ultimately, accelerating transformation will require the secretary of defense to substantially increase investment in concept development and experimentation by both the services and the Joint Forces Command. It will also require a change in the military's zero-defect culture—that is, the perception that one misstep or mistake will end a promising career—to one that fosters and rewards innovation.

Even at a time when the nation seems willing to spend whatever it takes on defense, we simply cannot afford to spend money on programs we do not need. The Department of Defense must set priorities and make tough trade-offs to ensure that additional monies made available for defense as a result of September 11 are spent where they are needed most. This means scrapping unnecessary programs and infrastructure as well as reengineering inefficient business practices so that resources can be shifted toward those that will truly transform the U.S. military's ability to deal with the new threats we face.

9. The secretary of defense should establish a new commander in chief for homeland defense and make homeland defense the primary mission of the National Guard.

The U.S. military must be better organized to support homeland defense. Historically, assigning responsibility for an area or function to a commander in chief (CINC) has been the most effective way to ensure that it receives priority attention in the military's planning, training, and resource allocation. Creating a new CINC for homeland defense would put all the military assets required to support homeland security—air defense forces, missile defense forces, civil support units, and others—under the command of a single four-star general or admiral. It would create a senior go-to person within the U.S. military whose sole job, day and night, would be to prepare the military for operations to protect against or respond to threats to the U.S. homeland. No such person or focal point currently exists. Practically speaking, creating a new homeland defense CINC would most likely involve reorienting and expanding the missions and resources of either Joint Forces Command or Space Command. In either case, the challenge would be to balance the desire to put all of the military's homeland defense missions into one CINC's basket, with the need to ensure that the resulting CINC has a manageable set of missions and span of control.

In addition, homeland defense should be made the primary mission of the U.S. Army and Air National Guard, and elements of the guard should be reorganized, properly trained, and equipped to undertake this mission. Specifically, the Air National Guard should be given air and missile defense of the United States as its primary mission and should be restructured accordingly. The Army National Guard should be reoriented, reorganized, trained, and equipped to focus on consequence management in the event of a major terrorist attack (especially one involving chemical, biological, or nuclear materials), maintaining civil order, and augmenting civilian capabilities for protecting critical infrastructure. Geographically dispersed, with deep ties to local communities and well-established relationships with state governments, the National Guard is ideally suited to be the military's primary contribution to these missions. Reorienting the Army National Guard in this way would reorder its current priorities and would make acting as a strategic reserve in the event of a long or difficult major war overseas a secondary mission. Over the longer term, the strategic reserve mission might be assigned to a restructured Army Reserve.

10. The president should reinvigorate and recast the original Bush Doctrine to make clear that any regime that uses nuclear, biological, or chemical weapons against the United States, its forces, or its interests or that supplies such weapons to terrorists will be removed from power.

In January 1991, President George H. W. Bush wrote a letter to Saddam Hussein that stated that "the United States will not tolerate the use of chemical or biological weapons . . . [and that] the American people would demand the strongest possible response. You and your country will pay a terrible price if you order unconscionable actions of this sort."[1] This policy that a regime's use of nuclear, biological, or chemical weapons would effectively end its existence subsequently became known as the Bush Doctrine.

In the aftermath of September 11 and the subsequent anthrax attacks, we see this doctrine through a new lens: We now know that such weapons could be used not only against U.S. forces and interests abroad but also against the American people on American soil. This new reality—or perhaps this newly recognized reality—calls for a new version of the Bush Doctrine. The new doctrine should make clear that any regime that (a) uses nuclear, biological, or chemical weapons against the United States, its forces, or its vital interests or (b) provides such nuclear, biological, or chemical capabilities to terrorists will be removed from power. Given the credibility and the seriousness of the threat of such an attack on the U.S. homeland, the revised doctrine should also address the issue of preemption: The United States reserves the right to destroy, disable, or seize any regime's nuclear, biological, or chemical capabilities if the United States has credible evidence that the use of these weapons against the United States is imminent or that the regime is providing these capabilities to terrorist organizations.

There may be little or nothing we can do to deter terrorists who are willing to commit suicide for their cause, but the United States can and should do everything in its power to deter states who would contemplate using nuclear, biological, or chemical weapons against us or providing the necessary means to terrorist organizations for their use.

11. The president and the Congress should redouble U.S. initiatives to prevent the proliferation of nuclear, biological, and chemical weapons, materials, and know-how and to reduce the risk that these could fall into the hands of terrorists.

Horrific as the events of September 11 were, the potential for greater destruction is real. Al Qaeda is known to have sought to acquire weapons of mass destruction. Part of our effort to prevent future tragedies must be to bolster international nonproliferation and counterproliferation efforts—particularly in Russia, where the largest source of dangerous materials and weapons of mass destruction know-how is found. Every effort must be made to ensure that nuclear, biological, and chemical weapons and materials do not fall into the hands of terrorists.

Specifically, the United States should work with Russia and key allies to broaden and deepen cooperation on nonproliferation and Nunn-Lugar-type programs. When looking to revitalize Nunn-Lugar and other threat reduction programs, we must take into account what has transpired in the past—what has worked, what has not, and why. We must also seek to expand these programs in light of September 11 and the subsequent anthrax attacks in the United States. Specifically, U.S. leaders should urge Russia to fully disclose the size and composition of its stockpiles of chemical and biological agents and to explore ways the United States and others could assist Russia in accelerating the destruction of excess agents, enhancing the security of stockpiles and facilities that remain, and enhancing the security of its borders and its export control system. The United States should also explore ways to expand ongoing cooperation with Russia on the safety, security, and disposal of nuclear materials and to initiate a threat reduction program for tactical nuclear weapons. The United States should also ask its European allies and Japan to increase their financial support for expanded threat reduction programs aimed at reducing the chances that chemical, biological, or nuclear weapons materials could fall into the hands of terrorist organizations or their state sponsors.

12. The president and the secretary of state should launch a major global initiative in order to strengthen international norms against terrorism.

The U.S. government should work to broaden and deepen a clear set of norms and international legal instruments to combat terrorism. Far from constraining America's ability to act, these norms can help sustain the coalitions necessary to prosecute a long-term antiterror campaign. A clear and effective international legal framework would facilitate participation of states with considerable domestic political constraints, especially in the Islamic and the broader developing world. It would placate European allies that often seek (and, in the case of Germany, need) a legal basis for cooperation in military efforts.

A first step is securing U.S. ratification of the 1997 Convention for the Suppression of Terrorist Bombing and the 1999 Convention for the Suppression of the Financing of Terrorism and ensuring that enough other states ratify these conventions for their early entry into force. Next, the United States should spearhead an effort to negotiate a 13th UN convention to strengthen implementation and fill in gaps in the 12 UN-sponsored antiterrorism conventions passed between 1963 and 1999.

Strengthening international norms against terrorism does not require that the United States seek UN approval for all its actions against terrorism. Article 51 of the UN Charter already establishes the right of self defense. While the United States is thus free to directly combat those who attacked it, Security Council resolutions specifically identifying parties who have violated the abovementioned norms will assist the United States in securing the broadest support possible for its actions.

13. The United States should launch an initiative to enhance the international community's funding and capabilities to rebuild failed states.

Failed states and postconflict societies often serve as sanctuaries from which terrorist organizations can operate with relative impunity: witness Afghanistan, Somalia, and Sudan. Central to the long-term success of the campaign against terrorism will be reducing the number of such states through international reconstruction efforts.

Rebuilding failed states involves addressing the security, economic, and social well-being, justice and reconciliation, and governance needs of the states in question, with the aim of restoring a functioning state that can look after the needs of its people and provide security within its own borders. Viewed in this light, reconstruction is a means of reducing direct threats to the security of the United States and its coalition partners. In the past, however, international efforts to assist countries in rebuilding in the aftermath of conflict have suffered from a number of shortfalls, including inadequate civilian capabilities in a number of critical areas, poor coordination among key actors in capitals and on the ground, and chronic underfunding.

It is therefore imperative that the United States work with donor countries, international financial institutions, and international organizations to determine an appropriate division of labor, a common understanding of requirements, and a game plan for addressing critical capability shortfalls. Within the U.S. government, particular attention should be paid to creating rapidly deployable civilian capabilities that would enable the United States to reduce its reliance on military forces that could be better used to meet other national security needs. The United States now has a compelling interest in working with other governments, international financial institutions, international organizations, regional organizations, and nongovernmental organizations to enhance the resources, capabilities, and coordination mechanisms available for rebuilding failed states.

14. The president and Congress should work together to fundamentally rewrite the U.S. Foreign Assistance Act, reinvigorate development assistance programs, and substantially increase the levels of foreign assistance the United States provides to key countries and regions.

Increasing and refocusing U.S. support to the economic and political development of key countries around the world is critical to ameliorating the conditions that contribute to global terrorism. It would also communicate the fact that the campaign against terrorism involves not only a strategy for waging war on the terrorists and those who support them, but also a constructive agenda. The president should commission a small bipartisan group of foreign assistance experts and senior political figures to design a new foreign assistance program.

While the process should bear the direct stamp of the president, the powers granted to Congress under the Constitution must be respected, and congressional leadership should be part of the process every step of the way.

A 10-point agenda should establish the fundamentals of the new approach:

- **Focused and clear objectives.**

  - Reduce transnational threats using a developmental approach to build international law enforcement capacity and fund specific antiterror, anticrime, and antinarcotics programs to complement traditional security assistance;
  - Improve sustainable development, including a focus on both economic growth and poverty alleviation;
  - Increase humanitarian programs, including refugee assistance, disaster assistance, and food assistance;
  - Promote democracy, political pluralism, and governance capacity;
  - Work toward conflict prevention; and
  - Increase trade and investment programs.

- **Coherence of strategic vision.** Put forward a coherent strategic vision of how various priorities are related and redefine funding and oversight authorities to correspond with that vision. Ensure that all development assistance, both bilateral and multilateral, is provided through the same account and overseen by the same committees in Congress.

- **Balancing types of assistance.** Reexamine how best to use foreign assistance to advance security and other goals simultaneously. Find a better balance between security and nonsecurity assistance and, within the latter, establish the right balance among lump-sum program assistance, food aid, and project assistance.

- **Program effectiveness and cost-effectiveness.** End the practice of excessive earmarking. Enable the administration, in consultation with Congress, to respond to changing needs. Lift some of the more rigid buy-American requirements in the contracting process. Move from uniform single-year appropriations for foreign assistance programs to a mixture of single-year to multiyear appropriations as needed to correspond with specific programs and funding cycles.

- **Efficiency and timeliness.** Reduce excessive reporting requirements and multiple layers of bureaucracy.
- **Interagency rationalization and coordination.** Provide a mechanism for coordinating the numerous agencies involved in foreign assistance, especially in the field.
- **Leverage investments.** Seek more opportunities to leverage limited U.S. bilateral monies by seeking partnerships with other bilateral and multilateral donors and using foreign assistance to more quickly bring private capital to bear to solve crucial problems.
- **Presence.** Increase the number of U.S. government personnel doing economic development work in the field—particularly USAID and the Peace Corps—and increase the authority of field representatives to make decisions.
- **Accountability.** Define and enhance a rigorous system of accountability for all funds provided. Adopt results-based budgeting, with clear lines of authority so that both agencies and individuals can be held accountable for results.
- **Resource levels.** Commit to funding foreign assistance at no less than 0.2 percent of gross national product—essentially double the current level—and, in the longer term, commit to a goal of 0.3 percent of gross national product—the average amount of U.S. foreign assistance between 1962 and 1979.

Ultimately, the foreign assistance program must change because it does not work. The imperative for a new program is only partially related to the fight against terrorism; most of these modifications are needed regardless. But now that a global threat to U.S. interests and ideals is once again a major part of the equation, it is more important than ever to recognize that promoting development is security by other means.

Writing a new foreign assistance act and reinvigorating development assistance programs would help alleviate real problems in the developing world, addressing some of the conditions that are conducive to terrorism. It would also help deepen cooperation with the developing world—and, in fact, would likely improve cooperation with other industrialized countries as well since they have been highly critical of the United States for abdicating its leadership role in this area for far too long. It would give the lie to terrorists' and their supporters' arguments that the United States represents only increasing inequality. And it would be a cost-effective investment in a better, safer world. By casting our lot with others around the globe and helping them lift their own lives, the United States will better define who we are as a country—to people and governments abroad and to ourselves.

15. The president should pursue a new U.S. strategy toward the Middle East and seek to win support for this strategy from Congress and key allies.

In the wake of September 11, U.S. strategy in the Middle East must be reoriented toward assisting—and, if necessary, pressuring—various regimes to create more modern governments responsive to the needs of their people, more pluralistic civil societies that provide average citizens greater opportunities for political participation, and more dynamic economies that create alternatives to frustration and violence, especially for younger generations. At the same time, the United States should aggressively seek to reduce its reliance on petroleum products from the region and to encourage its allies in Europe and Asia to do the same.

Working with Congress and key allies, the president should pursue a new U.S. strategy toward the Middle East to address some of the conditions that have enabled global terrorism to take root and grow. Any U.S. strategy in the Middle East and Persian Gulf is bound to be controversial and difficult to implement. Yet, in the aftermath of September 11, the outlines of a new approach and an integrated set of steps are emerging, requiring a new bipartisan vision and a durable diplomatic commitment. In the immediate aftermath of the first phase of military operations in Afghanistan, the United States must be prepared to move on a broad range of fronts to begin to put into place a multifaceted and long-term plan:

- Begin to put pressure on various Middle Eastern regimes to adopt fundamental political reforms and to move toward more representative forms of government and more open civil societies. Such reforms might include the release of political prisoners, the revision of draconian security laws and practices, the establishment of universal suffrage, tolerance of open political debate in a free press, and eventually the holding of free and fair democratic elections at all levels of government. Specifically, U.S. leaders should engineer a series of broad and sustained strategic dialogues with the leadership of various Middle Eastern states about the need for fundamental change.

- Reassert leadership in the Middle East peace process in an effort to get Israel and the Palestinians to return to the negotiating table. Pressure the Palestinian Authority to stop the attacks emanating from areas under its control and pressure Israel to stop conducting raids on Palestinian villages and expanding settlements in the occupied territories. Clarify U.S. support for both Israel's security and the establishment of a viable Palestinian state. Reviving the peace process will be exceedingly difficult after all that has happened since the parties walked away from the table, but failing to do so is intolerable and not in anyone's long-term interests.

- Engage a broader range of Middle Eastern leaders inside and outside of government, including scholars, clerics, and other opinion leaders, from moderates to fundamentalists.

- Redirect aid and investment flows to a broader civil society and commercial sector in the Middle East, deemphasizing direct grants to central government authorities. Strongly encourage structural economic reforms and diversification through targeted aid, trade agreements, and other measures to build up the private sector and encourage international investment.

- Provide assistance for educational reform in the region, particularly the establishment of Western-style universities, as an investment in future generations.

- Conduct a comprehensive review of U.S. military posture and bases in the Middle East to determine whether any changes should be made to reduce tensions and enhance our long-term standing in the region.

- Seek to reorient international sanctions against Iraq to focus on limiting Saddam Hussein's military buildup and weapons of mass destruction without crippling Iraq's economy and development.

Be prepared to strike Iraq militarily if evidence of collusion in terrorist attacks against the United States is credible.

- Move away from dual containment of Iraq and Iran in favor of a modest and careful political opening toward Iran. This can be undertaken only with a clear recognition that even though Iran appears to be in the later phase of its revolution, segments of Iranian society still see the United States as the Great Satan. Begin with expanded trade, some political dialogue, and modest people-to-people exchanges.
- On the home front, undertake steps such as adopting more aggressive conservation measures, developing more fuel-efficient vehicles and industrial processes, and further diversifying energy supplies to reduce U.S. reliance on Middle Eastern oil. Strongly encourage allies and friends in Europe and Asia to do the same.

The conditions that allowed Al Qaeda's brand of global terrorism to flourish—and to find sympathy, support, or at least tolerance in many quarters across the Middle East—must be addressed. From this point on, U.S. strategy toward the Middle East must recognize and seek to alter these realities while also reducing U.S. dependence on Persian Gulf oil.

16. The United States should initiate a long-term dialogue between religious and moral leaders from Western and Islamic societies in an effort to identify issues that link humanity instead of divide civilizations.

The campaign against terrorist organizations like Al Qaeda and the regimes that give them support and sanctuary is not a war between the West and Islam. Although members of Al Qaeda and their supporters may see the conflict in those terms, the prevailing view in the United States and Europe is very different. This war is not a clash of civilizations; rather, this is a clash between civilization—be it Judeo-Christian or Islamic—and a form of extremism that cloaks itself in the language of Islam even as it betrays some of that faith's most fundamental teachings.

How we characterize this campaign and how others understand it will likely have profound implications for our ability to succeed in the long term. Given the stakes involved, the U.S. government should fund a group of nongovernmental organizations to launch an independent initiative to bring together religious and moral leaders from both Western and Islamic societies to begin a series of dialogues on issues of common concern. The principal objective of these dialogues would be to find areas of common ground and then develop projects that would build on and communicate that common interest to a larger audience. Ideally, these dialogues should yield opportunities for people not only to meet together over time but also to work together on issues of mutual interest.

17. The president should promptly appoint a bipartisan commission to make recommendations for improving the development and delivery of public diplomacy.

The president and the secretary of state must make it clear that information is a strategic resource and that U.S. public diplomacy is critical to the success of the campaign against terrorism. The success of our foreign policy is inexorably linked to America's ability to understand, inform, and influence foreign publics.

The purpose of this commission would be to evaluate the state of public diplomacy and make concrete recommendations for improving its development and delivery. The commission should include experts in communications from the private sector (for example, television programmers, film writers and directors, and advertising specialists) and academics with a deep understanding of the Arab and Islamic worlds. Specifically, the commission should consider whether, and how to,

- prioritize public diplomacy in the foreign policy process;
- strengthen foreign public opinion research;
- develop a rapid response capability to counter misinformation about America and its policies;
- empower and equip U.S. ambassadors, embassies, and foreign policy officers to compete in the war of ideas;
- create American-presence posts outside of foreign capitals;
- take better advantage of media in the Arab and Muslim worlds;
- bolster international broadcasting programs and better utilize the Internet;

- develop and support outside validators;
- cultivate foreign opinion leaders;
- sustain and strengthen foreign exchange programs;
- develop message campaigns with the private sector;
- engage Arab-Americans and Muslim Americans in communicating America's message and policies; and
- undermine censorship and constraints on the media around the world.

Upon completion, the president and secretary of state should promptly review the commission's findings, decide which to accept, and order periodic progress reports on their implementation.

To prevail in the war against terrorism and then to secure the peace, the United States must begin a substantial, sustained effort to change hearts and minds in the Arab and Muslim worlds. Not to do so would sell America short in a war that is as much about persuasion as it is about coercion.

18. The administration should launch a public education campaign to better explain to the American people the objectives and nature of the long-term campaign.

Ensuring that the American people understand the campaign against terrorism—what it is trying to accomplish, how it is being conducted, how it is expected to unfold, the potential costs or sacrifices it may entail, and how best to deal with the continued threat of further terrorist attacks—is critical to sustaining our national resolve over the longer term. The administration has both an opportunity and an obligation to provide the American people with the information they need to stay committed to this campaign, even when the going gets rough.

This is particularly important with regard to homeland security, where government officials should aim to arm the public with information that will give the average citizen a greater sense of control—as the postal service has sought to do in letting people know what a suspicious package might look like. Local police should proactively inform residents how to recognize and report suspicious activity. Health officials should spread the word about disease prevention, symptom recognition, and treatment protocols for pathogens that could be used in a bioterrorism attack. And federal officials should raise public awareness about what used to be called civil defense measures, such as evacuation plans and preparation to remain sheltered in residences for an extended period. Such measures would not only help in the event of a terrorist attack (not to mention other natural or man-made disasters) but could also foster a sense of participation that would help sustain the national mood of collective purpose and unity.

The prevailing assumption should be that the public is mature enough to handle information, even when it is frightening. What causes people to distrust their leaders is feeling as though they are not being given the essential knowledge they need to protect themselves and their families. This reaction was palpable in the wake of the deaths of postal workers who had not immediately been put on antibiotics after it became clear that anthrax was being delivered through the U.S. mail.

A proactive public information campaign can also go a long way toward counteracting the conspiracy theories and hyperbolic rumors that inevitably proliferate to fill the vacuum of established facts and that can undermine national resolve.

In a democracy, the public has a right to know, and government leaders ignore that axiom at their peril. If the support of the American people for the campaign against global terrorism is to be deepened and sustained over time, the administration will need to develop a much more deliberate, comprehensive, and sophisticated approach to providing the American people with information. Providing information is essential to maintaining trust, and maintaining the public's trust is essential to prevailing in this campaign.

A Concluding Thought

In considering these findings and recommendations, one sobering conclusion is clear: If this moment in history is ripe with potential, it is also rich with risk.

What if the United States is blamed for the deaths of hundreds of thousands of Afghan refugees and internally displaced persons because of starvation and exposure this winter? What if U.S. military actions in Afghanistan tip the fragile political balance in Pakistan and extremists seize power and that country's nuclear arsenal? What if the United States widens its military operations in a way that is perceived as unjustified, fracturing the coalition and choking off international cooperation in critical areas like intelligence sharing and law enforcement? What if new surveillance and law enforcement measures undermine the civil liberties that define American society?

Even as we pursue the imperative to prevail, the United States must take great care not to overplay its hand; we must be prepared to respond rapidly to reduce the negative effects of any unintended consequences that should occur; and we must take great care to ensure that our short-term actions remain consistent with our long-term objectives over the life of the campaign.

We stand at a delicate moment in history—a turning point after which the United States could emerge even stronger, with the civilized world united against terrorism and our relations transformed for the better with friends and former foes alike; or after which events could spiral out of our control and plunge us into a period of fractious relations, intensified anti-Americanism, and a prolonged period in which our very way of life could be fundamentally threatened.

The stakes are as high as they come for this generation and the next. In managing this campaign—and this moment in history—we must prevail.

Note

[1] Statement by Press Secretary Fitzwater on President Bush's Letter to President Saddam Hussein of Iraq, January 12, 1991, http://bushlibrary. tamu.edu/papers/1991/91011201.html.

Appendixes

Selected Public Addresses on and after September 11, 2001

President George W. Bush
The White House
Washington, D.C.
September 11, 2001

Good evening. Today, our fellow citizens, our way of life, our very freedom came under attack in a series of deliberate and deadly terrorist acts. The victims were in airplanes, or in their offices; secretaries, businessmen and women, military and federal workers; moms and dads, friends and neighbors. Thousands of lives were suddenly ended by evil, despicable acts of terror.

The pictures of airplanes flying into buildings, fires burning, huge structures collapsing, have filled us with disbelief, terrible sadness, and a quiet, unyielding anger. These acts of mass murder were intended to frighten our nation into chaos and retreat. But they have failed; our country is strong.

A great people has been moved to defend a great nation. Terrorist attacks can shake the foundations of our biggest buildings, but they cannot touch the foundation of America. These acts shattered steel, but they cannot dent the steel of American resolve.

America was targeted for attack because we're the brightest beacon for freedom and opportunity in the world. And no one will keep that light from shining.

Today, our nation saw evil, the very worst of human nature. And we responded with the best of America—with the daring of our rescue workers, with the caring for strangers and neighbors who came to give blood and help in any way they could.

Immediately following the first attack, I implemented our government's emergency response plans. Our military is powerful, and it's prepared. Our emergency teams are working in New York City and Washington, D.C., to help with local rescue efforts.

Our first priority is to get help to those who have been injured, and to take every precaution to protect our citizens at home and around the world from further attacks.

The functions of our government continue without interruption. Federal agencies in Washington which had to be evacuated today are reopening for essential personnel tonight, and will be open for business tomorrow. Our financial institutions remain strong, and the American economy will be open for business, as well.

The search is underway for those who are behind these evil acts. I've directed the full resources of our intelligence and law enforcement communities to find those responsible and to bring them to justice. We will make no distinction between the terrorists who committed these acts and those who harbor them.

I appreciate so very much the members of Congress who have joined me in strongly condemning these attacks.

And on behalf of the American people, I thank the many world leaders who have called to offer their condolences and assistance.

America and our friends and allies join with all those who want peace and security in the world, and we stand together to win the war against terrorism. Tonight, I ask for your prayers for all those who grieve, for the children whose worlds have been shattered, for all whose sense of safety and security has been threatened. And I pray they will be comforted by a power greater than any of us, spoken through the ages in Psalm 23: "Even though I walk through the valley of the shadow of death, I fear no evil, for You are with me."

This is a day when all Americans from every walk of life unite in our resolve for justice and peace. America has stood down enemies before, and we will do so this time. None of us will ever forget this day. Yet, we go forward to defend freedom and all that is good and just in our world.

Thank you. Good night, and God bless America.

President George W. Bush
Address to a Joint Session of Congress
and the American People
United States Capitol
Washington, D.C.
September 20, 2001

Mr. Speaker, Mr. President Pro Tempore, members of Congress, and fellow Americans:

In the normal course of events, Presidents come to this chamber to report on the state of the Union. Tonight, no such report is needed. It has already been delivered by the American people.

We have seen it in the courage of passengers, who rushed terrorists to save others on the ground—passengers like an exceptional man named Todd Beamer. And would you please help me to welcome his wife, Lisa Beamer, here tonight.

We have seen the state of our Union in the endurance of rescuers, working past exhaustion. We have seen the unfurling of flags, the lighting of candles, the giving of blood, the saying of prayers—in English, Hebrew, and Arabic. We have seen the decency of a loving and giving people who have made the grief of strangers their own.

My fellow citizens, for the last nine days, the entire world has seen for itself the state of our Union—and it is strong.

Tonight we are a country awakened to danger and called to defend freedom. Our grief has turned to anger, and anger to resolution. Whether we bring our enemies to justice, or bring justice to our enemies, justice will be done.

I thank the Congress for its leadership at such an important time. All of America was touched on the evening of the tragedy to see Republicans and Democrats joined together on the steps of this Capitol, singing "God Bless America." And you did more than sing; you acted, by delivering $40 billion to rebuild our communities and meet the needs of our military.

Speaker Hastert, Minority Leader Gephardt, Majority Leader Daschle and Senator Lott, I thank you for your friendship, for your leadership and for your service to our country.

And on behalf of the American people, I thank the world for its outpouring of support. America will never forget the sounds of our

National Anthem playing at Buckingham Palace, and on the streets of Paris, and at Berlin's Brandenburg Gate.

We will not forget South Korean children gathering to pray outside our embassy in Seoul, or the prayers of sympathy offered at a mosque in Cairo. We will not forget moments of silence and days of mourning in Australia and Africa and Latin America.

Nor will we forget the citizens of 80 other nations who died with our own: dozens of Pakistanis; more than 130 Israelis; more than 250 citizens of India; men and women from El Salvador, Iran, Mexico and Japan; and hundreds of British citizens. America has no truer friend than Great Britain. Once again, we are joined together in a great cause—so honored the British Prime Minister has crossed an ocean to show his unity of purpose with America. Thank you for coming, friend.

On September the 11th, enemies of freedom committed an act of war against our country. Americans have known wars—but for the past 136 years, they have been wars on foreign soil, except for one Sunday in 1941. Americans have known the casualties of war—but not at the center of a great city on a peaceful morning. Americans have known surprise attacks—but never before on thousands of civilians. All of this was brought upon us in a single day—and night fell on a different world, a world where freedom itself is under attack.

Americans have many questions tonight. Americans are asking: Who attacked our country? The evidence we have gathered all points to a collection of loosely affiliated terrorist organizations known as al Qaeda. They are the same murderers indicted for bombing American embassies in Tanzania and Kenya, and responsible for bombing the USS *Cole.*

Al Qaeda is to terror what the mafia is to crime. But its goal is not making money; its goal is remaking the world—and imposing its radical beliefs on people everywhere.

The terrorists practice a fringe form of Islamic extremism that has been rejected by Muslim scholars and the vast majority of Muslim clerics—a fringe movement that perverts the peaceful teachings of Islam. The terrorists' directive commands them to kill Christians and Jews, to kill all Americans, and make no distinction among military and civilians, including women and children.

This group and its leader—a person named Osama bin Laden—are linked to many other organizations in different countries, including the Egyptian Islamic Jihad and the Islamic Movement of Uzbekistan. There are thousands of these terrorists in more than 60 countries. They are recruited from their own nations and neighborhoods and brought to camps in places like Afghanistan, where they are trained in the tactics of terror. They are sent back to their homes or sent to hide in countries around the world to plot evil and destruction.

The leadership of al Qaeda has great influence in Afghanistan and supports the Taliban regime in controlling most of that country. In Afghanistan, we see al Qaeda's vision for the world.

Afghanistan's people have been brutalized—many are starving and many have fled. Women are not allowed to attend school. You can be jailed for owning a television. Religion can be practiced only as their leaders dictate. A man can be jailed in Afghanistan if his beard is not long enough.

The United States respects the people of Afghanistan—after all, we are currently its largest source of humanitarian aid—but we condemn the Taliban regime. It is not only repressing its own people, it is threatening people everywhere by sponsoring and sheltering and supplying terrorists. By aiding and abetting murder, the Taliban regime is committing murder.

And tonight, the United States of America makes the following demands on the Taliban: Deliver to United States authorities all the leaders of al Qaeda who hide in your land. Release all foreign nationals, including American citizens, you have unjustly imprisoned. Protect foreign journalists, diplomats and aid workers in your country. Close immediately and permanently every terrorist training camp in Afghanistan, and hand over every terrorist, and every person in their support structure, to appropriate authorities. Give the United States full access to terrorist training camps, so we can make sure they are no longer operating.

These demands are not open to negotiation or discussion. The Taliban must act, and act immediately. They will hand over the terrorists, or they will share in their fate.

I also want to speak tonight directly to Muslims throughout the world. We respect your faith. It's practiced freely by many millions of Americans, and by millions more in countries that America counts as friends. Its teachings are good and peaceful, and those who commit evil in the name of Allah blaspheme the name of Allah. The terrorists are traitors to their own faith, trying, in effect, to hijack Islam itself. The enemy of America is not our many Muslim friends; it is not our many Arab friends. Our enemy is a radical network of terrorists, and every government that supports them.

Our war on terror begins with al Qaeda, but it does not end there. It will not end until every terrorist group of global reach has been found, stopped and defeated.

Americans are asking, why do they hate us? They hate what we see right here in this chamber—a democratically elected government. Their leaders are self-appointed. They hate our freedoms—our freedom of religion, our freedom of speech, our freedom to vote and assemble and disagree with each other.

They want to overthrow existing governments in many Muslim countries, such as Egypt, Saudi Arabia, and Jordan. They want to drive Israel out of the Middle East. They want to drive Christians and Jews out of vast regions of Asia and Africa.

These terrorists kill not merely to end lives, but to disrupt and end a way of life. With every atrocity, they hope that America grows fearful, retreating from the world and forsaking our friends. They stand against us, because we stand in their way.

We are not deceived by their pretenses to piety. We have seen their kind before. They are the heirs of all the murderous ideologies of the 20th century. By sacrificing human life to serve their radical visions— by abandoning every value except the will to power—they follow in the path of fascism, and Nazism, and totalitarianism. And they will follow that path all the way, to where it ends: in history's unmarked grave of discarded lies.

Americans are asking: How will we fight and win this war? We will direct every resource at our command—every means of diplomacy, every tool of intelligence, every instrument of law enforcement, every financial influence, and every necessary weapon of war—to the disruption and to the defeat of the global terror network.

This war will not be like the war against Iraq a decade ago, with a decisive liberation of territory and a swift conclusion. It will not look like the air war above Kosovo two years ago, where no ground troops were used and not a single American was lost in combat.

Our response involves far more than instant retaliation and isolated strikes. Americans should not expect one battle, but a lengthy campaign, unlike any other we have ever seen. It may include dramatic strikes, visible on TV, and covert operations, secret even in success. We will starve terrorists of funding, turn them one against another, drive them from place to place, until there is no refuge or no rest. And we will pursue nations that provide aid or safe haven to terrorism. Every nation, in every region, now has a decision to make. Either you are with us, or you are with the terrorists. From this day forward, any nation that continues to harbor or support terrorism will be regarded by the United States as a hostile regime.

Our nation has been put on notice: We are not immune from attack. We will take defensive measures against terrorism to protect Americans. Today, dozens of federal departments and agencies, as well as state and local governments, have responsibilities affecting homeland security. These efforts must be coordinated at the highest level. So tonight I announce the creation of a Cabinet-level position reporting directly to me—the Office of Homeland Security.

And tonight I also announce a distinguished American to lead this effort, to strengthen American security: a military veteran, an effective governor, a true patriot, a trusted friend—Pennsylvania's Tom Ridge. He will lead, oversee and coordinate a comprehensive national strategy to safeguard our country against terrorism, and respond to any attacks that may come.

These measures are essential. But the only way to defeat terrorism as a threat to our way of life is to stop it, eliminate it, and destroy it where it grows.

Many will be involved in this effort, from FBI agents to intelligence operatives to the reservists we have called to active duty. All deserve our thanks, and all have our prayers. And tonight, a few miles from the damaged Pentagon, I have a message for our military: Be ready. I've called the Armed Forces to alert, and there is a reason. The hour is coming when America will act, and you will make us proud.

This is not, however, just America's fight. And what is at stake is not just America's freedom. This is the world's fight. This is civilization's fight. This is the fight of all who believe in progress and pluralism, tolerance and freedom.

We ask every nation to join us. We will ask, and we will need, the help of police forces, intelligence services, and banking systems around the world. The United States is grateful that many nations and many international organizations have already responded—with sympathy and with support. Nations from Latin America, to Asia, to Africa, to Europe, to the Islamic world. Perhaps the NATO Charter reflects best the attitude of the world: An attack on one is an attack on all.

The civilized world is rallying to America's side. They understand that if this terror goes unpunished, their own cities, their own citizens may be next. Terror, unanswered, can not only bring down buildings, it can threaten the stability of legitimate governments. And you know what—we're not going to allow it.

Americans are asking: What is expected of us? I ask you to live your lives, and hug your children. I know many citizens have fears tonight, and I ask you to be calm and resolute, even in the face of a continuing threat.

I ask you to uphold the values of America, and remember why so many have come here. We are in a fight for our principles, and our first responsibility is to live by them. No one should be singled out for unfair treatment or unkind words because of their ethnic background or religious faith.

I ask you to continue to support the victims of this tragedy with your contributions. Those who want to give can go to a central source of information, libertyunites.org, to find the names of groups providing direct help in New York, Pennsylvania, and Virginia.

The thousands of FBI agents who are now at work in this investigation may need your cooperation, and I ask you to give it.

I ask for your patience, with the delays and inconveniences that may accompany tighter security; and for your patience in what will be a long struggle.

I ask your continued participation and confidence in the American economy. Terrorists attacked a symbol of American prosperity. They did not touch its source. America is successful because of the hard work, and creativity, and enterprise of our people. These were the true strengths of our economy before September 11th, and they are our strengths today.

And, finally, please continue praying for the victims of terror and their families, for those in uniform, and for our great country. Prayer has comforted us in sorrow, and will help strengthen us for the journey ahead.

Tonight I thank my fellow Americans for what you have already done and for what you will do. And ladies and gentlemen of the Congress, I thank you, their representatives, for what you have already done and for what we will do together.

Tonight, we face new and sudden national challenges. We will come together to improve air safety, to dramatically expand the number of air marshals on domestic flights, and take new measures to prevent hijacking. We will come together to promote stability and keep our airlines flying, with direct assistance during this emergency.

We will come together to give law enforcement the additional tools it needs to track down terror here at home. We will come together to strengthen our intelligence capabilities to know the plans of terrorists before they act, and find them before they strike.

We will come together to take active steps that strengthen America's economy, and put our people back to work.

Tonight we welcome two leaders who embody the extraordinary spirit of all New Yorkers: Governor George Pataki, and Mayor Rudolph Giuliani. As a symbol of America's resolve, my administration will work with Congress, and these two leaders, to show the world that we will rebuild New York City.

After all that has just passed—all the lives taken, and all the possibilities and hopes that died with them—it is natural to wonder if America's future is one of fear. Some speak of an age of terror. I know there are struggles ahead, and dangers to face. But this country will define our times, not be defined by them. As long as the United States of America is determined and strong, this will not be an age of terror; this will be an age of liberty, here and across the world.

Great harm has been done to us. We have suffered great loss. And in our grief and anger we have found our mission and our moment. Freedom and fear are at war. The advance of human freedom—the great achievement of our time, and the great hope of every time—now depends on us. Our nation—this generation—will lift a dark threat of violence from our people and our future. We will rally the world to this cause by our efforts, by our courage. We will not tire, we will not falter, and we will not fail.

It is my hope that in the months and years ahead, life will return almost to normal. We'll go back to our lives and routines, and that is good. Even grief recedes with time and grace. But our resolve must not pass. Each of us will remember what happened that day, and to whom it happened. We'll remember the moment the news came—where we were and what we were doing. Some will remember an image of a fire, or a story of rescue. Some will carry memories of a face and a voice gone forever.

And I will carry this: It is the police shield of a man named George Howard, who died at the World Trade Center trying to save others. It was given to me by his mom, Arlene, as a proud memorial to her son. This is my reminder of lives that ended, and a task that does not end.

I will not forget this wound to our country or those who inflicted it. I will not yield; I will not rest; I will not relent in waging this struggle for freedom and security for the American people.

The course of this conflict is not known, yet its outcome is certain. Freedom and fear, justice and cruelty, have always been at war, and we know that God is not neutral between them.

Fellow citizens, we'll meet violence with patient justice—assured of the rightness of our cause, and confident of the victories to come. In all that lies before us, may God grant us wisdom, and may He watch over the United States of America.

Thank you.

Secretary-General Kofi Annan
United Nations General Assembly
New York, N.Y.
September 24, 2001 (excerpts)

Two weeks ago, as you will all remember, we were looking forward to this day, as the day when we would begin our General Debate.

Many of you expected to be represented here by your head of State or government, or by your foreign minister.

I had, myself, hoped to set out for you what I see as the main priorities for the work of the Organization over the next five years.

But alas, Mr. President, that was two weeks ago.

Thirteen days ago—on a day none of us is likely to forget—our host country, and our beloved host city, were struck by a blow so deliberate, so heartless, malicious and destructive, that we are all still struggling to grasp its enormity.

In truth, this was a blow not against one city or one country, but against all of us.

It was not only an attack on our innocent fellow citizens—well over 60 Member States are affected, including, I am sad to say, my own country—but an attack on our shared values.

It struck at everything this Organization stands for: peace, freedom, tolerance, human rights, and the very idea of a united human family.

It struck at all our efforts to create a true international society, based on the rule of law.

Let us respond by reaffirming, with all our strength, our common humanity and the value that we share. We shall not allow them to be overthrown.

On the very day after the onslaught, the Security Council rightly identified it as a threat to international peace and security.

Let us therefore respond to it in a way that strengthens international peace and security—by cementing the ties among nations, and not subjecting them to new strains. . . .

So let us respond by reaffirming the rule of law, on the international as well as the national levels.

No effort should be spared in bringing the perpetrators to justice, in a clear and transparent process that all can understand and accept.

Let us uphold our own principles and standards, so that we can make the difference unmistakable, for all the world to see, between those who resort to terrorism and those who fight against it.

Responding appropriately to this vicious onslaught is indeed a vital task. But we must not let it distract us from the rest of the work we have to do.

In no way do these tragic events make the broader mission of the United Nations less relevant.

On the contrary—and especially if we allow them to succeed in tipping the world economy into recession—these events will make that mission even more urgent. . . .

International cooperation is needed now, more than ever, in managing the world economy—and in ensuring that the costs of adjustment do not, once again, fall most heavily on developing countries.

We must not allow these events to set us back in our fulfillment of the pledges given, one year ago, by our heads of State and government in their Millennium Declaration—such as the promise to halve, by 2015, the proportion of the world's people whose income is less than one dollar a day; to ensure universal primary education for girls and boys alike; to halt and begin reversing the spread of HIV/AIDS; and to preserve the planet for future generations by adopting a new ethic of conservation and stewardship.

Those tasks remain as urgent as they ever were—if anything more so; and this Organization's work to advance them—which is described in detail in the report you have before you—remains as important as ever.

These longer-term issues of development can and must be addressed during this session of the Assembly. Our understandable preoccupation with the fight against terrorism must not lead us to neglect them.

The social and economic evils in our world are all too real—as is the need to make globalization work for all the peoples of the world, by embedding the new global economy in a global society, based on shared global values of solidarity, social justice, and human rights.

But these things cannot be achieved by violence. . . .

Let us reject the path of violence, which is the product of nihilism and despair.

Let us prove by our actions that there is no need to despair; that the political and economic problems of our time can be solved peacefully; and that no human life should be sacrificed, because every human being has cause to hope.

That, I believe, Mr. President, is the true business of this Assembly, and the true mission of this Organization.

Mayor Rudolph Giuliani of New York
United Nations General Assembly
New York, N.Y.
October 1, 2001 (excerpts)

On September 11th 2001, New York City—the most diverse City in the world—was viciously attacked in an unprovoked act of war. More than five thousand innocent men, women, and children of every race, religion, and ethnicity are lost. Among these were people from 80 different nations. To their representatives here today, I offer my condolences to you as well on behalf of all New Yorkers who share this loss with you.

This was the deadliest terrorist attack in history. It claimed more lives than Pearl Harbor or D-Day. This was not just an attack on the City of New York or on the United States of America. It was an attack on the very idea of a free, inclusive, and civil society.

It was a direct assault on the founding principles of the United Nations itself. The Preamble to the U.N. Charter states that this organization exists "to reaffirm faith in fundamental human rights, in the dignity and worth of the human person...to practice tolerance and live together in peace as good neighbors...[and] to unite our strength to maintain international peace and security."

Indeed, this vicious attack places in jeopardy the whole purpose of the United Nations.

Terrorism is based on the persistent and deliberate violation of fundamental human rights. With bullets and bombs—and now with hijacked airplanes—terrorists deny the dignity of human life. Terrorism preys particularly on cultures and communities that practice openness and tolerance. Their targeting of innocent civilians mocks the efforts of those who seek to live together in peace as neighbors. It defies the very notion of being a neighbor.

This massive attack was intended to break our spirit. It has not done that. It has made us stronger, more determined and more resolved. . . .

The strength of America's response, please understand, flows from the principles upon which we stand.

Americans are not a single ethnic group. Americans are not of one race or one religion. Americans emerge from all your nations.

We are defined as Americans by our beliefs—not by our ethnic origins, our race or our religion. Our beliefs in religious freedom, political freedom, and economic freedom—that's what makes an American. Our belief in democracy, the rule of law, and respect for human life—that's how you become an American. It is these very principles—and the opportunities these principles give to so many to create a better life for themselves and their families—that make America, and New York, a "shining city on a hill."

There is no nation, and no City, in the history of the world that has seen more immigrants, in less time, than America. People continue to come here in large numbers to seek freedom, opportunity, decency, and civility.

Each of your nations—I am certain—has contributed citizens to the United States and to New York. I believe I can take every one of you someplace in New York City, where you can find someone from your country, someone from your village or town, that speaks your language and practices your religion. In each of your lands there are many who are Americans in spirit, by virtue of their commitment to our shared principles.

It is tragic and perverse that it is because of these very principles— particularly our religious, political and economic freedoms—that we find ourselves under attack by terrorists. . . .

Each of you is sitting in this room because of your country's commitment to being part of the family of nations. We need to unite as a family as never before—across all our differences, in recognition of the fact that the United Nations stands for the proposition that as human beings we have more in common than divides us.

If you need to be reminded of this, you don't need to look very far. Just go outside for a walk in the streets and parks of New York City. You can't walk a block in New York City without seeing somebody that looks different than you, acts different than you, talks different than you, believes different than you. If you grow up in New York City, you learn that. And if you're an intelligent or decent person, you learn that all those differences are nothing in comparison to the things that unite us.

We are a City of immigrants—unlike any other City—within a nation of immigrants. Like the victims of the World Trade Center attack, we are of every race, religion, and ethnicity. Our diversity has always been our greatest source of strength. It's the thing that renews us and revives us in every generation—our openness to new people from all over the world.

So from the first day of this attack, an attack on New York and America, and I believe an attack on the basic principles that underlie this organization, I have told the people of New York that we should not allow this to divide us, because then we would really lose what this City is all about. We have very strong and vibrant Arab and Muslim communities in New York City. They are an equally important part of the life of our City. We respect their religious beliefs. We respect everybody's religious beliefs—that's what America's about, that's what New York City is about. I have urged New Yorkers not to engage in any form of group blame or group hatred. This is exactly the evil that we are confronting with these terrorists. And if we are going to prevail over terror, our ideals, principles, and values must transcend all forms of prejudice. This is a very important part of the struggle against terrorism.

This is not a dispute between religions or ethnic groups. All religions, all decent people, are united in their desire to achieve peace, and understand that we have to eliminate terrorism. We're not divided about this. . . .

Freedom from Fear is a basic human right. We need to reassert our right to live free from fear with greater confidence and determination than ever before, here in New York City, across America, and around the World. With one clear voice, unanimously, we need to say that we will not give in to terrorism.

Surrounded by our friends of every faith, we know that this is not a clash of civilizations; it is a conflict between murderers and humanity.

This is not a question of retaliation or revenge. It is a matter of justice leading to peace. The only acceptable result is the complete and total eradication of terrorism.

New Yorkers are strong and resilient. We are unified. And we will not yield to terror. We do not let fear make our decisions for us. We choose to live in freedom.

Prime Minister Tony Blair of Great Britain
Labour Party Conference
Brighton, England
October 2, 2001 (excerpts)

In retrospect, the Millennium marked only a moment in time. It was the events of September 11 that marked a turning point in history, where we confront the dangers of the future and assess the choices facing humankind.

It was a tragedy. An act of evil. From this nation, goes our deepest sympathy and prayers for the victims and our profound solidarity with the American people.

We were with you at the first. We will stay with you to the last. . . .

Round the world, 11 September is bringing Governments and people to reflect, consider and change. And in this process, amidst all the talk of war and action, there is another dimension appearing.

There is a coming together. The power of community is asserting itself. We are realizing how fragile are our frontiers in the face of the world's new challenges.

Today conflicts rarely stay within national boundaries. Today a tremor in one financial market is repeated in the markets of the world. Today confidence is global; either its presence or its absence.

Today the threat is chaos; because for people with work to do, family life to balance, mortgages to pay, careers to further, pensions to provide, the yearning is for order and stability and if it doesn't exist elsewhere, it is unlikely to exist here.

I have long believed this interdependence defines the new world we live in.

People say: we are only acting because it's the USA that was attacked. Double standards, they say. But when Milosevic embarked on the ethnic cleansing of Muslims in Kosovo, we acted.

The skeptics said it was pointless, we'd make matters worse, we'd make Milosevic stronger and look what happened, we won, the refugees went home, the policies of ethnic cleansing were reversed and one of the great dictators of the last century, will see justice in this century.

And I tell you if Rwanda happened again today as it did in 1993, when a million people were slaughtered in cold blood, we would have a moral duty to act there also. We were there in Sierra Leone when a murderous group of gangsters threatened its democratically elected Government and people.

And we as a country should, and I as Prime Minister do, give thanks for the brilliance, dedication and sheer professionalism of the British Armed Forces.

We can't do it all. Neither can the Americans.

But the power of the international community could, together, if it chose to. . . .

We know this also. The values we believe in should shine through what we do in Afghanistan.

To the Afghan people we make this commitment. The conflict will not be the end. We will not walk away, as the outside world has done so many times before.

If the Taliban regime changes, we will work with you to make sure its successor is one that is broad-based, that unites all ethnic groups, and that offers some way out of the miserable poverty that is your present existence.

And, more than ever now, with every bit as much thought and planning, we will assemble a humanitarian coalition alongside the military coalition so that inside and outside Afghanistan, the refugees, millions on the move even before September 11, are given shelter, food and help during the winter months.

The world community must show as much its capacity for compassion as for force.

The critics will say: but how can the world be a community? Nations act in their own self-interest. Of course they do. But what is the lesson of the financial markets, climate change, international terrorism, nuclear proliferation or world trade? It is that our self-interest and our mutual interests are today inextricably woven together. This is the politics of globalization.

I realize why people protest against globalization. We watch aspects of it with trepidation. We feel powerless, as if we were now pushed to and fro by forces far beyond our control.

But there's a risk that political leaders, faced with street demonstrations, pander to the argument rather than answer it. The demonstrators are right to say there's injustice, poverty, environmental degradation. But globalization is a fact and, by and large, it is driven by people. Not just in finance, but in communication, in technology, increasingly in culture, in recreation. In the world of the Internet, information technology and TV, there will be globalization. And in trade, the problem is not there's too much of it; on the contrary there's too little of it. The issue is not how to stop globalization. The issue is how we use the power of community to combine it with justice. If globalization works only for the benefit of the few, then it will fail and will deserve to fail.

But if we follow the principles that have served us so well at home—that power, wealth and opportunity must be in the hands of the many, not the few—if we make that our guiding light for the global economy, then it will be a force for good and an international movement that we should take pride in leading. Because the alternative to globalization is isolation.

President George W. Bush
The White House
Washington, D.C.
October 7, 2001

Good afternoon. On my orders, the United States military has begun strikes against al Qaeda terrorist training camps and military installations of the Taliban regime in Afghanistan. These carefully targeted actions are designed to disrupt the use of Afghanistan as a terrorist base of operations, and to attack the military capability of the Taliban regime.

We are joined in this operation by our staunch friend, Great Britain. Other close friends, including Canada, Australia, Germany and France, have pledged forces as the operation unfolds. More than 40 countries in the Middle East, Africa, Europe and across Asia have granted air transit or landing rights. Many more have shared intelligence. We are supported by the collective will of the world.

More than two weeks ago, I gave Taliban leaders a series of clear and specific demands: Close terrorist training camps; hand over leaders of the al Qaeda network; and return all foreign nationals, including American citizens, unjustly detained in your country. None of these demands were met. And now the Taliban will pay a price. By destroying camps and disrupting communications, we will make it more difficult for the terror network to train new recruits and coordinate their evil plans.

Initially, the terrorists may burrow deeper into caves and other entrenched hiding places. Our military action is also designed to clear the way for sustained, comprehensive and relentless operations to drive them out and bring them to justice.

At the same time, the oppressed people of Afghanistan will know the generosity of America and our allies. As we strike military targets, we'll also drop food, medicine and supplies to the starving and suffering men and women and children of Afghanistan.

The United States of America is a friend to the Afghan people, and we are the friends of almost a billion worldwide who practice the Islamic faith. The United States of America is an enemy of those who aid terrorists and of the barbaric criminals who profane a great religion by committing murder in its name.

This military action is a part of our campaign against terrorism, another front in a war that has already been joined through diplomacy, intelligence, the freezing of financial assets and the arrests of known terrorists by law enforcement agents in 38 countries. Given the nature and reach of our enemies, we will win this conflict by the patient accumulation of successes, by meeting a series of challenges with determination and will and purpose.

Today we focus on Afghanistan, but the battle is broader. Every nation has a choice to make. In this conflict, there is no neutral ground. If any government sponsors the outlaws and killers of innocents, they have become outlaws and murderers, themselves. And they will take that lonely path at their own peril.

I'm speaking to you today from the Treaty Room of the White House, a place where American Presidents have worked for peace. We're a peaceful nation. Yet, as we have learned, so suddenly and so tragically, there can be no peace in a world of sudden terror. In the face of today's new threat, the only way to pursue peace is to pursue those who threaten it.

We did not ask for this mission, but we will fulfill it. The name of today's military operation is Enduring Freedom. We defend not only our precious freedoms, but also the freedom of people everywhere to live and raise their children free from fear.

I know many Americans feel fear today. And our government is taking strong precautions. All law enforcement and intelligence agencies are working aggressively around America, around the world and around the clock. At my request, many governors have activated the National Guard to strengthen airport security. We have called up Reserves to reinforce our military capability and strengthen the protection of our homeland.

In the months ahead, our patience will be one of our strengths—patience with the long waits that will result from tighter security;

patience and understanding that it will take time to achieve our goals; patience in all the sacrifices that may come.

Today, those sacrifices are being made by members of our Armed Forces who now defend us so far from home, and by their proud and worried families. A Commander-in-Chief sends America's sons and daughters into a battle in a foreign land only after the greatest care and a lot of prayer. We ask a lot of those who wear our uniform. We ask them to leave their loved ones, to travel great distances, to risk injury, even to be prepared to make the ultimate sacrifice of their lives. They are dedicated, they are honorable; they represent the best of our country. And we are grateful.

To all the men and women in our military—every sailor, every soldier, every airman, every coastguardsman, every Marine—I say this: Your mission is defined; your objectives are clear; your goal is just. You have my full confidence, and you will have every tool you need to carry out your duty.

I recently received a touching letter that says a lot about the state of America in these difficult times—a letter from a 4th-grade girl, with a father in the military: "As much as I don't want my Dad to fight," she wrote, "I'm willing to give him to you."

This is a precious gift, the greatest she could give. This young girl knows what America is all about. Since September 11, an entire generation of young Americans has gained new understanding of the value of freedom, and its cost in duty and in sacrifice.

The battle is now joined on many fronts. We will not waver; we will not tire; we will not falter; and we will not fail. Peace and freedom will prevail.

Thank you. May God continue to bless America.

Senator John McCain
United States Naval Academy
Annapolis, Md.
October 9, 2001 (excerpts)

On September 11, our country was attacked by a depraved, malevolent force that hates ever0y value Americans hold dear. It was a terrible blow that no one alive today will ever forget. But we will survive it. Our enemies will not. I have every confidence that the American people and their government will remain resolute in waging the war that has been declared on us. We have been attacked and we are fighting back. And woe to anyone who dares oppose us.

We have now begun the first phase of military operations against our enemies. As President Bush has explained, this war will have many components, diplomatic, financial, intelligence. It will include both overt and covert operations. But American military power is essential to our success. There should be no confusion about that. Nor should Mr. bin Laden or anyone who wishes this country harm have any doubt about what America can accomplish by force when we are obliged to use it. They wrongly believed they could destroy the way we live our lives. They are now just beginning to understand just how radically their lives are going to change.

The professionalism and power of our armed forces, stronger by a magnitude of ten than any other nation on earth, is something only a fool would underestimate. When it is brought to bear in great and terrible measure it is a thing to strike terror into the heart of anyone who opposes it. No mountain is big enough, no cave deep enough to hide from the fury of American military power when we are committed to victory. We must not shrink from using it, in whatever measure necessary, to defeat our enemies, wherever they are.

I agree that we will have to use force wisely to avoid inflaming the hatred for America that our enemies have been allowed to sow in the Islamic world. Toward that end, we should try hard to minimize non-combatant casualties. If we can use means other than force in some countries to achieve our goal, then we should. But we must keep our attention firmly fixed on our primary goal. Our goal is to vanquish terrorism, not reduce it, not change its operations, not temporarily subdue it, but vanquish it. All other concerns are secondary. It is a difficult, demanding task we have undertaken. We must expect and prepare for our enemies to strike us again before they are vanquished. Some of this war will be fought at home. And the casualties that we will suffer may again include civilians. We must keep our nerve at all costs. We should use no more force than necessary, but no less than necessary. Fighting this war in half measures will only give our enemies time and opportunity to strike us again. We must change and change permanently the mindset of terrorists, those who give them sanctuary and support, and those parts of Islamic populations who believe the terrorist conceit that they will ultimately prevail in a conflict with the West, that America has not the stomach to wage a relentless, long term, and, at times, ruthless war to destroy them.

We are at war, a new kind of war as the President has rightly called it. It might not involve nations clashing in conventional sea, land and air battles, although it is possible that it could come to that. I should add that I don't consider the operations in Afghanistan that commenced on Sunday to be a war against a nation, much less a war against the Muslim world. The Taliban and Al Qaeda are not legitimate representatives of that country, they are terrorists, period, who represent evil, not nations. But whatever this war's unique attributes, it is war nonetheless, and like all wars it will require sacrifice and hardship and casualties. And like all wars it will occasion great heroism.

This war will still be underway, in one form or another, when some of you, perhaps all of you, receive your commissions. Eighty thousand sailors and marines have already been summoned to war. Over three dozen warships, including the carriers *Enterprise, Carl Vinson, Theodore Roosevelt* and the *Kitty Hawk* have been deployed. Four battle groups, including Marine Corps Amphibious Ready Groups, destroyers, cruisers, submarines and support ships, are on station. We know that much of the air campaign to date has been waged from American and British ships. And although this war cannot and will not be fought only with cruise missiles and from 15,000 feet in the air, the Navy and Marine Corps are always an essential instrument of American power, and your service will be essential to our victory, in Afghanistan and beyond if necessary. It is your duty and your honor to defend the greatest nation in history in its hour of need. I envy you.

I say that fully aware of the hardships and risks that we impose on those we send to fight for us. I say that fully aware of the horrors that war inevitably visits on the innocent. I don't think war is glorious. I don't know a veteran who cherishes a romantic remembrance of war. All wars are awful. When nations must defend themselves by force of arms, a million tragedies ensue. Nothing, not the valor with which it is fought nor the nobility of the cause it serves, can glorify the cruel and merciless reality of warfare. That's what makes war a thing to be avoided if possible. But it is not possible now. There was no avoiding the war we are in today anymore than we could have avoided world war after the bombing of Pearl Harbor.

In truth, this war was declared by our enemies long before the attacks of September 11. And our reluctance to recognize this reality, and commit ourselves to unconditional victory, has been a very costly mistake. Because the only things worse than war are the consequences of refusing to wage and win it when our vital interests and founding ideals are at stake.

Our enemies have now made plain to us the clear and present danger they pose to our physical security and to the very essence of our culture, liberty. Only the most willfully deluded Americans could doubt the necessity of this war. We must fight. And we must prevail. . . .

Until the end of time, will there ever be a nation such as ours? I cannot imagine that any other nation's history will ever so profoundly affect the progress of the human race. That is not boastful chauvinism. It is a profession of faith in the American creed, and in the patriots who understood what history expects of us, and who saw to it that America exceeded even the loftiest aspirations of our founders.

We are not a perfect nation. Prosperity and power might delude us into thinking we have achieved that distinction, but challenges unforeseen a mere generation ago command every good citizen's concern and labor. But what we have achieved in our brief history is irrefutable proof that a nation conceived in liberty will prove stronger than any nation ordered to exalt the few at the expense of the many or made from a common race or culture or to preserve traditions that have no greater attribute than longevity. As blessed as we are, as empowered by liberty as we are, no nation complacent in its greatness can long sustain it. We are an unfinished nation. And we are not a people of half-measures. We must all take our place, give our counsel, direct our passion to the enduring task of national greatness.

I believe we were all shaken from whatever complacency we may have felt before September 11. And that is one good thing to have arisen from the ashes of the World Trade Center. But it is only good so long as the absence of complacency does not provoke an absence of confidence. What our enemies have sought to destroy is beyond their reach. We must all have faith in that truth. Armed with the power of our faith, we can endure whatever trials we must face.

Appendix B

Compendium of Major International Terrorist Organizations

The following list of foreign terrorist organizations is adapted from the U.S. Department of State's List of Foreign Terrorist Organizations, with descriptions provided by the State Department's *Patterns of Global Terrorism 2000*. This information is updated annually and is available at www.state.gov. Note that the names of some of the groups listed in this appendix are spelled differently from the way they are spelled in the text, as the appendix uses State Department transliterations.

Abu Nidal Organization (ANO) a.k.a. Fatah Revolutionary Council, Arab Revolutionary Brigades, Black September, and Revolutionary Organization of Socialist Muslims
  Description: International terrorist organization led by Sabri al-Banna. Split from PLO in 1974. Made up of various functional committees, including political, military, and financial.
  Activities: Has carried out terrorist attacks in 20 countries, killing or injuring almost 900 persons. Targets include the United States, the United Kingdom, France, Israel, moderate Palestinians, the PLO, and various Arab countries. Major attacks included the Rome and Vienna airports in December 1985, the Neve Shalom synagogue in Istanbul and the Pan Am flight 73 hijacking in Karachi in September 1986, and the City of Poros day-excursion ship attack in Greece in July 1988. Suspected of assassinating PLO deputy chief Abu Iyad and PLO security chief Abu Hul in Tunis in January 1991. ANO assassinated a Jordanian diplomat in Lebanon in January 1994 and has been linked to the killing of the PLO representative there. Has not attacked Western targets since the late 1980s.

Strength: A few hundred plus limited overseas support structure.
Location/Area of Operation: Al-Banna relocated to Iraq in December 1998, where the group maintains a presence. Has an operational presence in Lebanon, including in several Palestinian refugee camps. Financial problems and internal disorganization have reduced the group's activities and capabilities. Authorities shut down the ANO's operations in Libya and Egypt in 1999. Has demonstrated ability to operate over wide area, including the Middle East, Asia, and Europe.
External Aid: Has received considerable support, including safehaven, training, logistic assistance, and financial aid from Iraq, Libya, and Syria (until 1987), in addition to close support for selected operations.

Abu Sayyaf Group (ASG)

Description: The ASG is the smallest and most radical of the Islamic separatist groups operating in the southern Philippines. Some ASG members have studied or worked in the Middle East and developed ties to mjuahidin while fighting and training in Afghanistan. The group split from the Moro National Liberation Front in 1991 under the leadership of Abdurajik Abubakar Janjalani, who was killed in a clash with Philippine police on 18 December 1998. Press reports place his younger brother, Khadafi Janjalani, as the nominal leader of the group, which is composed of several factions.
Activities: Engages in bombings, assassinations, kidnappings, and extortion to promote an independent Islamic state in western Mindanao and the Sulu Archipelago, areas in the southern Philippines heavily populated by Muslims. Raided the town of Ipil in Mindanao in April 1995—the group's first large-scale action—and kidnapped more than 30 foreigners, including a U.S. citizen, in 2000.
Strength: Believed to have about 200 core fighters, but more than 2,000 individuals motivated by the prospect of receiving ransom payments for foreign hostages allegedly joined the group in August.
Location/Area of Operation: The ASG primarily operates in the southern Philippines with members occasionally traveling to Manila, but the group expanded its operations to Malaysia this year when it abducted foreigners from two different resorts.

External Aid: Probably receives support from Islamic extremists in the Middle East and South Asia.

Armed Islamic Group (GIA)

Description: An Islamic extremist group, the GIA aims to overthrow the secular Algerian regime and replace it with an Islamic state. The GIA began its violent activities in 1992 after Algiers voided the victory of the Islamic Salvation Front (FIS)—the largest Islamic opposition party—in the first round of legislative elections in December 1991.

Activities: Frequent attacks against civilians and government workers. Between 1992 and 1998 the GIA conducted a terrorist campaign of civilian massacres, sometimes wiping out entire villages in its area of operation. Since announcing its campaign against foreigners living in Algeria in 1993, the GIA has killed more than 100 expatriate men and women—mostly Europeans—in the country. The group uses assassinations and bombings, including car bombs, and it is known to favor kidnapping victims and slitting their throats. The GIA hijacked an Air France flight to Algiers in December 1994. In late 1999 several GIA members were convicted by a French court for conducting a series of bombings in France in 1995. The Salafi Group for Call and Combat (GSPC) splinter faction appears to have eclipsed the GIA since approximately 1998 and is currently assessed to be the most effective remaining armed group inside Algeria. Both the GIA and GSPC leadership continue to proclaim their rejection of President Bouteflika's amnesty, but in contrast to the GIA, the GSPC has stated that it limits attacks on civilians. The GSPC's planned attack against the Paris-Dakar Road Rally in January 2000 demonstrates, however, that the group has not entirely renounced attacks against high-profile civilian targets.

Strength: Unkown; probably several hundred to several thousand.

Location/Area of Operation: Algeria.

External Aid: Algerian expatriates and GSPC members abroad, many of whom reside in Western Europe, provide financial and logistic support. In addition, the Algerian government has accused Iran and Sudan of supporting Algerian extremists.

Aum Supreme Truth (Aum) a.k.a. Aum Shinrikyo, Aleph
   Description: A cult established in 1987 by Shoko Asahara, the Aum aimed to take over Japan, then the world. Approved as a religious entity in 1989 under Japanese law, the group ran candidates in a Japanese parliamentary election in 1990. Over time the cult began to emphasize the imminence of the end of the world and stated that the United States would initiate Armageddon by starting World War III with Japan. The Japanese government revoked its recognition of the Aum as a religious organization in October 1995, but in 1997 a government panel decided not to invoke the Anti-Subversive Law against the group, which would have outlawed the cult. In 2000, Fumihiro Joyu took control of the Aum following his three-year jail sentence for perjury. Joyu was previously the group's spokesman and Russia Branch leader. Under Joyu's leadership the Aum changed its name to Aleph and claims to have rejected the violent and apocalyptic teachings of its founder.
   Activities: On 20 March 1995, Aum members simultaneously released the chemical nerve agent sarin on several Tokyo subway trains, killing 12 persons and injuring up to 6,000. (Recent studies put the number of persons who suffered actual physical injuries closer to 1,300, with the rest suffering from some form of psychological trauma.) The group was responsible for other mysterious chemical accidents in Japan in 1994. Its efforts to conduct attacks using biological agents have been unsuccessful. Japanese police arrested Asahara in May 1995, and he remained on trial, facing 17 counts of murder at the end of 2000. Since 1997 the cult continued to recruit new members, engage in commercial enterprise, and acquire property, although the cult scaled back these activities significantly in 2000 in response to public outcry. The cult maintains an Internet homepage.
   Strength: The Aum's current membership is estimated at 1,500 to 2,000 persons. At the time of the Tokyo subway attack, the group claimed to have 9,000 members in Japan and up to 40,000 worldwide.
   Location/Area of Operation: The Aum's principal membership is located only in Japan, but a residual branch comprising an unknown number of followers has surfaced in Russia.
   External Aid: None.

Basque Fatherland and Liberty (ETA) a.k.a. Euzkadi Ta Askatasuna
   Description: Founded in 1959 with the aim of establishing an independent homeland based on Marxist principles in the northern Spanish provinces of Vizcaya, Guipuzcoa, Alava, and Navarra and the southwestern French departments of Labourd, Basse-Navarra, and Soule.
   Activities: Primarily bombings and assassinations of Spanish government officials, especially security and military forces, politicians, and judicial figures. ETA finances its activities through kidnappings, robberies, and extortion. The group has killed more than 800 persons since it began lethal attacks in the early 1960s. In November 1999, ETA broke its "unilateral and indefinite" cease-fire and began an assassination and bombing campaign that killed 23 individuals and wounded scores more by the end of 2000.
   Strength: Unknown; may have hundreds of members, plus supporters.
   Location/Area of Operation: Operates primarily in the Basque autonomous regions of northern Spain and southwestern France, but also has bombed Spanish and French interests elsewhere.
   External Aid: Has received training at various times in the past in Libya, Lebanon, and Nicaragua. Some ETA members allegedly have received sanctuary in Cuba while others reside in South America. Also appears to have ties to the Irish Republican Army through the two groups' legal political wings.

Al-Gama'a al-Islamiyya (IG) a.k.a. Islamic Group
   Description: Egypt's largest militant group, active since the late 1970s; appears to be loosely organized. Has an external wing with a worldwide presence. The group issued a cease-fire in March 1999, but its spiritual leader, Shaykh Umar Abd al-Rahman, incarcerated in the United States, rescinded his support for the cease-fire in June 2000. The Gama'a has not conducted an attack inside Egypt since August 1998. Rifa'i Taha Musa—a hardline former senior member of the group—signed Usama bin Ladin's February 1998 fatwa calling for attacks against U.S. civilians. The IG since has publicly denied that it supports Bin Ladin and frequently differs with public statements made by Taha Musa. Taha Musa has in the last year sought to push the group toward a return to armed operations, but

the group, which still is led by Mustafa Hamza, has yet to break the unilaterally declared cease-fire. In late 2000, Taha Musa appeared in an undated video with Bin Ladin and Ayman al-Zawahiri threatening retaliation against the United States for Abd al-Rahman's continued incarceration. The IG's primary goal is to overthrow the Egyptian government and replace it with an Islamic state, but Taha Musa also may be interested in attacking U.S. and Israeli interests.

Activities: Group specialized in armed attacks against Egyptian security and other government officials, Coptic Christians, and Egyptian opponents of Islamic extremism before the cease-fire. From 1993 until the cease-fire, al-Gama'a launched attacks on tourists in Egypt, most notably the attack in November 1997 at Luxor that killed 58 foreign tourists. Also claimed responsibility for the attempt in June 1995 to assassinate Egyptian president Hosni Mubarak in Addis Ababa, Ethiopia. The Gama'a has never specifically attacked a U.S. citizen or facility but has threatened U.S. interests.

Strength: Unknown. At its peak the IG probably commanded several thousand hard-core members and a like number of sympathizers. The 1998 cease-fire and security crackdowns following the attack in Luxor in 1997 probably have resulted in a substantial decrease in the group's numbers.

Location/Area of Operation: Operates mainly in the Al-Minya, Asyu't, Qina, and Sohaj Governorates of southern Egypt. Also appears to have support in Cairo, Alexandria, and other urban locations, particularly among unemployed graduates and students. Has a worldwide presence, including Sudan, the United Kingdom, Afghanistan, Austria, and Yemen.

External Aid: Unknown. The Egyptian government believes that Iran, Bin Ladin, and Afghan militant groups support the organization. Also may obtain some funding through various Islamic nongovernmental organizations.

HAMAS a.k.a. Islamic Resistance Movement

Description: Formed in late 1987 as an outgrowth of the Palestinian branch of the Muslim Brotherhood. Various HAMAS elements have used both political and violent means, including terrorism, to pursue the goal of establishing an Islamic Palestinian state in place of Israel. Loosely structured, with some elements working clandestinely and others working openly through mosques and social service institutions to recruit members, raise money, organize activities, and distribute propaganda. HAMAS's strength is concentrated in the Gaza Strip and a few areas of the West Bank. Also has engaged in peaceful political activity, such as running candidates in West Bank Chamber of Commerce elections.

Activities: HAMAS activists, especially those in the Izz el-Din al-Qassam Brigades, have conducted many attacks—including large-scale suicide bombings—against Israeli civilian and military targets. In the early 1990s, they also targeted suspected Palestinian collaborators and Fatah rivals. Claimed several attacks during the unrest in late 2000.

Strength: Unknown number of hard-core members; tens of thousands of supporters and sympathizers.

Location/Area of Operation: Primarily the occupied territories, Israel. In August 1999, Jordanian authorities closed the group's Political Bureau offices in Amman, arrested its leaders, and prohibited the group from operating on Jordanian territory.

External Aid: Receives funding from Palestinian expatriates, Iran, and private benefactors in Saudi Arabia and other moderate Arab states. Some fundraising and propaganda activities take place in Western Europe and North America.

Harakat ul-Mujahidin (HUM)

Description: Formerly known as the Harakat al-Ansar, the HUM is an Islamic militant group based in Pakistan that operates primarily in Kashmir. Long-time leader of the group, Fazlur Rehman Khalil, in mid-February stepped down as HUM emir, turning the reins over to the popular Kashmiri commander and his second-in-command, Farooq Kashmiri. Khalil, who has been linked to Bin Ladin and signed his fatwa in February 1998 calling for attacks on U.S. and Western interests, assumed the position of HUM Secretary General. Continued to operate terrorist training camps in eastern Afghanistan.

Activities: Has conducted a number of operations against Indian troops and civilian targets in Kashmir. Linked to the Kashmiri militant group al-Faran that kidnapped five Western tourists in Kashmir

in July 1995; one was killed in August 1995 and the other four reportedly were killed in December of the same year. The new millennium brought significant developments for Pakistani militant
groups, particularly the HUM. Most of these sprang from the hijacking of an Indian airliner on 24 December by militants believed
to be associated with the HUM. The hijackers negotiated the release of Masood Azhar, an important leader in the former Harakat
ul-Ansar imprisoned by the Indians in 1994. Azhar did not, however, return to the HUM, choosing instead to form the Jaish-e-
Mohammed (JEM), a rival militant group expressing a more radical line than the HUM.

Strength: Has several thousand armed supporters located in Azad
Kashmir, Pakistan, and India's southern Kashmir and Doda regions.
Supporters are mostly Pakistanis and Kashmiris and also include
Afghans and Arab veterans of the Afghan war. Uses light and heavy
machine guns, assault rifles, mortars, explosives, and rockets. HUM
lost some of its membership in defections to the JEM.

Location/Area of Operation: Based in Muzaffarabad, Rawalpindi,
and several other towns in Pakistan and Afghanistan, but members
conduct insurgent and terrorist activities primarily in Kashmir. The
HUM trains its militants in Afghanistan and Pakistan.

External Aid: Collects donations from Saudi Arabia and other Gulf
and Islamic states and from Pakistanis and Kashmiris. The sources
and amount of HUM's military funding are unknown.

Hizballah (Party of God) a.k.a. Islamic Jihad, Revolutionary Justice
Organization, Organization of the Oppressed on Earth, and Islamic
Jihad for the Liberation of Palestine
Description: Radical Shia group formed in Lebanon; dedicated to
increasing its political power in Lebanon and opposing Israel and
the Middle East peace negotiations. Strongly anti-West and anti-
Israel. Closely allied with, and often directed by, Iran but may have
conducted operations that were not approved by Tehran.
Activities: Known or suspected to have been involved in numerous
anti-U.S. terrorist attacks, including the suicide truck bombing of
the U.S. Embassy and U.S. Marine barracks in Beirut in October
1983 and the U.S. Embassy annex in Beirut in September 1984.
Elements of the group were responsible for the kidnapping and

detention of U.S. and other Western hostages in Lebanon. The group also attacked the Israeli Embassy in Argentina in 1992 and is a suspect in the 1994 bombing of the Israeli cultural center in Buenos Aires. In fall 2000, it captured three Israeli soldiers in the Shabaa Farms and kidnapped an Israeli noncombatant whom it may have lured to Lebanon under false pretenses.

Strength: Several thousand supporters and a few hundred terrrorist operatives.

Location/Area of Operation: Operates in the Bekaa Valley, the southern suburbs of Beirut, and southern Lebanon. Has established cells in Europe, Africa, South America, North America, and Asia.

External Aid: Receives substantial amounts of financial, training, weapons, explosives, political, diplomatic, and organizational aid from Iran and Syria.

Islamic Movement of Uzbekistan (IMU)

Description: Coalition of Islamic militants from Uzbekistan and other Central Asian states opposed to Uzbekistani President Islom Karimov's secular regime. Goal is the establishment of an Islamic state in Uzbekistan. The group's propaganda also includes anti-Western and anti-Israeli rhetoric.

Activities: Believed to be responsible for five car bombs in Tashkent in February 1999. Took hostages on several occasions in 1999 and 2000, including four U.S. citizens who were mountain climbing in August 2000, and four Japanese geologists and eight Kyrgyzstani soldiers in August 1999.

Strength: Militants probably number in the thousands.

Location/Area of Operation: Militants are based in Afghanistan and Tajikistan. Area of operation includes Uzbekistan, Tajikistan, Kyrgyzstan, and Afghanistan.

External Aid: Support from other Islamic extremist groups in Central and South Asia. IMU leadership broadcasts statements over Iranian radio.

Al-Jihad a.k.a. Egyptian Islamic Jihad, Jihad Group, Islamic Jihad

Description: Egyptian Islamic extremist group active since the late 1970s. Close partner of Bin Ladin's al-Qaida organization. Suffered setbacks as a result of numerous arrests of operatives worldwide, most recently in Lebanon and Yemen. Primary goals are to overthrow the Egyptian government and replace it with an Islamic state and attack U.S. and Israeli interests in Egypt and abroad.

Activities: Specializes in armed attacks against high-level Egyptian government personnel, including cabinet ministers, and car-bombings against official U.S. and Egyptian facilities. The original Jihad was responsible for the assassination in 1981 of Egyptian president Anwar Sadat. Claimed responsibility for the attempted assassinations of Interior Minister Hassan al-Alfi in August 1993 and Prime Minister Atef Sedky in November 1993. Has not conducted an attack inside Egypt since 1993 and has never targeted foreign tourists there. Responsible for Egyptian Embassy bombing in Islamabad in 1995; in 1998, planned attack against U.S. Embassy in Albania was thwarted.

Strength: Not known but probably has several hundred hard-core members.

Location/Area of Operation: Operates in the Cairo area. Has a network outside Egypt, including Yemen, Afghanistan, Pakistan, Sudan, Lebanon, and the United Kingdom.

External Aid: Not known. The Egyptian government claims that both Iran and Bin Ladin support the Jihad. Also may obtain some funding through various Islamic nongovernmental organizations, cover businesses, and criminal acts.

Kach and Kahane Chai

Description: Stated goal is to restore the biblical state of Israel. Kach (founded by radical Israeli-American rabbi Meir Kahane) and its offshoot Kahane Chai, which means "Kahane Lives" (founded by Meir Kahane's son Binyamin following his father's assassination in the United States), were declared to be terrorist organizations in March 1994 by the Israeli cabinet under the 1948 Terrorism Law. This followed the groups' statements in support of Dr. Baruch Goldstein's attack in February 1994 on the al-Ibrahimi Mosque— Goldstein was affiliated with Kach—and their verbal attacks on the Israeli government. Palestinian gunmen killed Binyamin Kahane and his wife in a drive-by shooting on 31 December in the West Bank.

Activities: Organize protests against the Israeli government. Harass and threaten Palestinians in Hebron and the West Bank. Have threatened to attack Arabs, Palestinians, and Israeli government officials. Have vowed revenge for the death of Binyamin Kahane and his wife.

Strength: Unknown.

Location/Area of Operation: Israel and West Bank settlements, particularly Qiryat Arba' in Hebron.

External Aid: Receives support from sympathizers in the United States and Europe.

Kurdistan Workers' Party (PKK)

Description: Founded in 1974 as a Marxist-Leninist insurgent group primarily composed of Turkish Kurds. The group's goal has been to establish an independent Kurdish state in southeastern Turkey, where the population is predominantly Kurdish. In the early 1990s, the PKK moved beyond rural-based insurgent activities to include urban terrorism. Turkish authorities captured Chairman Abdullah Ocalan in Kenya in early 1999; the Turkish State Security Court subsequently sentenced him to death. In August 1999, Ocalan announced a "peace initiative," ordering members to refrain from violence and withdraw from Turkey and requesting dialogue with Ankara on Kurdish issues. At a PKK Congress in January 2000, members supported Ocalan's initiative and claimed the group now would use only political means to achieve its new goal, improved rights for Kurds in Turkey.

Activities: Primary targets have been Turkish government security forces in Turkey. Conducted attacks on Turkish diplomatic and commercial facilities in dozens of West European cities in 1993 and again in spring 1995. In an attempt to damage Turkey's tourist industry, the PKK bombed tourist sites and hotels and kidnapped foreign tourists in the early-to-mid-1990s.

Strength: Approximately 4,000 to 5,000, most of whom currently are located in northern Iraq. Has thousands of sympathizers in Turkey and Europe.

Location/Area of Operation: Operates in Turkey, Europe, and the Middle East.

External Aid: Has received safehaven and modest aid from Syria, Iraq, and Iran. The Syrian government expelled PKK leader Ocalan and known elements of the group from its territory in October 1998.

Liberation Tigers of Tamil Eelam (LTTE). Other known front organizations: World Tamil Association (WTA), World Tamil Movement (WTM), the Federation of Associations of Canadian Tamils (FACT), the Ellalan Force, the Sangilian Force.

Description: Founded in 1976, the LTTE is the most powerful Tamil group in Sri Lanka and uses overt and illegal methods to raise funds, acquire weapons, and publicize its cause of establishing an independent Tamil state. The LTTE began its armed conflict with the Sri Lankan government in 1983 and relies on a guerrilla strategy that includes the use of terrorist tactics.

Activities: The Tigers have integrated a battlefield insurgent strategy with a terrorist program that targets not only key personnel in the countryside but also senior Sri Lankan political and military leaders in Colombo and other urban centers. The Tigers are most notorious for their cadre of suicide bombers, the Black Tigers. Political assassinations and bombings are commonplace. The LTTE has refrained from targeting foreign diplomatic and commercial establishments.

Strength: Exact strength is unknown, but the LTTE is estimated to have 8,000 to 10,000 armed combatants in Sri Lanka, with a core of trained fighters of approximately 3,000 to 6,000. The LTTE also has a significant overseas support structure for fundraising, weapons procurement, and propaganda activities.

Location/Area of Operation: The Tigers control most of the northern and eastern coastal areas of Sri Lanka but have conducted operations throughout the island. Headquartered in northern Sri Lanka, LTTE leader Velupillai Prabhakaran has established an extensive network of checkpoints and informants to keep track of any outsiders who enter the group's area of control.

External Aid: The LTTE's overt organizations support Tamil separatism by lobbying foreign governments and the United Nations. The LTTE also uses its international contacts to procure weapons, communications, and any other equipment and supplies it needs. The LTTE exploits large Tamil communities in North America, Europe, and Asia to obtain funds and supplies for its fighters in Sri

Lanka. Information obtained since the mid-1980s indicates that some Tamil communities in Europe are also involved in narcotics smuggling. Tamils historically have served as drug couriers moving narcotics into Europe.

Mujahedin-e Khalq Organization (MEK or MKO) a.k.a. The National Liberation Army of Iran (NLA, the militant wing of the MEK), the People's Mujahidin of Iran (PMOI), National Council of Resistance (NCR), Muslim Iranian Student's Society (front organization used to garner financial support)

Description: Formed in the 1960s by the college-educated children of Iranian merchants, the MEK sought to counter what it perceived as excessive Western influence in the Shah's regime. Following a philosophy that mixes Marxism and Islam, has developed into the largest and most active armed Iranian dissident group. Its history is studded with anti-Western activity, and, most recently, attacks on the interests of the clerical regime in Iran and abroad.

Activities: Worldwide campaign against the Iranian government stresses propaganda and occasionally uses terrorist violence. During the 1970s the MEK staged terrorist attacks inside Iran and killed several U.S. military personnel and civilians working on defense projects in Tehran. Supported the takeover in 1979 of the U.S. Embassy in Tehran. In April 1992 conducted attacks on Iranian embassies in 13 different countries, demonstrating the group's ability to mount large-scale operations overseas. The normal pace of anti-Iranian operations increased during the "Operation Great Bahman" in February 2000, when the group claimed it launched a dozen attacks against Iran. During the remainder of the year, the MEK regularly claimed that its members were involved in mortar attacks and hit-and-run raids on Iranian military, law enforcement units, and government buildings near the Iran-Iraq border. The MEK also claimed six mortar attacks on civilian government and military buildings in Tehran.

Strength: Several thousand fighters based in Iraq with an extensive overseas support structure. Most of the fighters are organized in the MEK's National Liberation Army (NLA).

Location/Area of Operation: In the 1980s the MEK's leaders were forced by Iranian security forces to flee to France. Most resettled in

Iraq by 1987. In the mid-1980s the group did not mount terrorist operations in Iran at a level similar to its activities in the 1970s. In the 1990s, however, the MEK claimed credit for an increasing number of operations in Iran.

External Aid: Beyond support from Iraq, the MEK uses front organizations to solicit contributions from expatriate Iranian communities.

National Liberation Army (ELN)—Colombia

Description: Marxist insurgent group formed in 1965 by urban intellectuals inspired by Fidel Castro and Che Guevara. Began a dialogue with Colombian officials in 1999 following a campaign of mass kidnappings—each involving at least one U.S. citizen—to demonstrate its strength and continuing viability and to force the Pastrana administration to negotiate. Bogota and the ELN spent most of 2000 discussing where to establish an ELN safehaven in which to hold peace talks. A proposed location in north central Colombia faces stiff local and paramilitary opposition.

Activities: Kidnapping, hijacking, bombing, extortion, and guerrilla war. Modest conventional military capability. Annually conducts hundreds of kidnappings for ransom, often targeting foreign employees of large corporations, especially in the petroleum industry. Frequently assaults energy infrastructure and has inflicted major damage on pipelines and the electric distribution network.

Strength: Approximately 3,000 to 6,000 armed combatants and an unknown number of active supporters.

Location/Area of Operation: Mostly in rural and mountainous areas of north, northeast, and southwest Colombia and Venezuela border regions.

External Aid: Cuba provides some medical care and political consultation.

The Palestine Islamic Jihad (PIJ)

Description: Originated among militant Palestinians in the Gaza Strip during the 1970s. Committed to the creation of an Islamic Palestinian state and the destruction of Israel through holy war. Because of its strong support for Israel, the United States has been identified as an enemy of the PIJ, but the group has not specifically conducted attacks against U.S. interests in the past. In July 2000, however, publicly threatened to attack U.S. interests if the U.S. Embassy is moved from Tel Aviv to Jerusalem. Also opposes moderate Arab governments that it believes have been tainted by Western secularism.

Activities: Conducted at least three attacks against Israeli interests in late 2000, including one to commemorate the anniversary of former PIJ leader Fathi Shaqaqi's murder in Malta on 26 October 1995. Conducted suicide bombings against Israeli targets in the West Bank, Gaza Strip, and Israel.

Strength: Unknown.

Location/Area of Operation: Primarily Israel and the occupied territories and other parts of the Middle East, including Jordan and Lebanon.Headquartered in Syria.

External Aid: Receives financial assistance from Iran and limited logistic assistance from Syria.

Palestine Liberation Front (PLF)

Description: Broke away from the PFLP-GC in mid-1970s. Later split again into pro-PLO, pro-Syrian, and pro-Libyan factions. Pro-PLO faction led by Muhammad Abbas (Abu Abbas), who became member of PLO Executive Committee in1984 but left it in 1991.

Activities: Abu Abbas-led faction is known for aerial attacks against Israel. Abbas's group also was responsible for the attack in 1985 on the cruise ship *Achille Lauro* and the murder of U.S. citizen Leon Klinghoffer. A warrant for Abu Abbas's arrest is outstanding in Italy.

Strength: Unknown.

Location/Area of Operation: PLO faction based in Tunisia until *Achille Lauro* attack. Now based in Iraq.

External Aid: Receives support mainly from Iraq. Has received support from Libya in the past.

Popular Front for the Liberation of Palestine (PFLP)

Description: Marxist-Leninist group founded in 1967 by George Habash as a member of the PLO. Joined the Alliance of Palestinian Forces (APF) to oppose the Declaration of Principles signed in 1993 and suspended participation in the PLO. Broke away from the APF, along with the DFLP, in 1996 over ideological differences. Took part in meetings with Arafat's Fatah party and PLO representatives in

1999 to discuss national unity and the reinvigoration of the PLO but continues to oppose current negotiations with Israel.

Activities: Committed numerous international terrorist attacks during the 1970s. Since 1978 has conducted attacks against Israeli or moderate Arab targets, including killing a settler and her son in December 1996.

Strength: Some 800.

Location/Area of Operation: Syria, Lebanon, Israel, and the occupied territories.

External Aid: Receives safehaven and some logistic assistance from Syria.

Popular Front for the Liberation of Palestine–General Command (PFLP-GC)

Description: Split from the PFLP in 1968, claiming it wanted to focus more on fighting and less on politics. Violently opposed to Arafat's PLO. Led by Ahmad Jabril, a former captain in the Syrian Army. Closely tied to both Syria and Iran.

Activities: Carried out dozens of attacks in Europe and the Middle East during 1970s–1980s. Known for cross-border terrorist attacks into Israel using unusual means, such as hot-air balloons and motorized hang gliders. Primary focus now on guerrilla operations in southern Lebanon, small-scale attacks in Israel, West Bank, and Gaza Strip.

Strength: Several hundred.

Location/Area of Operation: Headquartered in Damascus with bases in Lebanon.

External Aid: Receives logistic and military support from Syria and financial support from Iran.

al-Qa'ida

Description: Established by Usama Bin Ladin in the late 1980s to bring together Arabs who fought in Afghanistan against the Soviet invasion. Helped finance, recruit, transport, and train Sunni Islamic extremists for the Afghan resistance. Current goal is to establish a pan-Islamic Caliphate throughout the world by working with allied Islamic extremist groups to overthrow regimes it deems "non-Islamic" and expelling Westerners and non-Muslims from Muslim countries. Issued statement under banner of "the World Islamic

Front for Jihad Against the Jews and Crusaders" in February 1998, saying it was the duty of all Muslims to kill U.S. citizens—civilian or military—and their allies everywhere.

Activities: Plotted to carry out terrorist operations against U.S. and Israeli tourists visiting Jordan for millennial celebrations. (Jordanian authorities thwarted the planned attacks and put 28 suspects on trial.) Conducted the bombings in August 1998 of the U.S. Embassies in Nairobi, Kenya, and Dar es Salaam, Tanzania, that killed at least 301 persons and injured more than 5,000 others. Claims to have shot down U.S. helicopters and killed U.S. servicemen in Somalia in 1993 and to have conducted three bombings that targeted U.S. troops in Aden, Yemen, in December 1992. Linked to the following plans that were not carried out: to assassinate Pope John Paul II during his visit to Manila in late 1994, simultaneous bombings of the U.S. and Israeli Embassies in Manila and other Asian capitals in late 1994, the midair bombing of a dozen U.S. trans-Pacific flights in 1995, and to kill President Clinton during a visit to the Philippines in early 1995. Continues to train, finance, and provide logistic support to terrorist groups in support of these goals.

Strength: May have several hundred to several thousand members. Also serves as a focal point or umbrella organization for a worldwide network that includes many Sunni Islamic extremist groups such as Egyptian Islamic Jihad, some members of al-Gama'at al-Islamiyya, the Islamic Movement of Uzbekistan, and the Harakat ul-Mujahidin.

Location/Area of Operation: Al-Qaida has a worldwide reach, has cells in a number of countries, and is reinforced by its ties to Sunni extremist networks. Bin Ladin and his key lieutenants reside in Afghanistan, and the group maintains terrorist training camps there.

External Aid: Bin Ladin, son of a billionaire Saudi family, is said to have inherited approximately $300 million that he uses to finance the group. Al-Qaida also maintains moneymaking front organizations, solicits donations from like-minded supporters, and illicitly siphons funds from donations to Muslim charitable organizations.

Revolutionary Armed Forces of Colombia (FARC)
Description: Established in 1964 as the military wing of the Colombian Communist Party, the FARC is Colombia's oldest, largest,

most capable, and best-equipped Marxist insurgency. The FARC is governed by a secretariat, led by septuagenarian Manuel Marulanda, a.k.a. "Tirofijo," and six others, including senior military commander Jorge Briceno, a.k.a. "Mono Jojoy." Organized along military lines and includes several urban fronts. In 2000, the group continued a slow-moving peace negotiation process with the Pastrana administration, which has gained the group several concessions, including a demilitarized zone used as a venue for negotiations.

Activities: Bombings, murder, kidnapping, extortion, hijacking, as well as guerrilla and conventional military action against Colombian political, military, and economic targets. In March 1999 the FARC executed three U.S. Indian rights activists on Venezuelan territory after it kidnapped them in Colombia. Foreign citizens often are targets of FARC kidnapping for ransom. Has well-documented ties to narcotics traffickers, principally through the provision of armed protection.

Strength: Approximately 9,000 to 12,000 armed combatants and an unknown number of supporters, mostly in rural areas.

Location/Area of Operation: Colombia with some activities—extortion, kidnapping, logistics, and R&R—in Venezuela, Panama, and Ecuador.

External Aid: Cuba provides some medical care and political consultation.

Revolutionary Organization 17 November (17 November)

Description: Radical leftist group established in 1975 and named for the student uprising in Greece in November 1973 that protested the military regime. Anti-Greek establishment, anti-U.S., anti-Turkey, anti-NATO, and committed to the ouster of U.S. bases, removal of Turkish military presence from Cyprus, and severing of Greece's ties to NATO and the European Union (EU).

Activities: Initial attacks were assassinations of senior U.S. officials and Greek public figures. Added bombings in 1980s. Since 1990 has expanded targets to include EU facilities and foreign firms investing in Greece and has added improvised rocket attacks to its methods. Most recent attack claimed was the murder in June 2000 of British defense attaché Stephen Saunders.

Strength: Unknown, but presumed to be small.

Location/Area of Operation: Athens, Greece.

Revolutionary People's Liberation Party/Front (DHKP/C) a.k.a. Devrimci Sol (Revolutionary Left), Dev Sol

Description: Originally formed in 1978 as Devrimci Sol, or Dev Sol, a splinter faction of the Turkish People's Liberation Party/Front. Renamed in 1994 after factional infighting, it espouses a Marxist ideology and is virulently anti-U.S. and anti-NATO. Finances its activities chiefly through armed robberies and extortion.

Activities: Since the late 1980s has concentrated attacks against current and retired Turkish security and military officials. Began a new campaign against foreign interests in 1990. Assassinated two U.S. military contractors and wounded a U.S. Air Force officer to protest the Gulf War. Launched rockets at U.S. Consulate in Istanbul in 1992. Assassinated prominent Turkish businessman and two others in early 1996, its first significant terrorist act as DHKP/C. Turkish authorities thwarted DHKP/C attempt in June 1999 to fire light antitank weapon at U.S. Consulate in Istanbul. Series of safehouse raids, arrests by Turkish police over last two years has weakened group significantly. Turkish security forces stormed prison wards controlled by the DHKP/C in December 2000, transferring militants to cell-type penitentiaries and further undermining DHKP/C cohesion.

Strength: Unknown.

Location/Area of Operation: Conducts attacks in Turkey, primarily in Istanbul, Ankara, Izmir, and Adana. Raises funds in Western Europe.

External Aid: Unknown.

Sendero Luminoso (Shining Path, or SL)

Description: Former university professor Abimael Guzman formed Sendero Luminoso in the late 1960s, and his teachings created the foundation of SL's militant Maoist doctrine. In the 1980s, SL became one of the most ruthless terrorist groups in the Western Hemisphere—approximately 30,000 persons have died since Shining Path took up arms in 1980. Its stated goal is to destroy existing Peruvian institutions and replace them with a communist peasant revolutionary regime. It also opposes any influence by foreign governments, as well as by other Latin American guerrilla groups, especially the Tupac Amaru Revolutionary Movement (MRTA). In 2000, government authorities continued to arrest and prosecute active SL members, including, in April, commander Jose Arcela Chiroque, a.k.a. Ormeno. Counterterrorist operations targeted pockets of terrorist activity in the Upper Huallaga River Valley and the Apurimac/ Ene River Valley, where SL columns continued to conduct periodic attacks.

Activities: Conducted indiscriminate bombing campaigns and selective assassinations. Detonated explosives at diplomatic missions of several countries in Peru in 1990, including an attempt to car-bomb the U.S. Embassy in December. SL continued in 2000 to clash with Peruvian authorities and military units in the countryside and conducted periodic raids on villages. Despite numerous threats, the remaining active SL guerrillas were unable to cause any significant disruption to the Peruvian national elections held on 9 April.

Strength: Membership is unknown but estimated to be 100 to 200 armed militants. SL's strength has been vastly diminished by arrests and desertions.

Location/Area of Operation: Peru, with most activity in rural areas.

External Aid: None.

United Self-Defense Forces/Group of Colombia (AUC–Autodefensas Unidas de Colombia)

Description: The AUC—commonly referred to as autodefensas or paramilitaries—is an umbrella organization formed in April 1997 to consolidate most local and regional paramilitary groups, each with the mission to protect economic interests and combat insurgents locally. The AUC—supported by economic elites, drug traffickers, and local communities lacking effective government security—claims its primary objective is to protect its sponsors from insurgents. The AUC now asserts itself as a regional and national counterinsurgent force. It is adequately equipped and armed and reportedly pays its members a monthly salary. AUC leader Carlos Castaño in 2000 claimed 70 percent of the AUC's operational costs were financed with drug-related earnings, the rest from "donations" from its sponsors.

Activities: AUC operations vary from assassinating suspected insurgent supporters to engaging guerrilla combat units. Colombian National Police reported the AUC conducted 804 assassinations,

203 kidnappings, and 75 massacres with 507 victims during the first 10 months of 2000. The AUC claims the victims were guerrillas or sympathizers. Combat tactics consist of conventional and guerilla operations against main force insurgent units. AUC clashes with military and police units are increasing, although the group has traditionally avoided government security forces. The paramilitaries have not taken action against U.S. personnel.

Strength: In early 2001, the government estimated there were 8,000 paramilitary fighters, including former military and insurgent personnel.

Location/Areas of Operation: AUC forces are strongest in the north and northwest: Antioquia, Cordoba, Sucre, Bolivar, Atlantico, and Magdalena Departments. Since 1999, the group demonstrated a growing presence in other northeastern and southwestern departments and a limited presence in the Amazon plains. Clashes between the AUC and the FARC insurgents in Putumayo in 2000 demonstrated the range of the AUC to contest insurgents throughout Colombia.

External Aid: None.

About the Authors

Zeyno Baran is director of the Georgia Forum and the Caucasus Project at CSIS and a fellow in the CSIS Russia and Eurasia Program.

Daniel Benjamin is a senior fellow in the CSIS International Security Program. He previously served on the National Security Council staff, including as director for transnational threats.

Antony Blinken is a senior fellow and writer-in-residence in the CSIS International Security Program. He previously served on the National Security Council staff, including as senior director for European affairs.

Kurt M. Campbell is senior vice president and director of the International Security Program at CSIS and deputy director of the Aspen Strategy Group. He previously served as deputy assistant secretary of defense for Asian and Pacific affairs and was associate professor at the John F. Kennedy School of Government at Harvard University.

Anthony Cordesman holds the Arleigh A. Burke Chair in Strategy at CSIS.

Robert Ebel is director of the CSIS Energy Program. He has served with the Central Intelligence Agency and as vice president of international affairs for Enserch Corporation.

Michèle A. Flournoy is a senior adviser in the CSIS International Security Program and former principal deputy assistant secretary of defense for strategy and threat reduction and deputy assistant secretary of defense for strategy.

George W. Handy is director of the CSIS Action Commissions Program. He was a senior executive at United Technologies Corp. and served 24 years in the U.S. Army.

Shireen Hunter is director of the CSIS Islam Program and a former visiting scholar at the Centre for European Policy Studies in Brussels.

Sherman Katz is director of the International Finance and Economics Program at CSIS, where he holds the William M. Scholl Chair in International Business. He practiced international law in Washington, D.C., for 30 years prior to joining CSIS.

James A. Lewis is a senior fellow and director of the Technology and Public Policy Program at CSIS. He had assignments at the State Department, the National Security Council, and the Department of Commerce, among others, before leaving federal service.

Sarah E. Mendelson is a senior fellow in the Russia and Eurasia Program at CSIS and assistant professor of international politics at the Fletcher School of Law and Diplomacy, Tufts University.

Derek Mitchell is a senior fellow in the CSIS International Security Program and former special assistant for Asian and Pacific affairs in the Office of the Secretary of Defense.

J. Stephen Morrison is director of the CSIS Africa Program and previously served on the policy planning staff at the U.S. Department of State.

Clark A. Murdock is a senior fellow in the CSIS International Security Program. He previously served as the deputy director of strategic planning in the Air Force and held positions at the Office of the Secretary of Defense, the National Security Council, the CIA, and the House Armed Services Committee.

Robert C. Orr is a senior fellow in the CSIS International Security Program. He was formerly Washington deputy to U.S. Ambassador to the United Nations Richard Holbrooke and director of multilateral and global affairs at the National Security Council.

Erik Peterson is senior vice president and director of studies at CSIS, where he also holds the William A. Schreyer Chair in Global Analysis.

Christopher Sands is a fellow in the CSIS Americas Program and director of the program's Canada Project.

Teresita Schaffer is director of the CSIS South Asia Program. During her 30-year career in the U.S. Foreign Service, she served in most of the capitals in the South Asian region and as deputy assistant secretary of state for the Near East and South Asia.

Simon Serfaty is director of the CSIS Europe Program and a senior professor in U.S. foreign policy at Old Dominion University.

Walter Slocombe is a distinguished adviser at CSIS and former under secretary of defense for policy.

Celeste A. Wallander is director and senior fellow of the CSIS Russia and Eurasia Program. She was previously a senior fellow at the Council on Foreign Relations and associate professor of government at Harvard University.

Murray Weidenbaum is a distinguished visiting scholar at CSIS. He is on leave from Washington University in St. Louis, where he holds the Mallinckrodt Distinguished University Professorship.

Sidney Weintraub is director of the Americas Program at CSIS, where he holds the William E. Simon Chair in Political Economy. He is also Dean Rusk Professor Emeritus at the Lyndon B. Johnson School of Public Affairs of the University of Texas at Austin.